CFA Institute

CW01677906

DERIVATIVES

CFA® Program Curriculum

2026 • LEVEL I • VOLUME 7

WILEY

ISBN 978-1-961409-89-7

May 2025

Please visit our website at
www.WileyGlobalFinance.com.

WILEY

CONTENTS

How to Use the CFA Program Curriculum

The CFA® Program exams measure your mastery of the core knowledge, skills, and abilities required to succeed as an investment professional. These core competencies are the basis for the Candidate Body of Knowledge (CBOK™). The CBOK consists of four components:

A broad outline that lists the major CFA Program topic areas (www.cfainstitute.org/programs/cfa/curriculum/cbok/cbok)

Topic area weights that indicate the relative exam weightings of the top-level topic areas (www.cfainstitute.org/en/programs/cfa/curriculum)

Learning outcome statements (LOS) that tell you the specific knowledge, skills, and abilities you should gain from each curriculum topic area. You will find these statements at the start of each learning module and lesson. We encourage you to review the information about the LOS on our website (www.cfainstitute.org/programs/cfa/curriculum/study-sessions), including the descriptions of LOS "command words" on the candidate resources page at www.cfainstitute.org/-/media/documents/support/programs/cfa-and-cipm-los-command-words.ashx.

The CFA Program curriculum that candidates receive access to upon exam registration.

Therefore, the key to your success on the CFA exams is studying and understanding the CBOK. You can learn more about the CBOK on our website: www.cfainstitute.org/programs/cfa/curriculum/cbok.

The curriculum, including the practice questions, is the basis for all exam questions. The curriculum is selected/developed specifically to provide candidates with the knowledge, skills, and abilities reflected in the CBOK.

CFA INSTITUTE LEARNING ECOSYSTEM (LES)

Your exam registration fee includes access to the CFA Institute Learning Ecosystem (LES). This digital learning platform provides access to all the curriculum content and practice questions. The LES is organized as a series of learning modules consisting of short online lessons and associated practice questions. This tool is your source for all study materials, including practice questions and mock exams. The LES is the primary method by which CFA Institute delivers your curriculum experience. Here, you will find additional practice questions to test your knowledge, including some interactive questions.

DESIGNING YOUR PERSONAL STUDY PROGRAM

An orderly, systematic approach to exam preparation is critical. You should dedicate a consistent block of time every week to reading and studying. Review the LOS both before and after you study curriculum content to ensure you can demonstrate the knowledge, skills, and abilities described by the LOS and the assigned learning module. Use the LOS as a self-check to track your progress and highlight areas of weakness for later review.

Successful candidates report an average of more than 300 hours preparing for each exam. Your preparation time will vary based on your prior education and experience, and you will likely spend more time on some topics than on others.

ERRATA

The curriculum development process is rigorous and involves multiple rounds of reviews by content experts. Despite our efforts to produce a curriculum that is free of errors, we must make corrections in some instances. Curriculum errata are periodically updated and posted by exam level and test date on the Curriculum Errata webpage (www.cfainstitute.org/en/programs/submit-errata). If you believe you have found an error in the curriculum, you can submit your concerns through our curriculum errata reporting process found at the bottom of the Curriculum Errata webpage.

OTHER FEEDBACK

Please send any comments or suggestions to info@cfainstitute.org, and we will review your feedback thoughtfully.

Derivatives

LEARNING MODULE

1

Derivative Instrument and Derivative Market Features

LEARNING OUTCOMES

Mastery	*The candidate should be able to:*
□	define a derivative and describe basic features of a derivative instrument
□	describe the basic features of derivative markets, and contrast over-the-counter and exchange-traded derivative markets

INTRODUCTION

1

Earlier lessons described markets for financial assets related to equities, fixed income, currencies, and commodities. These markets are known as **cash markets** or **spot markets** in which specific assets are exchanged at current prices referred to as **cash prices** or **spot prices**. Derivatives involve the future exchange of cash flows whose value is derived from or based on an underlying value. The following lessons define and describe features of derivative instruments and derivative markets.

LEARNING MODULE OVERVIEW

- A derivative is a financial contract that derives its value from the performance of an underlying asset, which may represent a firm commitment or a contingent claim.
- Derivative markets expand the set of opportunities available to market participants beyond the cash market to create or modify exposure to an underlying.
- The most common derivative underlyings include equities, fixed income and interest rates, currencies, commodities, and credit.
- Over-the-counter (OTC) derivative markets involve the initiation of customized, flexible contracts between derivatives end users and financial intermediaries.

- Exchange-traded derivatives (ETDs) are standardized contracts traded on an organized exchange, which requires collateral on deposit to protect against counterparty default.
- For derivatives that are centrally cleared, a central counterparty (CCP) assumes the counterparty credit risk of the derivative counterparties and provides clearing and settlement services.

LEARNING MODULE SELF-ASSESSMENT

These initial questions are intended to help you gauge your current level of understanding of this learning module.

1. Which of the following statements does **not** provide an argument for using a derivative instrument?

   A. Issuers may offset the financial market exposure associated with a commercial transaction.

   B. Derivatives typically have lower transaction costs than transacting directly in the underlying.

   C. Large exposures to an underlying can be created with derivatives for a similar cash outlay.

   Solution:

   C is correct. Derivative contracts create an exposure to the underlying with a small cash outlay, so this is the statement that does not provide an argument for using a derivative instrument. Statements A and B are statements that are valid arguments for using derivatives.

2. Which of the following words makes the following statement correct? Market participants use derivative agreements to exchange cash flows in the future based on a(n) ________________.

   A. Underlying

   B. Option

   C. Hedge

   Solution:

   A is correct. Market participants use derivative agreements to exchange cash flows in the future based on an *underlying*. B is incorrect because *option* refers to a specific derivative contract type. C is incorrect because *hedge* refers to a specific purpose of using a derivative contract.

3. Which of the following is a significant difference between exchange-traded derivative (ETD) and over the counter (OTC) derivative contracts?

   A. ETDs create counterparty credit risk for derivative users, while OTC derivatives do not.

   B. ETDs are standardized contracts, while OTC derivatives are customized.

   C. ETDs have higher transaction costs compared to OTC derivatives.

   Solution:

   B is correct. Exchanges standardize contracts to facilitate trading volume. However, users often require specific customized features, and the OTC market can accommodate these needs. A is incorrect because exchanges bear the counterparty credit risk of derivatives. C is incorrect because ETDs have lower transaction costs compared to OTC derivatives.

4. If a corporate issuer enters into a centrally cleared OTC derivative contract, which of the following risks is likely of most concern to the issuer and other participants in this market?

   A. Interest rate risk

   B. Counterparty credit risk

   C. Systemic risk

   Solution:

   C is correct. Because all the credit risk is taken on by the CCP, all participants in this market are most concerned that the CCP is able to satisfy its obligations to all contracts. A is incorrect because interest rate risk is an underlying risk that can be hedged or managed with certain OTC derivative contracts. B is incorrect because the CCP assumes the credit risk from all parties to the contracts.

DERIVATIVE FEATURES 2

☐ define a derivative and describe basic features of a derivative instrument

Definition and Features of a Derivative

A **derivative** is a financial instrument that derives its value from the performance of an underlying asset. The asset in a derivative is called the **underlying**. The underlying may not be an individual asset but rather a group of standardized assets or variables, such as interest rates or a credit index.

Market participants use derivative agreements to exchange cash flows in the future based on an underlying value. For example, Exhibit 1 shows the one-time future exchange of publicly traded shares of stock at a fixed price in a derivative known as a **forward contract**.

Exhibit 1: Forward Contract

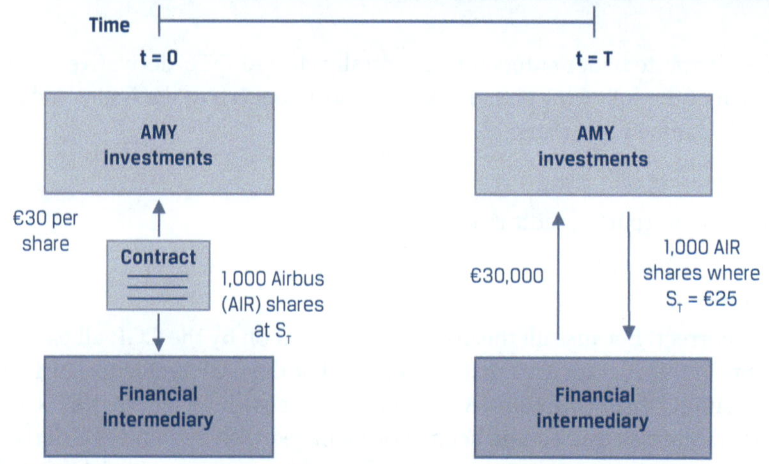

A derivative does not directly pass through the returns of the underlying but transforms the performance of the underlying. In Exhibit 1, AMY Investments agrees today ($t = 0$) to deliver 1,000 shares of Airbus (AIR) at a fixed price of €30 per share on a future date ($t = T$), which in our example is in six months. The forward contract allows AMY to transfer the price risk of underlying AIR shares to a second party, or a **counterparty**, by entering into this derivative contract. If the spot price of AIR (S_T) is €25 per share at time T in six months, AMY will either receive €30,000 from its counterparty, a financial intermediary, for 1,000 AIR shares now worth just €25,000, or simply settle with the intermediary the €5,000 difference in cash. Derivative transactions usually involve at least one financial intermediary as a counterparty. As we will see later, **counterparty credit risk**, or the likelihood that a counterparty is unable to meet its financial obligations under the contract, is an important consideration for these instruments.

A **derivative contract** is a legal agreement between counterparties with a specific **maturity**, or length of time until the closing of the transaction, or **settlement**. The buyer of a derivative enters a contract whose value changes in a way similar to a **long** position in the underlying, and the seller has exposure similar to a **short** position. The **contract size** (sometimes referred to as notional principal or amount) is agreed upon at the outset and may remain constant or change over time.

Exhibit 1 is an example of a **stand-alone derivative**, a distinct derivative contract, such as a derivative on a stock or bond. An **embedded derivative** is a derivative within an underlying, such as a callable, puttable, or convertible bond. Exhibit 2 provides a sample term sheet that includes key features of AMY Investment's stand-alone forward contract with a financial intermediary.

Exhibit 2: Sample Forward Contract Term Sheet

Contract Type: Firm commitment or contingent right to exchange future cash flows	**Forward Transaction Term Sheet**	
Maturity: Final date upon which payment or settlement occurs	**Start Date:** **Maturity Date:**	[Spot start] [Six months from Start Date]

Counterparties: Legal entities entering the derivative contract	**Forward Purchaser:**	[Financial Intermediary]
	Forward Seller:	AMY Investments
Underlying: Reference asset or variable used as source for contract value **Contract Size:** Amount(s) used for calculation to price and value the derivative	**Forward Delivery:**	1,000 shares of Airbus (AIR) common stock traded on the Frankfurt Stock Exchange
Underlying Price: Pre-agreed price for commitment or contingent claim settlement	**Forward Price:**	€30 per share
Contract Details	**Business Days:**	Frankfurt
	Documentation:	ISDA Agreement and credit terms acceptable to both parties

The derivative between AMY and the financial intermediary is a **firm commitment**, in which a pre-determined amount is agreed to be exchanged at settlement. Firm commitments include forward contracts, futures contracts, and **swaps** involving a periodic exchange of cash flows. Another type of derivative is a **contingent claim**, in which one of the counterparties determines whether and when the trade will settle. An **option** is the primary contingent claim.

Derivative markets expand the set of opportunities available to market participants to create or modify exposure to an underlying in several ways:

- Investors can sell short to benefit from an expected decline in the value of the underlying.
- Investors may use derivatives as a tool for portfolio diversification.
- Issuers may offset the financial market exposure associated with a commercial transaction.
- Market participants may create large exposures to an underlying with a relatively small cash outlay.
- Derivatives typically have lower transaction costs and are often more liquid than underlying spot market transactions.

Issuers and investors use derivatives to increase or decrease financial market exposures. For example, use of a derivative to offset or neutralize existing or anticipated exposure to an underlying is referred to as **hedging**, with the derivative itself commonly described as a **hedge** of the underlying transaction.

QUESTION SET

Derivative Features

1. Identify one reason why an issuer may use a derivative instrument.

   Solution:

   An issuer may use a derivative to offset the financial market exposure associated with a commercial transaction. An issuer may also use a derivative to offset or neutralize existing or anticipated exposure to an underlying.

2. Identify which example corresponds to each of the following stand-alone or embedded derivative contract types:

A. Firm commitment	1. Callable bond
B. Contingent claim	2. Fixed-price natural gas delivery contract
C. Neither a firm commitment nor a contingent claim exchange-traded fund (ETF)	3. Purchase of a FTSE 100 Index

Solution:

1. B is correct. A callable bond is an example of an embedded derivative within an underlying, which is a contingent claim.

2. A is correct. A fixed-price gas delivery contract is an example of a contract, which is a firm commitment with natural gas as the underlying.

3. C is correct. A FTSE 100 Index exchange-traded fund (ETF) is neither a firm commitment nor a contingent claim but rather an example of a cash or spot market transaction.

3. Determine the correct answers to fill in the blanks: Equities are an example of a derivative ____________, and a _______________ is a legal entity entering a derivative contract.

Solution:

Equities are an example of a derivative *underlying*, and a *counterparty* is a legal entity entering a derivative contract.

4. Describe the use of a derivative for hedging purposes.

Solution:

Use of a derivative for hedging purposes involves offsetting or neutralizing an existing or anticipated exposure to an underlying, referred to as hedging.

5. Explain the settlement of a forward contract.

Solution:

A forward contract is a firm commitment. This contract results in a settlement payment on the maturity date equal to the difference between the current market price and a pre-agreed forward price.

3 DERIVATIVE UNDERLYINGS

☐ define a derivative and describe basic features of a derivative instrument

Derivatives are typically grouped by the underlying from which their value is derived. A derivative contract may reference more than one underlying. The most common derivative underlyings include equities, fixed income and interest rates, currencies, commodities, and credit.

Equities

Equity derivatives usually reference an individual stock, a group of stocks, or a stock index, such as the FTSE 100. Options are the most common derivatives on individual stocks. Index derivatives are commonly traded as options, forwards, futures, and swaps.

Index swaps, or equity swaps, allow the investor to pay the return on one stock index and receive the return on another index or interest rate. An investment manager can use index swaps to increase or reduce exposure to an equity market or sector without trading the individual shares. These swaps are widely used in top-down asset allocation strategies. Finally, options, futures, and swaps are available based upon the realized *volatility* of equity index prices over a certain period. These contracts allow market participants to manage the risk, or dispersion, of price changes separately from the direction of equity price changes.

Options on individual stocks are purchased and sold by investors and frequently used by issuers as compensation for their executives and employees. Stock options are granted to provide incentives to work toward stronger corporate performance in the expectation of higher stock prices. Stock options can result in companies paying lower cash compensation. Companies may also issue warrants, which are options granted to employees or sold to the public that allow holders to purchase shares at a fixed price in the future directly from the issuer.

Fixed-Income Instruments

Bonds are a widely used underlying, and related derivatives include options, forwards, futures, and swaps. Government issuers, such as the US Treasury or Japanese Ministry of Finance, usually have many bond issues outstanding. A single standardized futures contract associated with such bonds therefore often specifies parameters that allow more than one bond issue to be delivered to settle the contract.

An interest rate is not an asset but rather a fixed-income underlying used in many interest rate derivatives, such as forwards, futures, and options. Interest rate swaps are a type of firm commitment frequently used by market participants to convert from fixed to floating interest rate exposure over a certain period. For example, an investment manager can use interest rate swaps to increase or reduce portfolio duration without trading bonds. An issuer, on the other hand, might use an interest rate swap to alter the interest rate exposure profile of its liabilities.

A **market reference rate (MRR)** is the most common interest rate underlying used in interest rate swaps. These rates typically match those of loans or other short-term obligations. Survey-based Libor rates used as reference rates in the past have been replaced by rates based on a daily average of observed market transaction rates. For example, the Secured Overnight Financing Rate (SOFR) is an overnight cash borrowing rate collateralized by US Treasuries. Other MRRs include the euro short-term rate (€STR) and the Sterling Overnight Index Average (SONIA).

Currencies

Market participants frequently use derivatives to hedge the exposure of commercial and financial transactions that arise due to foreign exchange risk. For example, exporters often enter into forward contracts to sell foreign currency and purchase domestic currency under terms matching those of a delivery contract for goods or services in a foreign country. Alternatively, an investor might sell futures on a particular currency while retaining a securities portfolio denominated in that currency to benefit from a temporary decline in the value of that currency. Options, forwards, futures, and swaps based upon sovereign bonds and exchange rates are used to manage currency risk.

Commodities

Cash or spot markets for soft and hard commodities involve the physical delivery of the underlying upon settlement. **Soft commodities** are agricultural products, such as cattle and corn, and **hard commodities** are natural resources, such as crude oil and metals. Commodity derivatives are widely used to manage either the price risk of an individual commodity or a commodity index separate from physical delivery. For example, an airline, shipping, or freight company might purchase oil futures as a hedge against rising operating expenses due to higher fuel costs. An investor might purchase a commodity index futures contract to increase exposure to commodity prices without taking physical delivery of the underlying.

Credit

Credit derivative contracts are based upon the default risk of a single issuer or a group of issuers in an index. Credit default swaps (CDS) allow an investor to manage the risk of loss from borrower default separately from the bond market. CDS contracts trade on a spread that represents the likelihood of default. For example, an investor might buy or sell a CDS contract on a high-yield index to change its portfolio exposure to high-yield credit without buying or selling the underlying bonds. Alternatively, a bank may purchase a CDS contract to offset existing credit exposure to an issuer's potential default.

Other

Other derivative underlyings include weather, cryptocurrencies, and longevity, all of which can influence the financial performance of various market participants. For example, longevity risk is important to insurance companies and defined benefit pension plans that face exposure to increased life expectancy. Derivatives based upon these underlyings are less common and more difficult to price. Exhibit 3 provides a summary of common underlyings.

Exhibit 3: Common Derivative Underlyings

Asset Class	Examples	Sample Uses
Equities	Individual stocks Equity indexes Equity price volatility	Change exposure profile (Investors) Employee compensation (Issuers)
Interest Rates	Sovereign bonds (domestic) Market reference rates	Change duration exposure (Investors) Alter debt exposure profile (Issuers)
Foreign Exchange	Sovereign bonds (foreign) Market exchange rates	Manage global portfolio risks (Investors) Manage global trade risks (Issuers)
Commodities	Soft and hard commodities Commodity indexes	Manage operating risks (Consumers/Producers) Portfolio diversification (Investors)

Asset Class	Examples	Sample Uses
Credit	Individual refence entities Credit indexes	Portfolio diversification (Investors) Manage credit risk (Financial Intermediaries)
Other	Weather Cryptocurrencies Longevity	Manage operating risks (Issuers) Manage portfolio risks (Investors)

RARE EARTH FUTURES AND THE LME LITHIUM CONTRACT

Derivative underlyings continue to adapt to the growing importance of environmental, social, and governance (ESG) factors affecting commercial and financial markets. For example, as the automotive industry shifts from internal combustion engine technology to electric vehicle (EV) production due to environmental concerns, demand for rare earth metals, such as lithium, as inputs into the EV battery production process are of increasing importance.

In response to growing demand from commodity producers and end users as well as investors, the London Metal Exchange (LME) introduced a lithium futures contract in 2021. The LME lithium contract is cash settled in USD against a weekly published spot price for battery-grade lithium hydroxide monohydrate deliverable in China, Japan, and Korea based upon a lot size of one metric ton per contract.

Investor Scenarios

The following scenarios consider the specific goals of two parties and review the most appropriate derivative contract for each.

Scenario 1: Hightest Capital

Hightest Capital is a US-based investment fund with a well-diversified domestic equity portfolio. Hightest's senior portfolio manager believes that health care stocks will significantly outperform the overall index over the next six months. Ace Limited is a financial intermediary and member of the Chicago Board Options Exchange (CBOE).

Hightest purchases an option based upon a standardized contract on the S&P 500 Health Care Select Sector Index (SIXV) with Ace as the financial intermediary and the spot SIXV price as the underlying. SIXV is comprised of approximately 60 health care equities included in the S&P 500 Index. The contract is a contingent claim, which grants Hightest the right to purchase SIXV at a 5% premium to the current market price (spot SIXV × 1.05) in six months.

Scenario 2: Esterr Inc.

Esterr Inc. is a Toronto-based public company with a CAD250 million floating-rate term loan. The loan has a remaining maturity of three and a half years and is priced at three-month MRR (which is CORRA, or the Canadian Overnight Reference Rate Average) plus 150 bps. Esterr's treasurer is concerned about higher Canadian interest rates over the remaining life of the loan and would like to fix Esterr's interest expense.

Esterr enters into a CAD250 million interest rate swap contract with a financial intermediary with MRR as the underlying. Under the swap, Esterr agrees to pay a fixed interest rate and receive three-month MRR on a notional principal of CAD250 million for three and a half years based upon payment dates that match the term loan. The swap contract is a firm commitment.

QUESTION SET

Derivative Underlyings

1. Describe how and why an underlying may be used in employee compensation.

   Solution:

   Derivatives with an equity underlying, in particular the stock of a particular issuer, may be included in the compensation of that company's employees. Stock options are granted to provide incentives to work toward stronger corporate performance in the expectation of a higher stock price, which will cause the options to increase in value.

2. Explain how a UK-based importer of goods from the euro zone might use a derivative with a currency underlying to mitigate risk.

   Solution:

   A UK-based importer of goods from the euro zone will likely pay EUR for goods that she intends to sell for GBP. To address this currency mismatch, she may consider entering a firm commitment to purchase EUR in exchange for GBP at a pre-determined price in the future based upon terms matching the import contract to offset risk to changes in the underlying spot exchange rate (i.e., GBP depreciation against EUR).

3. Identify A, B, and C in the following diagram, as in Exhibit 1, for the interest rate swap in Scenario 2 for Esterr Inc.

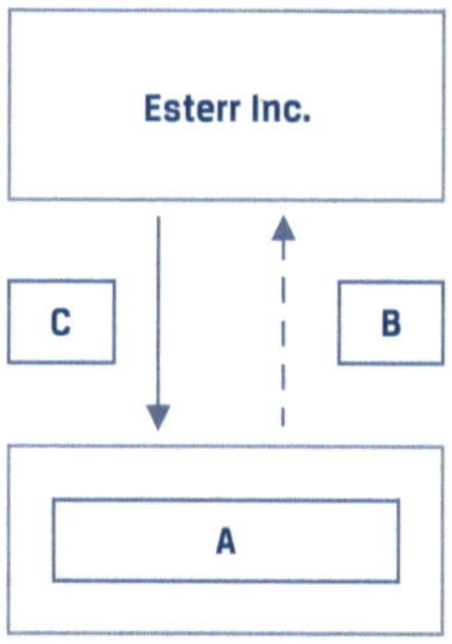

   Solution:

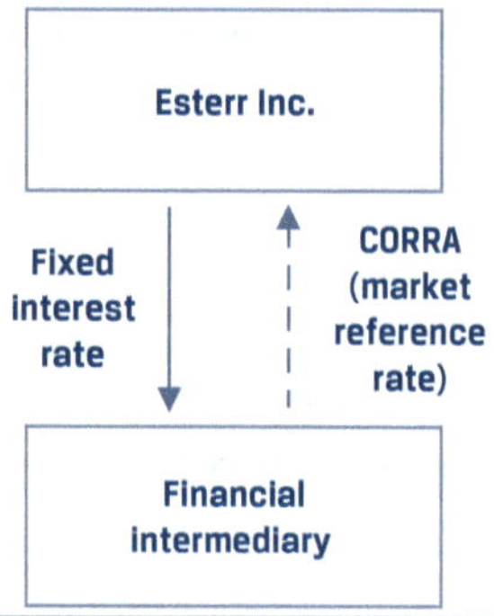

4. Identify and describe the derivative features for the Esterr Inc. interest rate swap using the following term sheet, as in Exhibit 2.

Interest Rate Swap Term Sheet

Start Date:	[Spot start]
Maturity Date:	[Three years and six months from Start Date]
Notional Principal:	CAD250,000,000
Fixed-Rate Payer:	Esterr Inc.
Fixed Rate:	2.05% on a semiannual, Act/365 basis
Floating-Rate Payer:	[Financial Intermediary]
Floating Rate:	Three-month Canadian Overnight Repo Rate Average (CORRA) as published each Business Day by the Bank of Canada
Payment Dates:	Semiannual exchange on a net basis
Business Days:	Toronto
Documentation:	ISDA Agreement and credit terms to match Esterr Inc. Term Loan

A. Underlying: ______________________

B. Counterparties: ________________ and ________________

C. Contract size: ______________________

D. Contract type: ______________________

Solution:

A. Underlying: Interest rate (Canadian market reference rate, CORRA)

B. Counterparties: Esterr Inc. and Financial Intermediary

C. Contract size: CAD250,000,000

D. Contract type: Firm commitment (interest rate swap)

5. Identify which example corresponds to each derivative underlying type.

A. Soft commodities	1. Aluminum futures
B. Hard commodities	2. SOFR futures
C. Neither soft nor hard commodities	3. Soybean options

Solution:

1. B is correct. Aluminum futures are an example of a metals contract, which is a derivative with a hard commodity underlying.

2. C is correct. SOFR futures are an example of an interest rate contract, not a commodity-based derivative contract.

3. A is correct. Soybean options are an example of a derivative contract with an agricultural, or soft, commodity underlying.

4 DERIVATIVE MARKETS

☐ describe the basic features of derivative markets, and contrast over-the-counter and exchange-traded derivative markets

Derivatives usage was historically dominated by exchange-traded futures markets in soft and hard commodities. Derivatives were expanded to **over-the-counter (OTC)** financial derivatives in interest rates and currencies in the 1980s, then credit derivatives in the 1990s.

Over-the-Counter (OTC) Derivative Markets

OTC markets can be formal organizations, such as NASDAQ, or informal networks of parties that buy from and sell to one another, as in the US fixed-income markets. OTC derivative markets involve contracts entered between derivatives end users and **dealers**, or financial intermediaries, such as commercial banks or investment banks. OTC dealers, known as **market makers**, typically enter into offsetting bilateral transactions with one another to transfer risk to other parties. The terms of OTC contracts can be customized to match a desired risk exposure profile. This flexibility is important to end users seeking to hedge a specific existing or anticipated underlying exposure based upon non-standard terms. The structure of the OTC derivative markets is shown in Exhibit 4.

Exhibit 4: Over-the-Counter Derivative Markets

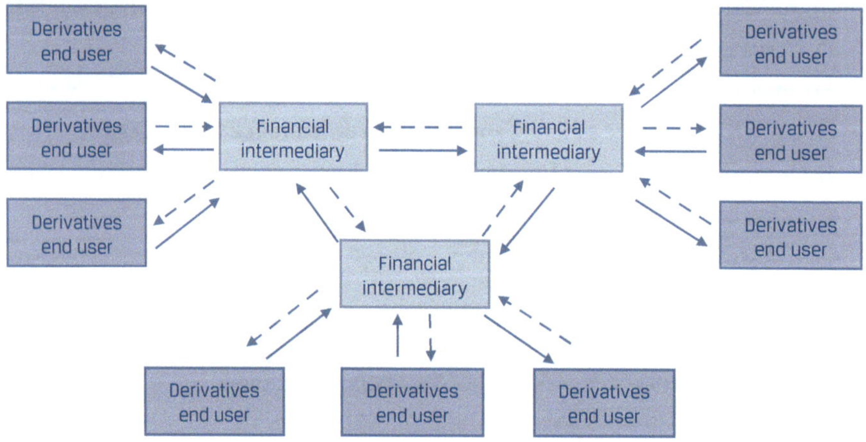

Exchange-Traded Derivative (ETD) Markets

An **exchange-traded derivative (ETD)** includes futures, options, and other financial contracts available on exchanges, such as the National Stock Exchange (NSE) in India or the Brasil, Bolsa, Balcão (B3) exchange in Brazil. ETD contracts are more formal and standardized, which facilitates a more liquid and transparent market. Terms and conditions—such as the size of each contract, type, quality, and location of underlying for commodities and maturity date—are set by the exchange. Exhibit 5 shows the key terms of the London Metals Exchange (LME) lithium futures contract described earlier.

Exhibit 5: LME Lithium Futures Contract Specifications

Contract Maturities:	Monthly [from 1 month to 15 months]
Contract Size:	One metric ton
Delivery Type:	Cash settled
Price Quotation:	USD per metric ton
Final Maturity:	Last LME business day of contract month
Daily Settlement:	LME Trading Operations calculates daily settlement values based on its published procedures
Final Settlement:	Based on the reported arithmetic monthly average of Fastmarkets' lithium hydroxide monohydrate 56.5% LiOH.H2O min, battery grade, spot price cif China, Japan, and Korea, USD/kg price, which is available from Fastmarkets from 16.30 London time on the last trading day

Exchange memberships are held by market makers (or dealers) that stand ready to buy at one price and sell at a higher price. With standard terms and an active market, they are often able to buy and sell simultaneously, earning a small bid–offer spread. When dealers cannot find a counterparty, risk takers (sometimes referred to as speculators) are often willing to take on exposure to changes in the underlying price.

Standardization also leads to an efficient clearing and settlement process. **Clearing** is the exchange's process of verifying the execution of a transaction, exchange of payments, and recording the participants. Settlement involves the payment of final amounts and/or delivery of securities or physical commodities between the counterparties based upon exchange rules. Derivative exchanges require collateral on deposit upon inception and during the life of a trade in order to minimize counterparty credit risk. This deposit is paid by each counterparty via a financial intermediary to the exchange, which then provides a guarantee against counterparty default. Finally, ETD markets have transparency, which means that full information on all transactions is disclosed to exchanges and national regulators.

OTC and ETD markets differ in several ways. OTC derivatives offer greater flexibility and customization than ETD. However, OTC instruments have less transparency, usually involve more counterparty risk, and may be less liquid. ETD contracts are more standardized, have lower trading and transaction costs, and may be more liquid than those in OTC markets, but their greater transparency and reduced flexibility may be a disadvantage to some market participants. The structure of the ETD markets is shown in Exhibit 6.

Exhibit 6: Exchange-Traded Derivative Markets

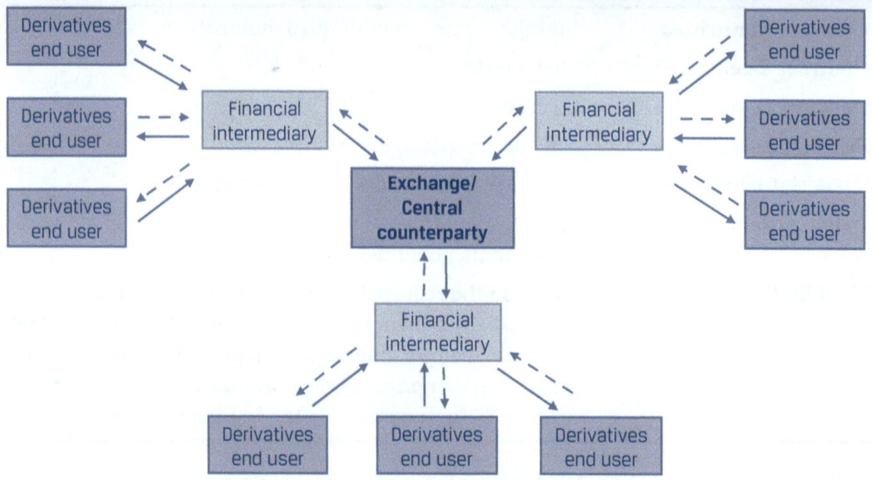

Central Clearing

Following the 2008 global financial crisis, global regulatory authorities instituted a **central clearing mandate** for most OTC derivatives. This mandate requires that a **central counterparty (CCP)** assume the credit risk between derivative counterparties, one of which is typically a financial intermediary. CCPs provide clearing and settlement for most derivative contracts. Issuers and investors are able to maintain the flexibility and customization available in the OTC markets when facing a financial intermediary, while the management of credit risk, clearing, and settlement of transactions between financial intermediaries occurs in a way similar to ETD markets. This arrangement seeks to benefit from the transparency, standardization, and risk reduction features of ETD markets. However, the systemic credit risk transfer from financial intermediaries to CCPs also leads to centralization and concentration of risks. Proper safeguards must be in place to avoid excessive risk being held in CCPs.

Exhibit 7 shows the central clearing process for interest rate swaps which also applies to other swaps and derivative instruments. Under central clearing, a derivatives trade is executed in Step 1 on a **swap execution facility (SEF)**, a swap trading platform accessed by multiple dealers. The original SEF transaction details are shared with the CCP in Step 2, and the CCP replaces the existing trade in Step 3. This **novation process** substitutes the initial SEF contract with identical trades facing the CCP. The CCP serves as counterparty for both financial intermediaries, eliminating bilateral counterparty credit risk and providing clearing and settlement services.

Exhibit 7: Central Clearing for Interest Rate Swaps

Step 1: Trade executed on an SEF

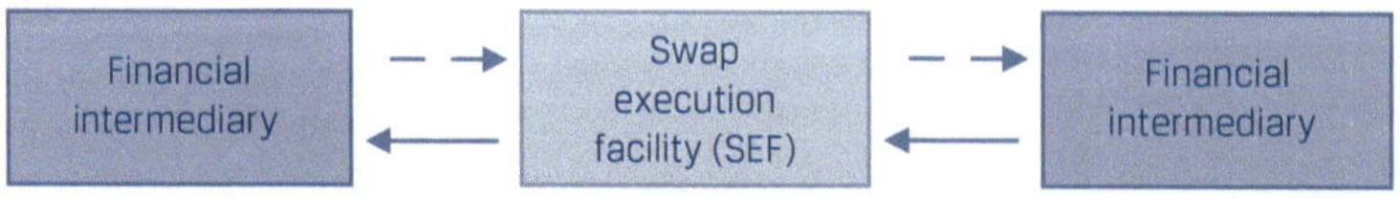

Step 2: SEF trade information submitted to CCP

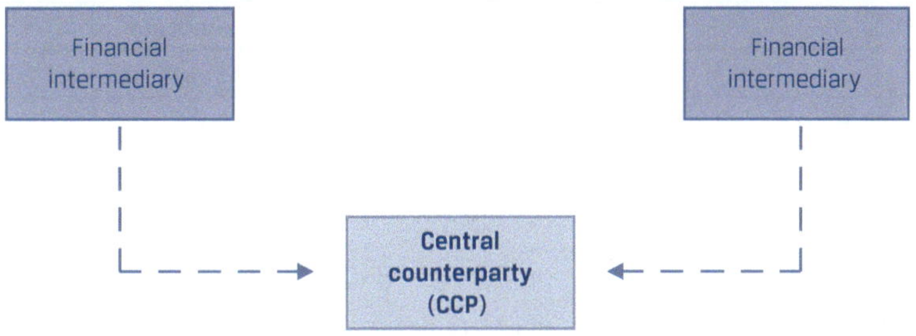

Step 3: CCP replaces (novates) existing trade, acting as new counterparty to both financial intermediaries

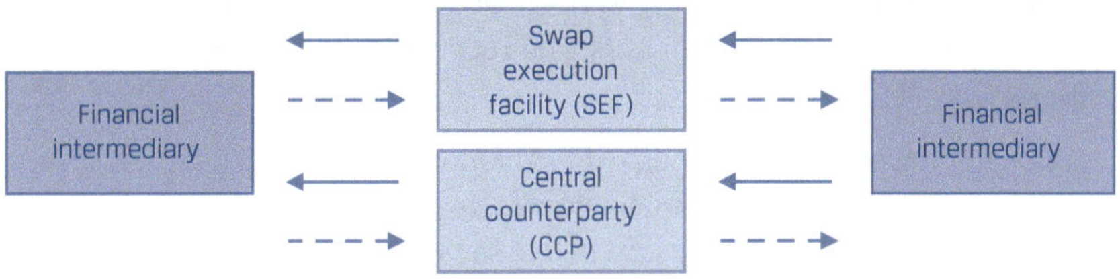

Investor Scenarios

In this section, we assess the most appropriate derivative markets for the scenarios presented in the previous lesson.

Scenario 1. Hightest Capital.

Hightest's index option contract would most likely be traded on the ETD derivative market. The trade has a standard size, exercise price, and maturity date.

Scenario 2. Esterr Inc.

Esterr's interest rate swap is likely to be traded in the OTC market. The swap contract terms are tailored to match the payment dates and remaining maturity of Esterr's term loan. Esterr's counterparty will be a financial intermediary that executes the offsetting hedge on an SEF and then novates the original SEF trade to face a CCP, which serves as the credit risk intermediary between dealers.

QUESTION SET

Derivative Markets

1. Describe the risk transfer process in OTC derivative markets.

   Solution:

   OTC dealers, known as market makers, typically enter into offsetting transactions with one another to transfer the risk of derivative contracts entered with end users.

2. Identify which of the following derivative markets corresponds to the following characteristics.

A. ETD	1. Standardized contracts
B. OTC	2. Includes market makers
C. Both ETD and OTC	3. Greater confidentiality

Solution:

1. A—ETD markets use standardized contracts.
2. C—Both ETD and OTC markets use market makers.
3. B—OTC markets have greater privacy.

3. Determine the correct answers to fill in the blanks: ____________ involves the payment of final amounts and/or delivery of securities or physical commodities, while __________ is the process of verifying the execution of a transaction, exchange of payments, and recording the participants.

Solution:

Settlement involves the payment of final amounts and/or delivery of securities or physical commodities, while *clearing* is the process of verifying the execution of a transaction, exchange of payments, and recording the participants.

4. Identify one potential risk concern about the central clearing of derivatives.

Solution:

The central clearing mandate transfers the systemic risk of derivatives transactions from the counterparties, typically financial intermediaries, to the CCPs. One concern is the centralization and concentration of risks in CCPs. Careful oversight must occur to ensure that these risks are properly managed.

5. Describe the steps for clearing a credit default swap.

Solution:

The counterparties are financial intermediaries that first execute the trade on an SEF (swap execution facility). Then, trade details are shared with a CCP; the novation process substitutes the original contract with another where the CCP steps into the trade and acts as the new counterparty for each original party. The CCP clears and settles the trade.

PRACTICE PROBLEMS

The following information relates to questions 1-5

Montau AG is a German capital goods producer that manufactures its products domestically and delivers its products to clients globally. Montau's global sales manager shares the following draft commercial contract with his Treasury team:

Montau AG Commercial Export Contract	
Contract Date:	[Today]
Goods Seller:	Montau AG, Frankfurt, Germany
Goods Buyer:	Jeon Inc., Seoul, Korea
Description of Goods:	A-Series Laser Cutting Machine
Quantity:	One
Delivery Terms:	Freight on Board (FOB), Busan Korea with all shipping, tax and delivery costs payable by Goods Buyer
Delivery Date:	[75 Days from Contract Date]
Payment Terms:	100% of Contract Price payable by Goods Buyer to Good Seller on Delivery Date
Contract Price:	KRW650,000,000

Montau AG's Treasury manager is tasked with addressing the financial risk of this prospective transaction.

1. Which of the following statements best describes why Montau AG should consider a derivative rather than a spot market transaction to manage the financial risk of this commercial contract?

   A. Montau AG is selling a machine at a contract price in KRW and incurs costs based in EUR.

   B. Montau AG faces a 75-day timing difference between the commercial contract date and the delivery date when Montau AG is paid for the machine in KRW.

   C. Montau AG is unable to sell KRW today in order to offset the contract price of machinery delivered to Jeon Inc.

2. Which of the following types of derivative and underlyings are best suited to hedge Montau's financial risk under the commercial transaction?

   A. Montau AG should consider a firm commitment derivative with currency as an underlying, specifically the sale of KRW at a fixed EUR price.

   B. Montau AG should consider a contingent claim derivative with the price of the machine as its underlying, specifically an A-series laser cutting machine.

C. Montau AG should consider a contingent claim derivative with currency as an underlying, specifically the sale of EUR at a fixed KRW price.

3. Identify A, B, and C in the correct order in the following diagram, as in Exhibit 1, for the derivative to hedge Montau's financial risk under the commercial transaction.

Exhibit 1

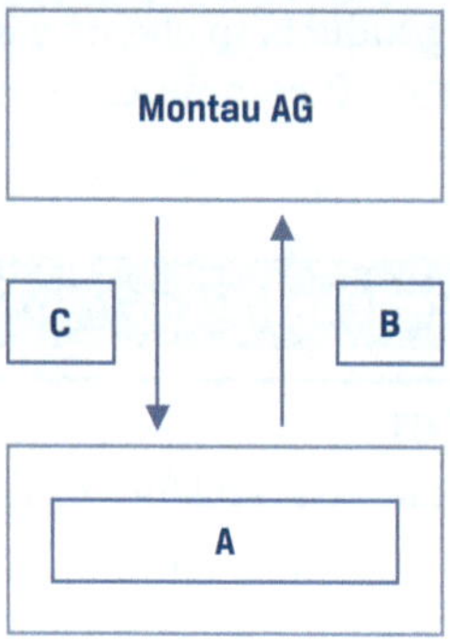

A. A: Financial intermediary, B: KRW650,000,000, C: Fixed EUR amount

B. A: Jeon Inc., B: KRW650,000,000, C: Fixed EUR amount

C. A: Financial intermediary, B: Fixed EUR amount, C: KRW650,000,000.

4. Which of the following statements about the most appropriate derivative market to hedge Montau AG's financial risk under the commercial contract is most accurate?

A. The OTC market is most appropriate for Montau, as it is able to customize the contract to match its desired risk exposure profile.

B. The ETD market is most appropriate for Montau, as it offers a standardized and transparent contract to match its desired risk exposure profile.

C. Both the ETD and OTC markets are appropriate for Montau AG to hedge its financial risk under the transaction, so it should choose the market with the best price.

5. If Montau enters into a centrally cleared derivative contract on the OTC market, which of the following statements about credit risk associated with the derivative is most likely correct?

A. Montau faces credit risk associated with the possibility that its counterparty to the contract may not fulfill its contractual obligation.

B. Montau poses a credit risk to its counterparty because it may fail to fulfill its contractual obligation.

C. Montau poses a credit risk to a derivative contract end user holding a contract with the opposite features of Montau's.

SOLUTIONS

1. B is correct. A 75-day timing difference exists between the commercial contract date and the delivery date when Montau AG is paid for the machine in KRW. A is true but does not explain why the use of a derivative is preferable to a spot market transaction. If as in C Montau were to sell the KRW it receives and buy EUR in a spot market transaction on the delivery date, it would be exposed to unfavorable changes in the KRW/EUR exchange rate over the 75-day period. A derivative contract in which the underlying KRW/EUR forward rate is agreed today and exchanged on the delivery date allows Montau to hedge or offset the EUR value of the future KRW payment. The derivative is therefore a more suitable contract to address the financial risk of the commercial transaction than a spot market sale of KRW.

2. A is correct. The derivative best suited to hedge Montau's financial risk is a firm commitment derivative in which a pre-determined amount is exchanged at settlement. The derivative underlying should be currencies, specifically the sale of KRW at a fixed EUR price in the future to offset or hedge the financial risk of the commercial contract. The machine price referenced under B is not considered an underlying, and C hedges the opposite of Montau's underlying exposure.

3. C is correct as per the following diagram:

Exhibit 1

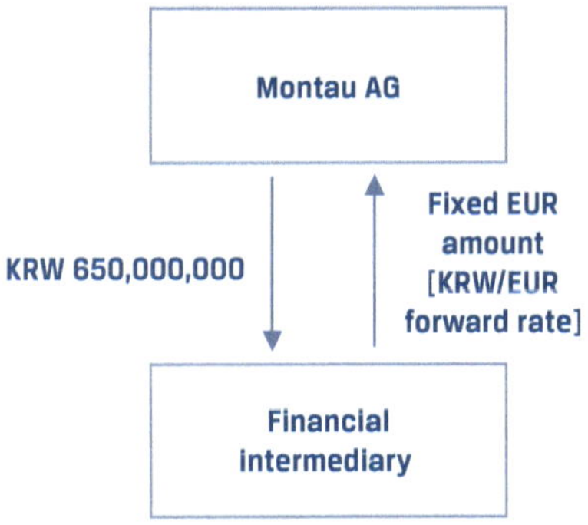

4. A is correct. The OTC market is most appropriate for Montau, as OTC contracts may be customized to match Montau's desired risk exposure profile. This is important to end users seeking to hedge a specific underlying exposure based upon non-standard terms. Montau would be unlikely to find an ETD contract under B that matches the exact size and maturity date of its desired hedge, which also makes C incorrect.

5. B is correct. In a centrally cleared OTC derivative contract, the central counterparty becomes the counterparty in all contracts and assumes the credit risk associated with individual derivative contracts. A is likely incorrect because the CCP takes actions to ensure that it can fulfill its obligations to its counterparties. C is incorrect because the CCP inserts itself between parties with opposite positions.

LEARNING MODULE

2

Forward Commitment and Contingent Claim Features and Instruments

LEARNING OUTCOMES

Mastery	The candidate should be able to:
☐	define forward contracts, futures contracts, swaps, options (calls and puts), and credit derivatives and compare their basic characteristics
☐	determine the value at expiration and profit from a long or a short position in a call or put option
☐	contrast forward commitments with contingent claims

INTRODUCTION

1

An earlier lesson established a derivative as a financial instrument that derives its performance from an underlying asset, index, or other financial variable, such as equity price volatility. Primary derivative types include a firm commitment in which a predetermined amount is agreed to be exchanged between counterparties at settlement and a contingent claim in which one of the counterparties determines whether and when the trade will settle. The following lessons define and compare the basic features of forward commitments and contingent claims and explain how to calculate their values at maturity.

LEARNING MODULE OVERVIEW

- Forwards, futures, and swaps represent firm commitments, or derivative contracts that require counterparties to exchange an underlying in the future based on an agreed-on price.
- Forwards are a flexible over-the-counter (OTC) derivative instrument, while futures are standardized and traded on an exchange with a daily settlement of contract gains and losses.
- Swap contracts are a firm commitment to exchange a series of cash flows in the future. Interest rate swaps are the most common type and involve the exchange of fixed interest payments for floating interest payments.

CFA Institute would like to thank Don Chance, PhD, CFA, for his contribution to this section, which includes material derived from material that appeared in *Derivative Markets and Instruments*, featured in the 2022 CFA® Program curriculum.

- Option contracts are contingent claims in which one of the counterparties determines whether and when a trade will settle. The option buyer pays a premium to the seller for the right to transact the underlying in the future at a pre-agreed exercise price.
- Option contract payoff and profit profiles are non-linear as the underlying price changes, as opposed to firm commitments, such as forwards, futures, and swaps, which are linear in underlying price changes.
- Market participants often create similar exposures to an underlying using firm commitments and contingent claims, although these derivative instrument types involve different payoff and profit profiles.

LEARNING MODULE SELF-ASSESSMENT

These initial questions are intended to help you gauge your current level of understanding of this learning module.

1. Which of the following statements correctly describes a difference between a forward contract and a futures contract?

   A. A forward contract sets an agreed-on price for buyer and seller, while a futures contract does not.

   B. A forward contract sets an agreed-on transaction date for the seller to deliver the underlying to the buyer, while a futures contract does not.

   C. A forward contract does not require daily settlement of gains and losses, while a futures contract does.

   Solution:

   C is correct. Futures contracts require daily settlement through the exchange clearinghouse mark-to-market process. Forward contracts are settled at their maturity date, although the two parties to the contract may customize alternative settlement procedures. A is incorrect because both forward and futures contracts set an agreed-on price for a future transaction. B is incorrect because both forwards and futures contracts include a maturity date when the underlying will be exchanged.

2. Identify which example fits each of the following firm commitments:

A. Futures contract purchaser	1. Agrees to make a single exchange in the future at a pre-agreed price under an OTC contract
B. Forward contract seller	2. Agrees to a single exchange in the future based on standardized terms set by an exchange
C. Fixed-rate payer on an interest rate swap	3. Agrees to a series of exchanges of interest fixed for floating interest payments

   Solution:

   1. B is correct. A forward contract seller agrees to make a single exchange in the future at a pre-agreed price under an OTC contract.

   2. A is correct. A futures contract purchaser agrees to a single exchange in the future based on standardized terms set by an exchange.

3. C is correct. A fixed-rate payer on an interest rate swap agrees to a series of exchanges of fixed for floating interest payments.

3. Identify which example fits each of the following contingent claims:

A. Put option purchaser	1. Seeks to gain from an increase in the underlying price
B. Call option purchaser	2. Allows the option to expire at maturity of the underlying price is above the exercise price
C. Both a put option purchaser and a call option purchaser	3. Pays an option premium to the option seller when the contract is agreed on

Solution:

1. B is correct. A call option purchaser seeks to gain from an increase in the underlying price.

2. A is correct. A put option purchaser will allow an option to expire at maturity without exercise if the underlying price is above the exercise price.

3. C is correct. Both a put option purchaser and a call option purchaser will pay a premium to the option seller when the option contract is executed.

4. An option to buy an underlying security at an exercise price of USD45 in three months trades at a premium of USD6. After three months, the underlying trades at USD50. Which of the following responses correctly describes the profit/loss position of the option buyer and seller?

   A. Option buyer earns USD5 profit, and option seller earns USD5 loss.

   B. Option buyer earns USD1 loss, and option seller earns USD1 profit.

   C. Option buyer earns USD5 profit, and option seller earns USD0.

Solution:

B is correct. The option buyer's position generates a payoff of USD5, equal to max(0, 50 – 45). The option buyer paid USD6 to buy the option position, and this cash flow more than offsets the positive payoff. Thus, the option buyer's overall profit is a loss of USD1 (i.e., 5 – 6). For the option seller, the option position creates a negative payoff of –USD5, equal to –max(0, 50 – 45). However, the option seller received the option premium of USD6, so the overall profit is USD1 (i.e., 6 – 5). A is incorrect because the USD5 amount reflects the option payoff only, not profits and losses accounting for the option premium. C is incorrect because the buyer's profit incorrectly states the payoff only to the option position, not the profit. The seller's profit would be correct only if the underlying traded at 51, not 50.

5. A put option buyer earns a positive profit in which of the following conditions?

   A. The price of the underlying at option expiration is less than the option's exercise price.

   B. The price of the underlying at option expiration is greater than the option's exercise price.

C. The price of the underlying is less than the option's exercise price minus the option's premium.

Solution:

C is correct. For a put option buyer to earn a positive profit, the underlying price must be sufficiently below the put option's exercise price such that (1) the put option can be exercised with a positive payoff and (2) the positive payoff is greater than the option premium paid. Thus, only if the underlying price falls below the exercise price minus the premium can this occur. A is incorrect because this condition only implies a positive payoff on the option but would include prices at which the payoff is not greater than the premium. B is incorrect because the put option would be out of the money and would generate zero payoff.

6. Which of the following positions on the same underlying benefit from opposite price movements in an underlying?

A. Long forward contract, short put option

B. Short forward contract, long put option

C. Short forward contract, short put option

Solution:

C is correct. A short forward position benefits as the underlying price declines, while a short put benefits only when the underlying price increases. A is incorrect because both a long forward and a short put benefit from underlying price increases. B is incorrect because both a short forward and a long put option benefit from underlying price decreases.

2 FORWARDS, FUTURES, AND SWAPS

☐ define forward contracts, futures contracts, swaps, options (calls and puts), and credit derivatives and compare their basic characteristics

Forwards, futures, and swaps are the most common derivative contracts which represent a firm commitment. This firm commitment is an obligation of both counterparties to perform under the terms of the derivative contract. Key common features of this type of derivative include the following:

- A specific contract size
- A specific underlying
- One or more exchanges of cash flows or underlying on a specific future date or dates
- Exchange(s) based on a pre-agreed price

Despite their similarities, forwards, futures, and swaps each have different features, which are the subject of this lesson.

A forward contract is an over-the-counter (OTC) derivative in which two counterparties agree that one counterparty, the buyer, will purchase an underlying from the other counterparty, the seller, in the future at a pre-agreed fixed price. As noted earlier, OTC derivatives offer greater flexibility and customization than exchange-traded derivatives (ETD), but also usually involve more counterparty risk. Forward contracts are advantageous for derivative end users seeking to hedge an existing or forecasted underlying exposure based on specific terms. For example, an importer may enter a forward contract to buy the foreign currency needed to satisfy the commercial terms of a future goods delivery contract. Forward contracts are more flexible as to the size, underlying details, maturity, and/or credit terms than a similar ETD. A forward contract buyer has a long position and will therefore benefit from price appreciation of the underlying over the life of the contract.

To gain a better understanding of forwards, we must examine their payoff profile. Assume a forward contract is agreed at time $t = 0$ and matures at time T. At time $t = 0$, the counterparties do not exchange a payment upfront but, rather, agree on delivery of the underlying at time T for a **forward price** of $F_0(T)$. The subscript refers to the date on which the underlying price in the future is set ($t = 0$), and the T in parentheses refers to the date of exchange ($t = T$). The spot price of the underlying at time T is S_T. Exhibit 1 shows the payoff from the forward buyer's perspective, which is a long forward position. Note that the payoff equals the profit, as no upfront payment is made.

Exhibit 1: Long Forward (Forward Buyer) Payoff Profile

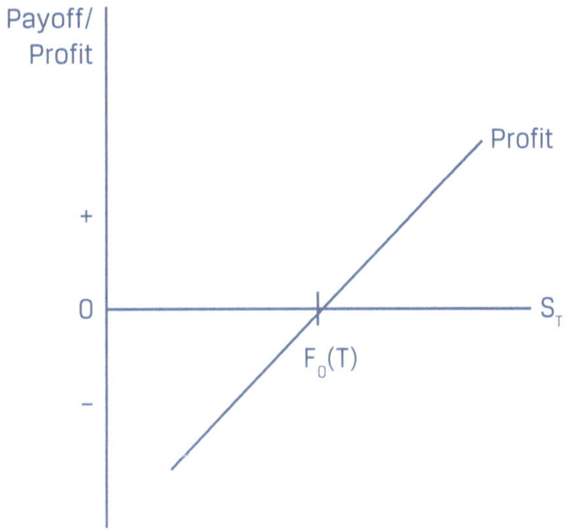

Outcome	Buyer Payoff	Seller Payoff
$S_T > F_0(T)$	$[S_T - F_0(T)] > 0$	$[F_0(T) - S_T] < 0$
$S_T < F_0(T)$	$[S_T - F_0(T)] < 0$	$[F_0(T) - S_T] > 0$

The symmetric payoff profile shown in Exhibit 1 is a common feature of firm commitments. Since the derivative price is a linear function of the underlying, firm commitments are also referred to as **linear derivatives**. At time T, the transaction is settled based on the difference between the forward price, $F_0(T)$, and the underlying price of S_T, or $[S_T - F_0(T)]$ from the buyer's perspective. That is, the buyer realizes a gain if she is able to take delivery of the underlying at a market value, S_T, that exceeds the pre-agreed price, $F_0(T)$. If the forward price exceeds the current market value $[F_0(T) > S_T]$, the buyer realizes a loss and must either take delivery of an asset at a loss of $[F_0(T) - S_T]$ or pay the seller this amount in cash. Forward contracts usually involve a single exchange in the future, as in Example 1.

EXAMPLE 1

Forward Gold Purchase

An investor, Procam Investments, enters a cash-settled forward contract with a financial intermediary to buy 100 ounces of gold at a forward price, $F_0(T)$, of \$1,792.13 per ounce in three months.

1. Today's spot gold price (S_0) is \$1,770 per ounce.
2. At contract maturity, the gold price (S_T) is \$1,780.50 per ounce.
3. The payoff, $S_T - F_0(T)$, is –\$11.63 = \$1,780.50 – \$1,792.13 per ounce.
4. Procam (the buyer) must pay the financial intermediary (the seller) \$1,163 (= 100 × \$11.63) to settle the forward contract at maturity.

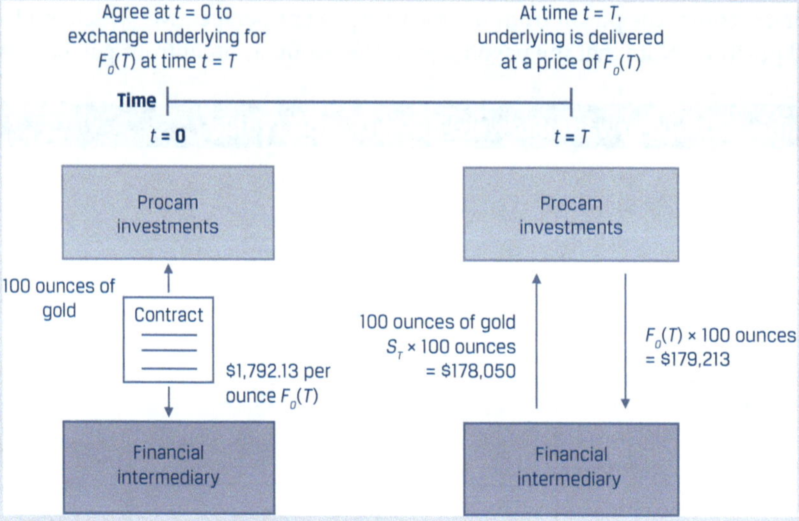

The contract may specify either the actual delivery of the underlying or a cash settlement. The settlement amount is equal to $[S_T - F_0(T)]$ from a buyer's perspective and $-[S_T - F_0(T)] = [F_0(T) - S_T]$ from a seller's perspective. Note that a buyer would have to pay S_0 at $t = 0$ and realize a return of $(S_T - S_0)$ at time T in order to create a similar exposure to the long forward position in the cash market.

QUESTION SET

Forwards

1. Describe a scenario in which a forward contract has cash settlement of zero at maturity and neither counterparty has defaulted.

   Solution:

   A forward contract will have a cash settlement of zero at maturity if $S_T = F_0(T)$ or the payoff from the buyer's perspective is $[S_T - F_0(T)] = 0$. This is often referred to as the **breakeven point** for the forward contract for both buyer and seller in the absence of transaction costs and is visually represented by the x-axis intercept of the profit line in Exhibit 1.

2. Determine the correct answers to fill in the blanks: An oil producer enters a derivative contract with an investor to sell 1,000 barrels of oil in two months at a forward price of \$64 per barrel. If the spot oil price at maturity

is \$58.50 per barrel, the investor realizes a __________ at maturity equal to __________.

Solution:

An oil producer enters a derivative contract with an investor to sell 1,000 barrels of oil in two months at a forward price of \$64 per barrel. If the spot oil price at maturity is \$58.50 per barrel, the investor realizes a *loss* at maturity equal to *\$5,500.*

The oil forward price, $F_0(T)$, under the contract equals \$64 per barrel.

At contract maturity, the spot oil price (S_T) is \$58.50 per barrel.

- Investor payoff per barrel:

$[S_T - F_0(T)]$ = \$58.50 – \$64.00 = –\$5.50 per barrel.

- Total amount the investor pays the oil producer to settle the forward contract for 1,000 barrels at maturity:

1,000 × \$5.50 = \$5,500.

3. Identify the most likely forward contract participants that correspond to the following statements:

A. forward contract purchaser	1. Seeks to benefit from underlying price depreciation
B. Forward contract seller	2. Realizes a gain if the initial spot price of the underlying, S_0, exceelds the forward price of $F_0(T)$
C. Neither a forward contract purchaser nor a seller	3. Receives a positive payoff at maturity if the spot price, S_T, exceeds the forward price of $F_0(T)$

Solution:

1. The correct answer is B. A forward seller pays $[F_0(T) - S_T]$ to the forward contract buyer at maturity and therefore benefits as the underlying spot price S_T declines over time.

2. The correct answer is C. Neither the buyer nor the seller of a forward contract realizes a gain if the initial spot price, S_0, exceeds the forward price of $F_0(T)$, as settlement is based on the future spot price, S_T.

3. The correct answer is A. The forward contract buyer realizes a gain at maturity if $S_T > F_0(T)$.

FUTURES 3

☐ define forward contracts, futures contracts, swaps, options (calls and puts), and credit derivatives and compare their basic characteristics

Futures contracts are forward contracts with standardized sizes, dates, and underlyings that trade on futures exchanges. Futures markets offer both greater liquidity and protection against loss by default by combining contract uniformity with an organized market with rules, regulations, and a central clearing facility.

The futures contract buyer creates a long exposure to the underlying by agreeing to purchase the underlying at a later date at a pre-agreed price. The seller makes the opposite commitment, creating a short exposure to the underlying by agreeing to sell the underlying asset in the future at an agreed-on price. This agreed-on price is called the **futures price,** $f_0(T)$. The frequency of futures contract maturities, contract sizes, and other details are established by the exchange based on buyer and seller interest.

The most important feature of futures contracts is the daily settlement of gains and losses and the associated credit guarantee provided by the exchange through its clearinghouse. At the end of each day, the clearinghouse engages in a practice called **mark to market (MTM)**, also known as the **daily settlement**. The clearinghouse determines an average of the final futures trading price of the day and designates that price as the end-of-day **settlement price**. All contracts are then said to be marked to the end-of-day settlement price.

As with forward contracts, no cash is exchanged when a futures contract is initiated by a buyer or seller. However, each counterparty must deposit a required minimum sum (or **initial margin**) into a **futures margin account** held at the exchange that is used by the clearinghouse to settle the daily mark to market. Futures contracts must be executed with specialized financial intermediaries that clear and settle payments at the exchange on behalf of counterparties, as shown in Example 2.

EXAMPLE 2

Purchase of a Gold Futures Contract

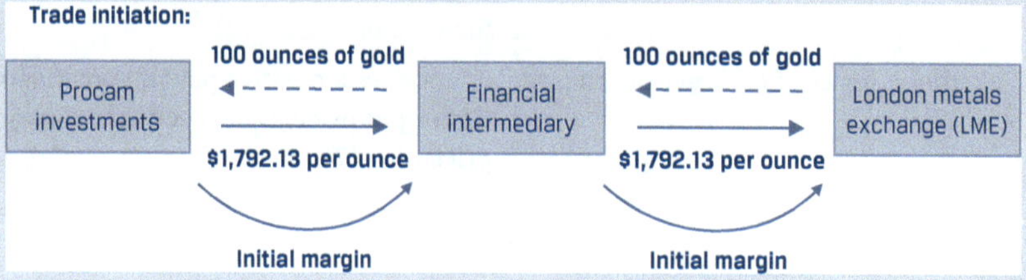

As in Example 1, Procam Investments enters a cash-settled contract to buy 100 ounces of gold at a price of $1,792.13 per ounce in three months. Instead of the forward in Example 1, Procam purchases a futures contract [$f_0(T)$ = $1,792.13] on the exchange via a financial intermediary. London Metals Exchange rules require an initial cash margin of $4,950 per gold contract (100 ounces) sold or purchased:

- Procam deposits $4,950 in required initial margin with the exchange.
- Today's spot gold price (S_0) is $1,770 per ounce, and the opening gold futures price, $f_0(T)$, is $1,792.13 per ounce.
- At today's close, the gold futures price, $f_1(T)$, settles at $1,797.13 per ounce.
- Procam realizes a $500 MTM gain, or $5 per ounce × 100 ounces. It receives a $500 futures margin account deposit from the clearinghouse.
- Procam's futures margin account has an ending balance for the day of $5,450, or $4,950 initial margin plus the $500 MTM gain.

Each futures contract specifies a **maintenance margin**, or minimum balance set below the initial margin, that each contract buyer and seller must hold in the futures margin account from trade initiation until final settlement at maturity. The clearinghouse moves funds daily between the buyer and seller margin accounts, crediting the accounts of those with mark to market gains and charging those with mark-to-market losses.

For example, London Metals Exchange rules require a maintenance margin of $4,500 per 100-ounce gold contract sold or purchased. Now consider the *seller* of a futures contract with a position that offsets that of Procam in Example 2.

- Seller deposits $4,950 in required initial margin with the exchange.
- Today's opening gold futures price, $f_0(T)$, is $1,792.13 per ounce.
- At the close, the gold futures price, $f_1(T)$, settles at $1,797.13 per ounce.
- Seller realizes a $500 MTM loss, or $5 per ounce × 100 ounces; $500 is deducted from its futures margin account by the clearinghouse.
- Seller's futures margin account has an ending balance of $4,450, or $4,950 initial margin less the $500 MTM loss.
- Seller's margin account is $50 below the required maintenance margin ($4,450 – $4,500) = –$50

The seller receives a **margin call**, or request to immediately deposit funds to return the account balance to the *initial margin*. The seller must deposit $500 in order to bring the margin account back to the $4,950 initial margin. The amount required to replenish the futures margin account is sometimes referred to as **variation margin**. If a counterparty fails to meet the margin call, it must close out the contract as soon as possible and cover any additional losses. If the counterparty cannot meet its obligations, the clearinghouse provides a guarantee that it will cover the loss itself by maintaining an insurance fund. Exhibit 2 shows the futures margining and settlement process, where $f_0(T)$ is the futures price at inception and $f_t(T)$ represents the futures price on day t.

Exhibit 2: Futures Margin and Settlement Process

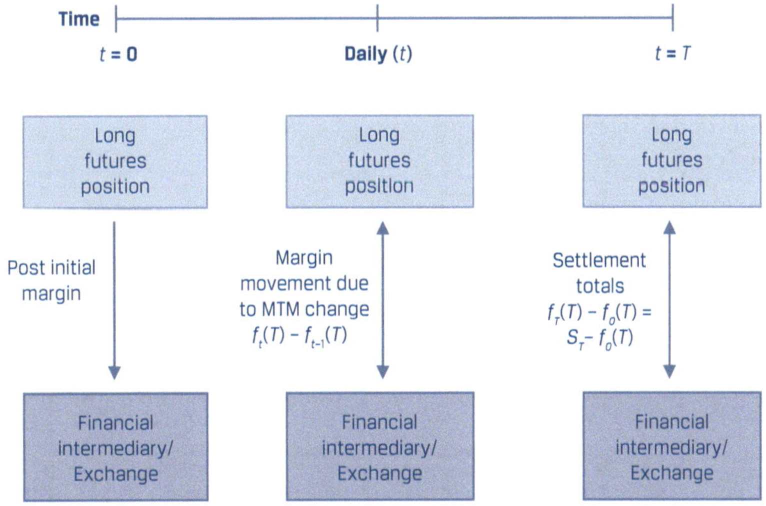

Exchanges reserve the right to impose more strict requirements than standard futures margin account rules to limit potential losses from counterparty default. For example, for large positions or a significant increase in price volatility of the underlying, an exchange may increase required margins and/or make margin calls on an intraday basis. Some futures contracts also limit daily price changes. These rules, called **price**

limits, establish a band relative to the previous day's settlement price within which all trades must occur. If market participants wish to trade at a price outside these bands, trading stops until two parties agree on a trade at a price within the prescribed range. In other cases, exchanges use what is called a **circuit breaker** to pause intraday trading for a brief period if a price limit is reached.

Similar to forward contracts, final settlement at maturity for futures contracts is based on the difference between the futures price, $f_0(T)$, and the underlying price of S_T, or $[S_T - f_0(T)]$ from the buyer's perspective. Because Procam has agreed to purchase gold now (at $t = T$) valued at $1,780.50 per ounce at a price of $1,792.13 per ounce, it owes $11.63 per ounce, or $1,163 [($1,780.50 – $1,792.13) × 100 oz.] under both the forward from Example 1 and this futures contract. The *net* payoff profile shown in Exhibit 1 is the same for a futures contract as for a forward assuming they have the same maturity date, with the difference being the *timing* of the cash flows due to the daily futures contract mark-to-market settlement, as shown in Example 3.

EXAMPLE 3

Final Settlement of a Gold Futures Contract

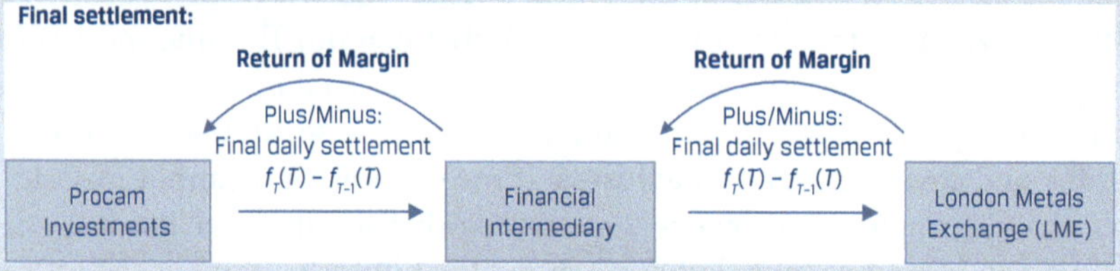

For purposes of exposition, we compress the three months of gold futures price changes from Example 2 into six days of trading in the following spreadsheet:

Exhibit 3

Procam's Futures Margin Account

Gold Contract	100	ounces
# of Contracts	1	
Initial Futures Price $f_0(T)$	$1,792.13	per ounce
Initial Position Value	$179,213	
Initial Margin	$4,950	
Maintenance Margin	$4,500	

Day	Futures Price	Day Gain (Loss)	Total Gain (Loss)	Margin Balance	Margin Call
$T - 6$	$1,792.13			$4,950	
$T - 5$	$1,797.13	$500	$500	$5,450	—
$T - 4$	$1,786.25	($1,088)	($588)	$4,362	$588
$T - 3$	$1,782.19	($406)	($994)	$4,544	—
$T - 2$	$1,777.45	($474)	($1,468)	$4,070	$880
$T - 1$	$1,779.50	$205	($1,263)	$5,155	—
T	$1,780.50	$100	**($1,163)**	$5,255	$1,468

Procam's Results from the Futures Contract	
Gold Contract	100
# of Contracts	1
Initial Futures Price $f_0(T)$	$1,792.13
Initial Position Value	$179,213
Total Gain (Loss)	($1,163)
Final Futures Price $F_T(T)$	$1,780.50
Final Position Value	$178,050
Sum of Margin Calls	$1,468
Beginning less Ending Margin Balance	($305)
Total Payments to Margin Account	$1,163

As the gold futures price, $f_0(t)$, falls and the margin balance drops below the $4,500 maintenance margin minimum over time, Procam must immediately replenish its balance to the $4,950 initial margin each time this occurs:

- On Day $T - 4$, gold futures fall $10.88 per ounce ($1,797.13 – $1,786.25). Procam's balance falls $1,088 (100 × $10.88) to $4,362 ($5,450 – $1,088). Procam faces a margin call of $588 ($4,950 – $4,362).
- On Day $T - 2$, gold futures fall $4.74 per ounce ($1,782.19 – $1,777.45). Procam's balance falls $474 (100 × $4.74) to $4,070 ($4,544 – $474). Procam faces a margin call of $880 ($4,950 – $4,070).

On the final trading day, Procam has paid a total of $1,468 ($588 + $880) in margin calls and its futures margin account balance is $5,155, or $205 in excess of the $4,950 initial margin. Procam has a cumulative MTM loss of $1,263 ($1,468 – $205) at the start of the last trading day.

- The prior day's gold futures settlement price, $f_{T-1}(T)$, is $1,779.50.
- Gold futures rise $1 per ounce on the final trading day to settle at $f_T(T)$ = $1,780.50 per ounce, the same as for the forward in Example 1.
- The daily change in Procam's margin account is an increase of $100 ($1 per ounce × 100 ounces), bringing the margin account to $5,255.
- Procam's futures margin balance of $5,255 is returned at settlement for a net return of $305 ($5,255 – $4,950) in margin.
- Procam receives a net return of $305 in margin at settlement for a cumulative loss upon settlement of $1,163 ($305 – $1,468).

Both the forward and futures contracts involve a $1,163 settlement loss, but the forward is fully settled at maturity while the futures contract is settled based on the daily MTM. The time value of money principle suggests that these forward and futures settlements are not equivalent amounts of money, but the differences are small for shorter maturities and low interest rates. Also note that under the forward contract in Example 1, the financial intermediary bears counterparty risk to Procam for the forward settlement. In practice, financial intermediaries often use collateral arrangements similar to futures margining for forwards or other derivatives to reduce counterparty credit risk.

At maturity, the number of outstanding contracts, or **open interest**, is settled via cash or physical delivery. A counterparty may instead choose to enter an offsetting futures contract before expiration to close out a position; for example, a futures contract buyer may simply sell the open contract. The clearinghouse marks the contract to the current price relative to the previous settlement price and closes out the participant's position.

Futures contracts specify whether physical delivery of an underlying or cash settlement occurs at expiration. For example, a commodity futures contract with physical delivery obligates the seller to deliver an underlying asset of a specific type, amount, and quality to a designated location. The buyer must accept and pay for delivery, which ensures that the futures price converges with the spot price at expiration.

QUESTION SET

Futures

1. Determine the correct answers to fill in the blanks: If a futures contract buyer's margin account falls below the ________ ________, or minimum balance that each contract buyer and seller must hold in the account from trade initiation until final settlement, the buyer must immediately deposit funds to return the account balance to the ________ ________.

   Solution:

   If a futures contract buyer's margin account falls below the *maintenance margin*, or minimum balance that each contract buyer and seller must hold in the account from trade initiation until final settlement, the buyer must immediately deposit funds to return the account balance to the *initial margin*.

2. Describe the mark-to-market process for a futures contract.

   Solution:

   The exchange clearinghouse determines an average of the final futures prices of the day and designates that price as the end-of-day settlement price. The daily settlement of gains and losses takes place via each counterparty's futures margin account.

3. Identify these futures contract participants that correspond to the following statements:

A Futures contract purchaser	1. Must make a margin deposit at contract initiation and maintain a minimum balance until maturity
B. Futures contract seller	2. Receives a margin account deposit if the futures price increases on any trading day
C. Both a futures contract purchaser and a seller	3. Receives a positive payoff if the spot price S_T is below the futures price, $f_0(T)$, at maturity

   Solution:

   1. The correct answer is C. Both futures contract buyers and sellers must deposit margin and maintain a minimum margin balance (maintenance margin) over the life of a contract.

   2. The correct answer is A. The futures contract buyer realizes a mark-to-market gain on any trading day when the futures price increases and receives a corresponding margin account deposit.

3. The correct answer is B. The futures contract seller realizes a positive payoff at maturity if $S_T < f_0(T)$.

SWAPS

4

☐ define forward contracts, futures contracts, swaps, options (calls and puts), and credit derivatives and compare their basic characteristics

A swap is a firm commitment under which two counterparties exchange a series of cash flows in the future. One set of cash flows is typically variable, or floating, and determined by a market reference rate that resets each period. The other cash flow stream is usually fixed or may vary based on a different underlying asset or rate. In this case, we refer to the counterparty paying the variable cash flows as the **floating-rate payer** (or fixed-rate receiver) and the counterparty paying fixed cash flows as the **fixed-rate payer** (floating-rate receiver), as shown in Exhibit 4.

Exhibit 4: Swap Mechanics

Swaps and forwards have similar features, such as a start date, a maturity date, and an underlying that are negotiated between counterparties and specified in a contract. Interest rate swaps in which a fixed rate is exchanged for a floating rate are the most common swap contract. For each period in the future, the market reference rate (MRR) paid by the floating-rate payer resets, while the fixed rate (referred to as the **swap rate**) is constant, as shown in Exhibit 5.

Exhibit 5: Swap as a Series of Forward Exchanges

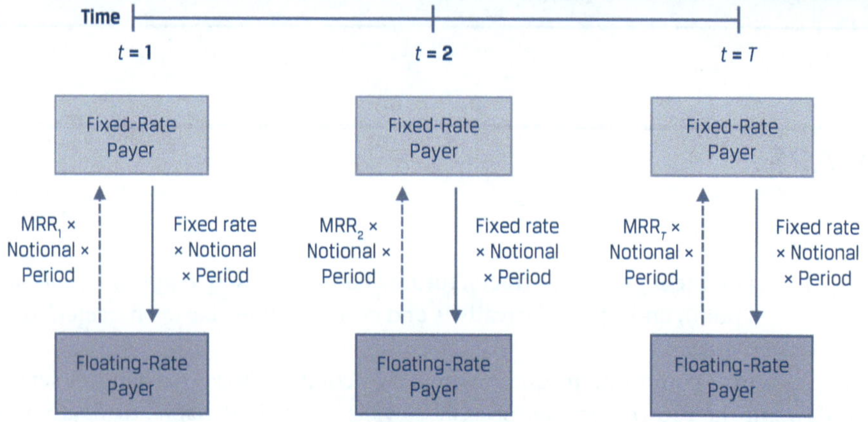

Counterparties usually exchange a net payment on fixed- and floating-rate payments on the swap as in Example 4.

EXAMPLE 4

Fyleton Investments Swap

Fyleton Investments has entered a five-year, receive-fixed GBP200 million interest rate swap with a financial intermediary to increase the duration of its fixed-income portfolio. Under terms of the swap, Fyleton has agreed to receive a semiannual GBP fixed rate of 2.25% and pay six-month MRR.

Calculate the first swap cash flow exchange if six-month MRR is set at 1.95%.

- The financial intermediary owes Fyleton a fixed cash flow payment of GBP2,250,000 (= GBP200 million × 0.0225/2).
- Fyleton owes the financial intermediary a floating cash flow payment of GBP1,950,000 (= GBP 200 million × 0.0195/2).
- The fixed and floating payments are netted against one another, and the net result is that the financial intermediary pays Fyleton GBP300,000 (= GBP2,250,000 – GBP1,950,000).

The notional principal is usually not exchanged but, rather, is used for fixed and floating interest payment calculations, as in Example 4. The example demonstrates how an investment manager might use an interest rate swap to change portfolio duration without trading bonds. Issuers often use swaps to alter the exposure profile of a liability, such as a term loan.

As with futures and forward contracts, no money is exchanged when a swap contract is initiated. The value of a swap at inception is therefore effectively zero, ignoring transaction costs. In an earlier fixed-income lesson, it was shown that implied forward rates may be derived from spot rates. Forward MRRs may be used to determine the expected future cash flows for the floating leg of an interest rate swap. The swap rate for the fixed leg payments is determined by solving for a constant fixed yield that equates the present value of the fixed and floating leg payments.

As market conditions change and time passes, the mark-to-market value of a swap will deviate from zero, resulting in a positive MTM to one counterparty and an offsetting negative MTM to the other. Swap credit terms are privately negotiated between counterparties in an over-the-counter agreement and may range from uncollateralized exposure, where each counterparty bears the full default risk of the other, to terms similar to futures margining for one or both counterparties. An event of counterparty default usually triggers swap termination and MTM settlement as for any other debt claim. Centrally cleared swaps between financial intermediaries and a central counterparty (CCP) include margin provisions similar to futures in order to standardize and reduce counterparty risk.

QUESTION SET

Swaps

1. Describe a similarity of and a difference between forward and swap contracts.

   Solution:

   Similarities: Both forwards and swaps represent firm commitments with an initial value of zero where cash flows are exchanged in the future at a pre-agreed price.

   Difference: Forwards usually involve one future exchange of cash flows, while a swap contract involves more than one exchange of future cash flows.

2. Determine the correct answers to fill in the blanks: Under a swap contract, we refer to the counterparty paying the variable cash flows as the ___-___ ___ and the counterparty paying fixed cash flows as the ___-___ ___.

   Solution:

   Under a swap contract, we refer to the counterparty paying the variable cash flows as the *floating-rate payer* (or *fixed-rate receiver*) and the counterparty paying fixed cash flows as the *fixed-rate payer* (or *floating-rate receiver*).

3. Identify the interest rate swap participants that correspond to the following statements:

A. Fixed-rate payer	1. Makes a payment each interest period based on a market reference rate
B. Floating-rate payer	2. May face a positive or a negative mark to market over the life of an interest rate swap contract
C. Both a fixed-rate payer and a floating-rate payer	3. Receives a net payment on the swap for any interest period for which the market reference rate exceeds the fixed rate

   Solution:

   1. The correct answer is B. A floating-rate payer on a swap makes a payment each period based on a market reference rate.

   2. The correct answer is C. Both a fixed-rate payer and a floating-rate payer may face a positive MTM or negative MTM on a swap contract.

3. The correct answer is A. A fixed-rate payer (also known as the floating-rate receiver) receives a net payment if the market reference rate exceeds the fixed rate for a given period.

5 OPTIONS

- ☐ define forward contracts, futures contracts, swaps, options (calls and puts), and credit derivatives and compare their basic characteristics
- ☐ determine the value at expiration and profit from a long or a short position in a call or put option
- ☐ contrast forward commitments with contingent claims

Contingent claims are a type of ETD or OTC derivative contract in which one of the counterparties has the right to determine whether a trade will settle based on the underlying value. Option contracts are the most common contingent claim. Similar to forwards and futures, options are derivative contracts between a buyer and a seller that specify an underlying, contract size, a pre-agreed execution price, and a maturity date. The option buyer has the right but not the obligation to transact the trade, and the option seller has the obligation to fulfill the transaction as chosen by the option buyer. As a consequence, the payoff to an option buyer is always zero or positive. It can never be negative.

Assume an option buyer pays a premium (c_0) of \$5 at $t = 0$ for the right—but not the obligation—to buy stock S at time T at a pre-agreed price (X) of \$30. The option buyer's decision at maturity depends on the stock price at maturity (S_T), as shown in the following two scenarios:

Scenario 1: Transact ($S_T > X$)

- If S_T = \$40, the option buyer chooses to exercise the option and buy the stock for X = \$30.
- The option buyer gains \$10 [($S_T - X$) = \$40 – \$30] on the transaction.
- The option buyer realizes a \$5 profit [($S_T - X$) – c_0 = (\$40 – \$30) – \$5].

Scenario 2: Do Not Transact ($S_T < X$)

- If S_T = \$25, the option buyer chooses not to exercise the option and buy the stock for X = \$30.
- The option buyer realizes a \$5 loss (c_0 = \$5).

Exhibit 6 shows the option mechanics for the case where the option buyer pays for the right to purchase an underlying stock S at a pre-agreed execution price of X in the future ($t = T$).

Exhibit 6: Call Option Mechanics

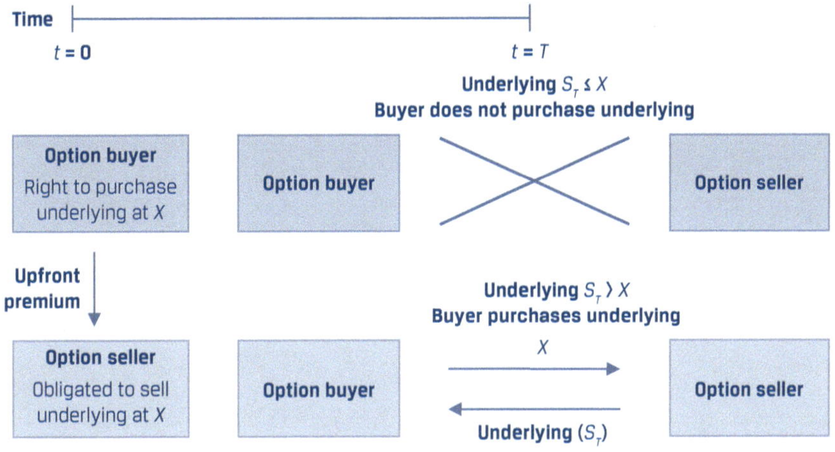

The decision to transact the underlying is referred to as an **exercise**, and the pre-agreed execution price is called the **exercise price** (or strike price). Option buyers may transact the underlying in the future at their sole discretion at the exercise price, a pre-agreed future spot price that may be above, at, or below the forward price, as shown in an earlier lesson. This right to exercise in the future has a value that is paid upfront to the option seller in the form of an **option premium**.

Option contract terms, such as the right to buy or sell, exercise price, maturity, and size, may either be agreed on between the counterparties in an over-the-counter transaction or executed on an exchange based on standardized terms. This lesson focuses on **European options**, or options that may be exercised only at maturity, although other option styles exist. **American options**, for example, may be exercised at any time from contract inception until maturity. Note the labels "European" and "American" refer not to where these options are used but, rather, to the difference in when they can be exercised.

Two primary option types exist—namely, (1) the right to buy an underlying known as a **call option** and (2) the right to sell the underlying, or a **put option**. An option buyer will exercise a call or put option only if it returns a positive payoff. If not exercised, the option expires worthless, and the option buyer's loss equals the premium paid.

One factor in an option's value prior to maturity ($t < T$) is the option's exercise value at time t, which is referred to as an option's **intrinsic value**.

We can say a call option is **in-the-money** at time t if the spot price, S_t, exceeds X, with an intrinsic value equal to ($S_t - X$). Both **out-of-the-money** options (where $S_t < X$) and **at-the-money** options ($S_t = X$) have zero intrinsic value, so their price, c_t, consists solely of time value.

Call option buyers will gain from a rise in the price of the underlying. Exhibit 7 shows the payoff and profit at maturity for a call option buyer.

Exhibit 7: Long Call Payoff Profile

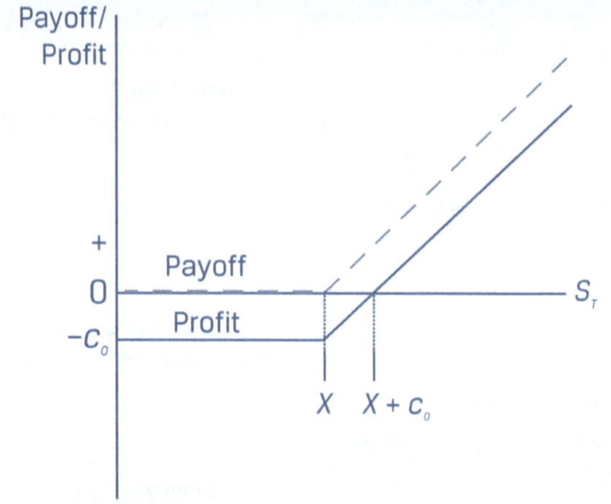

The option buyer pays a call option premium, c_0, at time $t = 0$ to the option seller and has the right to purchase the underlying, S_T, at an exercise price of X at time $t = T$. The exercise *payoff* $(S_T - X)$ is positive if $S_T > X$ and zero if $S_T \leq X$. The call option value at maturity, c_T, may be expressed as follows:

$$c_T = \max(0, S_T - X). \quad (1)$$

The call option buyer's *profit* equals the *payoff* minus the call premium, c_0 (ignoring the time value of money in this lesson):

$$\Pi = \max(0, S_T - X) - c_0. \quad (2)$$

This asymmetric payoff profile is a common feature of contingent claims, which are sometimes referred to as **non-linear derivatives**.

EXAMPLE 5

Hightest Capital—Call Option Purchase

Hightest Capital purchases a call option on the S&P 500 Health Care Select Sector Index (SIXV). This six-month exchange-traded option contract has a size of 100 index units and an exercise price of $1,240 per unit versus the initial SIXV spot price of $1,180.95. The option premium paid upfront is $24.85 per unit, or $2,485 (= $24.85 × 100). As the option nears maturity, a Hightest analyst is asked to determine the expected option payoff and profit per unit at maturity under different scenarios for the SIXV spot price on the exercise date.

She compiles the following table:

c_0 = Call option premium = $24.85 per unit.

= Exercise price at time T = $1,240 per unit.

S_T = Spot price per unit at time T.

SIXV Spot Price (S_T)	Exercise Price (X)	Payoff $\max(0, S_T - X)$	Profit $\max(0, S_T - X) - c_0$
$1,280	$1,240	$40	$15.15
$1,260	$1,240	$20	−$4.85

SIXV Spot Price (S_T)	Exercise Price (X)	Payoff max(0, $S_T - X$)	Profit max(0, $S_T - X$) − c_0
$1,240	$1,240	$0	−$24.85
$1,220	$1,240	$0	−$24.85

Example 5 raises another question regarding an option's value prior to maturity ($t < T$). The longer the time to option maturity, the more likely it is that a favorable change in the underlying price will increase both the likelihood and profitability of exercise. This **time value** of an option is always positive and declines to zero as an option reaches maturity.

In contrast to the call option buyer with unlimited upside potential and a loss limited to the premium paid, the call option seller receives a maximum of the premium and faces unlimited downside risk as the underlying appreciates above the exercise price. The short call payoff profile in Exhibit 8 is a mirror image of Exhibit 7.

Exhibit 8: Short Call Payoff Profile

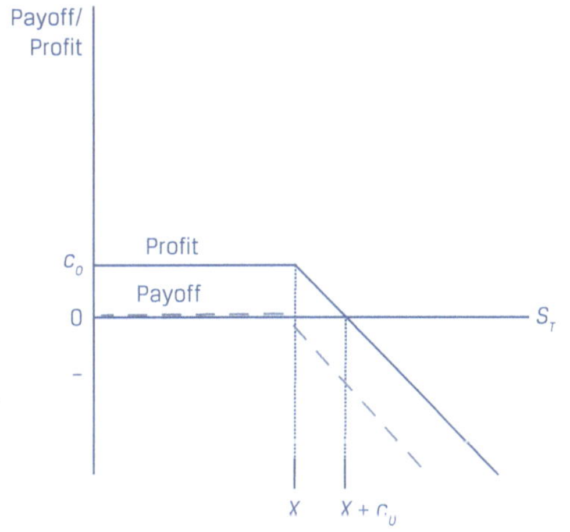

The option buyer and seller payoff profiles demonstrate the one-sided nature of counterparty credit risk for contingent claims. That is, the option seller has no credit exposure to the option buyer once the premium is paid. However, the option buyer faces the counterparty credit risk of the option seller equal to the option payoff at maturity.

Put option buyers benefit from a lower underlying price by selling the underlying at a pre-agreed exercise price. A put option buyer exercises when the underlying price is below the exercise price ($S_T < X$), as shown in Exhibit 9.

Exhibit 9: Long Put Payoff Profile

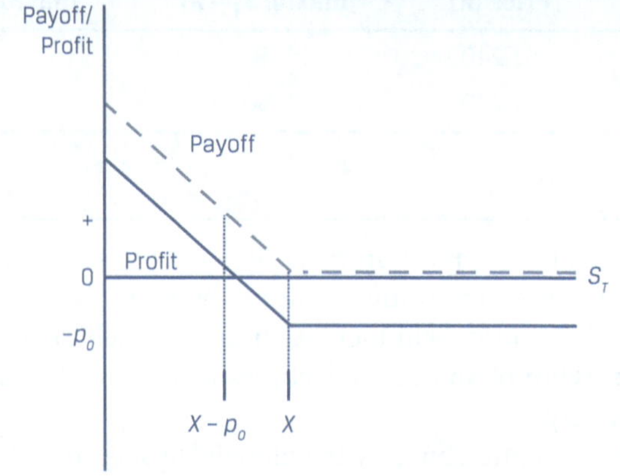

The put option buyer pays a premium of p_0 at inception to the option seller and will exercise the option only if $(X - S_T) > 0$. As in Equations 1 and 2, we may show the long put option *payoff* and *profit*, Π, as follows:

$$p_T = \max(0, X - S_T). \tag{3}$$

$$\Pi = \max(0, X - S_T) - p_0. \tag{4}$$

The payoff or profit from a put option seller's perspective is the opposite of the put option buyer's gain or loss for a given underlying price at expiration. As in the case of the call option seller, the put option seller has a maximum gain equal to the premium. However, although a call option seller faces unlimited potential loss as the underlying appreciates beyond the exercise price, the put option seller's loss is usually limited because the underlying price cannot fall below zero. The short put option *payoff* and *profit* are as follows:

$$-p_T = -\max(0, X - S_T). \tag{5}$$

$$\Pi = -\max(0, X - S_T) + p_0. \tag{6}$$

QUESTION SET

Options

1. Calculate the SIXV spot price at maturity from Example 5 at which Hightest Capital will reach a breakeven point and earn zero profit.

   Solution:

   The call purchaser has a profit equal to $\max(0, S_T - X) - c_0$. In the case of Hightest in Example 5, the SIXV exercise price is $1,240 and the initial call premium is $24.85. The breakeven or zero profit point is therefore equal to $1,240 + $24.85, or $1,264.85.

2. A put option seller receives a $5 premium for a put option sold on an underlying with an exercise price of $30. What is the option seller's maximum profit under the contract? What is the maximum loss under the contract?

Solution:

A put option seller receives a $5 premium ($p_0$) for a put option sold on an underlying with an exercise price (X) of $30. The put option seller's profit is $\Pi = -\max(0, X - S_T) + p_0$. If the option is unexercised, $-\max(0, X - S_T) = 0$ and the put seller earns $p_0 = \$5$. If the option is exercised and $S_T = 0$, then $\Pi = -\max(0, 30 - 0) + 5 = -\$25$. Therefore, the option seller's maximum profit under the contract is $5 and the maximum loss under the contract is $25.

3. Identify the option contract participants that correspond to the following statements:

A. Put option seller	1. Has no counterparty credit risk to the option buyer once the upfront premium has been paid
B. Call option seller	2. Earns a profit equal to the premium if the underlying price at maturity is less than the exercise price
C. Both a put option seller and a call option seller	3. Earns a profit equal to the premium if the underlying price at maturity exceeds the exercise price

Solution:

1. The correct answer is C. An option seller has no counterparty credit risk to the option buyer once the upfront premium has been paid.

2. The correct answer is B. A call option seller earns a profit equal to the premium if the underlying price at maturity is less than the exercise price.

3. The correct answer is A. A put option seller earns a profit equal to the premium if the underlying price at maturity is greater than the exercise price.

CREDIT DERIVATIVES

6

☐ define forward contracts, futures contracts, swaps, options (calls and puts), and credit derivatives and compare their basic characteristics

Credit derivative contracts are based on a credit underlying, or the default risk of a single debt issuer or a group of debt issuers in an index. The most common credit derivative contract is a credit default swap. CDS contracts allow an investor to manage the risk of loss from issuer default separately from a cash bond. CDS contracts trade based on a credit spread (**CDS credit spread**) similar to that of a cash bond. Credit spreads depend on the probability of default (POD) and the loss given default (LGD), as shown in an earlier lesson. A *higher* credit spread (or higher likelihood of issuer financial distress) corresponds to a *lower* cash bond price, and vice versa.

Despite their name, CDS contracts are contingent claims that share some features of firm commitments. Unlike the call and put options discussed earlier, both the timing of exercise and payment upon exercise under a CDS contract vary depending on the underlying issuer(s). As in the case of a standard interest rate swap, a CDS contract priced at a par spread has a zero net present value, and the notional amount is not exchanged but, rather, serves as a basis for spread and settlement calculations.

In a CDS contract, the credit protection buyer pays the credit protection seller to assume the risk of loss from the default of an underlying third-party issuer. If an issuer **credit event** occurs—usually defined as bankruptcy, failure to pay an obligation, or an involuntary debt restructuring—the credit protection seller pays the credit protection buyer to settle the contract. This contingent payment equals the issuer loss given default for the CDS contract notional amount. Exhibit 10 shows the periodic cash flows under a CDS contract.

Exhibit 10: Periodic Payments under a Credit Default Swap

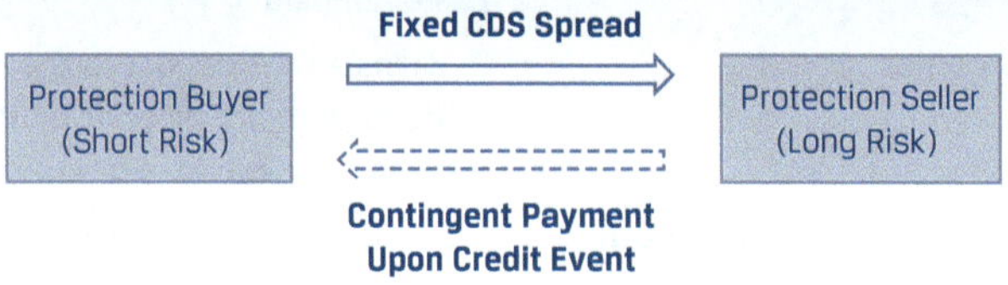

The underlying may be a corporate or sovereign issuer, an index of issuers, or a special purpose entity with a portfolio of loans, mortgages, or bonds.

A buyer can use a CDS contract as a hedge of existing credit exposure to the underlying issuer. The credit protection afforded by a CDS is similar to insurance for a buyer with an existing fixed-income exposure to the third-party issuer. The buyer may suffer a loss in value on its fixed-income exposure from the credit event but will receive a payment from the CDS contract that will offset that loss.

A credit protection buyer without the corresponding fixed-income exposure who buys a CDS is seeking to gain from higher credit spreads (which correspond to lower cash bond prices) for an underlying issuer and is therefore short credit risk.

The credit protection seller receives a periodic fixed spread payment in exchange for assuming the contingent risk of paying the credit protection buyer to offset the loss under a credit event. The contract structure is similar to insurance, with the periodic premium over the life of the contract agreed to upfront and with the timing and size of the loss under the credit event being unknown. The seller's position is therefore similar to that of a long risk position in the issuer's underlying bond.

For example, Exhibit 11 shows the CDS contract for an underlying issuer that experiences credit migration ($t = 1$) followed by a credit event ($t = 2$).

Exhibit 11: CDS Contract with Credit Migration and Credit Event

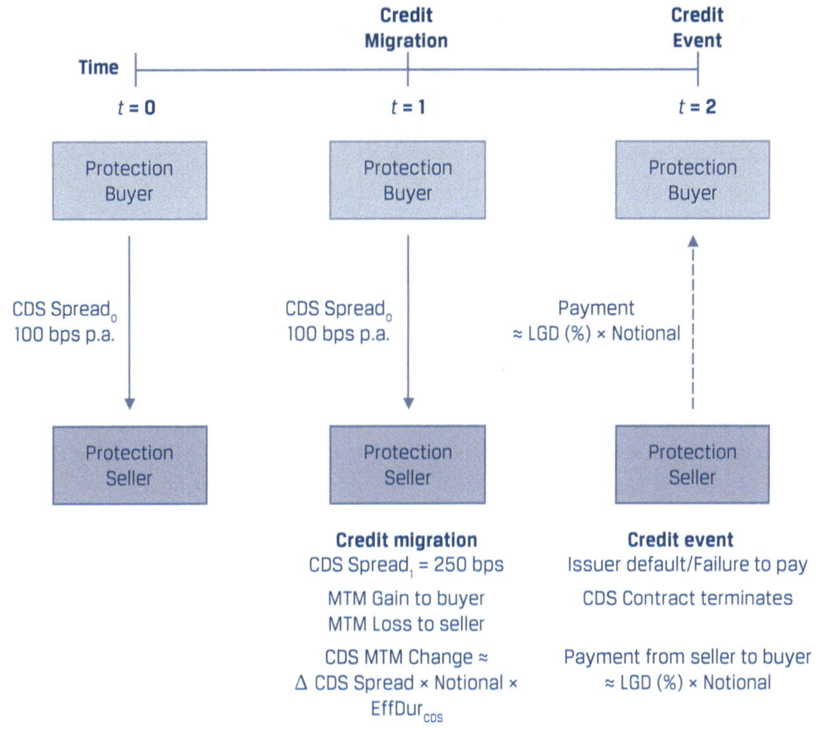

The protection buyer agrees to pay a fixed spread of 100 bps p.a. at $t = 0$ for the contract term. As the issuer's CDS spread widens to 250 bps p.a. at $t = 1$, the buyer gains on the CDS contract due to the low fixed spread paid while the seller loses due to the low fixed spread received relative to the current higher CDS market spread. As for any fixed-income instrument, the effective duration of the remaining contract may be used to approximate the MTM change. An issuer credit event at $t = 2$ causes the contract to terminate, and the seller must make a payment to the buyer equal to the percentage of loss (LGD) multiplied by the CDS contract notional.

QUESTION SET

Credit Derivatives

1. Determine the correct answer to fill in the blanks: The contingent payment under a credit default swap equals the ____ ____ ____ for the CDS notional amount specified in the contract.

   Solution:

   The contingent payment under a credit default swap equals the *loss given default* for the CDS notional amount specified in the contract.

2. Describe how a credit protection seller's position is similar to that of an underlying cash bond investment.

   Solution:

   A credit protection seller receives a periodic CDS spread payment in exchange for the contingent risk of payment to the buyer under an issuer credit event. A cash bond investor receives a periodic coupon that incorporates an issuer's credit spread in exchange for a potential loss if the issuer defaults. Under the CDS contract and the cash bond, this potential payment or loss equals the LGD. The credit protection seller's position is therefore similar to that of a long risk position in the issuer's underlying bond.

3. Identify the CDS contract participants that correspond to the following statements:

A. Credit protection buyer	1. Seeks to gain from higher issuer credit spreads
B. Credit protection seller	2. Enters into a derivative contract that transfers the risk of loss from a credit event of an underlying third-party issuer
C. Both a credit protection buyer and a credit protection seller	3. Faces an MTM gain on the CDS contract if the CDS spread of the underlying issuer falls

Solution:

1. The correct answer is A. A credit protection buyer seeks to gain from higher issuer credit spreads.

2. The correct answer is C. Both the credit protection buyer and credit protection seller enter into a derivative contract that transfers the risk of loss from a credit event of an underlying third-party issuer.

3. The correct answer is B. A credit protection seller faces an MTM gain on the CDS contract if the CDS spread of the underlying issuer falls. The decline in the issuer's CDS spread versus the original fixed spread on the CDS contract means that the protection seller is receiving an above-market spread. This above-market CDS spread more than compensates the seller for the new, lower level of credit risk and results in an MTM gain.

7 FORWARD COMMITMENTS VS. CONTINGENT CLAIMS

☐ contrast forward commitments with contingent claims

A firm commitment requires both counterparties to perform under a derivative contract, while an option buyer can decide whether to perform under the contract at maturity depending on the underlying price relative to the exercise price. Market participants often create similar exposures to an underlying using these different derivative instrument types. For example, both a long forward position and a long call option position will gain from an increase in the underlying price. Exhibit 12 contrasts the payoff and profit of these two derivative contracts, where the exercise price, X, equals the forward price, $F_0(T)$.

Exhibit 12: Long Forward and Long Call Option Payoff Profiles

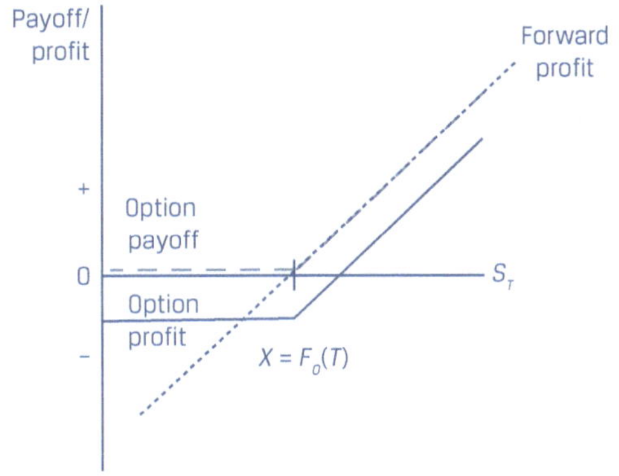

As shown earlier, both the long forward and the call option payoffs increase as S_T rises. In the case of a forward, this linear relationship is equal to $[S_T - F_0(T)]$, with the payoff equal to profit because no cash is exchanged at inception. For the buyer of a call option with an exercise price of $F_0(T)$, Equation 2 changes to

$$\Pi = \max[0, S_T - F_0(T)] - c_0.$$

Setting the forward payoff/profit $[S_T - F_0(T)]$ equal to the call option profit, Π, gives us the following relative profit profile between the forward and option:

- $S_T - F_0(T) > -c_0$ Forward profit exceeds option profit
- $S_T - F_0(T) = -c_0$ Forward profit equals call option profit
- $S_T - F_0(T) < -c_0$ Option profit exceeds forward profit

The side-by-side comparison in Exhibit 12 between the forward and call option profit diagrams shows the long call option's similarity to a long position in the underlying with downside protection in exchange for paying a premium.

Another contingent claim that benefits from a rise in the underlying price is the sold put option. While the long call option and long forward payoffs both rise when the underlying price is above the exercise price, the put option seller's profit is limited to the upfront premium. Exhibit 13 contrasts the short put payoff and profit with a long forward if the exercise price, X, equals $F_0(T)$.

Exhibit 13: Long Forward and Short Put Option Payoff Profile

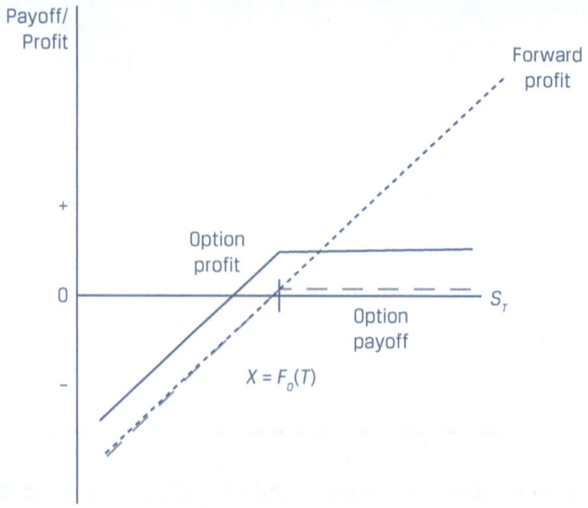

We can compare the long forward payoff/profit of $[S_T - F_0(T)]$ to a modified version of Equation 6:

$$\Pi = -\max[0, F_0(T) - S_T] + p_0.$$

Setting the forward profit $[S_T - F_0(T)]$ equal to the put option profit, Π, gives us the following relative profit profile between the forward and option:

- $S_T - F_0(T) > p_0$ Forward profit exceeds option profit
- $S_T - F_0(T) = p_0$ Forward profit equals option profit)
- $S_T - F_0(T) < p_0$ Option profit exceeds forward profit

The side-by-side comparison in Exhibit 13 of the forward and sold put option profit diagrams shows the sold put option's similarity to a long position in the underlying, with gains from price appreciation forgone in exchange for receiving a premium. The apparent symmetry between long call and short put positions and the long forward position will be examined in greater detail in a later lesson.

QUESTION SET

Firm Commitments and Contingent Claims

1. Determine the correct answers to fill in the blanks: A _____ forward position, a _____ call option position, and a _____ put option position will gain from a decrease in the underlying price.

   Solution:

   A *short* forward position, a *short* call option position, and a *long* put option position will gain from a decrease in the underlying price.

2. Identify the derivative positions that correspond to the following profit profiles at maturity assuming that the exercise price (X) equals $F_0(T)$:

A. Short forward position

1.

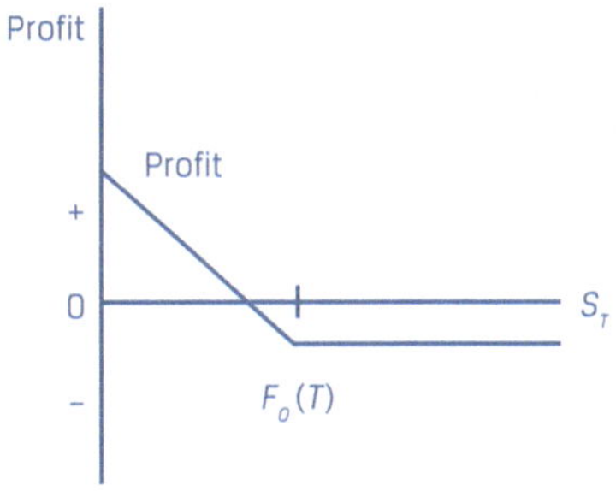

B. Long put position

2.

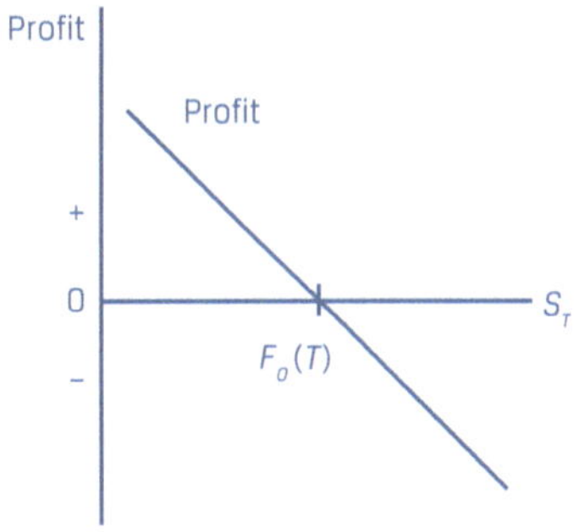

C. Short call position

3.

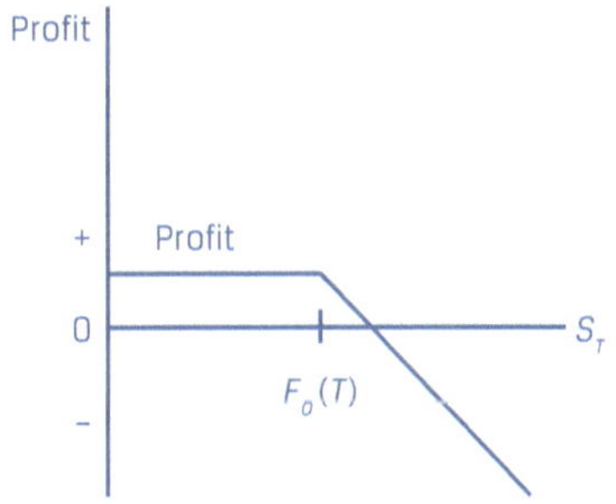

Solution:

1. The correct answer is B.
2. The correct answer is A.
3. The correct answer is C.

3. Describe the point at which a short forward and a long put with an exercise price (X) equal to the forward price, $F_0(T)$ have the same profit.

Solution:

The short forward and long put positions will have the same profit when $F_0(T) - S_T = -p_0$. A short forward position gains from a decline in the underlying price with a payoff/profit of $[F_0(T) - S_T]$, and a long put position has a profit of $\Pi = \max[0, F_0(T) - S_T] - p_0$, from Equation 4, with an exercise price equal to the forward price, $X = F_0(T)$.

PRACTICE PROBLEMS

The following information relates to questions 1-4

Biomian Limited is a Mumbai-based biotech company with common stock and listed futures and options on the National Stock Exchange (NSE). The Viswan Family Office (VFO) currently owns 10,000 Biomian common shares. VFO would like to reduce its long Biomian position and diversify its equity market exposure but will delay a cash sale of shares for tax reasons for six months.

1. Which of the following derivative contracts available to VFO's chief investment officer is best suited to reduce exposure to a decline in Biomian's stock price in the next six months?

   A. A short put position on Biomian stock that expires in six months

   B. A long call position on Biomian stock that expires in six months

   C. A short futures position in Biomian stock that settles in six months

2. VFO's market strategist believes that Biomian's share price will rise over the next six months but would like to protect against a decline in Biomian's share price over the period. Which of the following positions is best suited for VFO to manage its existing Biomian exposure based on this view?

   A. A long put position on Biomian stock that expires in six months

   B. A short call position on Biomian stock that expires in six months

   C. A long futures position in Biomian stock that settles in six months

3. Assume that Biomian shares rise over the next six months. Which of the following statements about VFO's derivative strategies under this scenario is most accurate?

   A. A forward sale of Biomian shares in six months would be more profitable than purchasing the right to sell Biomian shares in six months.

   B. Purchasing the right to sell Biomian shares in six months would be more profitable than a forward sale of Biomian shares in six months.

   C. We do not have enough information to determine whether a forward sale or the right to sell Biomian shares will be more profitable in six months.

4. VFO's market strategist is considering a six-month call option strategy on the NIFTY 50 benchmark Indian stock market index to increase broad market equity exposure. The NIFTY 50 price today is INR15,200, and the strategist observes that a call option with a INR16,000 exercise price (X) is trading at a premium of INR1,500. Which of the following represents the payoff and profit of this strategy just prior to maturity if the NIFTY 50 is trading at INR16,500?

   A. Payoff is INR500; profit is –INR1,000.

   B. Payoff is INR1,300; profit is INR800.

C. Payoff is INR1,300; profit is INR500.

SOLUTIONS

1. C is correct. VFO may consider either a short futures position in (or a forward sale of) Biomian shares in six months to achieve its objective. This firm commitment allows VFO to offset its long position with a short position in six months at a pre-agreed price. The futures contract is an exchange-traded derivative with standardized terms set by the exchange and requires initial margin and daily settlement. Answers A and B are contingent claims that can both potentially increase, not decrease, VFO's exposure to Biomian stock in six months.

2. A is correct. VFO should purchase a six-month put option on Biomian shares to manage its exposure based on the market strategist's view. This contingent claim grants VFO the right but not the obligation to sell Biomian shares at a pre-agreed exercise price in exchange for a premium. A put option buyer exercises the option at maturity when the underlying price is below the exercise price. This allows VFO to continue to benefit from a rise in Biomian's share price over the next six months with a limited downside. Neither B nor C provides VFO with downside protection if Biomian stock declines in six months.

3. C is correct. Under a forward sale of Biomian shares, the profit is $[F_0(T) - S_T]$. If the shares rise significantly over the next six months—that is, $S_T > F_0(T)$—then VFO's loss on the derivative is the difference between the Biomian forward price, $F_0(T)$, and the spot price, S_T. Under the long put option on Biomian shares, VFO's profit is $\max(0, X - S_T) - p_0$. If Biomian shares rise significantly over the next six months (i.e., $S_T > X$), then the option expires worthless and VFO's loss is limited to the put premium paid, p_0. If $[F_0(T) - S_T] > -p_0$, then VFO's loss would be greater under the firm commitment than under the contingent claim.

4. A is correct. The profit is equal to $\Pi = \max(0, S_T - X) - c_0$, and the payoff is equal to $\max(0, S_T - X)$. The exercise price is INR16,000, and the spot price just prior to maturity is INR16,500, so $\Pi = -1{,}000$ [= (16,500 – 16,000) – 1,500], and the payoff is equal to INR500 [= (16,500 – 16,000)].

LEARNING MODULE

3

Derivative Benefits, Risks, and Issuer and Investor Uses

LEARNING OUTCOMES

Mastery	The candidate should be able to:
☐	describe benefits and risks of derivative instruments
☐	compare the use of derivatives among issuers and investors

INTRODUCTION

1

Earlier lessons described how derivatives expand the set of opportunities available to market participants to create or modify exposure or to hedge the price of an underlying. This learning module describes the benefits and risks of using derivatives and compares their use among issuers and investors.

LEARNING MODULE OVERVIEW

- Derivatives allow market participants to allocate, manage, or trade exposure without exchanging an underlying in the cash market.
- Derivatives also offer greater operational and market efficiency than cash markets and allow users to create exposures unavailable in cash markets.
- Derivative instruments can involve risks such as a high degree of implicit leverage and less transparency in some cases than cash instruments, as well as basis, liquidity, and counterparty credit risks. Excessive risk taking in the past by market participants through the use of derivatives has contributed to market destabilization and systemic risk.
- Issuers typically use derivative instruments to offset or hedge market-based underlying exposures that impact their assets, liabilities, and earnings.

- Issuers usually seek hedge accounting treatment for derivatives to minimize income statement and cash flow volatility.
- Investors use derivatives to modify investment portfolio cash flows, replicate investment strategy returns in cash markets, and/or create exposures unavailable to cash market participants.

LEARNING MODULE SELF-ASSESSMENT

These initial questions are intended to help you gauge your current level of understanding of this learning module.

1. Which of the following statements does **not** describe a likely operational advantage of a futures market transaction as compared to a cash market transaction?

   A. It is easier to take a short position in the futures market than in the cash market.

   B. There is greater liquidity in the futures market than in the cash market.

   C. Cash requirements to buy in the cash market are lower than margin requirements to buy in the futures market.

   Solution:

   C is correct. The opposite is true: Margin requirements of a futures contract are typically only a small percentage of the cash requirement to buy the same amount of underlying in the cash market. A and B are both incorrect because both of these statements describe operational advantages of futures markets over cash markets.

2. Identify which derivative risk fits each of the following statements:

A. Basis risk	1. Potential divergence between the cash flow timing of a derivative versus an underlying or hedged transaction
B. Liquidity risk	2. Potential divergence between the expected value of a derivative versus an underlying or hedged transaction
C. Counterparty credit risk	3. Potential for a derivatives contract participant to fail to meet their obligations under an agreement

   Solution

   1. B is correct. Liquidity risk is the potential divergence between the cash flow timing of a derivative versus an underlying or hedged transaction.

   2. A is correct. Basis risk is the potential divergence between the expected value of a derivative versus an underlying or hedged transaction.

   3. C is correct. Counterparty credit risk is the potential for a derivatives contract participant to fail to meet their obligations under an agreement.

3. Identify which benefit of derivatives use fits each of the following examples:

A. Price discovery function	1. Equity market participants monitor index futures prior to the market open for an indication of the direction of cash market prices in early trading.
B. Operational advantages	2. An issuer may wish to lock in its future debt costs in advance of the maturity of an outstanding debt issuance.
C. Ability to allocate, transfer, and manage risk	3. Futures contracts in physical commodities eliminate the need to directly transport, insure, and store a physical asset in order to take a position in its underlying price.

Solution

1. A is correct. Equity market participants monitoring index futures prior to the market open for an indication of the direction of cash market prices in early trading is an example of the derivatives price discovery function.
2. C is correct. An issuer locking in its future debt costs in advance of the maturity of an outstanding debt issuance is an example of the ability to allocate, transfer, and manage risk.
3. B is correct. Futures contracts in physical commodities eliminating the need to directly transport, insure, and store a physical asset in order to take a position in its underlying price is an example of the operational advantages of a derivative.

4. Which of the following hedge accounting designations is appropriate for categorizing a corporate issuer's use of an interest swap converting a floating-rate debt into a fixed-rate debt?

A. Fair value hedge

B. Cash flow hedge

C. Net investment hedge

Solution:

B is correct. Cash flow hedge treatment is appropriate for instances in which a variable cash flow is converted to a fixed cash flow through the use of a derivative. A is incorrect because a fair value hedge is appropriate accounting treatment for derivative contracts that offset fluctuations in the fair value of the underlying. C is incorrect because a net investment hedge offsets the foreign currency risk of the value of a foreign subsidiary.

DERIVATIVE BENEFITS

2

☐ describe benefits and risks of derivative instruments

Earlier lessons demonstrated how market participants use derivative instruments as an alternative to cash markets to hedge or offset commercial risk as well as create or modify exposure to the price of an underlying. We now take a more detailed look at these and other benefits of the use of derivatives, while also considering several risks unique to derivative instruments.

Derivative instruments provide users the opportunity to allocate, transfer, and/or manage risk without trading an underlying. Cash or spot market prices for financial instruments and commercial goods and services are a critical source of information for the decision to buy or sell. However, in many instances, issuers and investors face a timing difference between an economic decision and the ability to transact in a cash market.

For example, issuers face the following timing differences when making operational and financing decisions:

- A manufacturer may need to order commodity inputs for its production process in advance of receiving finished-goods orders.
- A retailer may await a shipment of goods priced in a foreign currency before selling domestic currency to make payment.
- An issuer may wish to lock in its future debt costs in advance of the maturity of an outstanding debt issuance.

Investors may face similar timing issues when making portfolio decisions that are separate from cash market transactions, as in the following cases:

- An investor may seek to capitalize on a market view but lack the necessary cash on hand to transact in the spot market.
- In anticipation of a future stock dividend, debt coupon, or principal repayment, an investor may decide today how it will reinvest the proceeds in the future.

The ability to buy or sell a derivative instrument today at a pre-agreed price at a future date can bridge the timing gap between an economic decision and the ability to transact in underlying price risk under these scenarios. The use of forward commitments or contingent claims to allocate or transfer risk across time and among market participants able and willing to accept those exposures is a consistent theme in derivative markets. Example 1 builds on an earlier illustration of how an issuer may benefit from the use of a derivative associated with a commercial contract.

EXAMPLE 1

Foreign Exchange Risk Transfer of an Export Contract

Recall Montau AG, the German capital goods producer introduced earlier, which signs a commercial contract with Jeon, Inc., a Korean manufacturer, to deliver a laser cutting machine at a price of KRW650,000,000 in 75 days. Montau has fixed domestic currency (EUR) costs and therefore faces a timing mismatch between EUR costs incurred and EUR revenue realized upon the delivery of the machine and sale of KRW received in exchange for EUR in the spot FX market.

Describe Montau's currency exposure and how an FX forward contract may be used to mitigate its FX price risk.

Montau will receive KRW in 75 days, which it must sell to cover its EUR costs. This exposes the firm to KRW/EUR exchange rate changes for 75 days. Specifically, if the KRW depreciates versus the EUR, Montau will be able to purchase fewer EUR than expected with the KRW proceeds, resulting in a loss due to the FX timing mismatch. Montau's exposure profile due to the mismatch is as follows:

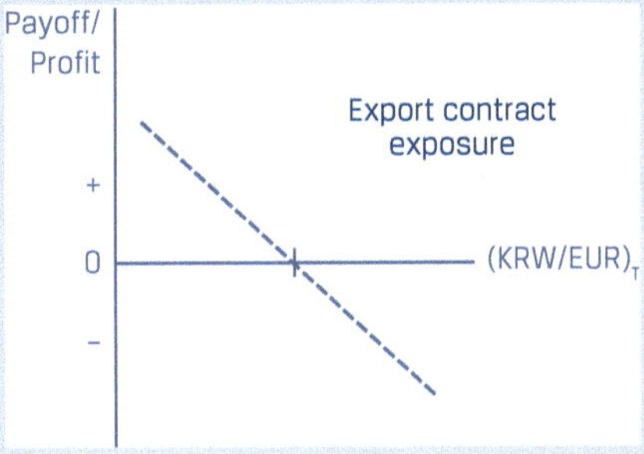

In order to mitigate its export contract exposure, Montau enters an FX forward to sell KRW and purchase EUR at a fixed price [$F_0(T)$] in 75 days to eliminate the KRW/EUR exchange rate mismatch arising from the export contract. The FX forward payoff and profit profile is as follows:

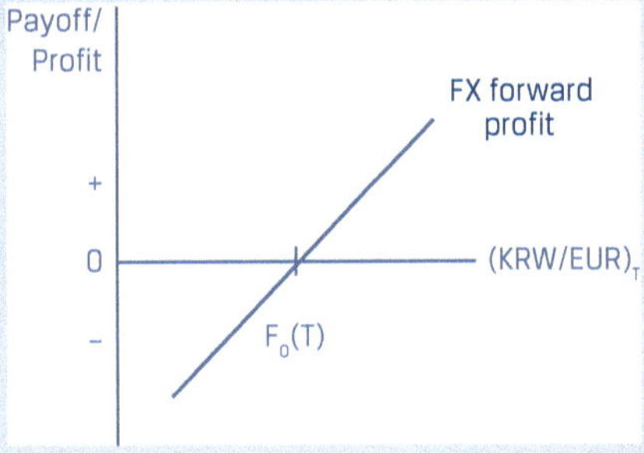

The FX forward payoff and profit profile offsets Montau's export contract exposure as a hedge, as shown in the following combined diagram:

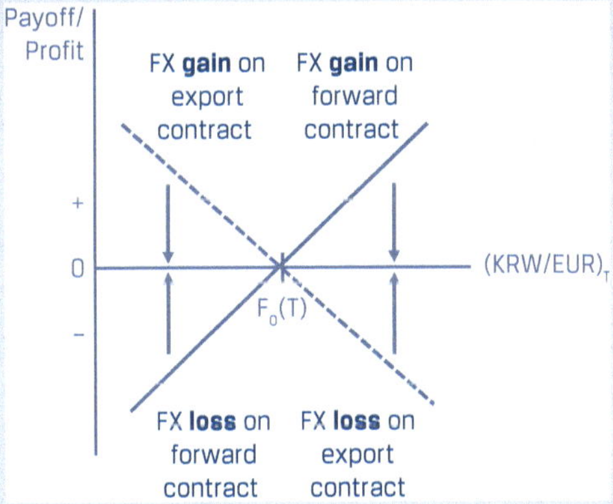

The ability to trade and/or manage risk using derivatives extends to the creation of exposure profiles, which are unavailable in cash markets. The following example combines a long cash position with a sold derivative to increase an investor's expected return, based on a specific market view.

EXAMPLE 2

Covered Call Option Strategy

South China Sprintwyck Investments (SCSI) has a Chinese equity portfolio that has outperformed in the first half of the year due to an overweight position in health care industry shares. SCSI holds a long position in the Shenzhen China Securities Index (CSI) 300 Health Care Index (CSI 300) traded on the China Financial Futures Exchange (CFFEX). SCSI's CIO expects volatility in the CSI

300 to decline and the CSI 300 price at year-end to be at or slightly above the current spot price. Rather than sell the CSI 300 position today in the cash market, she decides to sell a CSI 300 call option at an exercise price 5% above the current spot market price for the remaining six months of the year.

Describe the *difference* in SCSI's CSI 300 payoff profile between 1.) the long cash position and 2.) the sold call option plus long cash position (referred to as a **covered call** strategy) at the end of the year.

1. SCSI's long cash position will rise or fall in value as the CSI 300 spot price changes until the end of the year.

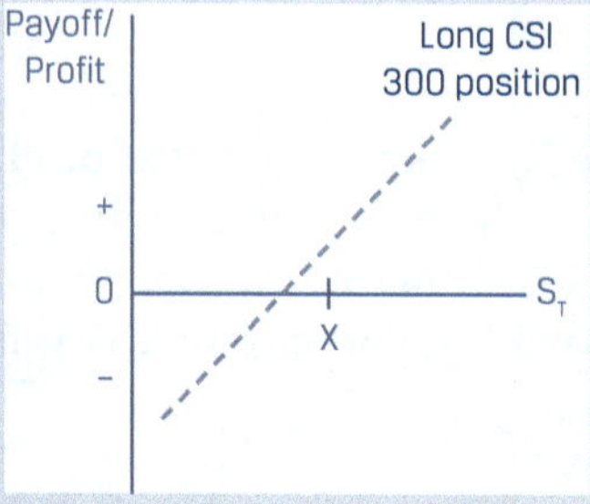

The *difference* between 1.) and 2.) is the sale of a CSI 300 call option. SCSI sells the call and receives an upfront premium. SCSI assumes unlimited downside risk as the CSI 300 price rises above the exercise price:

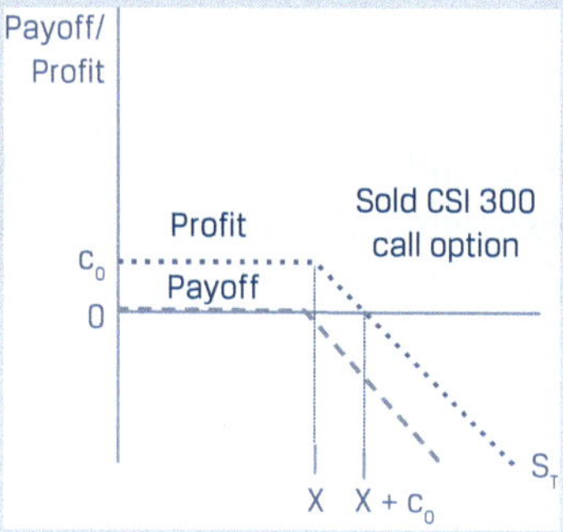

2. The combination of the long CSI 300 cash position and the short CSI 300 call option results in the profit profile represented by the solid line below:

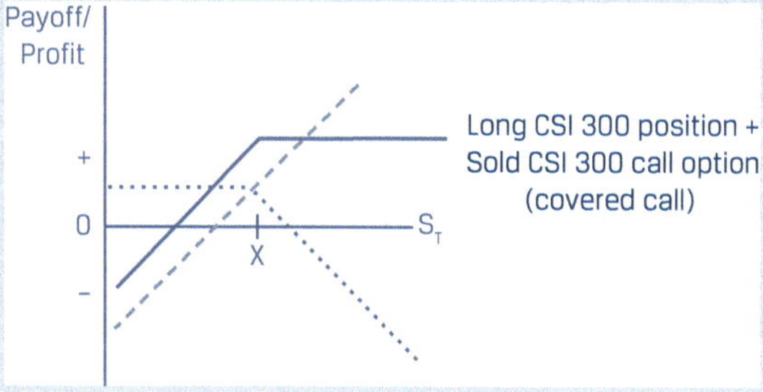

The covered call strategy payoff may be described as follows:

- **CSI 300 appreciates by less than 5%:** The call option expires unexercised. SCSI's profit equals the long CSI 300 position plus the call premium.
- **CSI 300 appreciates by more than 5%:** The call option is exercised. SCSI must pay the option buyer an amount equal to the gain on its long CSI 300 position above the exercise price. The option payoff is said to be "covered" by the long cash position. SCSI retains the call premium.

Derivative instrument prices serve a price discovery function beyond the underlying cash or spot market. For example, futures prices are often seen as revealing information about the direction of cash markets in the future, although they cannot be strictly considered an unbiased forecast of future spot prices.

Market participants often use futures prices to gauge the direction of cash markets in the future in the following ways:

- Equity market participants frequently monitor equity index futures prices prior to the stock market open for an indication of the direction of cash market prices in early trading.
- Analysts often use interest rate futures markets to extract investor expectations of a central bank benchmark interest rate increase or decrease at a future meeting.
- Commodity futures prices are a gauge of supply and demand dynamics between producers, consumers, and investors across maturities.

Example 3 provides a case of supply and demand effects on futures prices.

EXAMPLE 3

Negative Oil Futures Prices in 2020

In April 2020, the West Texas Intermediate (WTI) crude oil futures price fell below zero for the first time ever. The New York Mercantile Exchange (NYMEX) WTI crude oil futures contract has an underlying of 1,000 barrels of crude oil delivered to Cushing, Oklahoma, where energy companies store nearly 80 million barrels of oil. Widespread lockdowns in the wake of the COVID-19 pandemic caused demand to plummet, while producers could not cut oil production quickly enough in anticipation of the severe decline. Oil inventory in Cushing skyrocketed as a result.

NYMEX Oil Futures Price (USD per contract), January–June 2020

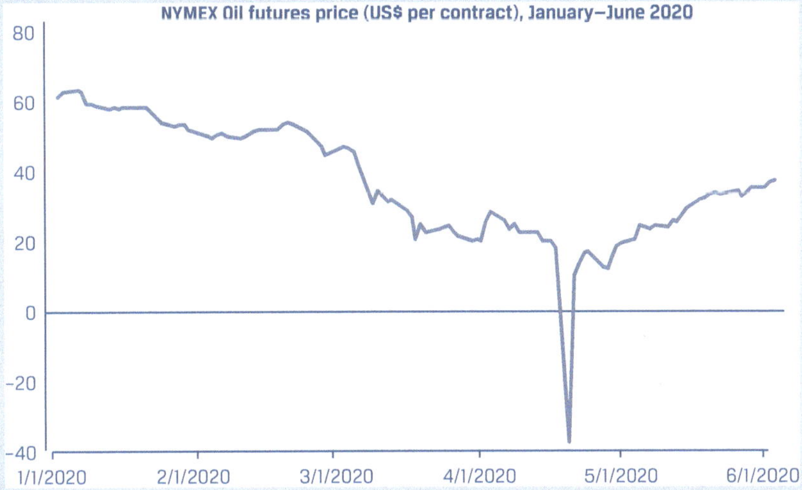

Source: Bloomberg.

As the May futures contract approached expiration in late April 2020, investors assuming the financial risk of oil prices were surprised as oil refiners avoided physical delivery of oil upon contract settlement due to a sharp rise in storage costs. This forced the May futures price sharply lower, to a closing price of –USD37.63 on 20 April 2020. Oil producers and refiners used this futures pricing information to adjust supply more quickly and reduce pressure on storage facilities.

The price discovery function of derivatives extends to contingent claims. As we will see in a later lesson, option prices reflect several characteristics of the underlying, including the expected price risk of the underlying, known as **implied volatility**. The implied volatility of an option may be derived from its current price and other option features and provides a measure of the general level of uncertainty in the price of the underlying.

Derivative transactions offer a number of operational advantages to cash or spot markets in many instances.

1. **Transaction Costs:** Commodity derivatives eliminate the need to transport, insure, and store a physical asset in order to take a position in its underlying price.
2. **Increased Liquidity:** Derivative markets typically have greater liquidity as a result of the reduced capital required to trade derivatives versus an equivalent cash position in an underlying.
3. **Upfront Cash Requirements:** Initial futures margin requirements and option premiums are low relative to the cost of a cash market purchase.
4. **Short Positions:** In the absence of a liquid derivative market, taking a short position involves the costly process of locating a cash owner willing to lend the underlying for a period sufficient to facilitate a short sale.

Example 4 contrasts the cash outlay of a spot trade with a futures contract based on transaction details familiar from an earlier lesson.

EXAMPLE 4

Purchase of Spot Gold versus a Gold Futures Contract

In an earlier example, Procam Investments enters a futures contract to buy 100 ounces of gold at a futures price [$f_0(T)$] of USD1,792.13 per ounce that expires in three months and must post USD4,950 in initial margin as required by the exchange. The spot gold price (S_0) at the time Procam enters the futures contract is USD1,770 per ounce. Assume that Procam is able to borrow funds from a financial intermediary at a rate of 5% per year. Contrast the expected opportunity cost of the initial margin for the three-month futures contract with a cash purchase of 100 ounces of gold for the same three-month period.

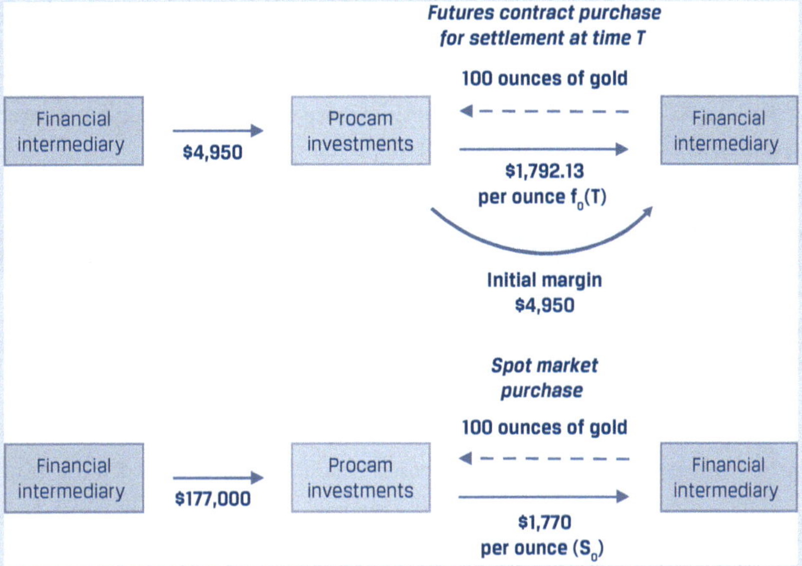

1. Procam borrows the USD4,950 initial margin from a financial intermediary at 5% for three months.

Opportunity (interest) cost of the initial margin:

= (USD4,950 × .05)/4 = USD61.88

2. Procam borrows USD177,000 (USD1,770 × 100 ounces) for the spot gold purchase from a financial intermediary at 5% for three months.

Opportunity (interest) cost of the cash gold purchase price:

= (USD177,000 × .05)/4 = USD2,212.50

Procam gains exposure to the underlying price of 100 ounces of gold in the futures market at a fraction of the spot market cost. This comparison ignores three points about the futures contract and spot gold transactions:

1. Procam's margin requirements change as the futures price fluctuates between t = 0 and t = T. Specifically, Procam faces margin calls if a lower futures price causes its margin account balance to fall below the maintenance margin. However, as the underlying price is usually bounded by zero, it is unlikely that Procam's borrowing cost for margin will exceed that of the spot cash purchase.
2. Procam's spot gold purchase involves physical gold. It must therefore cover the cost of delivery, storage, and insurance for three months.
3. The spot gold purchase takes place at a price of S_0 = USD1,770 per ounce, while the pre-agreed futures price [$f_0(T)$] = USD1,792.13 per ounce. At time T in three months, both the futures contract and the spot purchase result in a long position for Procam at a price of S_T. The expected cost and return for these two transactions should therefore be equal, but the prices agreed at t = 0 are not. In a later lesson, we will explore the relationship between the spot gold price (S_0) and the gold futures price [$f_0(T)$] and the effect of both borrowing and storage costs.

The operational efficiency of derivative markets also leads to greater market efficiency. When prices deviate from fundamental values, derivative markets offer less costly ways to exploit the mispricing. As noted earlier, less capital is required, transaction costs are lower, and short selling is easier. As a result of these market features, fundamental value is often reflected in derivative markets before it is restored in the underlying cash market. The existence of derivative markets therefore often causes financial markets in general to function more effectively. Exhibit 1 summarizes derivative market benefits for market participants.

Exhibit 1: Benefits of Derivative Instruments

Purpose	Description
Risk Allocation, Transfer, and Management	Allocate, trade, and/or manage underlying exposure without trading the underlying Create exposures unavailable in cash markets
Information Discovery	Deliver information regarding expected price in the future and information regarding expected risk of underlying
Operational Advantages	Reduced cash outlay, lower transaction costs versus the underlying, increased liquidity and ability to "short"
Market Efficiency	Less costly to exploit arbitrage opportunities or mispricing

QUESTION SET

Derivative Benefits

1. Describe a scenario in which an issuer faces a timing difference between an economic decision and an ability to transact in cash markets to manage price risk.

   Solution:

   An issuer may need to 1.) order commodity inputs for its production process in advance of receiving finished-goods orders, 2.) await a shipment of goods in a foreign currency before selling domestic currency to make payment, or 3.) lock in its future debt costs in advance of the maturity of an outstanding debt issuance.

2. Determine the correct answers to fill in the blanks: Derivative markets typically have greater _________ than the underlying spot markets, a result of the reduced _______ required to trade derivatives versus an equivalent cash position in an underlying.

   Solution:

   Derivative markets typically have greater *liquidity* than the underlying spot markets, a result of the reduced *capital* required to trade derivatives versus an equivalent cash position in an underlying.

3. Identify the proper derivative market benefits that correspond to the following statements:

A. Price discovery function	1. Futures margin requirements are quite low versus the cost of a cash market purchase.
B. Operational advantages	2. The ability to buy or sell a derivative today eliminates the timing mismatch between an economic decision and the ability to transact.
C. Risk transfer	3. Investors track an equity index futures price to gauge sentiment before the market opens.

Solution:

1. The correct answer is B. The low level of futures margin requirements versus the cost of a cash market purchase is an example of the operational advantage of using derivatives.
2. The correct answer is C. The ability to buy or sell a derivative contract today eliminates the timing mismatch between an economic decision and the ability to transact, which is an example of the risk transfer function of derivatives.
3. The correct answer is A. Investors use derivatives in a price discovery function when tracking an equity index futures price to gauge sentiment before the market opens.

DERIVATIVE RISKS

3

- [ ] describe benefits and risks of derivative instruments

While derivatives offer benefits such as the ability to efficiently hedge, allocate, and/or transfer risk as well as greater operational and market efficiency, the greater complexity of derivative instruments and positions also gives rise to greater potential risks associated with their use.

The greater operational efficiency of derivative strategies that limit an investor's initial cash outlay translates to a high degree of implicit leverage versus a similar cash market position. To illustrate this effect, we return to an earlier example to measure and compare the leverage between a futures contract and a cash market purchase with and without the use of borrowing.

EXAMPLE 5

Implicit Leverage of Spot versus Futures Purchases

In Example 4, we compared a spot purchase and a three-month futures contract purchase of 100 ounces of gold by Procam Investments.

- Procam's spot market purchase at S_0 = USD1,770 per ounce results in a purchase price of USD177,000 (USD1,770 × 100) paid in cash.

- Procam's three-month futures contract purchase at $f_0(T)$ = USD1,792.13 per ounce results in a purchase price of USD179,213 (USD1,792.13 × 100). This purchase requires a USD4,950 initial margin deposit at the exchange.

In three months, the spot gold price (S_T) is USD1,780.50 per ounce, and both the long cash position and the long futures contract position are valued at USD178,050 (USD1,780.50 × 100). We divide the value change by the initial cash outlay for each transaction to compare implicit leverages:

- Spot value change: 0.593% gain [(USD178,050 – USD177,000)/ USD177,000].
- Futures value change: 23.5% loss [(USD178,050 – USD179,213)/ USD4,950].

Note the large order-of-magnitude difference between the cash and futures transactions. As mentioned earlier, we will explore the relationship between borrowing costs, gold storage costs (ignored in this example), the spot gold price (S_0), and the gold futures price [$f_0(T)$] in a later lesson.

Implicit leverage is further magnified in an extreme case where only borrowed funds are used to enter the cash and futures transactions, as in Example 4:

- Spot value change versus borrowing cost: 47.5% gain [(USD178,050 – USD177,000)/ USD2,212.50].
- Futures value change versus borrowing cost: 1,879% loss [(USD178,050 – USD179,213)/ USD61.88].

This example emphasizes a very important point about derivatives: their inherent leverage magnifies the realized returns and risks and contributes to the severity of derivative-related losses.

Procam gains exposure to USD177,000 in underlying gold price risk with just USD61.88, implying a leverage ratio of 2,860. Procam benefits from this high leverage as gold prices rise, but its losses are rapidly magnified as gold prices decline. For example, as the futures price falls from USD179,213 to USD178,050, the modest –0.649% gold price change translates to a loss of USD1,163. Procam's actual loss on this transaction is both the interest payment (USD61.88) and the loss on the trade (USD1,163), for a total loss of USD1,224.88, nearly 20 times (USD1,224.88/ USD61.88) the cost of financing.

The same principle holds for non-linear derivatives such as sold options, where an option seller may face unlimited downside risk as underlying price changes make it more favorable for an option buyer to exercise for a gain far in excess of the premium paid.

Leverage in derivatives creates significant exposures for the counterparties involved. These risks are mitigated through a combination of trading and exposure risk management, daily marking to market, the use of collateral arrangements, transaction and exposure limits, and centralized counterparties.

Derivatives offer the flexibility to create exposures beyond cash markets, which can add significant portfolio complexity and involve risks that are not well understood by stakeholders. This risk increases when a combination of derivatives and/or embedded derivatives is involved. For example, **structured notes** are a broad category of securities that incorporate the features of debt instruments and one or more embedded derivatives designed to achieve a particular issuer or investor objective. For instance, structured notes designed to create a derivative-based payoff profile for individual investors may involve greater cost, lower liquidity, and less transparency than an equivalent stand-alone derivative instrument.

Derivative users hedging commercial or financial exposure usually assume that a derivative will be highly effective in offsetting the price risk of an underlying. However, in some instances, the expected value of a derivative differs unexpectedly from that of the underlying, in what is known as **basis risk**. Basis risk may arise if a derivative instrument references a price or index that is similar to, but does not exactly match, an underlying exposure such as a different market reference rate or an issuer CDS spread versus that of an actual bond. Basis risk is affected by supply and demand dynamics in derivative markets, among other factors.

A related risk that can arise for both hedgers and risk takers is **liquidity risk**, or a divergence in the cash flow timing of a derivative versus that of an underlying transaction. The daily settlement of gains and losses in the futures market can give rise to liquidity risk. If an investor or issuer using a futures contract to hedge an underlying transaction is unable to meet a margin call due to a lack of funds, the counterparty's position is closed out and the investor or issuer must cover any losses on the derivative trade.

Counterparty credit risk is of critical importance to derivative market participants. Unlike loan and bond markets, where credit exposures are predictably based on notional outstanding plus accrued interest, daily swings in the price of an underlying, among other factors affecting derivative prices, require more frequent exposure monitoring and management. Counterparty credit exposure varies by the derivative type and market in which a derivative is transacted. Exhibit 2 contrasts the counterparty credit risk of a contingent claim with that of a forward commitment, using the example of a purchased call option and a long forward position.

Exhibit 2: Counterparty Credit Risk of an Option versus a Forward

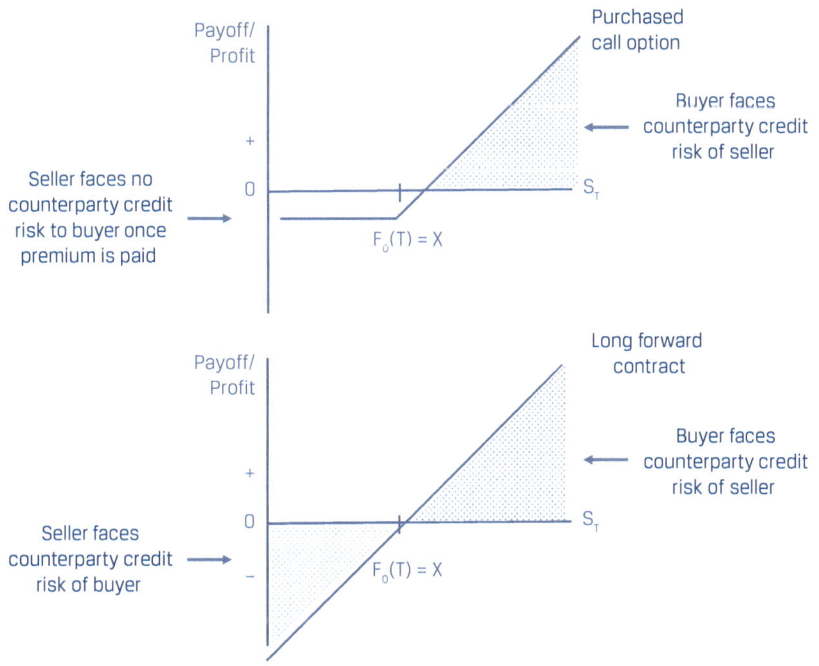

As for market type, the daily settlement of MTM gains and losses, which characterizes exchange-traded derivatives, substantially reduces counterparty credit risk. Exchanges reserve the right to increase margin requirements or require intraday margining for highly volatile or concentrated positions. In over-the-counter (OTC)

markets, credit terms privately arranged between counterparties vary from uncollateralized exposure to terms similar to futures margining for one or both counterparties using collateral.

Broader derivatives use among market participants has increased the focus of financial market supervisory authorities on the potential market-wide impact, or **systemic risk**, associated with these instruments. Regulators continue to specifically focus on the impact of financial innovation and financial conditions to ensure financial stability as they monitor risk taking and leverage among derivative market participants. Market reforms such as the central clearing mandate for swaps between financial intermediaries and a central counterparty (CCP), outlined earlier, include margin provisions similar to futures in order to standardize and reduce counterparty credit risk.

Exhibit 3 summarizes the key risks associated with derivative instruments and markets.

Exhibit 3: Risks of Derivative Instruments

Risk	Description
Greater Potential for Speculative Use	High degree of implicit leverage for some derivative strategies may increase the likelihood of financial distress.
Lack of Transparency	Derivatives add portfolio complexity and may create an exposure profile that is not well understood by stakeholders.
Basis Risk	Potential divergence between the **expected value** of a derivative instrument versus an underlying or hedged transaction
Liquidity Risk	Potential divergence between the **cash flow timing** of a derivative instrument versus an underlying or hedged transaction
Counterparty Credit Risk	Derivative instruments often give rise to **counterparty credit exposure**, resulting from differences in the current price versus the expected future settlement price.
Destabilization and Systemic Risk	Excessive risk taking and use of leverage in derivative markets may contribute to market stress, as in the 2008 financial crisis.

QUESTION SET

Derivative Risks

1. Determine the correct answers to fill in the blanks: The _______ operational efficiency of derivative strategies that limit an investor's initial cash outlay translates to a ____ degree of implicit leverage versus a similar cash market position.

   Solution:

   The *greater* operational efficiency of derivative strategies that limit an investor's initial cash outlay translates to a *high* degree of implicit leverage versus a similar cash market position.

2. Describe the counterparty credit risk faced by the seller of a call option.

Solution:

The seller of a call option receives an upfront premium in exchange for the obligation to sell the underlying asset at the exercise price if the option is exercised. Once the seller of a call option receives the premium from the option buyer, it has no further counterparty credit risk to the option buyer.

3. Match these derivative market risks to the following statements:

A. Liquidity risk	1. The risk that excessive risk taking and use of leverage in derivative markets contribute to market stress
B. Basis risk	2. The risk of a divergence in the cash flow timing of a derivative versus that of an underlying transaction
C. Systemic risk	3. The risk that the expected value of a derivative differs unexpectedly from that of the underlying

Solution:

1. The correct answer is C. Systemic risk involves excessive risk taking and use of leverage in derivative markets that contribute to market stress.
2. The correct answer is A. Liquidity risk is the divergence in the cash flow timing of a derivative versus that of an underlying transaction.
3. The correct answer is B. Basis risk involves the risk that the expected value of a derivative differs unexpectedly from that of an underlying.

ISSUER USE OF DERIVATIVES 4

☐ compare the use of derivatives among issuers and investors

Issuers, investors, and financial intermediaries use derivative instruments to increase, decrease, or modify exposure to an underlying to meet their financial objectives. Financial analysts must gain a deeper understanding of the various uses of derivatives among market participants in order to interpret and replicate the wide range of strategies encountered in practice.

Non-financial corporate issuers often face risks to their assets, liabilities, and earnings as a result of changes in the price of an underlying. For example, a corporate issuer that uses a traded commodity in its operations will face greater earnings volatility due to input price changes. The additional earnings volatility has the potential to increase the corporate issuer's cost of borrowing as well as to create difficulties for investors to estimate its future corporate earnings. The impact of foreign exchange volatility on corporate issuer earnings is illustrated by extending an earlier example.

EXAMPLE 6

Foreign Exchange Risk and Earnings Volatility

Recall from Example 1 that Montau AG will deliver a laser cutting machine for KRW650,000,000 in 75 days and has hedged its FX exposure by agreeing to sell the KRW it will receive and purchase EUR upon delivery in an over-the-counter FX forward with a financial intermediary.

Montau agrees to a KRW/EUR forward exchange rate [$F_0(T)$] of 1,350 (i.e., 1,350 KRW = 1 EUR), at which it will sell 650,000,000 KRW and receive 481,481 EUR (650,000,000/1,350) in 75 days. The production manager estimates the machine's cost to be €430,000. Montau's Treasury manager compiles the following profit margin scenarios at different KRW/EUR spot rates (S_T):

Spot KRW/ EUR (s_T)	Unhedged EUR Proceeds	Unhedged Profit Margin	Hedged EUR Proceeds	Hedged Profit Margin
1,525	€426,230	−1%	€481,481	11%
1,400	€464,286	7%	€481,481	11%
1,280	€507,813	15%	€481,481	11%
1,225	€530,612	19%	€481,481	11%

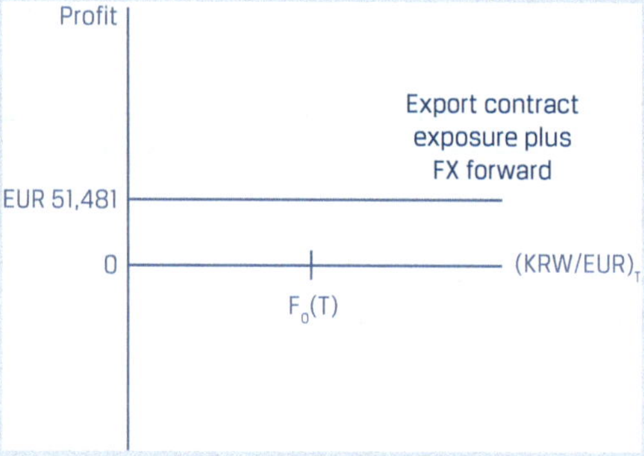

If Montau does not hedge its KRW/EUR exposure, its profit margin will fluctuate based on the KRW/EUR spot rate when the machine is delivered. A weaker KRW versus EUR results in a lower profit margin, while KRW appreciation results in a higher profit margin.

Example 6 illustrates one of the most common derivative strategies used by corporate issuers. The FX forward payoff offsets Montau's income statement and cash flow volatility due to currency changes.

Derivatives accounting has evolved from off-balance-sheet treatment to the reporting of these instruments on the balance sheet at their fair market value. This change aligns the recognition of derivative gains and losses with their designated risk management purpose, increasing transparency and disclosure of derivatives use. Many corporate issuers also establish risk management policies governing the objectives, guidelines, risk limits, and internal approval processes associated with derivatives use.

Derivatives accounting standards specify that any derivative purchased or sold must be marked to market through the income statement via earnings unless it is embedded in an asset or liability or qualifies for **hedge accounting**. Hedge accounting allows an issuer to offset a hedging instrument (usually a derivative) against a hedged transaction or balance sheet item to reduce financial statement volatility. Categorizing derivatives by hedge designation type sheds further light on both their intent and their expected financial statement impact, to the benefit of financial analysts and stakeholders.

For example, derivatives designated as absorbing the variable cash flow of a floating-rate asset or liability such as foreign exchange, interest rates, or commodities are referred to as **cash flow hedges**. Cash flow hedges may be either forward commitments or contingent claims. For instance, the FX forward in Example 6 is a cash flow hedge that offsets the variability of Montau's functional currency (EUR) proceeds from its commercial transaction in KRW. A swap to a fixed rate for a floating-rate debt liability is another example of a cash flow hedge.

A **fair value hedge** designation applies when a derivative is deemed to offset the fluctuation in fair value of an asset or liability. For example, an issuer might convert a fixed-rate bond issuance to a floating-rate obligation by entering into an interest rate swap to receive a fixed rate and pay a market reference rate through the bond's maturity. Alternatively, a commodities producer might sell its inventory forward in anticipation of lower future prices.

Net investment hedges occur when either a foreign currency bond or a derivative such as an FX swap or forward is used to offset the exchange rate risk of the equity of a foreign operation. Exhibit 4 summarizes these hedge designations.

Exhibit 4: Hedge Accounting Designation Types

Hedge Type	Description	Examples
Cash Flow	Absorbs variable cash flow of floating-rate asset or liability (forecasted transaction)	Interest rate swap to a fixed rate for floating-rate debt FX forward to hedge forecasted sales
Fair Value	Offsets fluctuation in fair value of an asset or liability	Interest rate swap to a floating rate for fixed-rate debt Commodity future to hedge inventory
Net Investment	Designated as offsetting the FX risk of the equity of a foreign operation	Currency swap Currency forward

Hedge accounting treatment for derivatives is highly desirable for corporate issuers, as it allows them to recognize derivative gains and losses at the same time as the associated underlying hedged transaction. Derivative mark-to-market changes are held within an equity account (Other Comprehensive Income) and released at the same time the underlying hedged transaction is recognized in earnings.

In order to qualify for this treatment, the dates, notional amounts, and other contract features of a derivative must closely match those of the underlying transaction. For this reason, issuers are far more likely to use OTC markets to create customized hedges to meet their specific needs. For example, Montau AG would face earnings volatility from the derivative position if it were to use a standardized two-month foreign exchange futures contract rather than the 75-day over-the-counter FX forward contract with a financial intermediary, as in Example 6.

QUESTION SET

Issuer Use of Derivatives

1. Describe hedge accounting treatment.

   Solution:

   Hedge accounting allows an issuer to offset a hedging instrument (usually a derivative) against a hedged transaction or balance sheet item to reduce financial statement volatility.

2. Match these hedge designation types to the following statements:

A. Cash flow hedge	1. A derivative used to offset the fluctuation in fair value of an asset or liability
B. Fair value hedge	2. A derivative designated as absorbing the variable cash flow of a floating-rate asset or liability
C. Net investment hedge	3. A derivative designated as offsetting the foreign exchange risk of the equity of a foreign operation

   Solution:

   1. The correct answer is B. A fair value hedge is a derivative used to offset the fluctuation in fair value of an asset or liability.
   2. The correct answer is A. A cash flow hedge is a derivative designated as absorbing the variable cash flow of a floating-rate asset or liability.
   3. The correct answer is C. A net investment hedge is a derivative designated as offsetting the foreign exchange risk of the equity of a foreign operation.

3. Describe an example of a fair value hedge an issuer might use.

   Solution:

   An issuer might convert a fixed-rate bond issuance to a floating-rate obligation by entering into an interest rate swap to receive a fixed rate and pay a market reference rate through the bond's maturity. Alternatively, a commodities producer might sell its inventory forward in anticipation of lower cash prices in the future.

5 INVESTOR USE OF DERIVATIVES

☐ compare the use of derivatives among issuers and investors

Issuers predominantly use derivatives to offset or hedge market-based underlying exposures incidental to their commercial operations and financing activities. In contrast, investors use derivatives to replicate a cash market strategy, hedge a fund's value against adverse movements in underlyings, or modify or add exposures using derivatives, which in some cases are unavailable in cash markets.

The greater liquidity and reduced capital required to trade derivatives may lead an investor to replicate a desired position using a derivative rather than cash. Alternatively, derivative hedges enable investors to isolate certain underlying exposures in the investment process while retaining a position in others. One example is the use of FX hedges when investing overseas in order to minimize the volatility of return due to currency fluctuations. Finally, the flexibility to take short positions or to increase or otherwise modify exposure using derivatives beyond cash alternatives is an attractive feature for portfolio managers targeting excess returns by using a variety of strategies.

An investment fund's prospectus typically specifies which derivative instruments may be used within a fund and for which purpose.

Several examples in earlier lessons illustrated the use of derivatives from an investor perspective using both forward commitments and contingent claims.

Forward Commitments

- Recall an earlier example in which Procam Investments purchased a three-month gold forward or futures contract. The derivatives contract increased Procam's exposure to the underlying price of gold in the future with no initial cash outlay and no requirement to take immediate delivery of the physical asset, as in the case of a cash purchase.
- In the example of Fyleton Investments, the fund entered into a GBP interest rate swap to increase the duration of its assets with no initial cash outlay.

Contingent Claims

- One example had Hightest Capital purchasing a call option to benefit from an expected increase in a health care stock index price above the exercise in exchange for an upfront premium.
- The SCSI long equity and short call (or covered call) example created an exposure profile under which SCSI realized a higher return than in its original long cash position if the underlying index price at the end of the year was stable to slightly higher, in accordance with the CIO's view.

In these and other instances throughout the curriculum, we find investors to be less focused than issuers on hedge accounting treatment, as an investment fund's derivative position is typically marked to market each day and included in the daily net asset value (NAV) of the portfolio or fund. This also explains why investors tend to transact more frequently in standardized and highly liquid exchange-traded derivative markets than do issuers.

QUESTION SET

Investor Use of Derivatives

1. Determine the correct answer to complete the following sentence: An investment fund's __________ typically specifies which derivative instruments may be used within a fund and for which purpose.

   Solution:

   An investment fund's *prospectus* typically specifies which derivative instruments may be used within a fund and for which purpose.

2. Describe two purposes of investor derivatives use within a fund.

Solution:

The purpose of investor derivatives use within a fund is usually to modify the fund's exposure to increase the return of the fund under specific market conditions and/or to offset or hedge the fund's value against adverse movements in underlyings, such as exchange rates, interest rates, and securities markets.

3. Match these derivative market participants to the following statements:

A. Investors	1. They use derivatives to offset or hedge market-based underlying exposures incidental to their commercial operations and financing activities.
B. Both issuers and investors	2. They tend to transact more frequently in exchange-traded derivative markets.
C. Issuers	3. They use derivatives to change their exposure to an underlying asset price without transacting in the cash market.

Solution:

1. The correct answer is C. Issuers use derivatives to offset or hedge market-based underlying exposures incidental to their commercial operations and financing activities.
2. The correct answer is A. Investors tend to transact more frequently in exchange-traded derivative markets.
3. The correct answer is B. Both issuers and investors use derivatives to change their exposure to an underlying asset price without transacting in the cash market.

PRACTICE PROBLEMS

The following information relates to questions 1-4

Consider the following structured note offered by Baywhite Financial:

Baywhite Financial LLC 80% Principal Protected Structured Note	
Description:	The Baywhite Financial LLC 80% Principal Protected Structured Note ("the Note") is linked to the performance of the S&P 500 Health Care Select Sector Index (SIXV).
Issuer:	Baywhite Financial LLC
Start Date:	[Today]
Maturity Date:	[Six months from Start Date]
Issuance Price:	102% of Face Value
Face Value:	Sold in a minimum denomination of USD1,000 and multiple units thereof
Payment at Maturity:	At maturity, you will receive a cash payment, for each USD1,000 principal amount note, of USD800 plus the Additional Amount, which may be zero.
Partial Principal Protection Percentage:	80% Principal Protection (20% Principal at Risk)
Additional Amount:	At maturity, you will receive the greater of 100% of the returns on the S&P 500 Health Care Select Sector Index (SIXV) in excess of 5% above the current spot price of the SIXV or zero.

As a financial analyst for a wealth management advisory firm, you have been tasked with comparing the features of the Baywhite Financial LLC Structured Note with those of a similar exchange-traded, stand-alone derivative instrument alternative in order to make a recommendation to the firm's clients.

1. Which of the following statements best describes the derivative instrument that is embedded in the Baywhite Financial LLC Structured Note?

   A. The Structured Note has an embedded long futures contract with the S&P 500 Health Care Select Sector Index (SIXV) as an underlying.

   B. The Structured Note has an embedded long call option contract with the S&P 500 Health Care Select Sector Index (SIXV) as an underlying.

   C. The Structured Note has an embedded short put option contract with the S&P 500 Health Care Select Sector Index (SIXV) as an underlying.

2. Which of the following statements best contrasts the credit risk of the Baywhite Financial LLC Structured Note with the counterparty credit risk of an investor

entering into the embedded exchange-traded derivative on a stand-alone basis?

A. An investor in the Baywhite Structured Note assumes the credit risk of Baywhite Financial LLC for 20% of the note's face value, as the remaining 80% is principal protected. An investor entering into the SIXV derivative on a stand-alone basis assumes the counterparty credit risk of a financial intermediary.

B. An investor in the Baywhite Structured Note assumes the credit risk of Baywhite Financial LLC for 80% of the note's face value, as the remaining 20% is associated with the embedded derivative. An investor entering into the SIXV derivative on a stand-alone basis assumes the counterparty credit risk of a financial intermediary.

C. An investor in the Baywhite Structured Note assumes the credit risk of Baywhite Financial LLC for 100% of the note's face value, while an investor entering into the SIXV derivative on a stand-alone basis assumes the counterparty credit risk of an exchange and its clearinghouse.

3. Which of the following statements most accurately describes the liquidity of the Baywhite Structured Note versus that of the embedded exchange-traded derivative?

A. The Baywhite Structured Note is likely to be more liquid than the stand-alone SIXV call option, as the Note has 80% principal protection while an investor in the stand-alone derivative may lose the entire option premium if it expires worthless at maturity.

B. The Baywhite Structured Note is likely to be more liquid than the stand-alone SIXV call option, as the Note is priced at a stated 2% premium above par while an investor in the stand-alone derivative faces the lack of transparency as well as basis, liquidity, and counterparty credit risks associated with derivative transactions.

C. Structured notes such as the Baywhite Financial LLC Structured Note often involve greater cost, lower liquidity, and less transparency than an equivalent stand-alone derivative instrument, while the exchange-traded SIXV derivative contract is standardized and trades in a liquid, transparent market.

4. Which of the following statements best describes how an investor should evaluate the terms of the Baywhite Financial LLC Structured Note as compared with the stand-alone derivative price in order to make a recommendation?

A. The Baywhite Financial LLC Structured Note issuance price of 2% above par value should be compared with the upfront premium for a six-month SIXV call option with an exercise price at 5% above the current SIXV spot price.

B. The Baywhite Financial LLC Structured Note 20% Principal at Risk should be compared with the upfront premium for a six-month SIXV call option with an exercise price at 5% above the current SIXV spot price.

C. The Baywhite Financial LLC Structured Note issuance price of 2% above par value *plus* the 20% Principal at Risk should be compared with the upfront premium for a six-month SIXV call option with an exercise price at 5% above the current SIXV spot price.

SOLUTIONS

1. B is correct. The Structured Note is linked to the performance of the S&P 500 Health Care Select Sector Index (SIXV). Note that the SIXV derivative is similar to that in the earlier SCSI CSI 300 example. The "Additional Amount" paid at maturity is equal to the greater of 100% of the returns on the S&P 500 Health Care Select Sector Index (SIXV) in excess of 5% above the current spot price of the SIXV or zero. This payoff profile [Max (0, S_T – X)] is identical to that of a purchased six-month SIXV call option with an exercise price (X) at 5% above today's SIXV spot price.

2. C is correct. The investor assumes the credit risk of Baywhite Financial LLC for the full value of the structured note as the structured note issuer. Under the purchased exchange-traded SIXV call option, the investor faces the risk of the exchange and its clearinghouse, which provides a guarantee of contract settlement backed by the exchange insurance fund.

3. C is correct. The Structured Note is likely to be far less liquid than the stand-alone SIXV call option, which is traded on a derivatives exchange. Recall from an earlier lesson that exchange-traded contracts are more formal and standardized, which facilitates a more liquid and transparent market. Note also that the Baywhite Financial LLC Structured Note is issued at 102% of face value, suggesting that an investor will likely forgo this premium if selling the note prior to maturity.

4. C is correct. The 20% Principal at Risk, or USD200 of Face Value for each USD1,000 (the minimum denomination), combined with the 2% (or USD20) issue premium, should be compared with the upfront premium for a six-month SIXV call option with an exercise price at 5% above the current SIXV spot price. The comparison should also consider the additional credit risk and liquidity risk of the Structured Note versus the exchange-traded option.

LEARNING MODULE

4

Arbitrage, Replication, and the Cost of Carry in Pricing Derivatives

LEARNING OUTCOMES	
Mastery	***The candidate should be able to:***
☐	explain how the concepts of arbitrage and replication are used in pricing derivatives
☐	explain the difference between the spot and expected future price of an underlying and the cost of carry associated with holding the underlying asset

INTRODUCTION

1

Earlier derivative lessons established the features of derivative instruments and markets and addressed both the benefits and risks associated with their use. Forward commitments and contingent claims were distinguished by their different payoff profiles and other characteristics. We now turn our attention to the pricing and valuation of these instruments. As a first step, we explore how the price of a forward commitment is related to the spot price of an underlying asset in a way that does not allow for arbitrage opportunities. Specifically, the strategy of replication shows that identical payoffs to a forward commitment can be achieved from spot market transactions combined with borrowing or lending at the risk-free rate. Finally, the second lesson demonstrates how costs or benefits associated with owning an underlying asset affect the forward commitment price.

LEARNING MODULE OVERVIEW

- Forward commitments are an alternative means of taking a long or short position in an underlying asset. A link between forward prices and spot prices exists to prevent investors from taking advantage of arbitrage opportunities across cash and derivative instruments.

CFA Institute would like to thank Don Chance, PhD, CFA, for his contribution to this section, which includes material derived from material that appeared in *Derivative Markets and Instruments*, featured in the 2022 CFA® Program curriculum.

- A forward commitment may be replicated with a long or short spot position in the underlying asset and borrowing or lending at a risk-free rate. Investors can recreate a variety of positions by using appropriate combinations of spot, forward, and risk-free positions.
- The risk-free rate provides a fundamental link between spot and forward prices for underlying assets with no additional costs or benefits of ownership.
- The cost of carry is the net of the costs and benefits related to owning an underlying asset for a specific period and must be factored into the difference between the spot price and a forward price of a specific underlying asset.
- The cost of carry may include costs, such as storage and insurance for physical commodities, or benefits of ownership, such as dividends for stocks and interest for bonds. Foreign exchange represents a special case in which the cost of carry is the interest rate differential between two currencies.
- Forward prices may be greater than or less than the underlying spot price, depending on the specific cost of carry associated with owning the underlying asset.

LEARNING MODULE SELF-ASSESSMENT

These initial questions are intended to help you gauge your current level of understanding of this learning module.

1. Which of the following statements correctly describes how to replicate a long forward position?

   A. Sell a risk-free bond, and buy a cash market position in the underlying.

   B. Buy a risk-free bond, and buy a cash market position in the underlying.

   C. Buy a risk-free bond, and sell a cash market position in the underlying.

   Solution:

   A is correct. Selling a risk-free bond provides the necessary cash to buy the underlying in the cash market. At the bond's maturity, the underlying is sold at the future spot price, and the proceeds are used to pay off the bond. The profit on this transaction is dependent on the future spot price of the underlying compared to the underlying cash market price multiplied by one plus the risk-free rate, and this profit position is identical to that of a long forward position in the underlying. B is incorrect because buying the risk-free bond creates a need for cash in addition to buying the underlying in the cash market. C is incorrect because this combination would replicate a short forward position.

2. Which of the following is closest to the arbitrage profit available to an investor who is able to buy an asset for a spot price of GBP50 at t = 0 and simultaneously sell a six-month forward commitment on the same asset at a forward price of GBP52.50? The risk-free rate of interest is 4%, and the asset has no additional costs or benefits.

   A. GBP0.99

   B. GBP0.48

C. GBP1.51

Solution:

C is correct. The investor borrows at 4% for six months to buy the asset today for GBP50. After six months, the investor pays the lender $S_0(1 + r)^T$, or GBP50.99 [= GBP50$(1.04)^{0.5}$] in principal and interest and delivers the asset to satisfy the forward commitment to sell at GBP52.50. The investor's arbitrage profit is GBP1.51 (= GBP52.50 – GBP50.99). A is incorrect because this answer reflects the difference between the no-arbitrage forward price and the current spot price. B is incorrect because this answer reflects the difference between the forward price discounted back one year (rather than six months) and the current spot price.

3. Which of the following statements correctly describes the relationship between a forward commitment price compared to the underlying spot price when the benefits of owning the underlying are greater than the costs of owning the underlying (including the opportunity interest costs)?

   A. Forward commitment price > spot price.

   B. Forward commitment price < spot price.

   C. Forward commitment price = spot price.

Solution:

B is correct. Greater benefits associated with the underlying will be associated with a higher spot price relative to the forward commitment price, and if these benefits are greater than the costs of owning the underlying, then the spot price will be greater than the forward commitment price. A is incorrect because this inequality would be true in the case of the costs exceeding the benefits. C is incorrect because an equality between the two prices describes the rare circumstance in which costs and benefits are exactly equal.

4. Which of the following statements best defines a convenience yield?

   A. Convenience yield reflects the preference that market participants exhibit for buying forward contracts to avoid having to pay cash up front.

   B. Convenience yield reflects the preference that market participants exhibit for buying in the spot market to avoid having to pay for storage.

   C. Convenience yield reflects the preference that market participants exhibit for buying in the spot market for non-cash reasons, including low inventories in the underlying cash market.

Solution:

C is correct. The convenience yield is a non-cash benefit associated with owning an underlying physical commodity that arises under certain economic conditions, including low inventories of the underlying. A is incorrect because the statement suggests convenience yield is a cost of owning the underlying. B is incorrect because the statement is contradictory in that it states that convenience yield causes market participants to prefer spot markets but incorrectly attributes this to a cost of owning the underlying.

2 ARBITRAGE

- ☐ explain how the concepts of arbitrage and replication are used in pricing derivatives

An earlier lesson on market efficiency established that market prices should not allow for the possibility of riskless profit or arbitrage in the absence of transaction costs. In its simplest form, an arbitrage opportunity arises if the "law of one price" does not hold, or an identical asset trades at the same time at different prices in different places.

In the case of a derivative contract whose value is derived from future cash flows associated with the price of an underlying asset, arbitrage opportunities arise either if two assets with identical *future cash flows* trade at different prices or if an asset with a known future price does not trade at the *present value* of its future price determined using an appropriate discount rate.

The first case of assets with identical future cash flows trading at different prices is illustrated in Exhibit 1.

Exhibit 1: Assets with Identical Future Cash Flows Trade at Different Prices

For example, assume the two assets are zero-coupon bonds with identical features and the same issuer. Both bonds mature on the same future date with a payoff of par and have the same risk of default between now and the maturity date.

1. Bond A has a price of EUR99 at time t = 0 ($S_0{}^A$ = EUR99).
2. Bond B has a price of EUR99.15 at time t = 0 ($S_0{}^B$ = EUR99.15).
3. Both bonds have an expected future price of EUR100 ($S_T{}^A$ = $S_T{}^B$ = EUR100).

This scenario represents an arbitrage opportunity for an investor.

- At time t = 0, the investor can:
  - Sell Bond B short to receive proceeds of EUR99.15 and purchase Bond A for EUR99;
  - Realize a net cash inflow at t = 0 of EUR0.15.
- At time t = T, when both bonds mature, the investor:
  - Receives EUR100 for Bond A and uses this to buy Bond B for EUR100 to cover the short position.
  - The offsetting cash flows at time T leave the investor with a riskless profit of the EUR0.15 price difference between Bonds A and B at time 0.

Other investors taking note of this discrepancy will also seek to earn a riskless profit at time $t = 0$ by selling Bond B, driving its price down, and buying Bond A, driving its price up, until the prices converge. The arbitrage opportunity disappears once the bonds have the same price ($S_0{}^A = S_0{}^B$).

A second type of derivative-related arbitrage opportunity arises when an asset with a known future price does not trade at the present value (PV) of its future price. An earlier time-value-of-money lesson distinguished between discrete and continuous compounding in calculating present versus future value. The future value of a single cash flow based on a *discrete* number of uniform periods follows the general formula in Equation 1:

$$\mathrm{FV}_N = \mathrm{PV}(1 + r)^N, \tag{1}$$

where r is the stated interest rate per *period* and N is the number of compounding periods. *Continuous compounding* is the case in which the length of the uniform periods approaches zero, so the number of periods per year approaches infinity and is calculated using the natural logarithm, as shown in Equation 2:

$$\mathrm{FV}_T = \mathrm{PV}e^{rT}. \tag{2}$$

While derivatives may be priced with either approach, for purposes of this and later lessons, we will use the discrete compounding method for individual underlying assets. However, for underlying assets that represent a portfolio, such as an equity, fixed-income, commodity, or credit index, or where the underlying involves foreign exchange where interest rates are denominated in two currencies, continuous compounding will be the preferred method. Ignoring additional costs or benefits associated with asset ownership, the appropriate discount rate, r, is the risk-free rate, as demonstrated in Example 1.

EXAMPLE 1

Spot vs. Discounted Known Future Price of Gold

In an earlier lesson, Procam Investments entered into a contract to buy 100 ounces of gold at an agreed-upon price of USD1,792.13 per ounce in three months. In this example, Procam does the opposite trade, given a discrepancy between spot and discounted known future gold prices. Assume that today's spot gold price (S_0) is USD1,770 per ounce, and the annualized risk-free interest rate (r) is 2%. For purposes of this example, we assume that Procam can borrow at the risk-free rate and gold may be stored at no cost. Under these conditions, we demonstrate how Procam can generate a riskless profit:

- At time $t = 0$:
- Procam borrows USD177,000 at 2.0% interest for three months and purchases 100 ounces of gold at today's spot price.
- Procam enters into a forward contract today to sell 100 ounces of gold at a price of USD1,792.13 per ounce in three months.

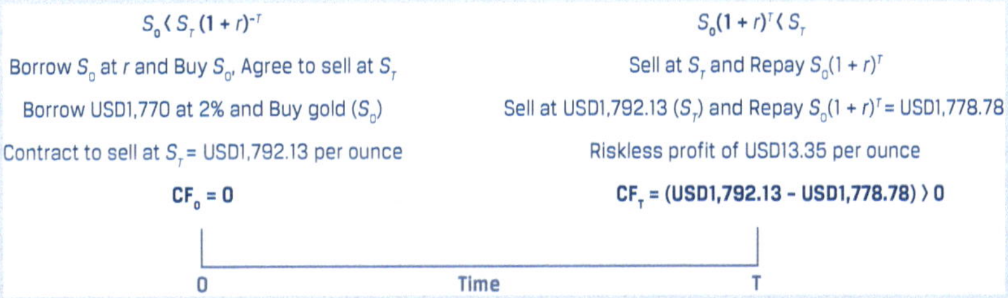

- At time $t = T$ (in three months):

- Procam delivers 100 ounces of gold under the forward contract and receives USD179,213 (= 100 × USD1,792.13).
- Procam repays the loan principal with interest:

USD177,878.44 = USD177,000$(1.02)^{0.25}$.

- Procam's riskless profit at time T is equal to the difference between the forward sale proceeds and the loan principal and interest: USD1,334.56 = USD179,213 – USD177,878.44.

In Example 1, the spot price of gold, S_0, is below the present value of the known future price of gold in three months' time ($S_0 < S_T(1 + r)^{-T}$, since USD1,770 < USD1,783.28). Procam earns a riskless profit of USD13.35 per ounce by borrowing and purchasing gold in the cash market and simultaneously selling gold in the forward market at an agreed-upon price. We would expect that as other investors recognize and pursue this opportunity, the spot price will increase (and the forward price will fall) until the spot price is equal to the discounted value of the known future price ($S_0 = S_T(1 + r)^{-T}$) to eliminate this arbitrage opportunity.

The two key arbitrage concepts used to price derivatives for an underlying with no additional cash flows may be summarized as follows:

- Identical assets or assets with identical cash flows traded at the same time must have the same price ($S_0^A = S_0^B$).
- Assets with a known future price must have a spot price that equals the future price discounted at the risk-free rate ($S_0 = S_T(1 + r)^{-T}$).

These arbitrage conditions establish the relationship between spot prices, forward commitment prices, and the risk-free rate shown in Exhibit 2.

Exhibit 2: Spot Prices, Forward Commitment Prices, and the Risk-Free Rate

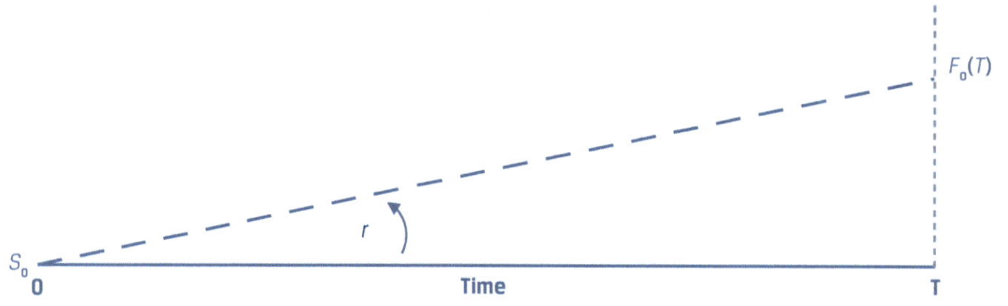

Exhibit 2 shows the case of $r > 0$ for an asset with no additional income or costs under discrete compounding. Note that for a given time T, the forward price will be higher relative to the spot price with a higher risk-free rate r. Also, for a given risk-free rate r, as T increases, the forward price will increase relative to the spot price. It is important to note that the relevant risk-free rate for most market participants is the repo rate, introduced in an earlier lesson, where borrowed funds are collateralized by highly liquid securities.

Recall from an earlier lesson that a forward commitment has a symmetric payoff profile. That is, at time T, the transaction is settled on the basis of the difference between the forward price $F_0(T)$ and the underlying price of S_T, or $F_0(T) - S_T$ from the seller's perspective, as in Exhibit 3.

Exhibit 3: Forward Commitment Seller Payoff Profile

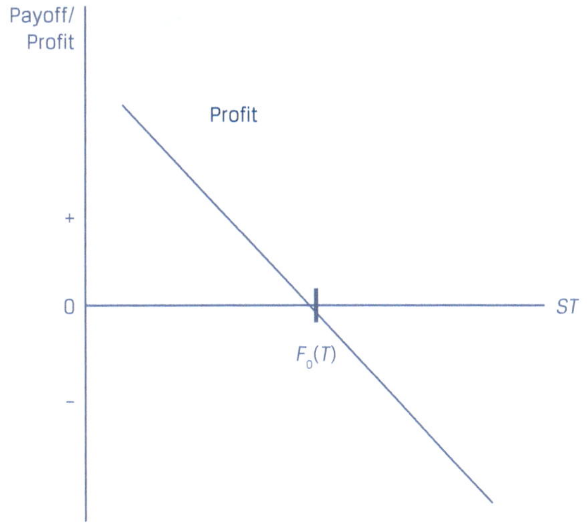

The forward seller realizes a gain if the seller is able to deliver the underlying at a market value (S_T) below the pre-agreed price, $F_0(T)$. In Example 1, Procam borrows to buy the underlying at a spot price below the present value of S_T to lock in a riskless gain. So far, we have taken the forward price, $F_0(T)$, as given. In what follows, we demonstrate how no-arbitrage conditions may be used to establish the relationship between spot and forward prices by replicating or recreating an exact offsetting position for a forward commitment.

REPLICATION 3

- [ ] explain how the concepts of arbitrage and replication are used in pricing derivatives

Replication is a strategy in which a derivative's cash flow stream may be recreated using a combination of long or short positions in an underlying asset and borrowing or lending cash. In contrast to the earlier arbitrage examples, replication is typically used to mirror or offset a derivative position when the law of one price holds and no riskless arbitrage profit opportunities exist. For example, Exhibit 4 compares a long forward commitment to the alternative of borrowing funds at the risk-free rate, r, to buy the underlying asset at today's spot price, S_0.

Exhibit 4: Forward Commitment Replication

Borrow S_0 and purchase at spot (S_0)	**Repay loan ($S_0(1 + r)^T$) and sell at spot (S_T)**
Borrow USD1,783.28 (S_0) today at $t = 0$	Repay USD1,792.13 ($S_0(1 + r)^T$) at $t = T$
Buy at S_0 = USD1,783.28	See at spot (S_T)
CF_0 = (USD1,783.28 – USD1,783.28) = 0	**CF_T = (S_T – $1,792.13)**
Enter long forward contact ($F_0(T)$)	**Settle long forward contact (S_T – $F_0(T)$)**
Agree to buy at USD1,792.13 ($F_0(T)$) at $t = T$	Settle contract (S_T – $F_0(T)$) at $t = T$
CF_0 = 0	**CF_T = (S_T – $1,792.13)**
0	T

Time

EXAMPLE 2

Replication of a Forward Commitment

In Example 1, we reintroduced Procam Investments, which borrowed and purchased gold in the spot market and simultaneously sold gold in the forward market to earn a riskless profit. Here we change the assumption about today's spot gold price (S_0). Specifically, the spot gold price has risen to USD1,783.28 (= USD1,792.13(1.02)$^{-0.25}$) to eliminate the earlier arbitrage opportunity when the spot price was USD1,770. Assume again that the risk-free interest rate (r) is 2% and gold can be stored at no cost.

1. Long forward commitment (agree to buy at $F_0(T)$ at $t = T$)
   - Procam enters a forward commitment to buy 100 ounces of gold in three months at a forward price, $F_0(T)$, of USD1,792.13 per ounce.
   - If S_T = USD1,900 per ounce,
   - Profit = USD10,787 = 100 × (USD1,900 – USD1,792.13).
   - If S_T = USD1,700 per ounce,
   - Profit = –USD9,213 = 100 × (USD1,700 –USD1,792.13).
2. Borrow and purchase (borrow S_0 and buy asset at S_0 at $t = 0$):
   - Procam borrows USD178,328 at 2% and buys 100 ounces of gold at today's spot price, S_0.
   - Procam sells the gold in three months at spot price S_T.
   - Procam repays the loan principal and interest: USD179,213 = USD178,328(1.02)$^{0.25}$.
   - If S_T = USD1,900,
   - Profit = USD10,787 = 100 × (USD1,900 – USD1,792.13).
   - If S_T = USD1,700,
   - Profit = –USD9,213 = 100 × (USD1,700 – USD1,792.13).

Note that the same profits are observed under Scenarios 1 and 2, which are equal to $S_T - F_0(T)$. If we set the forward price, $F_0(T)$, equal to the future value of the spot rate using the risk-free rate ($F_0(T) = S_0(1 + r)^T$), the no-arbitrage condition demonstrates that Procam generates the same cash flow at time T regardless of the direction of gold prices whether the company

1. enters into a long forward commitment settled at time T or
2. borrows at the risk-free rate, buys the underlying asset, and holds it until time T.

A separate but related form of replication pairing a long asset with a short forward is shown in Exhibit 5. The top half shows the profit/loss profile of the long asset, and the bottom half shows that of the short forward position. The long asset position produces a profit (loss) when $S_T > S_0$ ($S_T < S_0$). The short forward position produces a profit (loss) when $S_T < F_0$ ($S_T > F_0$).

Exhibit 5: Payoffs for Long Asset and Short Forward Positions

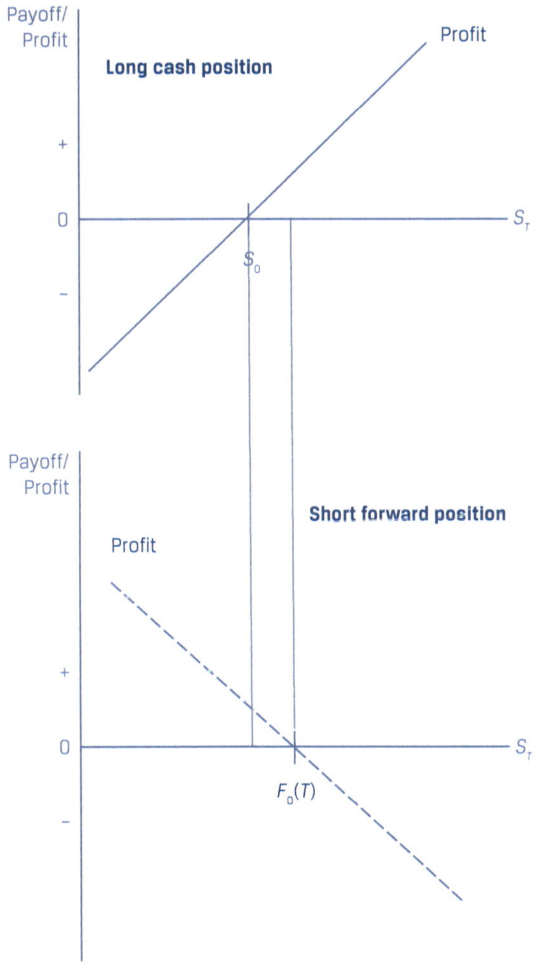

In contrast to Example 2, these positions appear to offset one another. The following example evaluates the return generated by these combined positions.

EXAMPLE 3

Risk-Free Trade Replication: Long Asset, Short Forward

Procam Investments buys 100 ounces of gold at today's spot price (S_0) of USD1,783.28 and simultaneously enters a forward commitment to sell gold at the forward price, $F_0(T)$, of USD1,792.13. Again, we assume that gold can be stored at no cost, and here we solve for Procam's rate of return.

- At $t = 0$, Procam's cash flow is $-S_0$ = –USD178,328.
- At $t = T$, Procam's cash flow is $F_0(T)$ = USD179,213.
- Solve for the rate of return on Procam's strategy, as follows:
  - USD179,213 = USD178,328$(1 + r)^{0.25}$.
  - r = 2.0%, which is equal to the risk-free rate.

This example demonstrates that Procam can hedge its long gold cash position with a short derivative (i.e., selling the forward contract) and earn the risk-free rate of return as long as the no-arbitrage condition ($F_0(T) = S_0(1 + r)^T$) holds. The combined return is shown in Exhibit 6. Note that if Procam borrows at the risk-free rate to purchase the underlying asset at S_0, it will earn zero.

Exhibit 6: Combined Long Asset and Short Forward Profit

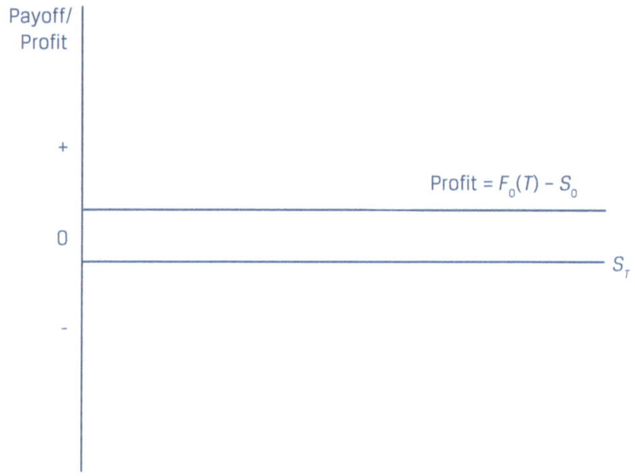

Because the forward price is assumed to be greater than the spot price in this example and r is positive, the risk-free profit is a positive amount and is the same (i.e., risk free) regardless of the price of the underlying (i.e., S_T). As we will see in the next lesson, there may be benefits or costs to owning an underlying asset that cause the risk-free return in Exhibit 6 to differ from $F_0(T) - S_0$ and possibly even be negative.

QUESTION SET

Arbitrage and Replication

1. Determine the correct answers to fill in the blanks: If the law of one price does not hold, a(n) ________ asset trades at the same time at ________ prices in different places.

   Solution:

   If the law of one price does not hold, a(n) *identical* asset trades at the same time at *different* prices in different places.

2. An investor observes that the spot price, S_0, of an underlying asset with no additional costs or benefits exceeds its known future price discounted at the risk-free rate, $S_T(1 + r)^{-T}$. Describe and justify an arbitrage strategy that generates a riskless profit for the investor.

   Solution:

   Since the spot price of the underlying asset exceeds the known future price discounted at the risk-free rate ($S_0 > F_0(T)(1 + r)^{-T}$), at $t = 0$, the investor:

   - Sells the underlying asset short in the spot market at S_0
   - Simultaneously enters a long forward contract at $F_0(T)$
   - Lends S_0 at the risk-free rate r to receive $S_0(1 + r)^T$ at time T.

   At time $t = T$, the investor:

   - Settles the long forward position and receives $S_T - F_0(T)$
   - Offsets the short underlying asset position at S_T, and
   - Retains $S_0(1 + r)^T - F_0(T)$ as a riskless profit regardless of the underlying spot price at time T.

3. Formulate a replication strategy for a three-month short forward commitment for 1,000 shares of a non-dividend-paying stock.

   Solution:

   The replication strategy for a three-month short forward commitment on a non-dividend-paying stock involves the short sale of 1,000 shares of stock at $t = 0$ and investment of proceeds at the risk-free rate, r. At time $t = T$, the short sale is covered at S_T, and under the no-arbitrage condition of $F_0(T) = S_0(1 + r)^T$, the return is equal to $F_0(T) - S_T$ for both the short forward and the replication strategy.

4. Calculate the arbitrage profit if a spot asset with no additional costs or benefits trades at a spot price of 100, the three-month forward price for the underlying asset is 102, and the risk-free rate is 5%.

   Solution:

   The forward price, $F_0(T) = S_0(1 + r)^T$, at which no-arbitrage opportunities would exist is 101.23 (= $100(1.05)^{0.25}$). With an observed forward price of 102, the arbitrage opportunity would be to sell the forward contract and buy the underlying, borrowing at the risk-free rate to fund the purchase. The arbitrage profit is the difference between the observed forward price and the no-arbitrage forward price of 0.77 (= 102 – 101.23).

5. Describe the relationship between the spot and forward price for an underlying asset if the risk-free rate is negative.

Solution:

The relationship between the spot and forward rate for an asset with no additional costs or benefits of ownership other than the opportunity cost (risk-free rate) is equal to $F_0(T) = S_0(1 + r)^T$. In a case where $r < 0$, $(1 + r)^T < 1$ and therefore the forward price, $F_0(T)$, is below the spot price, S_0, if the risk-free rate is negative.

4 COSTS AND BENEFITS ASSOCIATED WITH OWNING THE UNDERLYING

☐ explain the difference between the spot and expected future price of an underlying and the cost of carry associated with holding the underlying asset

In the prior lesson, replication was used to illustrate the basic relationship between entering into a spot transaction versus a forward commitment. The linkage between the spot price of an asset with no associated cash flows and a forward commitment on the same asset was shown to be the risk-free rate of interest, *r*. In this lesson, we discuss **cost of carry** as the net of the costs and benefits related to owning an underlying asset for a specific period.

In the forward commitment example from the prior lesson, where no costs or benefits were associated with the underlying asset, the following relationship between the spot and forward prices was established:

$$F_0(T) = S_0(1 + r)^T. \quad (3)$$

This relationship is shown under continuous compounding in Equation 4:

$$F_0(T) = S_0e^{rT}. \quad (4)$$

The risk-free rate, *r*, denotes the **opportunity cost** of holding ("**carrying**") the asset, whether or not the long investor borrows to finance the asset. This opportunity cost is present for all asset classes discussed below.

Equations 3 and 4 represent the special case of an underlying asset with no additional associated cash flows. However, many assets have additional costs or benefits of ownership that must be reflected in the forward commitment price in order to prevent riskless arbitrage opportunities from arising between underlying spot and derivative prices. Exhibit 7 demonstrates the effect of costs and benefits (usually dividend or interest income) on the spot price, forward commitment price, and risk-free rate relationships.

Exhibit 7: Spot Prices, Forward Commitment Prices, and the Risk-Free Rate with Underlying Asset Costs and Benefits

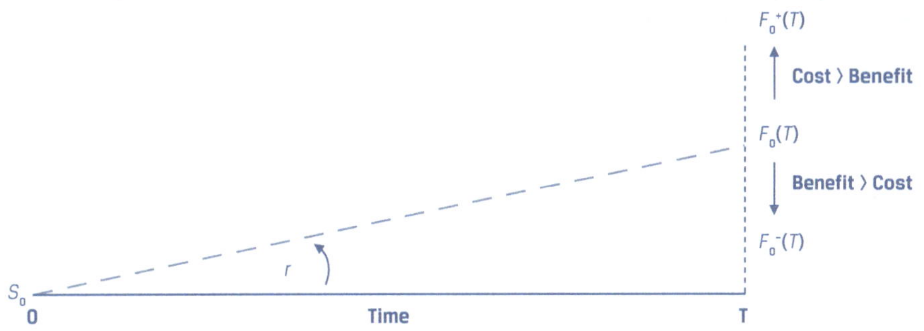

If an underlying asset owner incurs costs in addition to the opportunity cost, she should expect to be compensated for these added costs through a higher forward price, $F_0^+(T)$. Income or other benefits accrue to the underlying asset owner and therefore should reduce the forward price to $F_0^-(T)$.

For underlying assets with ownership benefits or income (I) or costs (C) expressed as a known *amount in present value terms at t = 0*—shown as $PV_0()$—the relationship between spot and forward prices in discrete compounding terms can be shown as

$$F_0(T) = [S_0 - PV_0(I) + PV_0(C)](1 + r)^T. \tag{5}$$

In other instances, the additional costs or benefits are expressed as a *rate of return* over the life of the contract. For income (i) and cost (c) expressed as rates of return, the relationship between spot and forward prices under continuous compounding is

$$F_0(T) = S_0 e^{(r+c-i)T}. \tag{6}$$

Whether expressed as a known amount in present value terms or as a rate of return, the forward price must incorporate the net effect of all costs and benefits associated with owning the underlying asset, including the following.

- **Opportunity cost (risk-free interest rate, r):** A positive risk-free rate causes a forward price to be greater than the underlying spot price, all else equal, and the higher the risk-free rate, the greater the positive difference between the two. This opportunity cost applies to any asset.
- **Other costs of ownership (C, c):** Owners of some underlying assets, such as physical commodities, must incur storage, transportation, insurance, and/or spoilage costs. An owner entering a contract for future delivery will expect to be compensated for these costs, resulting in a forward price that is therefore greater than the underlying spot price, all else equal.
- **Benefits of ownership (I, i):** Alternatively, the owners of some underlying assets enjoy cash flow or other benefits associated with owning the underlying asset as opposed to a derivative on the asset. A counterparty entering a derivative contract for future delivery of an underlying asset forgoes these benefits and will therefore reduce the forward price by this amount. Stock dividends or bond coupons are examples of cash flow benefits.

Exhibit 8 illustrates the relationship between forward and spot prices in the presence of costs and benefits. For example, when the opportunity cost and other costs of ownership exceed the benefits, the forward price will be above the underlying spot asset price.

Exhibit 8: Forward vs. Spot Price

Cost vs. Benefit	Forward vs. Spot Price
Opportunity and Other Cost > Benefit	$F_0(T) > S_0$
Opportunity and Other Cost < Benefit	$F_0(T) < S_0$
Opportunity and Other Cost = Benefit	$F_0(T) = S_0$

Each underlying asset type has different costs and benefits, which may vary over time and across markets. For example, owners of some individual equity securities receive the benefit of regular stock dividends, as in Example 4, while others do not. For equity indexes, the benefit is usually expressed as a rate of return, as shown in Example 5.

EXAMPLE 4

Hightest Equity Forward with Dividend

Assume Hightest Capital agrees to deliver 1,000 Unilever (UL) shares at an agreed-upon price to a financial intermediary in six months under a forward contract. Assume that UL has a spot price (S_0) of EUR50 and pays no dividend (I = 0), and assume a risk-free rate (r) of 5%. We may use Equation 3 to solve for the forward price, $F_0(T)$, in six months:

$$F_0(T) = S_0(1 + r)^T.$$

$$\text{EUR}51.23 = \text{EUR}50(1.05)^{0.5}.$$

Now assume instead that Unilever pays a quarterly dividend of EUR0.30, which occurs in exactly three months and again at time T, with other details unchanged. Use Equation 5 with $PV_0(C) = 0$ to solve for $F_0(T)$ in six months:

$$F_0(T) = [S_0 - PV_0(I)](1 + r)^T.$$

First, solve for the present value of the dividend per share, $PV_0(I)$, as follows:

$$PV_0(I) = \text{EUR}0.30(1.05)^{-0.25} + \text{EUR}0.30(1.05)^{-0.5}.$$

$$\text{EUR}0.5892 = 0.2964 + 0.2928.$$

Substitute $PV_0(I)$ = EUR0.5892 into Equation 5 to solve for $F_0(T)$:

$$F_0(T) = (\text{EUR}50 - \text{EUR}0.5892)(1.05)^{0.5}$$

$$= \text{EUR}50.6310.$$

Hightest's forward contract for 1,000 UL shares would therefore be priced at EUR50,631.00 (= 1,000 × EUR50.6310). The opportunity cost of borrowing at the risk-free rate is EUR1.23 per share for six months and equals $F_0(T) - S_0$ when Unilever pays no dividend. A EUR0.30 quarterly dividend reduces the difference between the forward and spot price to approximately EUR0.63.

EXAMPLE 5

Stock Index Futures with Dividend Yield

The Viswan Family Office (VFO) would like to enter into a three-month forward commitment contract to purchase the NIFTY 50 benchmark Indian stock market index traded on the National Stock Exchange. The spot NIFTY 50 index price is INR15,200, the index dividend yield is 2.2%, and the Indian rupee risk-free rate is 4%. Use Equation 6 (with $c = 0$) to solve for the forward price:

$$F_0(T) = S_0 e^{(r+c-i)T}$$

$$= 15{,}200e^{(0.04 - 0.022)0.25}$$

$$= \text{INR}15{,}268.55.$$

Foreign exchange requires some adjustments to establish the no-arbitrage condition between spot and forward prices, as shown in the prior lesson. First, it is important to distinguish the "price" of the underlying asset, which for equities, fixed income, or commodities refers to units of currency for each asset—for example, one share of stock or the principal amount for a bond. In contrast, the foreign exchange rate is expressed as a spot rate ($S_{0,f/d}$) specifying the number of units of a *price* currency (here denoted as f or foreign currency) in the numerator per *single* unit of a *base* currency (here shown as d or domestic currency) in the denominator. For example, for a USD/EUR spot rate ($S_{0,f/d}$) of 1.20, the US dollar is the price currency (f), and the euro is the base currency (d), with USD1.20 equal to EUR1.

An FX (foreign exchange) forward contract involves the sale of one currency and purchase of the other on a future date at a forward price ($F_{0,f/d}$) agreed on at inception. A *long* FX forward position involves the *purchase* of the base currency and the *sale* of the price currency. For example, a long USD/EUR FX forward position is the sale of US dollars and purchase of euros at a forward rate.

In the prior replication example, the derivative cash flow stream was recreated by combining a long or short position in an underlying asset and borrowing or lending cash. Here the foreign and domestic currency *each* has an opportunity cost—namely, the foreign risk-free rate (r_f) and the domestic risk-free rate (r_d), respectively.

EXAMPLE 6

AUD/USD Foreign Exchange Forward Replication

In order to replicate one currency's return in terms of the other for a given spot price today of $S_{0,f/d}$, we may solve for a forward rate $F_{0,f/d}(T)$ using the earlier arbitrage concept that assets with a known future price must have a spot price ($S_{0,f/d}$) equal to the future price discounted at the risk-free rate.

Assume the current AUD/USD spot price is 1.3335. The Australian dollar is the price currency or foreign currency, and the US dollar is the base or domestic currency (AUD1.3335 = USD1). The six-month Australian dollar risk-free rate is 0.05%, and the six-month US dollar risk-free rate is 0.20%.

- At time $t = 0$:
  1. Borrow USD1,000 at the 0.20% US dollar risk-free rate for six months.
  2. Purchase AUD1,333.50 at the AUD/USD spot rate ($S_{0,f/d} = 1.3335$).
  3. Lend the AUD1,333.50 received at the 0.05% Australian dollar risk-free rate for six months.

- At time $t = T$ in six months:

    4. Receive Australian dollar loan proceeds of 1,333.83 (= $1{,}333.50e^{(0.0005 \times 0.5)}$).
    5. Exchange Australian dollar proceeds for US dollars at $S_{T,f/d}$ to repay the US dollar loan.
    6. Repay the US dollar loan (with interest) of 1,001 (= $1{,}000e^{(0.002 \times 0.5)}$).

If the exchange in Step 5 at time T is at a spot price, $S_{T,f/d}$, at which the Australian dollar loan proceeds (Step 4) exactly offset the US dollar loan (Step 6), no riskless arbitrage opportunity exists. Solve for $S_{T,f/d}$ by dividing the Australian dollars in Step 4 by the US dollars in Step 6:

$S_{T,f/d}$ = 1.3325 (= AUD1,333.83/USD1,001).

The following diagram summarizes the cash flows at time $t = 0$ and time T:

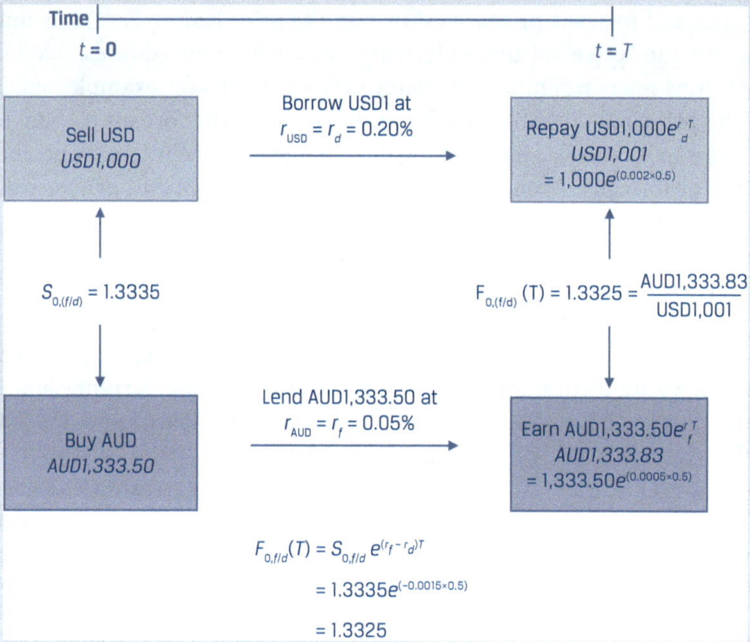

For the no-arbitrage condition to hold between the FX spot and forward price, the amount of Australian dollars necessary to purchase USD1 at time T ($F_{0,f/d}(T)$) must have a spot price ($S_{0,f/d}$) equal to the discounted future price. The relevant discount rate here involves the *difference* between the foreign and domestic risk-free rates, as shown in the following modified version of Equation 4:

$$F_{0,f/d}(T) = S_{0,f/d}e^{(r_f - r_d)T}. \tag{7}$$

Solve for $F_{0,AUD/USD}(T)$ in Example 6 as follows:

$F_{0,f/d}(T) = 1.3325$ (= $1.3335e^{(-0.0015 \times 0.5)}$).

From Equation 7, we see that it is the risk-free interest rate *differential* ($r_f - r_d$), rather than the absolute level of interest rates, that determines the spot versus forward FX price relationship. For example, in Example 6, the Australian dollar risk-free rate is 0.15% below the US dollar rate ($r_f - r_d < 0$). Borrowing at the higher US dollar rate and lending at the lower Australian dollar rate results in a no-arbitrage forward price at which *fewer* Australian dollars are required to purchase USD1 in the future, so the Australian dollar is said to trade at a *premium* in the forward market versus the US dollar. Exhibit 9 summarizes the relationship between forward and spot FX prices.

Exhibit 9: FX Forward vs. Spot Price Relationship

Interest Rate Differential	Forward vs. Spot Price	Foreign Currency Forward	FX Forward Premium/ Discount
$(r_f - r_d) > 0$	$F_{0,f/d}(T) > S_{0,f/d}$	Discount	Premium
$(r_f - r_d) < 0$	$F_{0,f/d}(T) < S_{0,f/d}$	Premium	Discount
$(r_f - r_d) = 0$	$F_{0,f/d}(T) = S_{0,f/d}$	Neither a premium nor a discount	Neither a premium nor a discount

We now examine this FX spot versus forward relationship in the case of the Montau AG example from an earlier lesson.

EXAMPLE 7

Montau AG's FX Forward Rate

An earlier lesson introduced Montau AG, a German capital goods producer. Montau signs a commercial contract with Jeon, Inc., a South Korean manufacturer, to deliver a laser cutting machine at a price of KRW650 million in 75 days. Montau faces a timing mismatch between domestic euro costs incurred and euro revenue realized upon the delivery of the machine and sale of South Korean won received in exchange for euros in the spot FX market. Montau enters a long KRW/EUR FX forward contract. That is, Montau agrees to sell South Korean won and purchase euros at a fixed price, $F_0(T)$, in 75 days to eliminate the KRW/EUR exchange rate mismatch arising from the export contract.

In this version of the Montau AG example, we use today's spot exchange rate and the domestic (r_d) and foreign (r_f) risk-free rates to solve for the KRW/EUR forward rate. As seen in Equation 7, the difference between spot and forward FX rates involves the *difference* in risk-free rates. In the KRW/EUR case, the South Korean won is the price currency or foreign currency and r_f is therefore the South Korean won interest rate. The euro is the base or domestic currency. We may therefore rewrite Equation 7 as follows:

$$F_{0,KRW/EUR}(T) = S_{0,KRW/EUR}e^{(r_{KRW} - r_{EUR})T}.$$

Assume a spot KRW/EUR rate (S_0) of 1,300 (that is, KRW1,300 = EUR1), a South Korean won risk-free rate of 0.75%, and a euro risk-free rate of –0.25% (r_d). Calculate the KRW/EUR forward rate in 75 days consistent with no arbitrage.

$$F_{0,KRW/EUR}(T) = 1{,}300 \times e^{(0.0075 + 0.0025) \times (75/365)}.$$

Solving for the KRW/EUR forward rate gives us $F_0(T)$ = 1,302.67. Notice that the 1% difference between South Korean won and euro interest rates leads to a forward price that is above the spot price ($F_{0,f/d}(T) > S_{0,f/d}$). That is, in six months' time, more South Korean won will be required to purchase a euro, and the South Korean won is said to trade at a forward discount versus the euro.

To demonstrate the no-arbitrage condition between the forward and spot rates, assume that Montau converts the KRW650 million into euros at the 1,300 KRW/EUR spot rate to receive EUR500,000 (= KRW650,000,000/1,300) and invests this for 75 days at a continuously compounded r_f = –0.25%:

$$\text{EUR}499{,}743.22 = \text{EUR}500{,}000 \times e^{[-0.0025 \times (75/365)]}.$$

Assume that Jeon Inc. invests the KRW650 million at the South Korean won risk-free rate (r_d = 0.75%) for 75 days to receive

$$\text{KRW}651{,}002{,}484.59 = \text{KRW}650{,}000{,}000 \times e^{[0.0075 \times (75/365)]}.$$

An arbitrage-free forward commitment price should therefore allow Montau to convert KRW651,002,484.59 into EUR499,743.22 after 75 days.

$F_0(T) = 651{,}002{,}484.59/499{,}743.22 = 1{,}302.67.$

This confirms that the two prices (spot and forward exchange rates) are consistent with the risk-free interest rate differential in the two different currencies.

In contrast to securities or cash stored electronically, commodities usually involve known costs associated with the storage, insurance, transportation, and potential spoilage (in the case of soft commodities) of these physical assets. A non-cash benefit of holding a physical commodity versus a derivative is known as a **convenience yield**. In physical goods markets, economic conditions may arise that cause market participants to prefer to own the physical commodity. As a simple example, if crude oil inventories are very low, refineries may bid up the spot oil price so that forward prices do not fully reflect storage costs and interest rates. The following example illustrates the impact of these carry costs on the relationship between spot and forward commitment prices for a commodity, as well as the possibility of a convenience yield.

EXAMPLE 8

Procam's Gold Forward Contract with Storage Costs

Recall from earlier examples that Procam borrowed and purchased gold in the spot market and simultaneously sold gold in the forward market for three months to earn a riskless profit. Under the assumption of a 2% risk-free rate, we demonstrated that the spot gold price (S_0) would need to rise to USD1,783.28 (= USD1,792.13$(1.02)^{-0.25}$) in order to eliminate the earlier arbitrage opportunity for a given USD1,792.13 forward price where gold may be stored at no cost.

Given the spot price of USD1,783.28, how would the forward gold price change to satisfy the no-arbitrage condition if we were to introduce a USD2 per ounce cost of gold storage and insurance payable at the end of the contract?

The forward commitment price for a commodity with known storage cost amounts may be determined using Equation 5, where $PV_0(I) = 0$:

$$F_0(T) = [S_0 + PV_0(C)](1 + r)^T.$$

First, solve for the present value of the storage cost per ounce $PV_0(C)$ as follows:

$$PV_0(C) = \text{USD}2(1.02)^{-0.25}$$

$$= \text{USD}1.99.$$

Substitute $PV_0(C)$ = USD1.99 into Equation 5 to solve for $F_0(T)$:

$$F_0(T) = (\text{USD}1{,}783.28 + \text{USD}1.99)(1.02)^{0.25}$$

$$= \text{USD}1{,}794.13.$$

Note that the addition of storage and insurance costs increases the difference between the spot and forward price. Finally, note that a forward price, $F_0(T)$, significantly *below* the no-arbitrage price may indicate the presence of a convenience yield.

The additional costs and benefits of underlying asset ownership are summarized in Exhibit 10.

Exhibit 10: Cost of Carry for Underlying Assets

Asset Class	Examples	Benefits (i)	Costs (r, c)
Asset without Cash Flows	Non-dividend-paying stock	None	Risk-free rate
Equities	Dividend-paying stocks	Dividend	Risk-free rate
	Equity indexes	Dividend yield	
Foreign Exchange	Sovereign bonds (foreign)	None	Difference between foreign and domestic risk-free rates ($r_f - r_d$)
	Market exchange rates		
Commodities	Soft and hard commodities	Convenience yield	Risk-free rate
	Commodity indexes		Storage cost
Interest Rates	Sovereign bonds (domestic)	Interest income	Risk-free rate
	Market reference rates		
Credit	Single reference entity	Credit spread	Risk-free rate
	Credit indexes		

Interest rates and credit have a term structure—that is, different prices or rates for different maturities. These forward contracts are addressed in a later lesson.

QUESTION SET

Cost of Carry

1. Describe the relationship between the spot and forward price for an underlying asset whose benefits exceed the opportunity and other costs of ownership.

   Solution:

   If the benefits for an owner of an underlying asset exceed the opportunity and other costs of owning the underlying asset, the spot price will be greater than the forward price.

2. Identify which example corresponds to each of the following relationships between the spot and forward rate:

1. $F_0(T) > S_0$	A. A fixed-coupon bond priced at par whose coupon is above the risk-free rate
2. $F_0(T) < S_0$	B. A foreign currency forward where the foreign risk-free rate is greater than the domestic risk-free rate
3. Not enough information to determine the relationship between $F_0(T)$ and S_0	C. A commodity with a convenience yield as well as storage and insurance costs

   Solution:

   1. B is correct. The FX forward rate is greater than the spot rate if the foreign risk-free rate is greater than the domestic risk-free rate.

2. A is correct. A fixed-coupon bond priced at par has an income that exceeds the opportunity cost of the risk-free rate, so $F_0(T) < S_0$.

3. C is correct. We do not have enough information to fully evaluate the benefit (convenience yield) versus the cost (risk-free rate, storage, and insurance) of holding the physical commodity asset in this example.

3. Determine the correct answers to fill in the blanks: A positive risk-free rate causes a forward price to be _______ than the underlying spot price, all else equal, and the higher the risk-free rate, the _______ the difference between the two.

Solution:

A positive risk-free rate causes a forward price to be *greater* than the underlying spot price, all else equal, and the higher the risk-free rate, the *greater* the difference between the two.

4. An analyst observes that the current spot MXN/USD exchange rate is 19.50, the Mexican peso six-month risk free rate is 4%, and the six-month US dollar risk free rate is 0.25%. Describe the relationship between the MXN/USD spot and six-month forward rate, and justify your answer.

Solution:

The relationship between the MXN/USD FX spot and forward price depends on the risk-free interest rate differential between the Mexican peso and the US dollar ($r_f - r_d > 0$, since 3.75% = 4.0% – 0.25%). Since the Mexican peso rate is 3.75% above the US dollar rate, we would expect that borrowing at a higher Mexican peso rate and lending at a lower US dollar rate would result in a no-arbitrage forward price at which more Mexican pesos are required to purchase USD1 in the future, so the Mexican peso is said to trade at a discount in the forward market versus the US dollar ($F_{0,MXN/USD}(T) > S_{0,MXN/USD}$).

We can show this using Equation 7 for the case of MXN/USD as follows:

$$F_{0,MXN/USD}(T) = S_{0,MXN/USD}e^{(r_{MXN} - r_{USD})T}.$$

Based on the current $S_{0,f/d}$ of 19.50, $r_f = 4\%$, $r_d = 0.25\%$, and T of 0.5, we may solve for the no-arbitrage forward price, $F_{0,f/d}$, as

$$F_{0,MXN/USD}(T) = 19.50e^{[(0.04 - 0.0025) \times 0.5]}$$

$$= 19.8691.$$

5. Assume that new, stricter environmental regulations associated with oil storage and insurance cause the cost of these services to increase sharply. Describe the anticipated effect of these increased costs on the relationship between oil spot and forward commitment prices.

Solution:

Owners of physical commodities who must incur storage and insurance costs over time expect to be compensated by higher forward commitment prices for future delivery of the underlying assets. Assuming other factors are constant, higher storage and insurance costs therefore lead to higher forward commitment prices and a greater difference between spot and forward prices. As shown in Equation 5, an increase in C increases $F_0(T)$ for a given S_0:

$$F_0(T) = [S_0 - \mathrm{PV}_0(I) + \mathrm{PV}_0(C)]\,(1 + r)^T. \tag{8}$$

LEARNING MODULE

5

Pricing and Valuation of Forward Contracts and for an Underlying with Varying Maturities

LEARNING OUTCOMES

Mastery	*The candidate should be able to:*
☐	explain how the value and price of a forward contract are determined at initiation, during the life of the contract, and at expiration
☐	explain how forward rates are determined for interest rate forward contracts and describe the uses of these forward rates.

INTRODUCTION

1

Earlier lessons introduced forward commitment features, payoff profiles, and concepts used in pricing these derivative instruments. In particular, the relationship between spot and forward commitment prices was established as the opportunity cost of owning the underlying asset (represented by the risk-free rate) as well as any additional cost or benefit associated with holding the underlying asset. This price relationship both prevents arbitrage and allows a forward commitment to be replicated using spot market transactions and risk-free borrowing or lending.

In the first lesson, we explore the pricing and valuation of forward commitments on a mark-to-market basis from inception through maturity. This analysis is essential for issuers, investors, and financial intermediaries alike to assess the value of any asset or liability portfolio that includes these instruments. The second lesson addresses forward pricing for the special case of underlying assets with different maturities such as interest rates, credit spreads, and volatility. The prices of these forward commitments across the so-called term structure are an important building block for pricing swaps and related instruments in later lessons.

LEARNING MODULE OVERVIEW

- A forward commitment price agreed upon at contract inception remains fixed and establishes the basis on which the underlying asset (or cash) will be exchanged in the future versus the spot price at maturity.
- For an underlying asset that does not generate cash flows, the value of a long forward commitment prior to expiration equals the current spot price of the underlying asset minus the present value of the forward price discounted at the risk-free rate. The reverse is true for a short forward commitment. Foreign exchange represents a special case in which the spot versus forward price is a function of the *difference* between risk-free rates across currencies.
- For an underlying asset with additional costs and benefits, the forward contract mark-to-market (MTM) value is adjusted by the sum of the present values of all additional cash flows through maturity.
- Underlying assets with a term structure, such as interest rates, have different rates or prices for different times-to-maturity. These zero or spot and forward rates are derived from coupon bonds and market reference rates and establish the building blocks of interest rate derivatives pricing.
- Implied forward rates represent a breakeven reinvestment rate linking short-dated and long-dated zero-coupon bonds over a specific period.
- A forward rate agreement (FRA) is a contract in which counterparties agree to apply a specific interest rate to a future period.

LEARNING MODULE SELF-ASSESSMENT

These initial questions are intended to help you gauge your current level of understanding of this learning module.

1. Match the following situations with their corresponding forward contract valuation for an asset with no additional costs or benefits.

1. At time $t = 0$, the spot price of the underlying asset rises instantaneously and other market parameters remain unchanged.	A. The forward contract buyer has an MTM gain.
2. At time t, the present value of the forward price discounted at the risk-free rate (r) equals the current spot price (S_t).	B. The forward contract seller has an MTM gain.
3. At time T, the forward contract price, $F_0(T)$, is greater than the current spot price, S_T.	C. The MTM value of the forward contract is zero.

Solution:

1. A is correct. In order to satisfy the no-arbitrage condition, the original spot price, S_0 at $t = 0$, must equal the present value of the forward price discounted at the risk-free rate, r. An immediate increase in the spot price to $S_0^+ > S_0$ results in an MTM gain for the forward buyer.

2. C is correct. At any time t, the MTM value, $V_t(T)$, is equal to the difference between the current spot price, S_t, and the present value of the forward price discounted at the risk-free rate, r, or $F_0(T)(1 + r)^{-(T-t)}$. When $S_t = F_0(T)(1 + r)^{-(T-t)}$, then $V_t(T) = 0$.

3. B is correct. The MTM value to the forward contract seller upon settlement at time T is equal to the settlement value of $F_0(T) - S_T$.

2. An increase in the risk-free rate, r, following the inception of a forward contract will cause which of the following to the forward contract's MTM value to the forward seller if other parameters remain unchanged.

   A. The forward contract's MTM value to the forward seller will be unchanged.

   B. The forward contract's MTM value to the forward seller will increase.

   C. The forward contract's MTM value to the forward seller will decrease.

   Solution:

   C is correct. The mark-to-market value from the forward seller's perspective is equal to Vt(T) in the following equation:

   $V_t(T) = F_0(T)(1 + r)^{-(T-t)} - S_t$.

   An increase in the risk-free rate, r, following the inception of a forward contract will cause the present value of the forward price, F0(T), to fall, and this will reduce the MTM value from the contract seller's perspective.

3. Which of the following is closest to the two-year zero rate given a 3% annual coupon bond priced at 99 per 100 face value if a one-year annual coupon bond from the same issuer has a yield-to-maturity of 2.50%?

   A. 3.5266%

   B. 3.5000%

   C. 3.5422%

   Solution:

   C is correct. The yield-to-maturity and the zero rate for a bond with a single cash flow at maturity in one period are identical, so the one-year zero rate, z1, equals 2.50%. Solve for the two-year zero rate (z2) in the following equation:

   $99 = 3/1.025 + 103/(1 + z_2)^2$.

   Solve for z_2 to get 3.5422%. A is incorrect because 3.5266% is the internal rate of return (IRR) solved for cash flows of -99 at $t = 0$, 3 at $t = 1$, and 103 at $t = 2$. This response assumes a flat term structure, which is not a correct assumption given the question. B is incorrect because this response implies that we can find the correct answer by assuming the coupon rate is the simple average of the one- and two-year zero rates.

4. Which of the following is a correct description of a 2y3y forward rate?

   A. The implied two-year rate beginning three years in the future.

   B. The implied three-year rate beginning two years in the future.

   C. The implied one-year rate beginning two years in the future.

   Solution:

   B is correct. In the terminology of forward rates, the first number reflects the point in time when a forward rate begins; thus, the forward rate stated above reflects a rate starting two years in the future. The second number reflects the maturity of the rate. Thus, the 2y3y forward rate reflects a three-year rate starting in two years. A is incorrect because this is the description of the 3y2y forward rate. C is incorrect because this is the description of the 2y1y rate.

2 PRICING AND VALUATION OF FORWARD CONTRACTS

☐ explain how the value and price of a forward contract are determined at initiation, during the life of the contract, and at expiration

Pricing versus Valuation of Forward Contracts

When counterparties enter into forward, futures, or swap contracts with one another, these contracts have an initial value of zero (ignoring trading and transaction costs as well as counterparty credit exposure). While forward commitments require no cash outlay at inception, their price incorporates the opportunity cost of a long cash position as measured by the risk-free rate. The forward price or forward rate established at inception remains fixed and determines the basis on which the underlying asset (or cash) will be exchanged in the future versus the spot price at maturity.

As time passes and/or the underlying asset spot price and other parameters change, the value of a forward contract changes. This mark-to-market value of a contract reflects the change in the underlying price and other factors that would result in a gain or loss to a counterparty if the forward contract were to be settled immediately. The MTM gain of the forward seller will equal the MTM loss of the forward buyer and vice versa. Recall that a key difference between exchange-traded futures and over-the-counter forwards is that the futures clearinghouse settles these MTM changes in cash on a daily basis, while forward contract settlement typically occurs at maturity.

Pricing and Valuation of Forward Contracts at Initiation

The prior learning module established that a forward contract agreed at time $t = 0$ occurs at a forward price, $F_0(T)$, that satisfies no-arbitrage conditions for the underlying spot price (S_0), the risk-free rate of return (r), and any additional costs or benefits associated with underlying asset ownership until the forward contract matures at time T. In an earlier example, AMY Investments agreed to purchase 1,000 Airbus (AIR) shares trading at the spot price (S_T) at maturity at an agreed upon forward price, $F_0(T)$, of EUR30 per share, as shown in Exhibit 1.

Exhibit 1: Forward Contract Value at Initiation

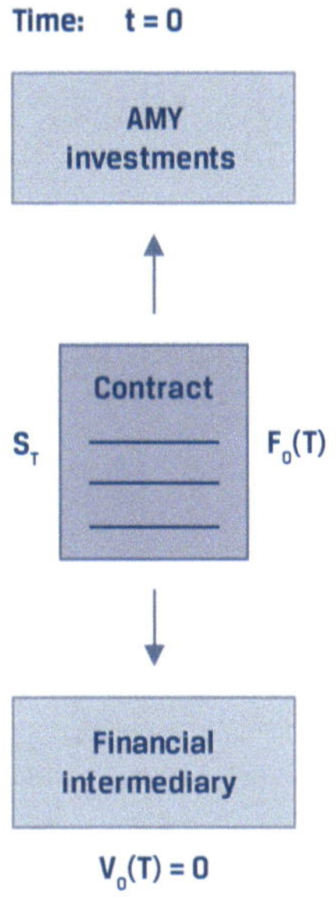

If we assume S_0 = EUR29.70, r = 1.00% and T is one year, $F_0(T)$ of EUR30 satisfies the no-arbitrage condition at t = 0 (ignoring transaction costs). The forward contract is neither an asset nor a liability to AMY Investments (the buyer) or the financial intermediary (the seller) and therefore has a value of zero to both parties:

$$V_0(T) = 0 \quad (1)$$

Pricing and Valuation of Forward Contracts at Maturity

Recall from an earlier lesson that a forward commitment has a symmetric payoff profile. That is, at time T a forward contract is settled based on the difference between the forward price, $F_0(T)$, and the underlying spot price, S_T, or $S_T - F_0(T)$, from the buyer's perspective, as shown in Exhibit 2.

Exhibit 2: Forward Contract Value at Maturity

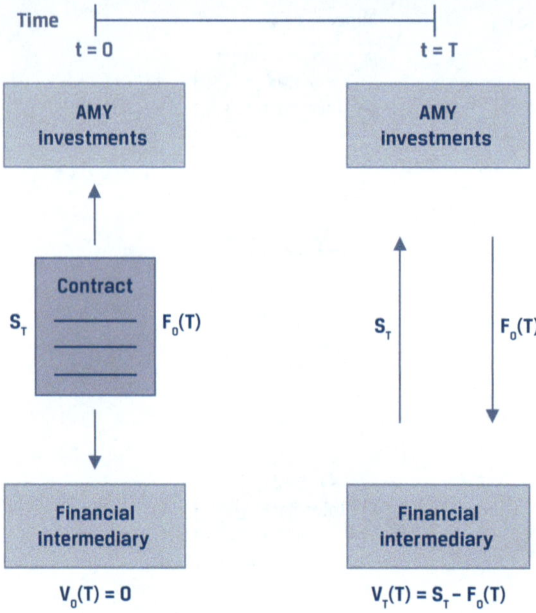

Outcome	$V_T(T)$ (long position)	$V_T(T)$ (short position)
$S_T > F_0(T)$	$S_T - F_0(T) > 0$	$F_0(T) - S_T < 0$
$S_T < F_0(T)$	$S_T - F_0(T) < 0$	$F_0(T) - S_T > 0$
$S_T = F_0(T)$	$S_T - F_0(T) = 0$	$F_0(T) - S_T = 0$

AMY must pay the agreed upon price of $F_0(T)$ in exchange for the underlying asset at the current spot price of S_T. Since the contract settles at maturity, its *value* at maturity is equal to the settlement amount from each counterparty's perspective. For example, at time $t = T$, the value of the forward contract at maturity, $V_T(T)$, from the perspective of AMY (the forward buyer) equals:

$$V_T(T) = S_T - F_0(T) \quad (2)$$

EXAMPLE 1

Value of Biomian Forward Positions at Maturity

The Viswan Family Office (VFO) currently owns 10,000 common non-dividend-paying shares of Biomian Limited, a Mumbai-based biotech company, at a spot price of INR 295 per share. VFO agrees to sell forward 1,000 shares of Biomian stock to a financial intermediary for INR300.84 per share in six months. Calculate the contract value at maturity, $V_T(T)$, from both the buyer's and the seller's perspective if the spot price at maturity (S_T) is:

(1) S_T = INR 287

(2) S_T = INR 312

Solution:

At contract inception, VFO enters into a forward contract with a financial intermediary to sell Biomian for $F_0(T)$ = INR 300.84. The forward contract value at initiation for both VFO and the financial intermediary, $V_0(T)$, is zero.

(1) S_T = INR287 and $F_0(T)$ = INR300.84. The contract value per share at maturity equals its settlement value from the perspective of both the financial intermediary (buyer) and VFO (seller), as follows:

- Buyer (long forward position): $V_T(T) = S_T - F_0(T)$
  $V_T(T)$ = –INR13.84 = 287 – 300.84
- Viswan Family Office (short forward position): $V_T(T) = F_0(T) - S_T$
  $V_T(T)$ = INR13.84 = 300.84 – 287

(2) S_T = INR312 and $F_0(T)$ = INR300.84. The contract value per share at maturity equals its settlement value from the perspective of both the financial intermediary (buyer) and VFO (seller), as follows:

- Buyer (long forward position): $V_T(T) = S_T - F_0(T)$
  $V_T(T)$ = INR11.16 = 312 – 300.84
- Viswan Family Office (short forward position): $V_T(T) = F_0(T) - S_T$
  $V_T(T)$ = –INR11.16 = 300.84 – 312

Pricing and Valuation of Forward Contracts during the Life of the Contract

Once a forward contract is initiated between two counterparties, the passage of time and changes in the underlying asset's spot price, among other factors, will cause the forward contract value to change. The mark-to-market value of a contract at any point in time from inception to maturity, $V_t(T)$, reflects the relationship between the current spot price at time t (S_t) and the present value of the forward price at time t discounted at the current risk-free rate. Exhibit 3 shows this relationship for the Airbus equity forward example from AMY Investments' perspective (the long forward position).

Exhibit 3: Forward Contract Value at Inception, over Time, and at Maturity

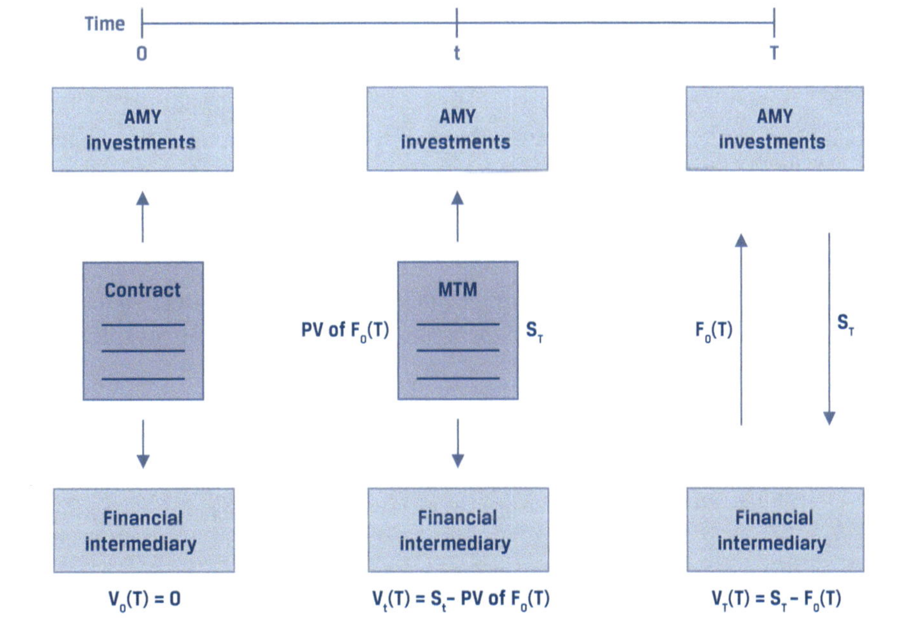

Recall that under no-arbitrage conditions, the forward price of an underlying asset with no additional cost or benefit of ownership equals the future value of the spot price at the risk-free rate, r:

$$F_0(\mathrm{T}) = S_0(1 + r)^T \quad (3)$$

At any time t over the life of the contract where $t < T$, we can show the present value of the forward price, $F_0(T)$, at time t as follows:

$$\mathrm{PV}_t \text{ of } F_0(T) = F_0(T)(1 + r)^{-(T-t)} \quad (4)$$

If S_t is the spot price of the underlying asset at time t, Equation 5 shows the forward contract MTM value at time t, $V_t(T)$, from the long forward position's perspective:

$$V_t(T) = S_t - F_0(T)(1 + r)^{-(T-t)} \quad (5)$$

Exhibit 4 shows the relationship between the spot price, the forward price, and the present value of the forward price, $F_0(T)(1 + r)^{-(T-t)}$, over time as represented by the dashed line. The slope of the dashed line is equal to r.

Exhibit 4: Present Value of the Forward Price over Time

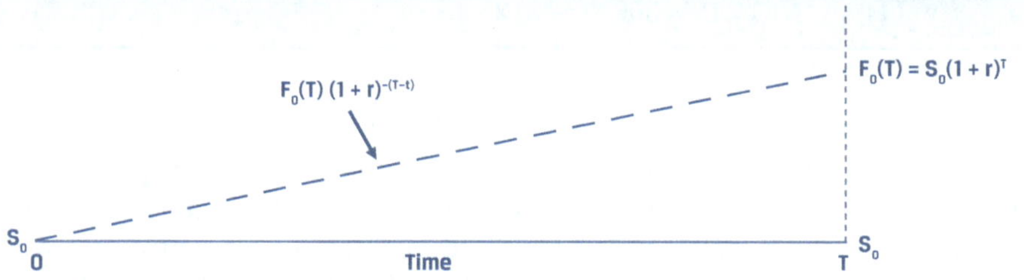

We explore these relationships, as well as the MTM impact of an instantaneous change in the spot price (S_0), in the following example.

EXAMPLE 2

Implied Risk-Free Rate and Biomian Forward Contract MTM

As in Example 1, VFO enters into a six-month forward contract with a financial intermediary to sell Biomian shares for $F_0(\mathrm{T})$ = INR300.84 per share. The current spot price is INR295 per share.

1. Calculate the risk-free rate implied by the spot and forward prices.
2. Calculate the forward contract MTM from VFO's perspective if Biomian's share price rises instantaneously to INR325 at contract inception (t = 0).

Solution:

1. We can use Equation 3—with S_0 = 295, $F_0(T)$ = 300.84, and T = 0.5—to solve for the risk-free rate, r:

$$F_0(T) = S_0(1 + r)^T$$

$$300.84 = 295(1 + r)^{0.5}$$

$$r = 0.04 \text{ or } 4\%$$

2. As the forward contract seller, we must rearrange Equation 5 to solve for the contract MTM value from VFO's perspective as follows:

$$V_t(T) = F_0(T)(1 + r)^{-(T-t)} - S_t$$

Note that if $t = 0$, $F_0(T)(1 + r)^{-(T-t)}$ simplifies to $F_0(T)(1 + r)^{-T} = S_0$, so the contract value from VFO's perspective can be shown simply as:

$$V_t(T) = S_0 - S_t$$

$$-\text{INR}30 = \text{INR}295 - \text{INR}325$$

If we consider the new higher Biomian price as $S_0^+ = \text{INR}325$, we can show this MTM change in the following diagram:

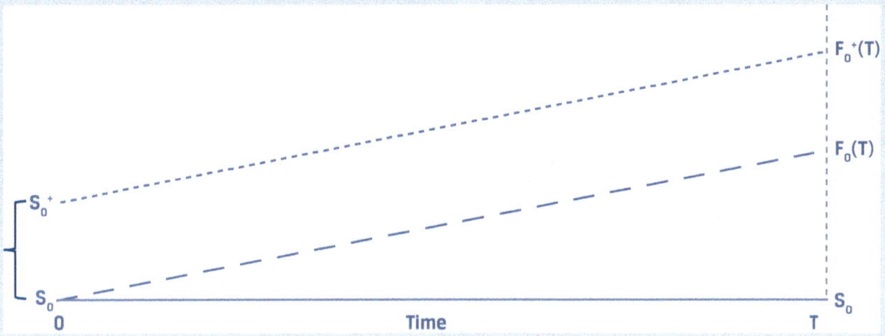

The combination of spot price changes over the life of a forward contract and the passage of time causes the MTM value of a forward contract to fluctuate over time, representing a gain or loss to contract participants so long as $S_t \neq F_0(T)(1 + r)^{-(T-t)}$. Exhibit 5 shows this relationship, assuming a constant risk-free rate over the life of a contract for long and short forward contract positions.

Exhibit 5: Forward Contract MTM

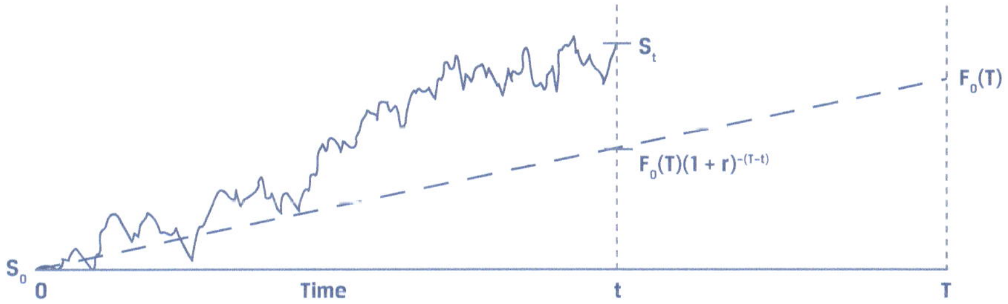

Outcome	$V_t(T)$ (long position)	$V_t(T)$ (short position)
$S_t > F_0(T)(1 + r)^{-(T-t)}$	MTM gain	MTM loss
$S_t < F_0(T)(1 + r)^{-(T-t)}$	MTM loss	MTM gain
$S_t = F_0(T)(1 + r)^{-(T-t)}$	No MTM gain or loss	No MTM gain or loss

Example 3 illustrates these combined effects for VFO's Biomian forward contract and examines the effect of a change in the risk-free rate.

EXAMPLE 3

Biomian Forward Contract MTM over Time and Changes in Risk-Free Rate

As in earlier examples, VFO enters into a six-month forward contract with a financial intermediary to sell Biomian shares at $F_0(\text{T})$ = INR300.84 per share. The spot price at $t = 0$ is INR295 per share and the risk-free rate is 4%.

1. Calculate the forward contract MTM from VFO's perspective in three months ($t = 0.25$) if Biomian's spot price (S_t) falls to INR285 per share.
2. Show the forward contract MTM from VFO's perspective in Question (1) if the risk-free rate doubles from 4% to 8%, and interpret the results.

Solution:

(1) From VFO's perspective as the forward contract seller, rearrange Equation 5 to solve for the contract MTM value as follows:

$V_t(T) = F_0(T)(1 + r)^{-(T-t)} - S_t$

Solve for $V_t(T)$ where $F_0(T) = 300.84$, $r = 0.04$, T = 0.5, $t = 0.25$, and $S_t = 285$:

$V_t(T) = 300.84(1.04)^{-(0.25)} - 285$

$V_t(T)$ = INR12.90 MTM gain

(2) Solve for $V_t(T)$ using the same equation and inputs as in Question (1) except that $r = 0.08$:

$V_t(T) = F_0(T)(1 + r)^{-(T-t)} - S_t$

Solve for $V_t(T)$ where $F_0(T) = 300.84$, $r = 0.08$, $T = 0.5$, $t = 0.25$, and $S_t = 285$:

$V_t(T) = 300.84(1.08)^{-(0.25)} - 285$

$V_t(T)$ = INR10.11 MTM gain

VFO's MTM gain on the contract has declined by INR2.79 (12.90 – 10.11). The *higher* risk-free rate increases the opportunity cost of a cash position and *lowers* the present value of the forward price, *reducing* VFO's MTM gain, $V_t(T)$, as represented by the present value of $F_0(T) - S_t$.

Pricing and Valuation of Forward Contracts with Additional Costs or Benefits

The pricing and valuation of forward contracts in this lesson have assumed that there are no cash flows associated with the underlying asset. We showed that the contract MTM value at any time t equals the difference between the current spot price and the present value of the forward price discounted at the risk-free rate. Now we turn our attention to how the cost of carry, or the net of all costs and benefits related to owning an underlying asset or index, affects the valuation of a forward contract. Recall the relationship between spot and forward prices for underlying assets with ownership benefits or income (I) or costs (C), which is expressed as a present value at time t = 0 in discrete compounding terms:

$$F_0(T) = (S_0 - \text{PV}_0(I) + \text{PV}_0(C))\,(1 + r)^T \quad (6)$$

Equation 6 incorporates the cost of carry and satisfies the no-arbitrage condition at t = 0 (ignoring transaction costs). A forward contract at a price, $F_0(T)$, that incorporates these known costs and benefits is neither an asset nor a liability to the buyer or seller at inception: $V_0(T) = 0$. Also, since the forward price, $F_0(T)$, incorporates the cost of carry, the value at maturity, $V_T(T)$, is equal to the difference between the spot price (S_T) at maturity and the original forward price, $F_0(T)$.

At any time t over the life of the contract, the MTM value of the forward contract, $V_t(T)$, will depend on the difference between the current spot price adjusted for any remaining costs or benefits from time t through maturity, $S_t - \text{PV}_t(I) + \text{PV}_t(C)$, and the present value of the forward price, $\text{PV}_t F_0(T) = F_0(T)(1 + r)^{-(T-t)}$. This result is shown in Equation 7 from the long forward counterparty's perspective:

$$V_t(T) = (S_t - \text{PV}_t(I) + \text{PV}_t(C)) - F_0(T)(1 + r)^{-(T-t)} \quad (7)$$

EXAMPLE 4

Hightest Equity Forward Valuation

In an earlier example, Hightest Capital agreed to deliver 1,000 Unilever (UL) shares to a financial intermediary in six months under a forward contract at a price of EUR 50,631.10, or EUR 50.6311 per share. Unilever pays a quarterly dividend of EUR 0.30 three months after contract inception and at time T, and the risk-free rate (r) is 5%. Calculate the forward contract breakeven price, S_t, where $V_t(T)$ = MTM = 0 four months after contract inception if the risk-free rate, r, remains unchanged at 5%.

Use Equation 7 with $\text{PV}_t(C) = 0$ to solve for $V_t(T) = 0$ four months after contract inception:

$$V_t(T) = (S_t - \text{PV}_t(I)) - F_0(T)(1 + r)^{-(T-t)}$$

First, solve for the present value of the dividend per share, $\text{PV}_t(I)$, given that the second dividend will be paid in two months:

$$\text{PV}_t(I) = \text{EUR}0.30(1.05)^{-0.167}$$
$$= \text{EUR}0.2976$$

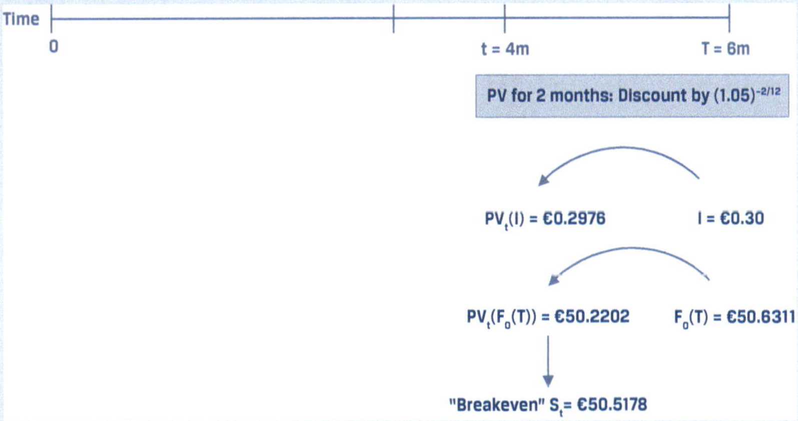

Substitute $\text{PV}_t(I)$ = EUR0.2976 into Equation 5 to solve for $V_t(T) = 0$:

$$0 = (S_t - 0.2976) - 50.6311(1.05)^{-0.167}$$
$$S_t = \text{EUR}50.2202 + \text{EUR}0.2976$$
$$= \text{EUR}50.5178$$

Hightest Capital's breakeven spot rate, S_t (i.e., where $V_t(T) = 0$), four months after inception of the forward contract is therefore EUR50.5178 per share.

Forward commitments on underlying indexes such as equity indexes or commodity indexes are predominantly exchange-traded index futures contracts. An earlier lesson used the *rate of return* over the life of the contract under continuous compounding to establish the relationship between spot and forward pricing for these instruments. The valuation of index futures and other futures contracts will be addressed in a later lesson.

Recall that for a foreign exchange forward, both spot ($S_{0,f/d}$) and forward ($F_{0,f/d}(T)$) prices are expressed in terms of units of a *price* currency (f or foreign currency) per *single* unit of a *base* currency (d or domestic currency). The spot price versus forward price relationship reflects the *difference* between the foreign risk-free rate, r_f, and the domestic risk-free rate, r_d, as shown in Equation 8:

$$F_{0,f/d}(T) = S_{0,f/d}\, e^{(r_f - r_d)T} \tag{8}$$

At trade inception at $t = 0$, the currency with the lower risk-free rate for the forward period is said to trade at a forward premium—that is, fewer units of currency are required to purchase one unit of the other—while the currency with the higher risk-free rate trades at a forward discount.

At any given time t, the MTM value of the FX forward is the difference between the *current* spot FX price ($S_{t,f/d}$) and the present value of the forward price discounted by the *current* difference in risk-free rates ($r_f - r_d$) for the remaining period through maturity, as shown in Equation 9:

$$V_t(T) = S_{t,f/d} - F_{0,f/d}(T)e^{-(r_f - r_d)(T-t)} \tag{9}$$

Changes in the interest rate differential ($r_f - r_d$) represent a change in the *relative* opportunity cost between currencies. As described in an earlier lesson, a price change of one currency in terms of another is referred to as *appreciation* or *depreciation*. For example, if fewer USD are required to purchase one EUR, then the USD/EUR exchange rate falls and the USD is said to *appreciate* against the EUR.

A greater interest rate differential—that is, an increase in ($r_f - r_d$)—causes the price, or foreign, currency to depreciate on a forward basis and the base, or domestic, currency to appreciate. The following example illustrates the effect of an interest rate change on the FX forward contract MTM value.

EXAMPLE 5

Rook Point Investors LLC FX Forward MTM

Rook Point Investors LLC has entered into a long one-year USD/EUR forward contract. That is, it has agreed to purchase EUR1,000,000 in exchange for USD1,201,000 in one year. At time $t = 0$ when the contract is initiated, the USD/EUR spot exchange rate is 1.192 (i.e., USD1.192 = EUR1), the one-year USD risk-free rate is 0.50%, and the one-year EUR risk-free rate is –0.25%.

Describe the MTM impact on the FX forward contract from Rook Point's perspective if the one-year USD risk-free rate instantaneously rises by 0.25% once the contract is initiated, with other details unchanged.

The instantaneous rise in the USD risk-free rate by 0.25% (from 0.5% to 0.75%) increases the difference between the foreign and domestic risk-free rates ($r_f - r_d$), *increasing* the discount rate used to calculate the present value of the forward rate, $F_{0,f/d}(T)$. Since $S_{0,f/d} > F_{0,f/d}(T)e^{-(r_f - r_d)(T-t)}$, $V_0(T) > 0$ from Rook Point's perspective and it realizes an MTM gain.

We can solve for the MTM value at time $t = 0$ by first rewriting Equation 9:

$$V_t(T) = S_{0,USD/EUR} - F_{0,USD/EUR}(T)e^{-(r_{USD} - r_{EUR})T}$$

Solve for $V_t(T)$ from Rook Point's perspective, with $S_{0,f/d} = 1.192$ USD/EUR, $F_{0,f/d} = 1.201$ USD/EUR, $r_f = 0.75\%$, $r_d = -0.25\%$, and $T = 1$.

$= 1.192 - 1.201e^{-(0.0075 + 0.0025)}$

$= 0.00295$ USD/EUR

Note that this positive exchange rate difference of 0.00295 USD/EUR can be shown in Equation 9 if we instead substitute the USD needed to purchase EUR1,000,000 to arrive at a USD contract value:

$= USD1,192,000 - USD1,201,000e^{-(0.0075 + 0.0025)}$
$= USD2,950.15$ MTM gain

In this and other examples involving interest rates, we have assumed constant risk-free rates both over time and across maturities. In the next lesson, we will explore how spot and forward prices change for variables, with different prices across maturities.

QUESTION SET

Pricing and Valuation of Forward Contracts

1. Identify which MTM situation corresponds to which forward price versus spot price relationship for an underlying asset with no additional costs or benefits.

1. At time $t = 0$ once the forward price is agreed, the spot price of the underlying asset immediately falls and other market parameters remain unchanged.	A. The forward contract seller has an MTM loss.
2. At time T, the forward contract price, $F_0(T)$, equals the current spot price, S_T.	B. The forward contract seller has an MTM gain.
3. At time T, the forward contract price, $F_0(T)$, is below the current spot price, S_T.	C. The MTM value of the forward contract is zero.

Solution:

1. B is correct. To satisfy the no-arbitrage condition, the original spot price, S_0 at $t = 0$, must equal the present value of the forward price discounted at the risk-free rate, r. Therefore, an immediate fall in the spot price to $S_0^- < S_0$ results in an MTM gain for the forward contract seller.

2. C is correct. At time T, the MTM value, $V_t(T)$, is equal to contract settlement, or the difference between $F_0(T)$ and S_T, which in this case is zero.

3. A is correct. The MTM value to the forward seller upon settlement at time T equals $F_0(T) - S_T$, so the seller has a loss if $F_0(T) < S_T$.

2. Identify the following statement as true or false and justify your answer:

At time t, a forward contract with no additional cash flows has a value equal to the difference between the current spot price and the present value of the forward price. Therefore, the MTM value of the forward contract from the seller's perspective is S_t – PV of $F_0(T)$.

Solution:

This statement is false. Although the forward contract MTM equals the difference between the current spot price and the present value of the forward price, the MTM value of the forward contract from the seller's perspective is PV of $F_0(T) - S_t$.

3. Assume that Hightest Capital enters into a six-month forward contract to purchase Unilever (UL) shares at EUR51.23. UL shares pay no dividend, and the risk-free rate across all maturities is 5%. Calculate the forward contract

MTM value from Hightest's perspective in three months' time if the current UL spot rate, S_t, is EUR50.50 and the risk-free rate does not change.

Solution:

Use Equation 5 to solve for the forward contract value in three months from Hightest's perspective:

$V_t(T) = S_t - F_0(T)(1 + r)^{-(T-t)}$

If S_t = EUR50.50, $F_0(T)$ = EUR51.23, r = 5%, and $T - t = 0.25$:

$V_t(T)$ = EUR50.50 – (EUR51.23)$(1.05)^{-0.25}$

= –EUR0.1089

Hightest therefore has an MTM loss of EUR0.11 on the forward contract in three months' time.

4. Match the following statements with their corresponding MTM situation for an underlying asset with additional costs and benefits.

1. At time *t*, the present value of the benefits of owning the underlying asset is *greater than* the present value of the costs.	A. The forward contract has an MTM value *equal to* the difference between the current spot price and the present value of the forward price.
2. At time *t*, the present value of the benefits of owning the underlying asset is *equal to* the present value of the costs.	B. The forward contract has an MTM value *greater than* the difference between the current spot price and the present value of the forward price.
3. At time *t*, the present value of the benefits of owning the underlying asset is *less than* the present value of the costs.	C. The forward contract has an MTM value *less than* the difference between the current spot price and the present value of the forward price.

Solution:

Recall the forward contract MTM value, $V_t(T)$, for underlying assets with additional costs and benefits from the long forward counterparty's perspective in Equation 7:

$V_t(T) = (S_t - \mathrm{PV}_t(I) + \mathrm{PV}_t(C)) - F_0(T)(1 + r)^{-(T-t)}$

1. C is correct. A higher present value of the benefits of owning the underlying asset versus the present value of the costs will reduce the MTM below the difference between the current spot price and the present value of the forward price. For Equation 7, if $\mathrm{PV}_t(C) - \mathrm{PV}_t(I) < 0$, then:

$V_t(T) < S_t - F_0(T)(1 + r)^{-(T-t)}$

2. A is correct. If the present values of the remaining benefits and costs of owning the underlying asset offset each other, then the forward contract MTM *equals* the difference between the current spot price and the present value of the forward price. For Equation 7, if $\mathrm{PV}_t(C) - \mathrm{PV}_t(I) = 0$, then:

$V_t(T) = S_t - F_0(\mathrm{T})(1 + r)^{-(T-t)}$

3. B is correct. A lower present value of the benefits of owning the underlying asset versus the present value of the costs will increase the MTM beyond the difference between the current spot price and the present value of the forward price. For Equation 7, if $\mathrm{PV}_t(C) - \mathrm{PV}_t(I) > 0$, then:

$V_t(T) > S_t - F_0(T)(1 + r)^{-(T-t)}$

5. Rook Point Investors LLC has entered into a six-month FX forward contract in which it agrees to sell South African rand (ZAR) and buy EUR at a

forward ZAR/EUR price of 17.2506 in six months. The ZAR/EUR spot price is 16.909, the six-month South African risk-free rate is 3.5%, and the six-month EUR risk-free rate is –0.5%. Describe the FX forward MTM impact from Rook Point's perspective of an immediate appreciation in ZAR/EUR to 16.5 if other parameters are unchanged.

Solution:

An immediate appreciation in the ZAR/EUR spot price after contract inception will result in an MTM loss from Rook Point's perspective as the forward seller of ZAR/EUR.

The FX forward MTM from Rook Point's perspective equals the present value of the forward price discounted at the interest rate differential between the foreign currency and the domestic currency minus the spot price:

$V_0(T) = F_{0,f/d}(T)\,e^{-(r_f - r_d)T} - S_{0,f/d}$

Note that ZAR is the price, or foreign, currency and EUR is the base, or domestic, currency, so we can rewrite the equation as:

$V_0(T) = F_{0,ZAR/EUR}(T)\,e^{-(r_{ZAR} - r_{EUR})T} - S_{0,ZAR/EUR}$

If the ZAR price ($S_{0,ZAR/EUR}$) appreciates from 16.909 to 16.5, we can show that Rook Point would have a 0.4090 loss, as follows:

$V_t(T) = 17.2506e^{-(0.035 - -0.005)\times(0.5)} - 16.5$

$= 16.909 - 16.5$

$= 0.4090$

PRICING AND VALUATION OF INTEREST RATE FORWARD CONTRACTS 3

☐ explain how forward rates are determined for interest rate forward contracts and describe the uses of these forward rates.

Interest Rate Forward Contracts

The relationship between spot and forward prices of underlying assets uses a constant risk-free interest rate as the opportunity cost of owning the underlying asset. Unlike equities and commodities, addressed earlier, interest rates are characterized by a term structure—that is, different interest rates exist for different times-to-maturity. While this lesson focuses on interest rates, similar principles apply to other underlying variables with a term structure, including credit spreads and implied volatility as well as foreign exchange, where two interest rate term structures are involved.

Spot Rates and Discount Factors

The relationships between spot and forward interest rates, established in earlier fixed-income lessons, are key building blocks for interest rate derivatives pricing. These building blocks are usually based on a government benchmark or market reference rate. While most fixed-income instruments have coupon cash flows prior to maturity, interest rate derivatives pricing and valuation are based on the price and yield of single cash flows on a future date. The transformation of these cash flows from one form into another is a first step in the process, as in the following example.

EXAMPLE 6

Zero Rate

Assume we observe three most recently issued annual fixed-coupon government bonds, with coupons and prices as follows:

Years to Maturity	Annual Coupon	PV (per 100 FV)
1	1.50%	99.125
2	2.50%	98.275
3	3.25%	98.000

Note that each bond trades at a discount (PV < FV). As a first step, we solve for each bond's yield-to-maturity (YTM) using the Excel RATE function (=RATE(nper, pmt, pv, [fv],[type])). For example, for the three-year bond, we use nper = 3, pmt = 3.25, pv = −98, fv = 100, and type = 0 (indicating payment at the end of the period) to solve for the three-year bond YTM of 3.9703%.

Years to Maturity	Annual Coupon	PV (per 100 FV)	YTM
1	1.50%	99.125	2.3960%
2	2.50%	98.275	3.4068%
3	3.25%	98.000	3.9703%

We can use these government yields-to-maturity to solve for a sequence of yields-to-maturity on zero-coupon bonds, or zero rates (z_1, ... z_N), where z_i is the zero rate for period i.

Starting with the one-year bond, which consists of a single cash flow at maturity, we can solve for the one-year zero rate (z_1) as follows:

One-year:

$$99.125 = \frac{101.5}{(1+z_1)^1}; z_1 = 2.3960\%$$

The yield-to-maturity rate and the zero rate for a bond with a single cash flow at maturity in one period are identical. Since all cash flows at time t = 1 are discounted at z_1, we can substitute z_1 into the two-year fixed-coupon bond calculation to solve for the zero-coupon rate at the end of the second period (z_2):

Two-year:

$$98.275 = \frac{2.5}{1.02396} + \frac{102.5}{(1+z_2)^2}; z_2 = 3.4197\%$$

We then substitute both z_1 and z_2 into the three-year bond equation to solve for the zero-coupon cash flow at the end of year three (z_3):

Three-year:

$$98.00 = \frac{3.25}{(1.02396)} + \frac{3.25}{(1.034197)^2} + \frac{103.25}{(1+z_3)^3}; z_3 = 4.0005\%$$

The zero rates are summarized in the following diagram:

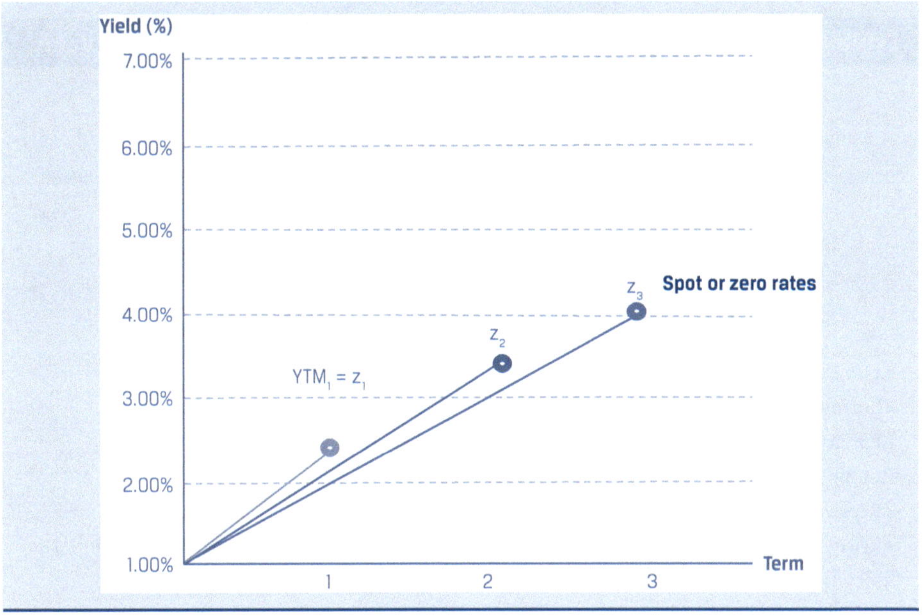

This process of deriving zero or spot rates from coupon bonds using forward substitution, as shown in Example 6, is sometimes referred to as bootstrapping. The *price* equivalent of a zero rate is the present value of a currency unit on a future date, known as a **discount factor**. The discount factor for period i (DF_i) is:

$$DF_i = \frac{1}{(1 + z_i)^i} \tag{10}$$

For each of the zero rates shown in Example 6, an equivalent discount factor can be derived as follows:

One-year: $DF_1 = 1/(1 + z_1)$; $DF_1 = 0.976601$

Two-year: $DF_2 = 1/(1 + z_2)^2$; $DF_2 = 0.934961$

Three-year: $DF_3 = 1/(1 + z_3)^3$; $DF_3 = 0.888982$

A discount factor may also be interpreted as the price of a zero-coupon cash flow or bond. We can use the discount factor for any period to demonstrate the same no-arbitrage condition from an earlier lesson—namely, that an asset with a known future price must trade at the present value of its future price as determined by using an appropriate discount rate.

For example, assume a two-year GBP risk-free zero rate (z_2) of 3.42% and a two-year zero-coupon bond with a face value of GBP100 trading at a price of GBP92.45. The no-arbitrage price of the zero-coupon bond is equal to GBP93.4955: GBP100/(1.0342)^2. In order to earn a riskless arbitrage profit, we can take the following steps, as shown in Exhibit 6.

Exhibit 6: Asset with Known Future Price Does Not Trade at Its Present Value

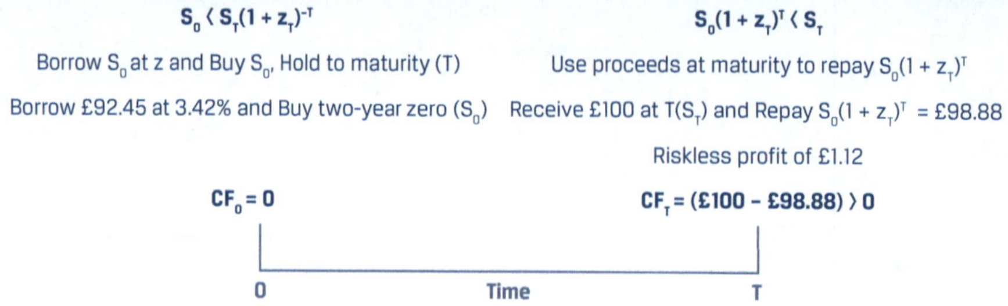

At time $t = 0$:

- Borrow GBP92.45 at the risk-free rate of 3.42%.
- Purchase the two-year zero-coupon note for GBP92.45.

At time $t = T$ (in two years):

- Receive GBP100 on the zero-coupon bond maturity date.
- Repay loan of GBP98.88—GBP92.45 × $(1.0342)^2$—and earn a riskless arbitrage profit of GBP1.12.

Forward Rates

As in the case of other underlying assets, the forward market for interest rates involves a delivery date beyond the usual cash market settlement date. Given the term structures of different interest rates for different maturities, an interest rate forward contract specifies both the *length* of the forward period and the tenor of the underlying rate.

For example, a two-year forward contract that references a three-year underlying interest rate (which starts at the end of year two and matures at the end of year five) is referred to as a "2y3y" forward rate, which we will denote as $F_{2,3}$. Short-term market reference rates (MRRs) usually reference a forward rate in months—for instance, $F_{3m,6m}$ references a six-month MRR that begins in three months and matures nine months from today.

The breakeven reinvestment rate linking a short-dated and a long-dated zero-coupon bond is an **implied forward rate**. That is, the implied forward rate is the interest rate for a period in the future at which an investor earns the same return from:

1. investing for a period from today until the forward start date and rolling over the proceeds at the implied forward rate, or
2. investing today through the final maturity of the forward rate.

The fact that these strategies have equal returns establishes the no-arbitrage condition for the implied forward rate. The following example demonstrates how spot rates can be used to derive forward rates.

EXAMPLE 7

Implied Forward Rate ($IFR_{1,1}$)

We return to the earlier example of three most recently issued annual fixed-coupon government bonds, with coupons and prices as well as yields-to-maturity and zero or spot rates as follows:

Years to Maturity	Annual Coupon	PV (per 100 FV)	YTM
1	1.50%	99.125	2.3960%
2	2.50%	98.275	3.4068%
3	3.25%	98.000	3.9703%

Years to Maturity	Zero Rate
1	2.3960%
2	3.4197%
3	4.0005%

Using the one-year and two-year zero rates from the prior example, an investor faces the following investment choices over a two-year period:

1. Invest USD100 for one year today at the zero rate (z_1) of 2.396% and reinvest the proceeds of USD102.40 at the one-year rate in one year's time, or the "1y1y" implied forward rate ($IFR_{1,1}$).
2. Invest USD100 for two years at the two-year zero rate (z_2) of 3.4197% to receive USD100$(1 + z_2)^2$, or USD106.96.

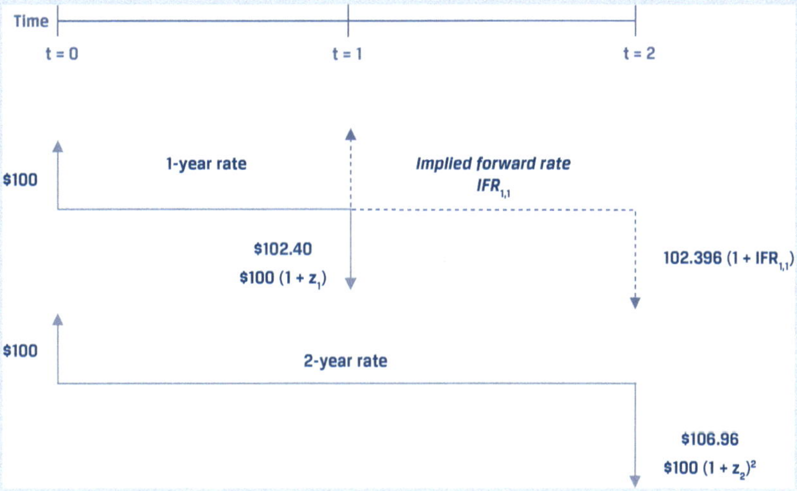

In order to arrive at the same return for investment choices 1.) and 2.), we set them equal to each other and solve for $IFR_{1,1}$ as follows:

$$\text{USD100} \times (1 + z_1) \times (1 + IFR_{1,1}) = \text{USD100} \times (1 + z_2)^2$$

$$\text{USD100} \times (1.02396) \times (1 + IFR_{1,1}) = \text{USD100} \times (1.034197)^2$$

$$IFR_{1,1} = 4.4536\%$$

We can demonstrate that the $\text{IFR}_{1,1}$ of 4.4536% creates identical returns for the first and second strategies by calculating the return on the first strategy as follows:

$$\text{USD100} \times (1.02396) \times (1.044536) = \text{USD106.96}$$

In general, assume a shorter-term bond matures in A periods and a longer-term bond matures in B periods. The yields-to-maturity per period on these bonds are denoted as z_A and z_B. The first bond is an A-period zero-coupon bond trading in the cash market. The second is a B-period zero-coupon cash market bond. The implied forward rate between period A and period B is denoted as $IFR_{A,B-A}$. It is a forward rate on a bond that starts in period A and ends in period B. Its tenor is $B - A$ periods.

Equation 11 is a general formula for the relationship between the two spot rates (z_A, z_B) and the implied forward rate ($IFR_{A,B-A}$):

$$(1 + z_A)^A \times (1 + IFR_{A,B-A})^{B-A} = (1 + z_B)^B \quad (11)$$

Exhibit 7 shows the possible implied forward rates over three periods.

Exhibit 7: Implied Forward Rate Example

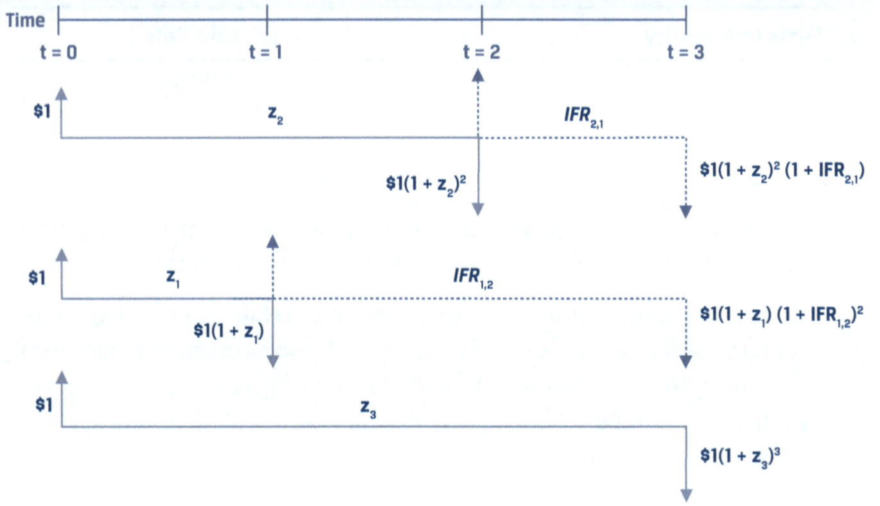

Using Equation 11, we can solve for the one-period rate in two periods ($IFR_{2,1}$) as follows:

$$(1 + z_2)^2 \times (1 + IFR_{2,1})^1 = (1 + z_3)^3$$

$$(1.034197)^2 \times (1 + IFR_{2,1}) = (1.040005)^3$$

$$IFR_{2,1} = 5.1719\%$$

A series of forward rates can be used to construct a forward curve of rates with the same time frame that are implied by cash market transactions or may be observed in the interest rate derivatives market. Exhibit 8 summarizes the relationship between spot or zero rates and the forward curve for one-year rates from the earlier government bond example.

Exhibit 8: Interest Rate Spot or Zero Curve and Forward Curve

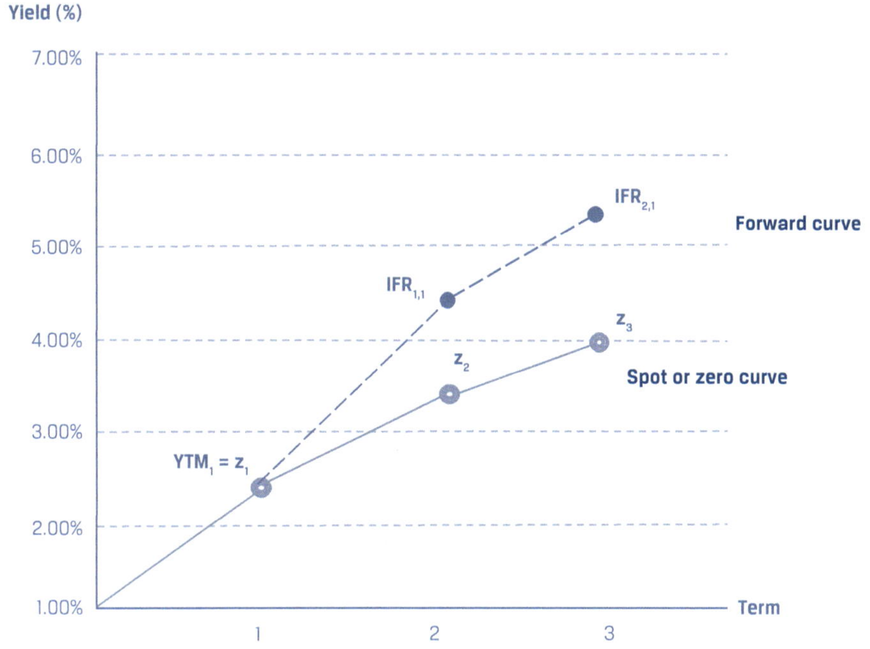

While our examples so far have focused on government benchmark rates, we now turn our attention to short-term market reference rates. Assume, for example, that today we observe a current three-month MRR of 1.25% and a current six-month MRR of 1.75%. How can we solve for the three-month implied forward MRR in three months' time ($IFR_{3m,\ 3m}$)?

In order to apply Equation 11 in this case, we must first ensure that the time frames, or periodicities, of the interest rates are the same. Here, the six-month rate has two periods per year and the three-month rate has four. Recall from an earlier fixed-income lesson that we can convert an annual percentage rate for m periods per year, denoted as APR_m, into an annual percentage rate for n periods per year, APR_n, as follows:

$$\left(1 + \frac{APR_m}{m}\right)^m = \left(1 + \frac{APR_n}{n}\right)^n. \quad (12)$$

First, we must convert the 1.75% semiannual MRR into a quarterly rate:

$$(1 + APR_4/4)^4 = (1 + 0.0175/2)^2$$

$$APR_4 = 1.74619\%$$

We can use this to solve Equation 11 for $IFR_{3m,3m}$:

$$(1 + z_{3m}/4) \times (1 + IFR_{3m,3m}/4) = (1 + z_{6m}/4)^2$$

$$(1 + 0.0125/4) \times (1 + IFR_{3m,3m}/4) = (1 + 0.0174619/4)^2$$

$$IFR_{3m,3m} = 2.24299\%$$

Our result can be confirmed by showing that CNY100,000,000 invested at:

1. 1.25% for three months and reinvested at 2.24299% for the following three months, or
2. 1.75% for six months

will both return CNY100,875,000 in six months:

1. CNY100,875,000 (= CNY100,000,000 × (1 + 0.0125/4) × (1 + 0.0224299/4))
2. CNY100,875,000 (= CNY100,000,000 × (1 + 0.0175/2))

As we will see in the next section, this breakeven reinvestment rate between zero rates of different maturities establishes a no-arbitrage price for a one-period interest rate forward contract.

Forward Rate Agreements (FRAs)

An OTC derivatives contract in which counterparties agree to apply a specific interest rate to a future period is a **forward rate agreement (FRA)**. The underlying is a hypothetical deposit of a notional amount in the future at a market reference rate that is fixed at contract inception ($t = 0$). The FRA buyer, or long position, agrees to pay the deposit interest based on the agreed upon fixed rate and receives deposit interest based on a market reference rate that begins in A periods and ends in B periods (with a tenor of $B - A$ periods) and is determined on or just before the forward settlement date at time $t = A$.

Exhibit 9 shows FRA mechanics at $t = 0$ and settlement at time A.

Exhibit 9: Forward Rate Agreement (FRA) Mechanics

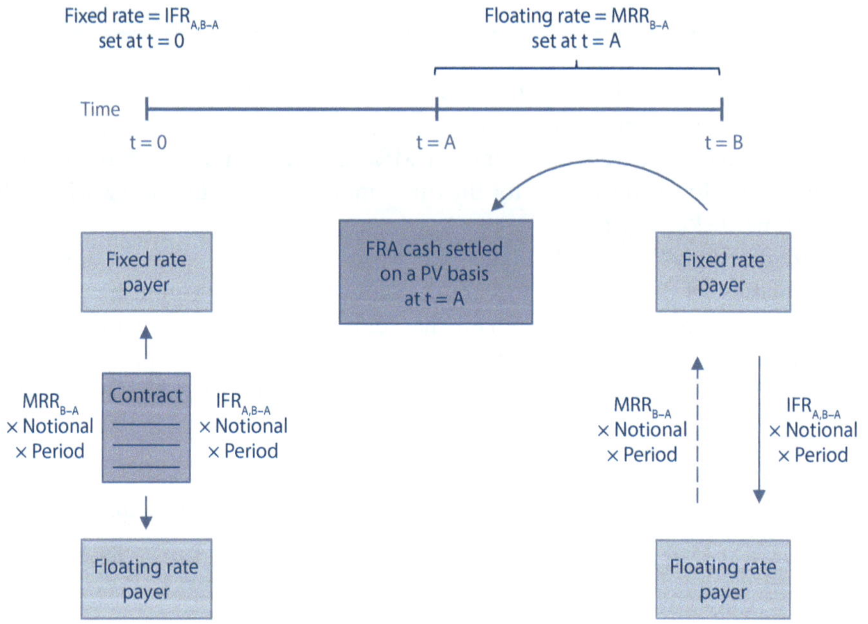

If Exhibit 9 looks familiar, it is because an FRA is a one-period version of the interest rate swap introduced as a *series* of exchanges in an earlier lesson. Similar to the swap, fixed versus floating payments on an FRA occur on a net basis and the notional is not exchanged but is used solely for interest calculations. The implied forward rates shown in the previous section represent the FRA fixed rate for a given period where no riskless profit opportunities exist. This no-arbitrage interest rate ensures that, similar to other forward contracts, the forward rate agreement has a value of zero ($V_0(T) = 0$) to both parties at inception. FRA settlement and other details are best demonstrated by extending our earlier implied forward rate example.

EXAMPLE 8

CNY Forward Rate Agreement

In a prior example, we solved for a three-month implied forward MRR in three months' time ($IFR_{3m,3m}$) of 2.24299%. Yangzi Bank enters into an agreement to pay the three-month rate in three months' time and receive MRR as in Exhibit 9. Yangzi Bank uses the FRA to offset or hedge an underlying liability in three months on which it will owe MRR.

Consider the following FRA term sheet:

Yangzi Bank CNY Forward Rate Agreement Term Sheet	
Start Date:	[Today]
Maturity Date:	[Three months from Start Date]
Notional Principal:	CNY 100,000,000
Fixed-Rate Payer:	Yangzi Bank
Fixed Rate:	2.24299% on a quarterly actual/360 basis
Floating-Rate Payer:	[Financial Intermediary]
Floating Rate:	Three-month CNY MRR on a quarterly actual/360 basis
Payment Date:	Maturity Date
Business Days:	Shanghai
Documentation:	ISDA Agreement and credit terms acceptable to both parties

Similar to forward agreements for other underlying assets, the FRA settlement amount is a function of the difference between $F_0(T)$ (here, a forward interest rate, $IFR_{A,B\text{-}A}$) and S_T (the market reference rate $MRR_{B\text{-}A}$, or the MRR for $B - A$ periods, which ends at time B). In our example, MRR_{3m} is the three-month market reference rate, which sets in three months' time. FRAs are usually cash settled at the beginning of the period during which the reference rate applies. We calculate the net payment amount from the perspective of Yangzi Bank (the FRA buyer or fixed-rate payer) at the *end* of the interest period as follows:

Net Payment = ($MRR_{B\text{-}A}$ – $IFR_{A,B\text{-}A}$) × Notional Principal × Period

If $MRR_{B\text{-}A}$ in three months' time sets at 2.15% and we assume a 90-day interest period, we calculate the net payment at the end of the period as follows:

Net Payment = ($MRR_{B\text{-}A}$ – $IFR_{A,B\text{-}A}$) × Notional Principal × Period

(2.15% – 2.24299%) × CNY100,000,000 × 90/360

= –CNY23,247.50

This is the net payment amount at the end of six months. However, the FRA settles at the *beginning* rather than the *end* of the interest period, which is three months in our example. We must therefore calculate the *present value* of the settlement amount to the beginning of the period during which the reference rate applies, using $MRR_{B\text{-}A}$ as the discount rate:

Cash Settlement (PV): –CNY23,123.21 = –CNY23,247.50/(1 + 0.0215/4)

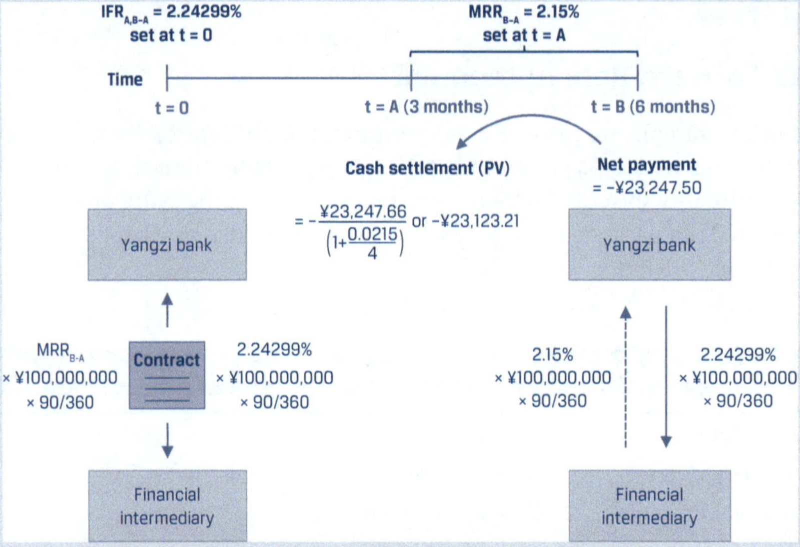

In this case, since $MRR_{B\text{-}A}$ sets below the fixed rate, as the fixed-rate payer and floating-rate ($MRR_{B\text{-}A}$) receiver, Yangzi Bank must make a net settlement payment to the financial intermediary. Because Yangzi Bank has used the FRA to offset or hedge an underlying liability on which it owes MRR, the net settlement payment it makes on the FRA is offset by a lower MRR payment on its liability.

Forward rate agreements are almost exclusively used by financial intermediaries to manage rate-sensitive assets or liabilities on their balance sheets. The forward rate agreement and its single-period swap equivalent that settles at the end of an interest period form the basic building blocks for interest rate swaps, which are more frequently used by issuers and investors to manage interest rate risk.

QUESTION SET

Interest Rate Forward Contracts

1. Determine the correct answers to complete the following sentences: The yield-to-maturity rate and the zero rate for a bond with a single cash flow at maturity in one period are ________. The *price* equivalent of a zero rate is the present value of a currency unit on a future date, known as a ____________.

   Solution:

   The yield-to-maturity rate and the zero rate for a bond with a single cash flow at maturity in one period are *identical*. The *price* equivalent of a zero rate is the present value of a currency unit on a future date, known as a *discount factor*.

2. An analyst observes three- and four-year government benchmark zero-coupon bonds priced at 93 and 90 per 100 face value, respectively. Calculate $IFR_{3,1}$ (the implied one-year forward rate in three years' time).

   Solution:

   First, use the three-year (DF_3) and four-year (DF_4) discount factors provided per unit of currency to derive three-year (z_3) and four-year (z_4) zero rates, which can be calculated as follows:

$$DF_i = \frac{1}{(1 + z_i)^i}$$

Therefore:

$0.93 = 1/(1 + z_3)^3$; $z_3 = 2.4485\%$

$0.90 = 1/(1 + z_4)^4$; $z_4 = 2.6690\%$

Solve for $IFR_{3,1}$ as follows:

$(1 + z_3)^3 \times (1 + IFR_{3,1}) = (1 + z_4)^4$

$(1.024485)^3 \times (1 + IFR_{3,1}) = (1.02669)^4$

$IFR_{3,1} = 3.3333\%$

3. Match the following descriptions with their corresponding interest rate derivative building block.

A. Forward rate agreement	1. The breakeven reinvestment rate linking a short-dated and long-dated zero-coupon bond
B. Implied forward rate	2. The present value of a currency unit on a future date
C. Discount factor	3. A derivative in which counterparties agree to apply a specific interest rate to a future time period

Solution:

1. B is correct. The breakeven reinvestment rate linking a short-dated and a long-dated zero-coupon bond is the implied forward rate.

2. C is correct. The price equivalent of a zero rate is the present value of a currency unit on a future date, known as a discount factor.

3. A is correct. A forward rate agreement is a derivative in which counterparties agree to apply a specific interest rate to a future period.

4. A trader observes one-year and two-year zero-coupon bonds that yield 4% and 5%, respectively, and would like to protect herself against a rise in one-year rates a year from now. Explain the position she should take in the FRA contract to achieve this objective and the forward interest rate she should expect on the contract.

Solution:

A forward rate agreement involves an underlying hypothetical future deposit at a market reference rate fixed at contract inception ($t = 0$). To protect against higher rates, the trader should enter into a fixed-rate payer FRA in order to realize a gain if one-year spot rates one year from now exceed the current forward rate. A long FRA position, or fixed-rate payer, agrees to pay interest based on the fixed rate and receives interest based on a variable market reference rate determined at settlement. The FRA is priced based on the implied forward rate, or breakeven reinvestment rate between a shorter and a longer zero rate. We can solve for $IFR_{1,1}$ as follows:

$(1 + z_1) \times (1 + IFR_{1,1}) = (1 + z_2)^2$

$(1.04) \times (1 + IFR_{1,1}) = (1.05)^2$

$IFR_{1,1} = 6.0096\%$

5. A counterparty agrees to be the FRA fixed-rate receiver on a one-month AUD MRR in three months' time based on a AUD150,000,000 notional amount. If $IFR_{3m,1m}$ at contract inception is 0.50% and one-month AUD MRR sets at 0.35% for settlement of the contract, calculate the settlement amount and interpret the results.

Solution:

A short FRA position, or fixed-rate receiver, agrees to pay interest based on a market reference rate determined at settlement and receives interest based on a pre-agreed fixed rate, the implied forward rate ($IFR_{3m,1m}$). Since AUD $MRR_{B\text{-}A}$ at settlement is below the pre-agreed fixed rate, the FRA fixed-rate receiver realizes a gain and receives a net payment based on the following calculation:

Net Payment = ($IFR_{A,B\text{-}A} - MRR_{B\text{-}A}$) × Notional Principal × Period

= (0.50% – 0.35%) × AUD150,000,000 × (1/12)

= AUD18,750 at the end of the period

Solve for the present value of settlement given the contract is settled at the beginning of the period, using $MRR_{B\text{-}A}$ as the discount rate:

Cash Settlement (PV) = AUD18,750.00/(1 + 0.35%/12)

= AUD18,744.53

PRACTICE PROBLEMS

The following information relates to questions 1-6

Baywhite Financial is a broker-dealer and wealth management firm that helps its clients manage their portfolios using stand-alone derivative strategies. A new Baywhite analyst is asked to evaluate the following client situations.

1. Match the following definitions with their corresponding forward pricing or valuation component.

1. Equal to the difference between the current spot price (adjusted by remaining costs and benefits through maturity) and the present value of the forward price	A. Forward contract MTM value at inception, $V_0(T)$
2. Future value of the underlying asset spot price (S_0) compounded at the risk-free rate incorporating the present value of the costs and benefits of asset ownership	B. Forward contract MTM value between inception and maturity, $V_t(T)$
3. Under no-arbitrage conditions for a given underlying spot price, S_0, adjusted by the costs and benefits, risk-free rate (r), and forward price, $F_0(T)$, this should be equal to zero (ignoring transaction costs).	C. Forward price, $F_0(T)$

2. A Baywhite client currently owns 5,000 common non-dividend-paying shares of Vivivyu Inc. (VIVU), a digital media company, at a spot price of USD173 per share. The client enters into a forward commitment to sell half of its VIVU position in six months at a price of USD175.58. Which of the following market events is most likely to result in the greatest gain in the VIVU forward contract MTM value from the client's perspective?

   A. An increase in the risk-free rate

   B. An immediate decline in the VIVU spot price following contract inception

   C. A steady rise in the spot price of VIVU stock over time

3. A Baywhite client has entered into a long six-month MXN/USD FX forward contract—that is, an agreement to sell MXN and buy USD. The MXN/USD spot exchange rate at inception is 19.8248 (MXN19.8248 = USD1), the six-month MXN risk-free rate is 4.25%, and the six-month USD risk-free rate is 0.5%. Baywhite's market strategist predicts that the Mexican central bank (Banco de Mexico) will surprise the market with a 50 bp short-term rate cut at its upcoming meeting. Which of the following statements best describes how the client's existing FX forward contract will be impacted if this prediction is realized and other parameters remain unchanged?

   A. The lower interest rate differential between MXN and USD will cause the MXN/USD contract forward rate to be adjusted downward.

B. The client will realize an MTM gain on the FX forward contract due to the decline in the MXN versus USD interest rate differential.

C. The lower interest rate differential between MXN and USD will cause the client to realize an MTM loss on the MXN/USD forward contract.

4. A client seeking advice on her fixed-income portfolio observes the price and yield-to-maturity of one-year (r_1) and two-year (r_2) annual coupon government benchmark bonds currently available in the market. Which of the following statements best describes how the analyst can determine a breakeven reinvestment rate in one year's time to help decide whether to invest now for one or two years?

   A. As the two-year rate involves intermediate cash flows, divide the square root of (1 + r_2) by (1 + r_1) and subtract 1 to arrive at a breakeven reinvestment rate for one year in one year's time.

   B. Since the first year's returns are compounded in the second year, set (1 + r_1) multiplied by 1 plus the breakeven reinvestment rate equal to $(1 + r_2)^2$ and solve for the breakeven reinvestment rate.

   C. Since the breakeven reinvestment involves a zero-coupon cash flow, first substitute the one-year rate (r_1) into the two-year bond price equation to solve for the two-year spot or zero rate (z_2), then set $(1 + r_1) \times$ (1 + breakeven reinvestment rate) = $(1 + z_2)^2$ and solve for the breakeven reinvestment rate.

5. Baywhite Financial seeks to gain a competitive advantage by making margin loans at fixed rates for up to 60 days to its investor clients. Since Baywhite borrows at a variable one-month market reference rate to finance these client loans, the firm enters into one-month FRA contracts on one-month MRR to hedge the interest rate exposure of its margin loan book. Which of the following statements best describes Baywhite's interest rate exposure and the FRA position it should take to hedge that exposure?

   A. Baywhite faces exposure to a *rise* in one-month MRR over the next 30 days, so it should enter into the FRA as a fixed-rate *payer* in order to benefit from a rise in one-month MRR above the FRA rate and offset its higher borrowing cost.

   B. Baywhite faces exposure to a *rise* in one-month MRR over the next 30 days, so it should enter into the FRA as a fixed-rate *receiver* in order to benefit from a rise in one-month MRR above the FRA rate and offset its higher borrowing cost.

   C. Baywhite faces exposure to a *decline* in one-month MRR over the next 30 days, so it should enter into the FRA as a fixed-rate *receiver* in order to benefit from a rise in one-month MRR above the FRA rate and offset its higher borrowing cost.

6. Baywhite observes that one-month MRR is 1.2% and two-month MRR is 1.5%. Which of the following rates is closest to the forward rate that Baywhite would expect on 1m1m forward rate agreement?

   A. 1.80%

   B. 1.35%

C. 3.55%

SOLUTIONS

1. 1. B is correct. The forward contract MTM value between inception and maturity, $V_t(T)$, is equal to the difference between the current spot price (adjusted by costs and benefits through maturity) and the present value of the forward price.

   2. C is correct. The forward price, $F_0(T)$, is the future value of the underlying asset spot price (S_0) compounded at the risk-free rate incorporating the present value of the costs and benefits of asset ownership.

   3. A is correct. Under no-arbitrage conditions for a given underlying spot price, S_0, adjusted by the costs and benefits, risk-free rate (r), and forward price, $F_0(T)$, the forward contract MTM value at inception, $V_0(T)$, should be equal to zero (ignoring transaction costs).

2. B is correct. The original VIVU spot price (S_0) at $t = 0$ must equal the present value of the forward price discounted at the risk-free rate, so an immediate fall in the spot price to $S_0^- < S_0$ results in an MTM gain for the forward contract seller. A is not correct, since a higher risk-free rate will reduce the contract MTM from the client's perspective by reducing the PV of $F_0(T)$, while C will also reduce the forward contract MTM from the seller's perspective.

3. C is correct. A decline in the interest rate differential between MXN and USD will cause the client to realize an MTM loss on the MXN/USD forward contract, while B states that this decline will result in an MTM gain. A is incorrect as the forward price, $F_0(T)$, is not adjusted during the contract life.

   Specifically, the original MXN/USD forward exchange rate at inception is equal to 20.20 (= $19.8248e^{(.0425 - 0.005) \times 0.5}$). If the MXN rate were to decline by 50 bps immediately after the contract is agreed, a new MXN/USD forward contract would be at a forward exchange rate of 20.15 (= $19.8248e^{(.0375 - 0.005) \times 0.5}$). The MXN would weaken or depreciate against the USD. Since the MXN seller has locked in a forward sale at the original 20.20 versus the new 20.15 rate, the seller's MTM loss is equal to 0.05, or MXN50,000 per MXN1,000,000 (= 0.05 × 1,000,000) notional amount.

4. C is correct. The one-year annual rate equals the one-year zero rate, as it involves a single cash flow at maturity ($z_1 = r_1$). Since the breakeven reinvestment rate involves a single cash flow at maturity, substitute the one-year rate (r_1) into the two-year bond price equation to solve for z_2, then set $(1 + r_1) \times$ (1 + breakeven reinvestment rate) = $(1 + z_2)^2$ and solve for the breakeven reinvestment rate ($IFR_{1,1}$).

5. A is correct. As Baywhite faces exposure to a rise in one-month MRR over the next 30 days, it should enter into the FRA as a fixed-rate payer in order to benefit from a rise in one-month MRR above the FRA rate and offset its higher borrowing cost. Both B and C are incorrect, as the fixed-rate *receiver* in an FRA does not benefit but rather must make a higher payment upon settlement if MRR rises.

6. A is correct. The APR of the monthly compounded two-month rate is 1.499%. Dividing $(1.01499/12)^2$ by (1.012/12) equals 1.001499. Subtracting 1 and then multiplying by 12 gives 1.7982%. Thus, the approximate forward rate is 1.80%. B is incorrect because this is a simple average of the two spot rates. C is incorrect because this result is derived from simply dividing (1.01499/12) by (1.012/12), then subtracting 1, and then multiplying by 12.

LEARNING MODULE

6

Pricing and Valuation of Futures Contracts

LEARNING OUTCOMES	
Mastery	*The candidate should be able to:*
☐	compare the value and price of forward and futures contracts
☐	explain why forward and futures prices differ

INTRODUCTION

1

Many of the pricing and valuation principles associated with forward commitments are common to both forward and futures contracts. For example, previous lessons demonstrated that forward commitments have a price that prevents market participants from earning riskless profit through arbitrage. It was also shown that long and short forward commitments may be replicated using a combination of long or short cash positions and borrowing or lending at the risk-free rate. Finally, both forward and futures pricing and valuation incorporate the cost of carry, or the benefits and costs of owning an underlying asset over the life of a derivative contract.

We now turn our attention to futures contracts. We discuss what distinguishes them from other forward commitments and how they are used by issuers and investors. We expand upon the daily settlement of futures contract gains and losses introduced earlier and explain the differences between forwards and futures. We also address and distinguish the interest rate futures market and its role in interest rate derivative contracts.

LEARNING MODULE OVERVIEW

- Futures are standardized, exchange-traded derivatives (ETDs) with zero initial value and a futures price $f_0(T)$ established at inception. The futures price, $f_0(T)$, equals the spot price compounded at the risk-free rate as in the case of a forward contract.
- The primary difference between forward and futures valuation is the daily settlement of futures gains and losses via a margin account. Daily settlement resets the futures contract value to zero at the current futures price $f_t(T)$. This process continues until contract maturity and the futures price converge to the spot price, S_T.

CFA Institute would like to thank Don Chance, PhD, CFA, for his contribution to this section, which includes material derived from material that appeared in *Derivative Markets and Instruments*, featured in the 2022 CFA® Program curriculum.

- The cumulative realized mark-to-market (MTM) gain or loss on a futures contract is approximately the same as for a comparable forward contract.
- Daily settlement and margin requirements give rise to different cash flow patterns between futures and forwards, resulting in a pricing difference between the two contract types. The difference depends on both interest rate volatility and the correlation between interest rates and futures prices.
- The futures price for short-term interest rate futures is given by (100 – yield), where yield is expressed in percentage terms. There is a price difference between interest rate futures and forward rate agreements (FRAs) due to convexity bias.
- The emergence of derivatives central clearing has introduced futures-like margining requirements for over-the-counter (OTC) derivatives, such as forwards. This arrangement has reduced the difference in the cash flow impact of ETDs and OTC derivatives and the price difference in futures versus forwards.

LEARNING MODULE SELF-ASSESSMENT

These initial questions are intended to help you gauge your current level of understanding of this learning module.

1. Which of the following responses is closest to the one-year futures price of a stock with a spot price (S_0) of €125 and an annual dividend of €2.50 paid at maturity if the risk-free rate is 1%?

   A. €123.75

   B. €122.50

   C. €126.25

   Solution:

   A is correct. The no arbitrage futures price for an underlying asset with known benefits, such as a dividend, may be determined using the following equation:

   $f_0(T) = [S_0 - PV_0(I)]\ (1 + r)^T.$

   First, solve for the present value of the dividend $PV_0(I)$ as follows:

   €2.48 = (€2.50 / 1.01).

   Substitute $PV_0(I)$ into the original equation to solve for $f_0(T)$:

   $f_0(T)$ = €123.75 = (€125 – €2.48)(1.01).

2. Which of the following statements regarding the gains or losses of a long forward contract position compared to a long futures contract position is most correct? Assume that the underlying is identical on both contracts and that both contracts have the same time until maturity.

   A. The daily realized gain or loss of the forward contract position and the futures contract position are equivalent.

   B. Before the contracts mature, the cumulative realized gains or losses of the forward contract position and the futures contract position are equivalent.

C. At contract maturity, the cumulative realized gains or losses of the forward contract position and the futures contract position are approximately equivalent.

Solution:

C is correct. The two contracts are similar in all respects except for the frequency with which contracts are marked to market. As a result, the cumulative gain or loss is approximately the same when the contracts mature. A is incorrect because the futures contract's daily mark-to-market (MTM) feature creates daily realized gains or losses while the forward contract's gains or losses are realized only at contract maturity. B is incorrect because the response refers to realized gains or losses, and the contracts have not yet matured. Thus, the forward contract has generated no realized gains or losses yet.

3. Identify which of the following situations leads to which relationship between forward and futures prices for forward commitment contracts with otherwise identical terms.

1. Futures prices are *positively* correlated with interest rates, and interest rates change over the contract period.	A. Forward prices are above futures prices: $F_0(T) > f_0(T)$.
2. Futures prices are *negatively* correlated with interest rates, and interest rates change over the contract period.	B. Forward and futures prices are the same: $F_0(T) = f_0(T)$.
3. Interest rates are constant over the forward commitment contract period.	C. Futures prices are above forward prices: $f_0(T) > F_0(T)$.

Solution:

1. C is correct. If futures prices are positively correlated with interest rates, then higher prices lead to futures profits reinvested at rising rates, and lower prices lead to losses that may be financed at lower rates.

2. A is correct. If futures prices are negatively correlated with interest rates, then higher prices lead to futures profits reinvested at lower rates, and lower prices lead to losses that must be financed at higher rates.

3. B is correct. If interest rates are constant over the forward commitment contract period, then forward and futures prices are the same.

4. Which of the following statements most correctly describes a development that has helped reduce the difference in the cash flow impact between forward and futures contracts?

A. Futures exchanges have moved away from daily mark-to-market recognition of gains and losses on futures contracts.

B. OTC derivatives have become increasingly subject to central clearing requirements.

C. Lower volatility in markets has reduced the magnitude of gains and losses in both types of contracts.

Solution:

B is correct. Under a central clearing framework for OTC derivatives, financial intermediaries that serve as counterparties are required to post daily margin or eligible collateral to the central counterparty (CCP) in a process very similar to futures margining. Dealers, therefore, often impose similar requirements on derivatives end users. A is incorrect because no such change has occurred in exchange-traded futures markets. C is incorrect because volatility changes over time are hard to categorize as higher or lower.

2 PRICING OF FUTURES CONTRACTS AT INCEPTION

☐ compare the value and price of forward and futures contracts

When a forward commitment is initiated, no cash is exchanged and the contract is neither an asset nor a liability to the buyer or seller. The value of both a forward contract and a futures contract at initiation is zero:

$$V_0(T) = 0. \quad (1)$$

An underlying asset with no cost or benefit has a futures price $f_0(T)$ at $t = 0$ of:

$$f_0(T) = S_0(1 + r)^T, \quad (2)$$

where r is the risk-free rate and T is the time to maturity. As in the case of a forward contract, the futures price is the spot price compounded at the risk-free rate over the life of the contract. This is shown in Exhibit 1, where the slope of the line is equal to the risk-free rate, r.

Exhibit 1: Futures Price at Initiation

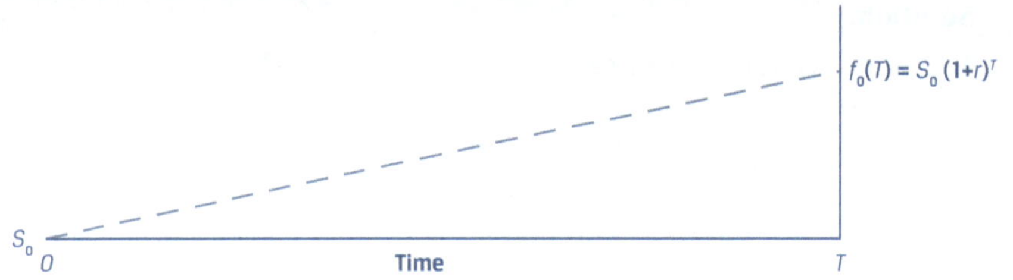

As for forwards, we use discrete compounding as in Equation 2 for futures on individual underlying assets. However, for underlying assets that are comprised of a portfolio—such as an equity, fixed-income, commodity, or credit index—or where the underlying involves foreign exchange with interest rates denominated in two currencies, continuous compounding is the preferred method, as shown in Equation 3:

$$f_0(T) = S_0e^{rT}. \quad (3)$$

EXAMPLE 1

Procam Investments - Gold Futures Contract

As shown in a previous lesson, Procam Investments purchases a 100-ounce gold futures contract. The current spot price is $1,770.00 per ounce, the risk-free rate is 2.0%, and we assume gold may be stored at no cost. Calculate the no arbitrage futures price, $f_0(T)$, for settlement in 91 days (T = 91/365 or 0.24932).

Solution

Using Equation 2: $f_0(T) = S_0(1 + r)^T$

$$\$1,778.76 \text{ per ounce} = \$1,770.00 \times (1.02)^{0.24932}$$

Contract price = \$177,876.04 (= 100 × \$1,778.76)

The futures price, $f_0(T)$, is identical to the forward price from a previous lesson.

As in the case of a forward, for underlying assets with ownership benefits or income (I) or costs (C) expressed as a known amount in present value terms at time t = 0, the spot versus futures price relationship using discrete compounding is shown in Equation 4 and Exhibit 2:

$$f_0(T) = [S_0 - \mathrm{PV}_0(I) + \mathrm{PV}_0(C)]\ (1 + \mathrm{r})^{\mathrm{T}}. \quad (4)$$

Exhibit 2: Futures Prices with Underlying Asset Costs and Benefits

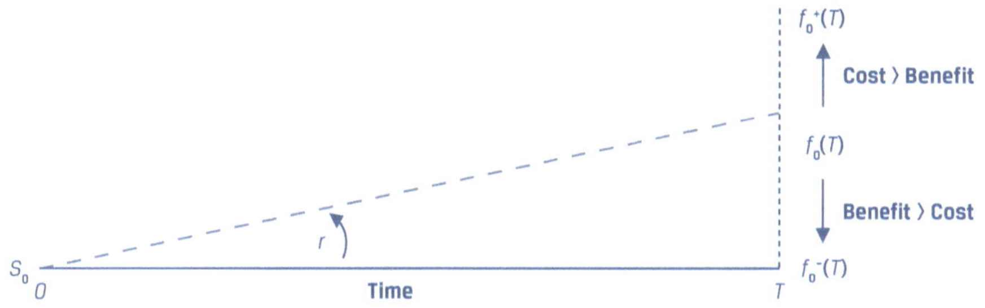

EXAMPLE 2

Procam's Gold Futures Contract with Storage Costs

Procam purchased a gold futures contract in Example 1 at $f_0(T)$ of \$177,876.04 (or \$1,778.76 per ounce) with S_0 equal to \$1,770 per ounce. How would $f_0(T)$ change to satisfy the no arbitrage condition if a \$2 per ounce cost of gold storage and insurance were payable at the end of the contract?

The futures price for a commodity with known storage cost amounts may be determined using Equation 4, where $\mathrm{PV}_0(I) = 0$:

$$f_0(T) = [S_0 + \mathrm{PV}_0(C)]\ (1 + r)^T.$$

First, solve for the present value of the storage cost per ounce, $\mathrm{PV}_0(C)$, as follows:

$$\mathrm{PV}_0(C) = \$1.99 = [\$2(1.02)^{-0.24982}].$$

Substitute $\mathrm{PV}_0(C)$ = \$1.99 into Equation 4 to solve for $f_0(T)$:

$$f_0(T) = (\$1,770.00 + \$1.99)(1.02)^{0.24982}$$

$$= \$1,780.78 \text{ per ounce}$$

The addition of storage and insurance costs increases the difference between the spot price and futures price. Finally, as in the case of forwards, a futures price, $f_0(T)$, significantly *below* the no arbitrage price including cash costs and benefits may indicate the presence of a convenience yield.

3 MTM VALUATION: FORWARDS VERSUS FUTURES

☐ compare the value and price of forward and futures contracts

Examples 1 and 2 show the similarities between forward and futures prices at contract inception. Over time, different forward and futures contract features lead to different MTM values for contracts with the same underlying assets and otherwise identical details. Example 3 shows how the daily settlement of gains and losses causes this difference to arise.

EXAMPLE 3

Procam Forward versus Futures Pricing and Valuation

We extend the earlier example to compare forward and futures pricing and valuation. In both cases, Procam Investments enters a cash-settled forward commitment to buy 100 ounces of gold at a price ($f_0[T] = F_0[T]$) of $1,778.76 per ounce in 91 days, with a risk-free rate of 2% and no gold storage cost.

Forward Contract

The forward price is $F_0(T)$ = $1,778.76 per ounce. No cash is exchanged or deposited at inception, and the contract value at inception, $V_0(T)$, is zero.

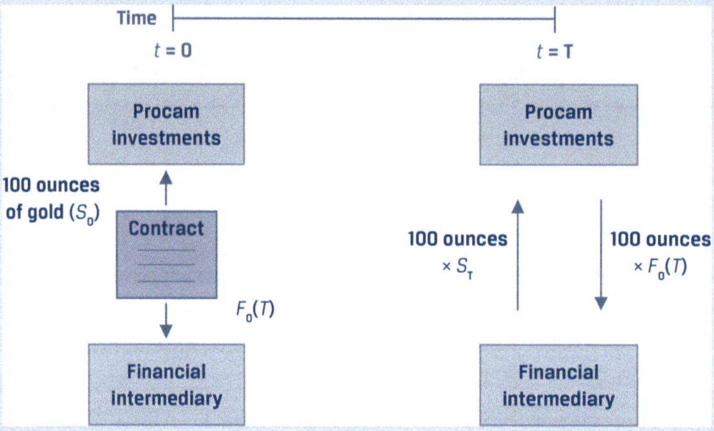

Over time, the forward price, $F_0(T)$, does not change, and the MTM at any time, $[V_t(T)]$, equals the difference between the current spot price, S_t, and the present value of the forward price, PV_t of $F_0(T)$, shown from Procam's (the forward buyer's) perspective:

$$V_t(T) = S_t - F_0(T)(1 + r)^{-(T-t)}.$$

For example, say 71 days have elapsed and 20 days remain to maturity, $T - t$ = 20/365 or 0.0548. If the gold spot price, (S_t), has fallen by $50 since inception to $1,720 per ounce, solve for $V_t(T)$ as follows:

$$V_t(T) = \$1,720 - \$1,778.76(1.02)^{-0.0548}$$

$$= -\$56.83 \text{ per ounce, or a } \$5,683 \text{ MTM loss } (= -\$56.83 \times 100 \text{ ounces}).$$

Under terms of the forward contract, no settlement of the MTM amount occurs until maturity. This process of resetting the contract value to zero each day makes it very unlikely that the futures contract would reach a similar MTM value.

Futures Contract

The futures price, $f_0(T)$, is \$1,778.76 per ounce. As per futures exchange daily settlement rules, the contract buyer and seller must post an initial cash margin of \$4,950 per gold contract (100 ounces) and maintain a maintenance margin of \$4,500 per contract. If a margin balance falls below \$4,500, a counterparty receives a margin call and must immediately replenish its account to the initial \$4,950.

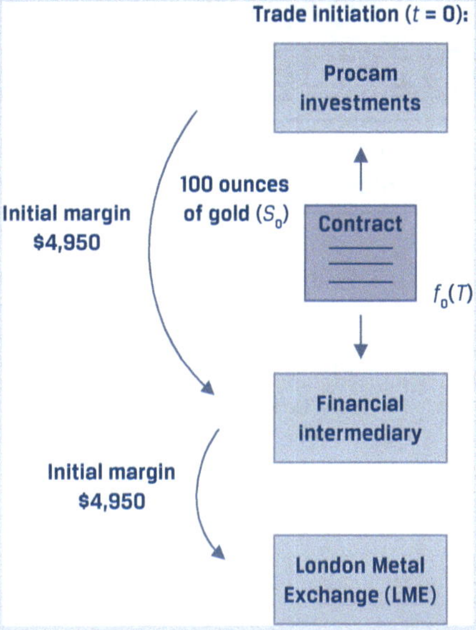

Consider the first day of trading, where the spot gold price, (S_0), is \$1,770 per ounce and the opening gold futures price, $f_0(T)$, is \$1,778.76 per ounce.

- Assume that the gold futures price, $f_1(T)$, falls by \$5 on the first trading day to \$1,773.76 and the spot price, S_1, ends the day at a no arbitrage equivalent of \$1,765.12 (= $\$1{,}773.76(1.02)^{-90/365}$).
- Procam realizes a \$500 MTM loss (= \$5 per ounce × 100 ounces) deducted from its margin account, leaving Procam with \$4,450.
- The MTM value of Procam's futures contract resets to zero at the futures closing price of \$1,773.76 per ounce.
- Since Procam's margin account balance has fallen below the \$4,500 maintenance level, it must deposit \$500 to return the balance to the \$4,950 initial margin.

Futures versus Forward Price and Value over Time

Using the same details, we compare the futures and forward price and value over two trading days. Assume that day two trading opens at day one's closing spot and futures prices. The following table shows the comparison:

Beginning of Day 2 Trading

Contract Type	Contract Price	Contract MTM	Realized MTM	Margin Deposit
Forward	$F_0(T)$ = \$177,876	–\$498	\$0	\$0
Futures	$f_1(T)$ = \$177,376	\$0	–\$500	\$4,950

The forward MTM contract value, $V_t(T)$, equals the difference between the current spot price, S_1 = \$1,765.12, and the present value of the original forward price, $PV_t[F_0(T)]$, here with 90 days remaining to maturity, $T - t = 90/365$ or 0.24657:

$V_t(T) = \$1,765.12 - \$1,778.76(1.02)^{-0.24657}$

$= \$4.98$ per ounce.

Extending our example to the beginning of day three at the prior day's close, assume a \$4 per ounce fall in the gold futures price on day two, $f_2(T)$, to \$1,769.76 and a no arbitrage equivalent spot price decline, S_2, to \$1,761.24 (= \$1,769.76[1.02]$^{-89/365}$). The following table shows the summary on day three:

Beginning of Day 3 Trading

Contract Type	Contract Price	Contract MTM	Realized MTM	Margin Deposit
Forward	$F_0(T)$ = \$177,876	–\$895	\$0	\$0
Futures	$f_2(T)$ = \$176,976	\$0	–\$400	\$4,550

The forward MTM contract value, $V_t(T)$, equals the difference between the current spot price, S_2 = \$1,761.24, and the present value of the original forward price, $PV_t[F_0(T)]$, here with 89 days remaining to maturity, $T - t$ = 89/365 or 0.24384:

$Vt(T) = \$1,761.24 - \$1,778.76(1.02)^{-0.24384}$

$= \$8.95$ per ounce.

Example 3 demonstrates the key differences in the price and value of forward and futures contracts over time. The forward contract price, $F_0(T)$, remains fixed until the contract matures. Forward contract MTM value changes are captured by the difference between the current spot price, S_t, and the present value of the forward price, $PV_t[F_0(T)]$. This forward contract MTM is not settled until maturity, giving rise to counterparty credit risk over time since no cash is exchanged from inception of the contract to its maturity or expiration. Futures contract prices fluctuate daily based upon market changes. The daily settlement mechanism resets the futures MTM to zero, and variation margin is exchanged to settle the difference, reducing counterparty credit risk. The *cumulative* realized MTM gain or loss on a futures contract is approximately the same as for a comparable forward contract. We will explore these differences in the next lesson after first turning our attention to forward and futures contracts on market reference rates.

4 INTEREST RATE FUTURES VERSUS FORWARD CONTRACTS

☐ compare the value and price of forward and futures contracts

In an earlier lesson on interest rate forward contracts, zero rates derived from coupon bonds were used to derive a future investment breakeven rate (or implied forward rate). The implied forward rate was shown to equal the no arbitrage fixed rate on a forward rate agreement (FRA) under which counterparties exchange a fixed-for-floating cash flow at a time in the future.

Futures markets on short-term interest rates offer market participants a highly liquid, standardized alternative to FRAs. Interest rate futures contracts are available for monthly or quarterly market reference rates for successive periods out to final contract maturities of up to ten years in the future. Although the underlying variable is the market reference rate (MRR) on a hypothetical deposit on a future date as for forward rate agreements, interest rate futures trade on a *price* basis as per the following general formula:

$$f_{A,B-A} = 100 - (100 \times \text{MRR}_{A,B-A}), \quad (5)$$

where $f_{A,B-A}$ represents the futures price for a market reference rate for B–A periods that begins in A periods ($\text{MRR}_{A,B-A}$), as shown in Exhibit 3.

Exhibit 3: Interest Rate Futures Contract Mechanics

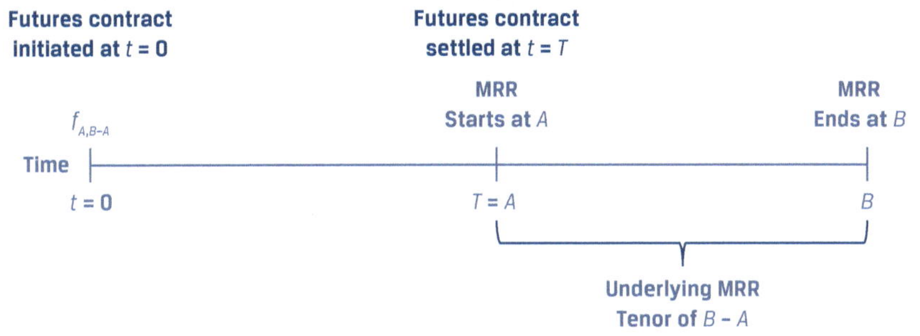

For example, we may solve for the implied three-month MRR rate in three months' time (where A = 3m, B = 6m, B – A = 3m) if an interest rate futures contract is trading at a price of 98.25 using Equation 5:

$$f_{3m,3m}\text{: } 98.25 = 100 - (100 \times \text{MRR}_{A,B-A})$$

$$\text{MRR}_{3m,3m} = 1.75\%.$$

This (100 – yield) price convention results in an inverse price/yield relationship but is *not* the same as the price of a zero-coupon bond at the contract rate. A long futures position involves earning or receiving MRR in A periods, whereas a short position involves paying MRR in A periods. The interest rate exposure profile for long and short futures contracts are as follows:

- Long futures contract (lender): Gains as prices rise, future MRR falls
- Short futures contract (borrower): Gains as prices fall, future MRR rises

In an earlier lesson, Yangzi Bank enters into an FRA as a fixed-rate payer to hedge a liability on which it owes MRR in the future, realizing a gain on the FRA contract as rates rise. Note that this would be equivalent to taking a *short* position on a CNY MRR futures contract if one were available. Exhibit 4 summarizes the relationship between futures and FRAs.

Exhibit 4: Interest Rate Futures versus FRAs

Contract Type	Gains from Rising MRR	Gains from Falling MRR
Interest rate futures	Short futures contract	Long futures contract
Forward rate agreement	Long FRA: FRA fixed-rate payer (FRA floating-rate receiver)	Short FRA: FRA floating-rate payer (FRA fixed-rate receiver)

Interest rate futures daily settlement occurs based on price changes, which translate into **futures contract basis point value (BPV)** as follows:

$$\text{Futures Contract BPV} = \text{Notional Principal} \times 0.01\% \times \text{Period}. \quad (6)$$

For example, assuming a $1,000,000 notional for three-month MRR of 2.21% for one quarter (or 90/360 days), the underlying deposit contract value would be:

$$\$1{,}005{,}525 = \$1{,}000{,}000 \times [1 + (2.21\% / 4)].$$

Consider how a one basis point (0.01%) change in MRR affects contract value:

$$\text{1 bp increase (2.22\%): } \$1{,}005{,}550 = \$1{,}000{,}000 \times [1 + (2.22\% / 4)].$$

$$\text{1 bp decrease (2.20\%): } \$1{,}005{,}500 = \$1{,}000{,}000 \times [1 + (2.20\% / 4)].$$

Both the increase and decrease in MRR by one basis point change the contract BPV by $25. Short-term interest rate futures are characterized by a fixed linear relationship between price and yield changes. The following example illustrates their use in practice.

EXAMPLE 4

Interest Rate Futures - Baywhite Margin Loan Book

In an earlier example, Baywhite Financial offered 60-day margin loans at fixed rates to its clients and borrowed at a variable one-month MRR to finance the loans. Describe Baywhite's residual interest rate exposure and how it may use interest rate futures as a hedge.

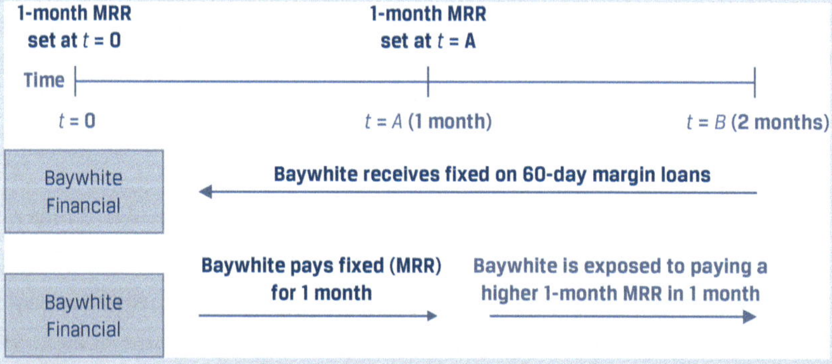

The diagram shows that Baywhite faces the risk of higher MRR in one month's time ($MRR_{1,1}$), which would reduce the return on its fixed margin loans. In the prior example, Baywhite entered an FRA where it agreed to pay fixed one-month MRR and receive floating. If Baywhite were to use an interest rate futures contract instead, it would *sell* a futures contract on one-month MRR. The futures contract BPV for a $50,000,000 notional amount is:

$$\text{Contract BPV} = \$416.67 \ (= \$50{,}000{,}000 \times 0.01\% \times [1/12]).$$

If Baywhite sells $f_{1,1}$ for \$98.75 (or $\text{MRR}_{1,1}$ = 1.25%) and settles at maturity at a price of \$97.75 ($\text{MRR}_{1,1}$ = 2.25%), it would expect to have a *cumulative* gain on the contract through maturity equal to \$41,667 (= Contract BPV × 100 bps).

QUESTION SET

Valuation and Pricing of Futures Contracts

1. Identify which of the following features corresponds to which type of forward commitment contract.

1. The daily change in contract price is used to determine and settle the MTM.	A. Forward contract
2. Inclusion of storage and insurance costs increases the difference between the spot and forward commitment contract price.	B. Futures contract
3. The contract price established at inception remains unchanged over time.	C. Both a forward and a futures contract

Solution:

1. B is correct. The futures contract price change at the close of each trading day is used to determine the daily MTM settlement via the margin account.

2. C is correct. Storage and insurance costs increase the forward commitment price for both forward and futures contracts.

3. A is correct. The forward contract price, $F_0(T)$, established at $t = 0$ remains unchanged and is used to calculate the MTM settlement at maturity.

2. Calculate the correct answer to fill in the blank and justify your response: An investor entered a short oil futures contract position three months ago on 1,000 barrels at an initial price of \$69.00 per barrel. The constant risk-free rate is 0.50%. Daily oil spot and futures prices for the final 10 days of trading are shown in the following table. The change in the investor's futures contract value on day $T - 5$ is closest to ______________.

Day	Crude Oil Spot Price (\$)	Crude Oil Futures Price (\$)
T-10	69.62	68.69
T-9	69.01	68.11
T-8	66.88	66.15
T-7	65.18	64.77
T-6	66.72	66.02
T-5	68.59	68.01
T-4	68.80	68.08
T-3	68.93	68.32
T-2	69.43	69.15

Day	Crude Oil Spot Price ($)	Crude Oil Futures Price ($)
T-1	69.36	69.18
T	70.03	70.03

Solution:

The answer is \$(1,990). The MTM of the investor's futures position is the daily futures price change on Day T – 5 per barrel multiplied by 1,000 barrels:

$$V_{T-5}(T) = -\left[-f_{T-5}(T) - f_{T-6}(T) -\right] \times 1{,}000 = -(68.01 - 66.02) \times 1{,}000$$
$$= -\$1{,}990.$$

Note the negative sign refers to the investor's short futures position. The investor realizes a loss as the futures price rises due to the short position.

3. Determine the correct answers to complete the following sentences: The daily settlement mechanism resets the futures MTM to __________, and margin is exchanged to settle the difference. The __________ realized MTM gain or loss on a futures contract is approximately the same as for a comparable forward contract.

   Solution:

   The daily settlement mechanism resets the futures MTM to *zero*, and margin is exchanged to settle the difference. The *cumulative* realized MTM gain or loss on a futures contract is approximately the same as for a comparable forward contract.

4. Identify the following statement as true or false and justify your answer: An FRA fixed-rate receiver (floating-rate payer) position is equivalent to a long interest rate futures contract on MRR, as both positions realize a gain as MRR falls below the initial fixed rate.

   Solution:

   The statement is true. An FRA fixed-rate receiver (floating-rate payer) position realizes a gain as MRR falls as the counterparty receives the fixed MRR and owes the floating MRR in the future. A long futures contract price is based on (100 – yield), which rises as yield-to-maturity (MRR) falls.

5. From May 2020 to January 2021, the three-month SONIA (Sterling Overnight Index Average) futures contract expiring in June 2021 traded at a price above 100. Describe the interest rate scenario implied by this futures price and justify your response.

   Solution:

   The future interest rate scenario implied by the futures price above 100 is a negative SONIA interest rate in June 2021. For example, if we consider the futures price for three-month SONIA one year forward as of June 2020 from Equation 5:

   $$f_{1y,3m} = 100 - (100 \times \text{MRR}_{1y,3m}).$$

   If $f_{1y,3m} > 100$, this implies that $\text{MRR}_{1y,3m} < 0$.

FORWARD AND FUTURES PRICE DIFFERENCES

5

- [ ] explain why forward and futures prices differ

Despite their similar symmetric payoff profile at maturity, differences exist between forward and futures valuation and pricing because of different cash flow profiles over the life of a futures versus a forward contract with otherwise similar characteristics. The distinguishing features of a futures contract are the posting of initial margin, daily mark-to-market, and settlement of gains and losses.

These features limit the MTM value of a futures contract to the daily gain or loss since the previous day's settlement. When that value is paid out in the daily settlement via the margin account, the futures price resets to the current settlement price and the MTM value goes to zero. Forward contracts, on the other hand, involve privately negotiated credit terms (which sometimes involve cash or securities collateral) and do not require daily MTM cash settlement. Forward contract settlement occurs at maturity in a one-time cash settlement of the cumulative change in contract value.

The different patterns of cash flows for forwards and futures can lead to a difference in the pricing of forwards versus futures. Forward and futures prices are identical under certain conditions, namely:

- if interest rates are constant, or
- if futures prices and interest rates are uncorrelated.

On the other hand, violations of these assumptions can give rise to differences in pricing between these two contracts. For example, if futures prices are positively correlated with interest rates, long futures contracts are more attractive than long forward positions for the same underlying and maturity. The reason is because rising prices lead to futures profits that are reinvested in periods of rising interest rates, and falling prices lead to losses that occur in periods of falling interest rates. The price differential will also vary with the volatility of interest rates.

A negative correlation between futures prices and interest rates leads to the opposite interpretation, with long forward positions being more desirable than long futures positions. In general, the more desirable contract will tend to have the higher price.

INTEREST RATE FORWARD AND FUTURES PRICE DIFFERENCES

6

- [ ] explain why forward and futures prices differ

The short maturity of most futures contracts and the ability of most market participants to borrow near risk-free rates for these maturities typically results in little to no distinction between futures and forward prices. An exception to this is the so-called **convexity bias**, which arises given the difference in price changes for interest rate futures versus forward contracts, as illustrated in the following example.

EXAMPLE 5

Interest Rate Forwards versus Futures

Let us return to an example from the prior lesson with an interest rate futures contract of $1,000,000 notional for three-month MRR of 2.21% for one quarter (or 90/360 days). Recall that the underlying deposit contract value was:

$$\$1{,}005{,}525 = \$1{,}000{,}000 \times [1 + (2.21\% / 4)].$$

The contract BPV was shown to be $25 (= $1,000,000 × 0.01% × [1/4]).

Consider in contrast a $1,000,000 notional FRA on three-month MRR in three months' time with an identical 2.21% rate. The net payment on the FRA is based upon the difference between MRR and the implied forward rate (IFR):

$$\text{Net Payment} = (\text{MRR}_{B-A} - \text{IFR}_{A,B-A}) \times \text{Notional Principal} \times \text{Period}.$$

For example, if the observed MRR in three months is 2.22% (+0.01%), the net payment *at maturity* would be $25 (= $1,000,000 × 0.01% × [1/4]). However, the settlement of an FRA is based upon the present value of the final cash flow discounted at MRR, so:

$$\text{Cash Settlement (PV): } \$24.86 = \$25 / (1 + 0.0222 / 4).$$

If we increase the magnitude of the MRR change at settlement and compare these changes between a long interest rate futures position and a short receive-fixed (pay floating) FRA contract, we arrive at the following result:

$MRR_{3m,3m}$	Short FRA Cash Settlement (PV)	Long Futures Settlement
2.01%	$497.50	$500
2.11%	$248.69	$250
2.21%	$0	$0
2.31%	($248.56)	($250)
2.41%	($497.01)	($500)

Although the settlement values differ due to different conventions across these instruments, note that while the futures contract has a fixed linear payoff profile for a given basis point change, the FRA settlement does not.

In the FRA contract in Example 5, we see that the percentage price change is greater (in absolute value) when MRR falls than when it rises. Although the difference here is very small due to the short forward period, note that this non-linear relationship is the convexity property, which characterizes fixed-income instruments from earlier lessons, as shown in Exhibit 5.

Exhibit 5: Convexity Bias

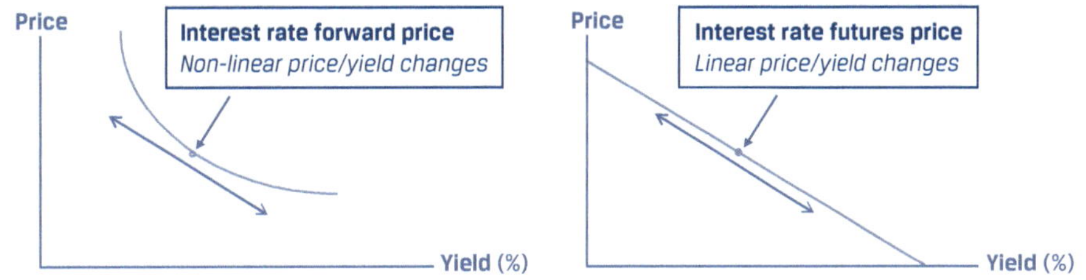

The discounting feature of the FRA, which is not present in the futures contract, leads to a convexity bias that is greater for longer discounting periods. You will recall from an earlier lesson that a discount factor is the *price* equivalent of a zero rate and is the present value of a currency unit on a future date, which may also be interpreted as the price of a zero-coupon cash flow or bond. We will show later how this discount factor is used to price interest rate swaps and other derivatives.

EFFECT OF CENTRAL CLEARING OF OTC DERIVATIVES 7

☐ explain why forward and futures prices differ

In periods of market and/or counterparty financial stress, large price movements combined with a derivative counterparty's inability to meet a margin call may force the closeout of a futures transaction prior to maturity. An OTC forward contract with more flexible credit terms, however, may remain outstanding.

The advent of derivatives central clearing, introduced in an earlier lesson, has created futures-like margining requirements for OTC derivative dealers who buy and sell forwards to derivatives end users. Dealers who are required to post cash or highly liquid securities to a central counterparty often impose similar requirements on derivatives end users. These dealer margin requirements reduce the difference in the cash flow impact of exchange-traded and OTC derivatives. This arrangement between dealers and their counterparties, shown in Exhibit 6, has been added to the original central clearing diagram from an earlier lesson.

Exhibit 6: Margin Requirements for Centrally Cleared OTC Derivatives

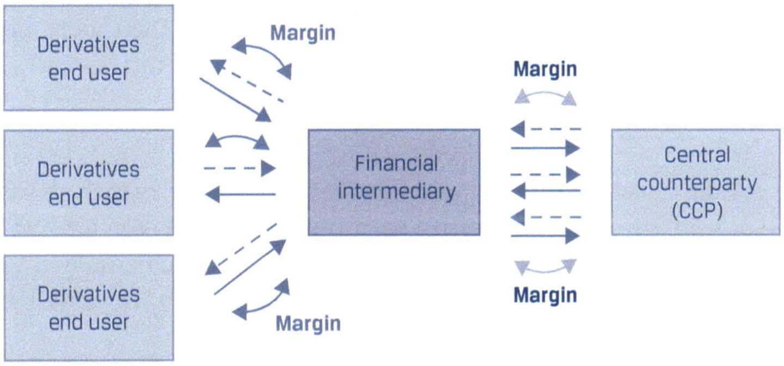

Investors who actively use both exchange-traded futures or OTC forwards must therefore maintain sufficient cash or eligible collateral to fulfill margin or collateral requirements. Market participants must also consider the financing, transaction, and administrative costs of maintaining these positions when using derivatives in a portfolio.

QUESTION SET

Forward and Futures Prices

1. Identify the following statement as true or false and justify your answer: If futures prices are positively correlated with interest rates, long futures contracts are more attractive than long forward positions for the same underlying and maturity.

   Solution:

   The statement is true. If futures contract prices rise as interest rates rise, a long futures contract holder can reinvest futures contract profits at higher interest rates.

2. An investor seeks to hedge its three-month MRR exposure on a £25,000,000 liability in two months and observes an implied forward rate today ($IFR_{2m,3m}$) of 2.95%. Calculate the settlement amounts if the investor enters a long pay-fixed (receive floating) FRA and a short futures contract, and compare and interpret the results if $MRR_{2m,3m}$ settles at 3.25%.

   Solution:

   Solve for the pay-fixed FRA Cash Settlement (PV) value as follows:

   Net Payment = $(MRR_{B-A} - IFR_{A,B-A}) \times$ Notional Principal $\times$ Period

   = £18,750 (= [3.25% − 2.95%] × £25,000,000 × [1/4]).

   The present value based upon $MRR_{2m,5m}$ of 3.25% is:

   = £18,598.88 (= £18,750 / [1 + 0.0325/4]).

   For the futures contract, contract BPV is equal to:

   Contract BPV = £625 (= £25,000,000 × 0.01% × [1/4]).

   For a 30-basis point increase in MRR (= 3.25% – 2.95%), the short futures contract will realize a price appreciation of £18,750 (= £625 x 30). Both contracts result in a gain from the investor's perspective as MRR rises. However, the futures settlement is larger due to the discounting of the FRA final payment to the settlement date.

3. Explain why short futures contracts are more attractive than short forward positions if futures prices are negatively correlated with interest rates for positions with the same underlying and maturity.

   Solution:

   The reason that short futures contracts are more attractive than short forward positions if futures prices are negatively correlated with interest rates is because falling prices lead to futures profits that are reinvested in periods of rising interest rates, and rising prices lead to losses that occur in periods of falling interest rates.

4. Identify the following statement as true or false and justify your answer:

   The convexity bias between interest rate futures and interest rate forwards causes the percentage price change to be greater (in absolute value) when MRR rises than when it falls for a forward than for a futures contract.

   Solution:

   The statement is false. The convexity bias between interest rate futures and interest rate forwards causes the percentage price change to be greater (in absolute value) when MRR *falls* than when it *rises* for a forward contract, as opposed to a futures contract.

5. Explain how central clearing of derivatives reduces the difference in futures and forward prices for the same underlying and maturity periods.

   Solution:

   The central clearing of derivatives has created futures-like margining requirements for OTC derivative dealers who buy and sell forwards to derivatives end users. Dealers who are required to post cash or highly liquid securities to a central counterparty often impose similar requirements on derivatives end users. This arrangement between derivative dealers and their counterparties will reduce the difference in the cash flow impact of ETD and OTC derivatives. Hence, any price difference between ETD futures and OTC forwards will be reduced.

PRACTICE PROBLEMS

The following information relates to questions 1-4

Ace Limited is a financial intermediary active in both futures and forward markets. You have been hired as an investment consultant and asked to review Ace's activities and answer the following questions.

1. Ace serves as a futures commission merchant to assist several of its commodity trading adviser (CTA) clients to clear and settle their futures margin positions with the futures exchange. Ace is reviewing the copper futures market for a CTA client considering a long copper futures position for the first time. Details of the copper futures market are as follows:

CME Copper Futures Contract Specifications

Contract Maturities:	Monthly [from 1 month to 15 months]
Contract Size:	25,000 pounds
Delivery Type:	Cash settled
Price Quotation:	$ per pound
Initial Margin:	$10,000 per contract
Maintenance Margin:	$6,000 per contract
Final Maturity:	Last CME business day of contract month
Daily Settlement:	CME Trading Operations calculates daily settlement values based on its published procedures

Today's copper spot price is $4.25 per pound, and the constant risk-free rate is 1.875%. Each contract has a $10 storage cost payable at the end of the month. Which of the following statements best characterizes the margin exposure profile of Ace's CTA client if it enters a one-month copper futures contract?

A. The CTA will be expected to post $10,000 initial margin and would receive a margin call if the copper futures price were to immediately fall below $4.10 per pound or below a price of $102,425 per contract.

B. The CTA would be expected to post $10,000 in initial margin and would receive a margin call at any time over the life of the contract if the copper futures price were to immediately fall below $3.86 per pound or below a price of $96,425 per contract.

C. The CTA will be expected to post $10,000 initial margin, but we cannot determine the exact futures price at which a margin call will occur as the futures MTM is settled each day and the contract value resets to zero.

2. One of Ace's investor clients has entered a long six-month forward transaction with Ace on 100 shares of Xenaliya (XLYA), a non-dividend-paying technology stock. The stock's spot price per share, S_0, is €85, and the risk-free rate is a constant 1% for all maturities. Ace has hedged the client transaction with a long

six-month XLYA futures contract at a price $f_0(T)$ of €85.42 and posted initial margin of €1,000. Three months after the forward and futures contracts are initiated, XYLA announces a strategic partnership with a major global technology firm, and its spot share price jumps €15 on the day's trading to close at €123.

Which of the following statements best characterizes the impact of the day's trading on the MTM value of the forward versus the futures contract?

A. Ace's client realizes an MTM gain of approximately €1,500 (= €15 × 100) on its margin account, which Ace must deposit at the end of the day to cover its margin call.

B. Ace's client benefits from an MTM unrealized gain on its forward contract with Ace, and Ace has a corresponding MTM gain of approximately €1,500 (= €15 × 100) deposited in its margin account by the exchange.

C. Because Ace has entered a hedge of its client's long forward position on XLYA by executing a futures contract with otherwise identical terms, the two contract MTM values exactly offset one another and no cash is exchanged on either transaction.

3. Identify which of the following corresponds to which description.

1. Long interest rate futures position	A. Results in a gain when MRR settles above the initial forward commitment rate at maturity
2. Pay fixed (receive floating) FRA contract	B. Results in a loss when MRR settles above the initial forward commitment rate at maturity
3. Receive fixed (pay floating) FRA contract	C. Has a forward commitment price that will increase as short-term interest rates fall

4. Ace's investor clients usually use OTC forward transactions that Ace must clear with a central counterparty. Which of the following statements related to the impact on Ace from clearing these positions is most accurate?

A. If Ace's counterparties enter long forward contracts whose prices are positively correlated with interest rates, Ace will have to post more collateral to central counterparties than for otherwise similar futures contracts, since rising prices will lead to counterparty MTM gains reinvested at higher rates.

B. If Ace's counterparties enter short forward contracts whose prices are negatively correlated with interest rates, Ace will have to post less collateral to central counterparties than for otherwise similar futures contracts, since falling prices will lead to counterparty MTM gains reinvested at higher rates.

C. Since Ace is required to post collateral (cash or highly liquid securities) to the central counterparty to clear its client forward transactions, Ace will face similar margining requirements to those of standardized exchange-traded futures markets.

SOLUTIONS

1. A is correct. The CTA will face a margin call if the copper contract price falls by more than \$4,000, or \$0.16 (= \$4,000/25,000) per pound. We may solve for the price at which the CTA receives a margin call by first solving for the initial futures contract price, $f_0(T)$, at contract inception as follows:

   $f_0(T) = [S_0 + \mathrm{PV}_0(C)]\ (1 + r)^T$.

   Solve for $\mathrm{PV}_0(C)$ per pound as follows:

   $\mathrm{PV}_0(C) = \$9.98\ (= \$10[1.01875^{-(1/12)}])$.

   Substitute $\mathrm{PV}_0(C) = \$9.98$ into Equation 4 to solve for $f_0(T)$:

   $f_0(T) = [(\$4.25 \times 25{,}000) + \$9.98](1.01875^{\ -(1/12)})$

   $f_0(T) = \$106{,}425$ per contract ($\approx$ \$4.257 per pound).

   So, \$106,425 – \$4,000 = \$102,425 per contract, and \$4.257 – \$0.16 = \$4.10 per pound.

   B is incorrect as it assumes there is no maintenance margin, and while C may be true under some circumstances, the change in *A* is immediate (occurs at trade inception).

2. B is correct. The long investor client forward position with Ace benefits from an MTM gain on its forward contract with Ace, but no cash is exchanged until maturity. Ace receives a deposit in its futures margin account equal to the daily MTM futures contract gain, which if spot and futures prices change by approximately the same amount will be equal to €1,500 (€15 × 100).

3. 1. C is correct. The futures contract price changes daily based upon a (yield – 100) quoting convention, so its price will increase as yields fall and vice versa. The fixed rate on an FRA does not change for the life of the contract.

   2. A is correct. An FRA fixed-rate payer (floating-rate receiver) will realize a gain on the contract upon settlement (equal to the present value of the difference between the fixed rate and MRR multiplied by the contract notional over the specified interest period) if MRR settles above the initial fixed rate on the contract.

   3. B is correct. If the MRR settles above the initial forward commitment rate at maturity, the FRA fixed-rate payer has an MTM loss on the contract.

4. C is correct. Mandatory central clearing requirements impose margin requirements on financial intermediaries similar to those of standardized exchange-traded futures markets, who often pass these costs and/or requirements on to their clients. Answers A and B are incorrect, as the MTM gains on the forward contracts are not realized until maturity.

LEARNING MODULE

7

Pricing and Valuation of Interest Rates and Other Swaps

LEARNING OUTCOMES

Mastery	*The candidate should be able to:*
☐	describe how swap contracts are similar to but different from a series of forward contracts
☐	contrast the value and price of swaps

INTRODUCTION

1

Swap contracts were introduced earlier as a firm commitment to exchange a series of cash flows in the future, with interest rate swaps where fixed cash flows are exchanged for floating payments being the most common type. Subsequent lessons addressed the pricing and valuation of forward and futures contracts across the term structure, which form the building blocks for swap contracts.

In this lesson, we will explore how swap contracts are related to these other forward commitment types. While financial intermediaries often use forward rate agreements or short-term interest rate futures contracts to manage interest rate exposure, issuers and investors usually prefer swap contracts, since they better match rate-sensitive assets and liabilities with periodic cash flows, such as fixed-coupon bonds, variable-rate loans, or known future commitments. It is important for these market participants not only to be able to match expected future cash flows using swaps but also to ensure that their change in value is consistent with existing or desired underlying exposures. The following lessons compare swap contracts with forward contracts and contrast the value and price of swaps.

LEARNING MODULE OVERVIEW

- A swap contract is an agreement between two counterparties to exchange a *series* of future cash flows, whereas a forward contract is a *single* exchange of value at a later date.

- Interest rate swaps are similar to forwards in that both contracts are firm commitments with symmetric payoff profiles and no cash is exchanged at inception, but they differ in that the fixed swap rate is constant, whereas a series of forward contracts has different forward rates at each maturity.
- A swap is priced by solving for the par swap rate, a fixed rate that sets the present value of all future expected floating cash flows equal to the present value of all future fixed cash flows.
- The value of a swap at inception is zero (ignoring transaction and counterparty credit costs). On any settlement date, the value of a swap equals the current settlement value plus the present value of all remaining future swap settlements.
- A swap contract's value changes as time passes and interest rates change. For example, a rise in expected forward rates increases the present value of floating payments, causing a mark-to-market (MTM) gain for the fixed-rate payer (floating-rate receiver) and an MTM loss for the fixed-rate receiver (floating-rate payer).

LEARNING MODULE SELF-ASSESSMENT

These initial questions are intended to help you gauge your current level of understanding of this learning module.

1. Identify which of the following characteristics matches which forward commitment contract.

1. Involves periodic settlements based on the difference between a fixed rate established for each period and market reference rate (MRR)	A. Both an interest rate swap and a series of forward rate agreements
2. Has a symmetric payoff profile and a value of zero to both counterparties at inception	B. A series of forward rate agreements (FRAs)
3. Involves periodic settlements based on the difference between a constant fixed rate and the MRR	C. Interest rate swap

Solution:

1. B is correct. A series of FRAs involves periodic settlements based on the difference between a fixed rate established for each period and the MRR.

2. A is correct. Both an interest rate swap and a series of forward rate agreements have a symmetric payoff profile and a value of zero to both counterparties at inception.

3. C is correct. An interest rate swap involves periodic settlements based on the difference between a constant fixed rate and the MRR.

2. Which of the following transactions would allow a fixed-income portfolio manager to gain from falling interest rates?

A. Buy a floating-rate bond

B. Enter into a receive-fixed, pay-floating interest rate swap

C. Enter into a pay-fixed, receive-floating interest rate swap

Solution:

B is correct. A fixed-income portfolio manager seeking to gain from falling interest rates may consider entering a *receive*-fixed, *pay*-floating interest rate swap rather than purchasing bonds. The fixed-rate payments become more valuable as interest rates decline A is incorrect as the floating-rate bond interest rate payments decline as interest rates decline, thus the bond does not increase in value. C is incorrect as the fixed interest rate payments become more costly as interest rates decline.

3. Which of the following statements provides a correct description of a pay-fixed, receive-floating interest rate swap position?

   A. Long a floating-rate note priced at the MRR and short a fixed-rate bond with a coupon equal to the fixed swap rate

   B. Long a fixed-rate bond with a coupon equal to the fixed swap rate and short a floating-rate note priced at the MRR

   C. Long a floating-rate note priced at the MRR

   Solution:

   A is correct. An interest rate swap is economically equivalent to a long and short position in underlying debt securities. In the case of a pay-fixed, receive-floating swap, the cash flow received reflects the long position. In this case, the party receives floating payments, so this is like buying a floating-rate note. The pay-fixed portion of the swap is like selling a fixed-rate bond and paying fixed coupons to the bond buyer. B is incorrect as this response is economically equivalent to entering into a receive-fixed, pay-floating swap. C is incorrect because the response does not reflect the short position.

4. An investor enters into a 10-year, pay-fixed EUR100 million swap at a rate of 1.12% versus six-month EUR MRR. Assume six-month EUR MRR sets today at 0.25%. Which of the following is closest to the correct calculation of the periodic settlement value of the swap from the investor's perspective in six months' time?

   A. EUR870,000

   B. –EUR870,000

   C. –EUR435,000

   Solution:

   C is correct. From the investor's (fixed-rate payer's) perspective, the periodic settlement value of the swap is equal to

   Periodic settlement value = (MRR – s_N) × Notional amount × Period

   = –EUR435,000 = (0.25% – 1.12%) × EUR100 million × 0.5 years.

   Since EUR MRR has set below the fixed swap rate, the fixed-rate payer must make a net payment to the fixed-rate receiver at the end of the interest period. Both A and B responses omit the period of the swap (0.5 years) so are incorrect. A is also incorrect because the reversed sign on the answer would properly reflect the counterparty's periodic settlement value, not the investor's.

2 SWAPS VS. FORWARDS

- [ ] describe how swap contracts are similar to but different from a series of forward contracts

A swap contract is an agreement between two parties to exchange a *series* of future cash flows, while a forward contract is an agreement for a *single* exchange of value at a later date. Although this lesson focuses on interest rate swaps, similar principles apply to other underlying variables where a series of cash flows are exchanged on a future date.

An earlier lesson showed how implied forward rates may be derived from spot rates. An implied forward rate for a given period in the future is equivalent to the forward rate agreement (FRA) fixed rate for that same period for which no riskless profit opportunities exist. The single cash flow of an FRA is similar to a single-period swap, as shown in Exhibit 1.

Exhibit 1: Swap and FRA Payoff Profile

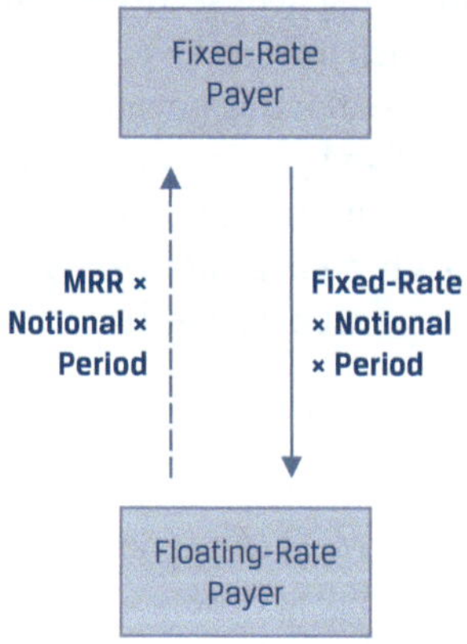

In each case, the net difference between a fixed rate agreed on at inception and an MRR set in the future is used as the basis for determining cash settlement on a given notional principal over a specific time period. For example, a fixed-rate payer on a swap or FRA will realize a gain if the MRR sets at a rate higher than the agreed-on fixed rate and will receive a net payment from the floating-rate payer. However, as we saw in an earlier lesson, the FRA has a single settlement, which occurs at the *beginning* of an interest period, while a standard swap has periodic settlements, which occur at the *end* of each respective period.

Other similarities between interest rate forwards and swaps include the symmetric payoff profile and the fact that no cash flow is exchanged upfront. Both interest rate forward and swap contracts involve counterparty credit exposure.

Since interest rates are characterized by a term structure, different FRA fixed rates usually exist for different times to maturity. In contrast, a standard interest rate swap has a *constant* fixed rate over its life, which includes multiple periods. This relationship is shown visually in Exhibit 2 and numerically in Example 1, which extends an earlier spot and forward rate example.

Exhibit 2: Series of FRAs vs. Standard Interest Rate Swap

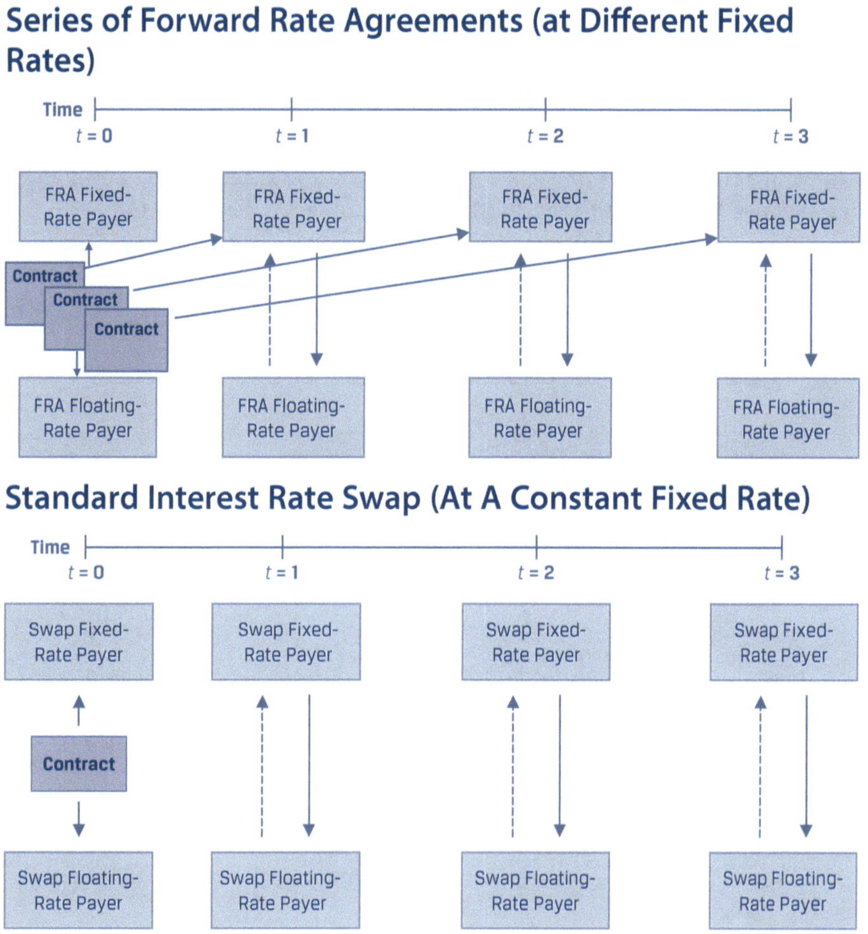

EXAMPLE 1

Swaps as a Combination of Forwards

Recall from an earlier lesson that three recently issued annual fixed-coupon government bonds had the following coupons, prices, yields-to-maturity, and zero (or spot) rates:

Years to Maturity	Annual Coupon	PV (per 100 FV)	YTM	Zero Rates
1	1.50%	99.125	2.3960%	2.3960%
2	2.50%	98.275	3.4068%	3.4197%
3	3.25%	98.000	3.9703%	4.0005%

We solve for the implied forward rate ($IFR_{A,B-A}$), the break-even reinvestment rate for a period starting in the future (at $t = A$) between short-dated (z_A) and longer-dated (z_B) zero rate using the following formula:

$$(1 + z_A)^A \times (1 + IFR_{A,B-A})^{B-A} = (1 + z_B)^B. \quad (1)$$

The respective spot rate at time $t = 0$ ($IFR_{0,1}$) and the implied forward rates in one year ($IFR_{1,1}$) and in two years ($IFR_{2,1}$) are as follows:

$IFR_{0,1}$ = 2.3960% = (1.023960) – 1.

$IFR_{1,1}$ = 4.4536% = $(1.034197)^2/(1.02396)$ – 1.

$IFR_{2,1}$ = 5.1719% = $(1.040005)^3/(1.034197)^2$ – 1.

One way to create a forward commitment for multiple periods with an initial value of zero would be to use a series of forward rate agreements, exchanging cash flows based on the respective implied forward rate (i.e., the FRA fixed rate) for each period. However, the fixed rate would *vary* for each period based on the term structure of interest rates. Instead, a standard interest rate swap is characterized by a *constant* fixed rate over multiple periods. These rates are shown for both alternatives below.

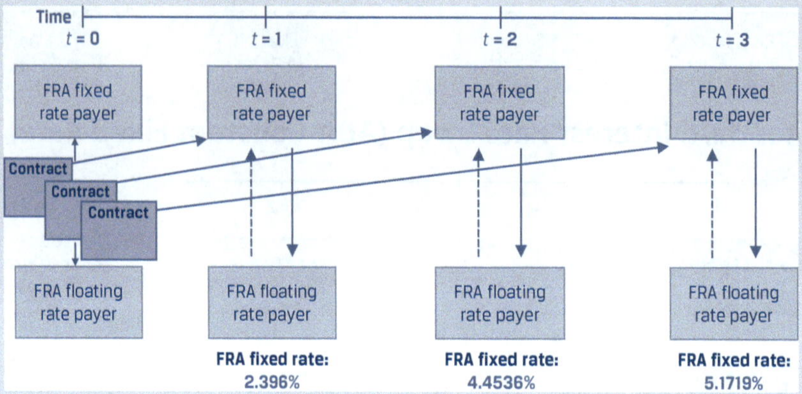

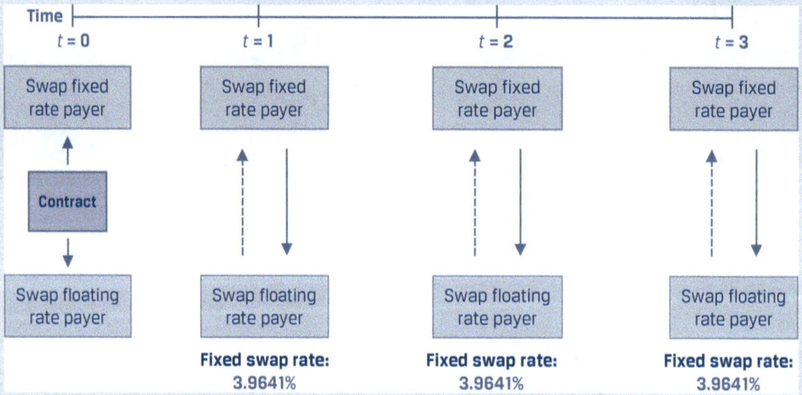

The method used to solve for a swap rate was introduced in an earlier fixed-income lesson. The *par rate* (PMT) was shown to be the fixed rate at which a fixed-coupon bond has a price equal to par (or 100) using a sequence of zero rates (z_i for period i) as market discount factors, as follows:

$$100 = \frac{PMT}{(1+z_1)^1} + \frac{PMT}{(1+z_2)^2} + \dots + \frac{PMT + 100}{(1+z_N)^N}. \quad (2)$$

A standard interest rate swap represents an exchange of fixed payments (with *no* final principal payment) at a constant rate for a series of floating-rate cash flows expected to equal the respective implied forward rates at time $t = 0$. We must therefore modify the par bond rate calculation in Equation 2 to solve for PMT as a **par swap rate.**

Exhibit 3: Par Swap Rate, Spot, and Forward Curve

The par swap rate is the fixed rate that equates the present value of all future expected floating cash flows to the present value of fixed cash flows.

Σ PV(Floating payments) = Σ PV(Fixed payments), or

$$\sum_{i=1}^{N} \frac{\text{IFR}}{(1+z_i)^i} = \sum_{i=1}^{N} \frac{s_i}{(1+z_i)^i}. \quad (3)$$

In our three-period example, we use the implied forward rates, IFR, to solve for s_3, or the three-year swap rate:

$$\frac{\text{IFR}_{0,1}}{(1+z_1)} + \frac{\text{IFR}_{1,1}}{(1+z_2)^2} + \frac{\text{IFR}_{2,1}}{(1+z_3)^3} = \frac{s_3}{(1+z_1)} + \frac{s_3}{(1+z_2)^2} + \frac{s_3}{(1+z_3)^3}.$$

Substitute each of these building blocks into Equation 3 to solve for s_3:

$$0.111017 = \frac{2.396\%}{1.02396} + \frac{4.4537\%}{(1.034197)^2} + \frac{5.1719\%}{(1.040005)^3}$$

$$= \frac{s_3}{1.02396} + \frac{s_3}{(1.034197)^2} + \frac{s_3}{(1.040005)^3}$$

$$0.111017 = 2.800545 \times s_3.$$

$$s_3 = 3.9641\%.$$

The three-year swap rate of 3.9641% may be interpreted as a multiperiod breakeven rate at which an investor would be indifferent to

- *paying* the fixed swap rate and *receiving* the respective forward rates or
- *receiving* the fixed swap rate and *paying* the respective forward rates.

For this reason, we may think of the fixed swap rate as an internal rate of return on the implied forward rates through the maturity of the swap as of $t = 0$. Exhibit 3 also demonstrates that while the combined value of the equivalent forward contracts is zero at time $t = 0$, some individual forward exchanges may have a positive present value and some will have a negative present value. For example, a fixed-rate receiver (floating-rate payer) on the swap in Example 1 would expect the following cash flow in one year's time:

- *Receive* the fixed swap rate (s_3) of 3.9641%.
- *Pay* the initial floating rate ($\text{IFR}_{0,1}$) of 2.396%.

- *Receive* a net payment of 1.5681% (= 3.9641% – 2.396%) on the notional for the period.

Derivative end users, such as issuers and investors, tend to use swaps more often than individual interest rate forward contracts for a number of reasons. For example, the ability to match cash flows of underlying assets or liabilities allows issuers to transform their exposure profile as in Example 2.

EXAMPLE 2

Esterr Inc. Swap to Fixed

Recall from an earlier lesson that Esterr Inc. has a CAD250 million floating-rate term loan at three-month Canadian MRR plus 150 basis points with three and a half years to maturity paid quarterly. Esterr enters into a CAD250 million interest rate swap contract to pay a fixed quarterly swap rate of 2.05% and receive a three-month floating MRR on a notional principal of CAD250 million based on payment dates that match the term loan. The combined loan and swap exposure may be shown as follows:

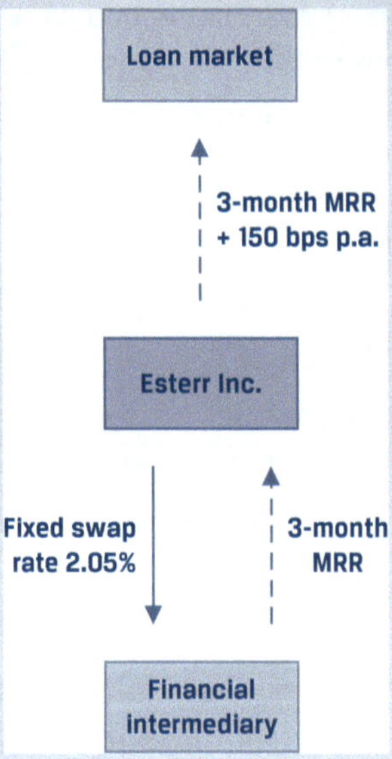

Under the swap arrangement, Esterr can fix its interest expense for the term loan and avoids the administrative burden of multiple forward contracts at different forward rates. Consider the following cash flow scenarios on the interest rate swap and term loan (assuming each interest period is 0.25 year):

Scenario 1:

CAD MRR sets at 3.75%. As the fixed-rate payer, Esterr

- pays the fixed swap rate of 2.05% and receives CAD MRR of 3.75%,
- *receives* a *net* swap payment of 1.70% for the quarter, and
- makes a term loan payment of 5.25% (= 3.75% + 1.50%).

Esterr's interest expense is 3.55% (= 5.25% paid – 1.70% received).

Scenario 2:

CAD MRR sets at 1.25%. As the fixed-rate payer, Esterr

- pays the fixed swap rate of 2.05% and receives CAD MRR of 1.25%,
- *pays* a *net* swap payment of 0.80% for the quarter, and

- makes a term loan payment of 2.75% (= 1.25% + 1.50%).

Esterr's interest expense is 3.55% (= 2.75% paid + 0.80% paid).

Regardless of where CAD MRR sets each period, Esterr's interest expense for each quarterly interest period is approximately CAD2,218,750 (= 3.55%, [equal to the 2.05% swap rate + 1.50% loan spread] × CAD250 million × 0.25 year).

As a fixed-income instrument with periodic fixed cash flows through maturity, an interest rate swap should be expected to have risk and return features similar to those of a fixed-coupon bond of a similar maturity. This feature makes interest rate swaps a more attractive alternative to forward rate agreements for investors in managing fixed-income exposures as well. Consider the following comparison of a cash bond position to paying or receiving a fixed swap rate:

Exhibit 4: Using Swaps to Manage Fixed-Income Exposure

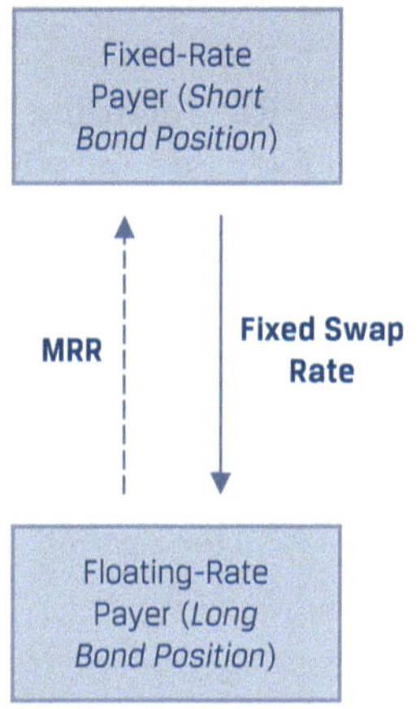

Instrument	Position	Higher interest rates	Lower interest rates
Cash bond	Long fixed bond	Loss	Gain
	Short floating-rate note		
Interest rate swap	Receive fixed	Loss	Gain
	Pay floating		
Cash bond	Short fixed bond	Gain	Loss
	Long floating-rate note		
Interest rate swap	Pay fixed	Gain	Loss
	Receive floating		

While the next lesson will explore the value and price of interest rate swaps in greater detail, Exhibit 4 demonstrates the similarity between a long (short) bond position and a receive (pay) fixed interest rate swap. Given their greater liquidity than and similar benchmark exposure profile to individual bond positions, active fixed-income portfolio managers often use swaps rather than underlying securities to adjust their interest rate exposure. For example, if interest rates are expected to fall, a portfolio manager may choose to receive fixed on a swap rather than purchase underlying bonds to realize a gain in a lower rate environment.

As mentioned earlier, FRAs are primarily used by financial intermediaries to manage their rate-sensitive positions on a period-by-period basis. Issuers and investors typically opt for the greater efficiency of interest rate swaps to manage their interest rate exposures. As we will see in later lessons, the greater liquidity of interest rate swaps has also led to their use both as a bond pricing benchmark and an underlying variable for other derivative instruments.

QUESTION SET

Interest Rate Swaps vs. Forward Contracts

1. Determine the correct answers to fill in the blanks: A fixed-rate payer on a swap or FRA will realize a(n) ______ if the MRR sets at a rate higher than the agreed-on fixed rate and will ______ a net payment ______ the floating-rate payer.

   Solution:

   A fixed-rate payer on a swap or FRA will realize a *gain* if the MRR sets at a rate higher than the agreed-on fixed rate and will *receive* a net payment *from* the floating-rate payer.

2. Identify which of the following characteristics matches which forward commitment contract.

1. The price of this contract is the implied forward rate, or the breakeven reinvestment rate, for a period starting in the future.	A. Interest rate swap
2. Involves counterparty credit risk	B. Forward rate agreement
3. Has a constant fixed rate for which the present value of future fixed versus floating cash flow exchanges is equal to zero	C. Both an interest rate swap and an interest rate forward contract

Solution:

1. B is correct. The breakeven reinvestment rate, or implied forward rate, is the no-arbitrage FRA fixed rate.
2. C is correct. Both an interest rate swap and a forward rate agreement involve counterparty credit risk.
3. A is correct. An interest rate swap has a constant fixed rate for which the present value of fixed versus floating cash flow exchanges equals zero.

3. Identify which of the following benefits of using swaps over forwards are most applicable to which derivative end users.

1. Swaps allow these end users to match the periodic cash flows of a specific balance sheet liability to transform their interest rate exposure profile.	A. Both issuers and investors
2. Swaps enable these end users to actively adjust their interest rate exposure profile without buying or selling underlying securities	B. Issuers
3. Swaps involving a series of cash flows enable these end users to avoid the administrative burden of entering into and managing multiple forward contracts.	C. Investors

Solution:

1. B is correct. Swaps allow issuers to match the periodic cash flows of a specific balance sheet liability to transform their interest rate exposure profile, as shown in Example 2.
2. C is correct. Swaps enable investors to actively adjust their interest rate exposure profile without buying or selling underlying securities.
3. A is correct. Both issuers and investors benefit from a reduced administrative burden of entering one interest rate swap for a series of cash flows rather than multiple individual forward contracts.

4. Identify the following statement as true or false, and justify your response: The market reference rate (MRR) is the internal rate of return on the implied forward rates over the life of an interest rate swap.

Solution:

False. The fixed swap rate is the internal rate of return on the implied forward rates over the life of an interest rate swap.

5. Explain how an active fixed-income portfolio manager might use an interest rate swap rather than underlying bonds to realize a gain in a lower–interest rate environment, and justify your response.

Solution:

A manager may choose to receive fixed, pay floating on an interest rate swap, with the fixed cash flow stream being similar to owning a fixed-coupon bond. If interest rates are expected to fall, the manager will realize an MTM gain in a lower-rate environment.

SWAP VALUES AND PRICES 3

☐ contrast the value and price of swaps

In the prior lesson, we showed a swap price (or par swap rate) to be a periodic fixed rate that equates the present value of all future expected floating cash flows to the present value of fixed cash flows. The swap rate (s_N for N periods) is equivalent to a forward rate, $F_0(T)$, that satisfies the no-arbitrage condition. Similar to other forwards, the initial contract value (ignoring transaction and counterparty credit costs) is zero ($V_0(T) = 0$).

In contrast to other forward commitments, which involve a *single* settlement at maturity, a swap contract involves a *series* of periodic settlements with a final settlement at contract maturity. Recall from an earlier lesson that the value of a forward contract at maturity from the long forward (or forward buyer's) perspective is $V_T(T) = S_T - F_0(T)$, where S_T is the spot price at maturity and $F_0(T)$ is the forward price. For a swap with periodic exchanges, the current MRR is the "spot" price and the fixed swap rate, s_N, is the forward price. Restating this result for the fixed-rate payer on a swap, the periodic settlement value is

$$\text{Periodic settlement value} = (\text{MRR} - s_N) \times \text{Notional amount} \times \text{Period}. \quad (4)$$

The value of a swap on any settlement date equals the current settlement value in Equation 4 *plus* the present value of all remaining future swap settlements. Although swap market conventions vary, for purposes of this lesson we will assume the MRR sets at the beginning of each interest period, with the same periodicity and day count convention as the swap rate. The fixed versus floating difference is exchanged at the end of each period.

EXAMPLE 3

Esterr Inc. Swap Value and Price

Esterr entered a 3.5-year CAD250 million interest rate swap contract under which it pays a fixed quarterly swap rate of 2.05% and receives three-month CAD MRR. The fixed swap *price* of 2.05% paid by Esterr remains constant over the life of the contract. While the first three-month CAD MRR is *known* at $t = 0$, the remaining 13 MRR settings are *unknown* but are *expected* to equal the respective implied forward rates (IFRs) for each period through maturity. A prior lesson showed how IFRs are derived from zero rates, which were then used to solve for the fixed swap rate by setting the present value of fixed payments equal to the present value of floating payments.

The *value* of Esterr's swap contract will change as time passes and interest rates change. We first consider the passage of time with no change to expected interest rates. That is, the MRR sets each period based on the implied forward rates at trade inception. Assume the following implied forward rates apply to Esterr's swap at $t = 0$:

Period	IFR	Rate
1	$IFR_{0,3m}$	0.50%
2	$IFR_{3m,3m}$	0.74%
3	$IFR_{6m,3m}$	0.98%
4	$IFR_{9m,3m}$	1.22%
5	$IFR_{12m,3m}$	1.46%
6	$IFR_{15m,3m}$	1.70%
7	$IFR_{18m,3m}$	1.94%
8	$IFR_{21m,3m}$	2.18%
9	$IFR_{24m,3m}$	2.43%
10	$IFR_{27m,3m}$	2.67%
11	$IFR_{30m,3m}$	2.91%
12	$IFR_{33m,3m}$	3.15%

Period	IFR	Rate
13	$IFR_{36m,3m}$	3.39%
14	$IFR_{39m,3m}$	3.78%

Based on these forward rates, Esterr expects to *make* a net swap payment each quarter through the seventh period—since (MRR – s_N) = (1.94% – 2.05%) < 0—and *receive* a net quarterly swap payment starting in the eighth period, where (MRR – s_N) = (2.18% – 2.05%) > 0. Using Equation 1, consider the periodic settlement values for the first two periods from Esterr's perspective as the fixed-rate payer:

- **Period 1:** –CAD968,750 = (0.5% – 2.05%) × CAD250 million × 0.25.
- **Period 2:** –CAD818,750 = (0.74% – 2.05%) × CAD250 million × 0.25.

What is the swap MTM *value* from Esterr's perspective immediately after the second periodic settlement if forward rates remain unchanged? Note that the swap *price* (the fixed swap rate of 2.05%) was set at inception to equate the present value of fixed versus floating payments.

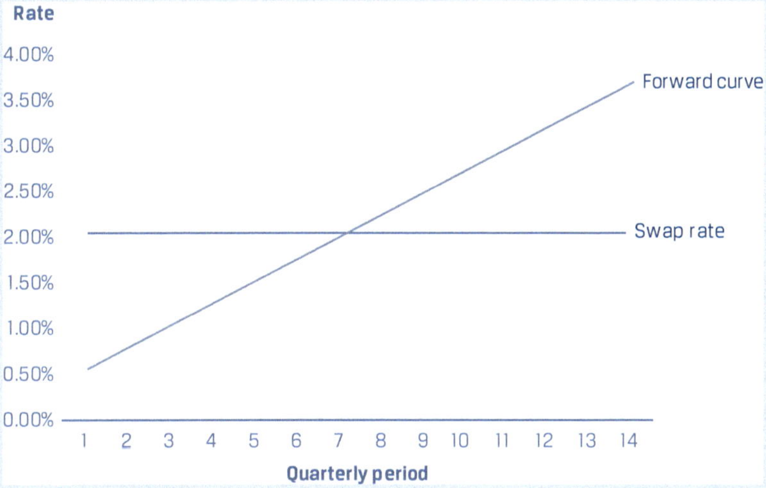

As we move forward in time with *no* change to interest rate expectations, the present value of remaining floating payments rises above the present value of fixed payments at 2.05%, as Esterr has made a net settlement payment in the first two periods.

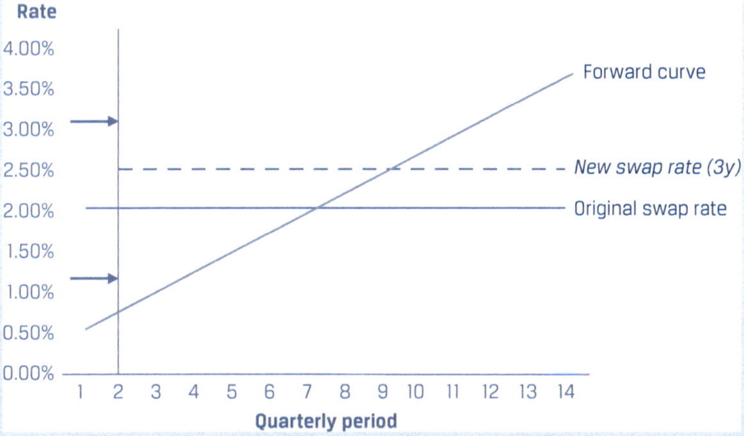

As the diagram shows, as time progresses, Esterr realizes an MTM gain on the swap, since

Σ PV(Floating payments received) > Σ PV(Fixed payments paid).

Note that this result depends on the relative level of IFRs and shape of the forward curve, which in this case is upward sloping.

If we instead consider interest rate changes only, from Esterr's perspective as the fixed-rate payer (and floating-rate receiver), we can show the conditions under which Esterr has a swap MTM gain or loss:

- Esterr realizes an MTM *gain* on the swap as the fixed-rate payer if

Σ PV(Floating payments received) > Σ PV(Fixed payments paid).

- Esterr realizes an MTM *loss* on the swap as the fixed-rate payer if

Σ PV(Floating payments received) < Σ PV(Fixed payments paid).

A rise in the expected forward rates after inception will increase the present value of floating payments, while the fixed swap rate will remain the same. We show the effect of an immediate change in interest rates following trade inception in the following diagram:

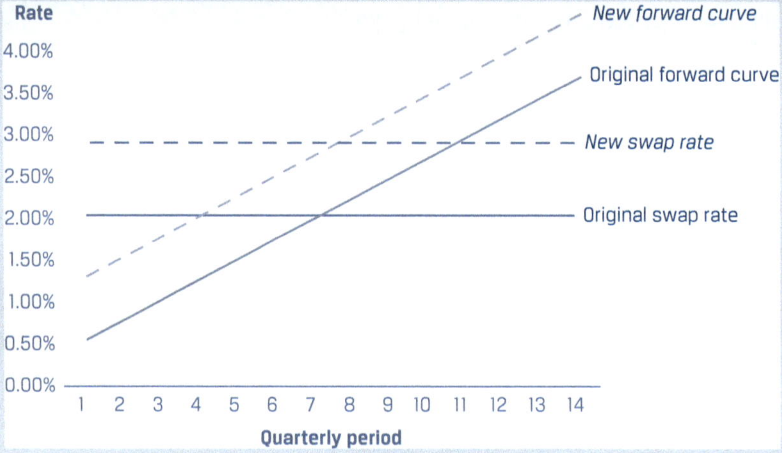

The new forward curve in this diagram is composed of higher IFRs. If we were to now solve for a fixed swap rate using these higher IFRs by setting floating and fixed cash flows equal to one another, the new swap rate would be above the original swap rate. However, since Esterr has locked in future fixed payments at the *lower* original swap rate while receiving higher expected future MRRs, the swap has a positive MTM value to Esterr.

Another interpretation of an interest rate swap is that the fixed-rate payer (floating-rate receiver) is *long* a floating-rate note (FRN) priced at the MRR and *short* a fixed-rate bond with a coupon equal to the fixed swap rate. Note that the combination of long and short bond positions causes both the purchase and sale prices of the two bonds at inception and the return of principal at maturity cancel one another out, and only the fixed versus variable coupon payments remain. The following example shows how the change in an interest rate swap's value is similar to that of a fixed-income security using an earlier investor swap example.

EXAMPLE 4

Fyleton Investments

Fyleton Investments entered a five-year, receive-fixed GBP200 million interest rate swap in an example from an earlier lesson to increase the duration of its fixed-income portfolio. Assume in this case that Fyleton receives a fixed swap rate of 2.38% on a semiannual basis versus six-month GBP MRR. Further assume that initial six-month GBP MRR sets at 0.71% and, as in the case of Esterr, the MRR forward curve is upward sloping. How will the value of Fyleton's swap change as time passes and interest rates change?

First, consider the passage of time with no rate changes. The first-period swap settlement value (in six months) from Fyleton's perspective as the fixed-rate receiver is

GBP1,670,000 = (2.38% – 0.71%) × GBP200 million × 0.5.

What is the MTM value from Fyleton's perspective immediately following the first settlement if implied forward rates remain the same as at trade inception?

As the fixed-rate *receiver*, Fyleton will realize an MTM *loss* on the swap, since

Σ PV(Floating payments paid) > Σ PV(Fixed payments received).

Second, consider a change in forward rates. A *decline* in expected forward rates immediately following trade inception will *reduce* the present value of floating payments, while the fixed swap rate will remain the same. Fyleton will realize an MTM gain as the fixed-rate receiver, since

Σ PV(Fixed payments received) > Σ PV(Floating payments paid).

This MTM gain is shown by the different size of the shaded areas under the original swap rate using the new forward curve in the following diagram.

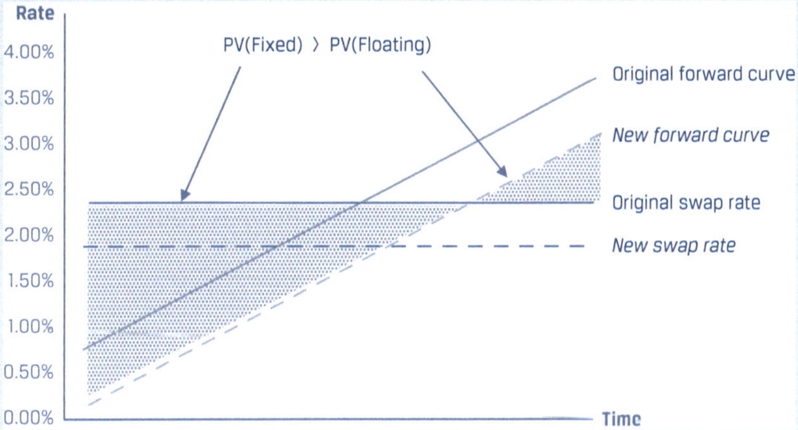

Note the similarity between the receive-fixed swap exposure profile and that of a long cash fixed-rate bond position. In the first instance, we would expect a fixed-rate par bond to be priced at a *discount* as time passes if rates rise as per an upward-sloping forward curve, while an FRN priced at the MRR would remain at par. In the second instance, a decline in implied forward rates (or downward shift in the forward curve) would cause a fixed-rate par bond to be priced at a *premium*, while the FRN price would not change. We will explore how term structure and yield curve changes affect swap values and bond prices in greater detail later in the curriculum.

QUESTION SET

Swap Prices and Values

1. Determine the correct answers to fill in the blanks: A rise in the expected forward rates after inception will ______ the present value of floating payments, causing a fixed-rate receiver to realize a(n) ______ in MTM value on the swap contract.

   Solution:

   A rise in the expected forward rates after inception will *increase* the present value of floating payments, causing a fixed-rate receiver to realize a *decline* in MTM value on the swap contract.

2. Identify the following statement as true or false, and justify your response: The fixed rate on an interest rate swap is priced such that the present value of the floating payments (based on respective implied forward rates for each period) is equal to the present value of the fixed payments at $t = 0$.

   Solution:

   This statement is true. The fixed rate on an interest rate swap may be solved by setting the present value of floating payments equal to the present value of fixed payments. We use zero rates to derive implied forward rates, or breakeven reinvestment rates, between a shorter and a longer zero rate. These IFRs represent the respective floating rates that are expected to apply for each future period at time $t = 0$.

3. Identify which of the following statements is associated with which position in an interest rate swap contract.

1. Establishes a set of certain net future cash flows on a swap contract at inception	A. Fixed-rate payer (Floating-rate receiver)
2. Realizes an MTM gain on a swap contract if the expected future floating-rate payments increase	B. Fixed-rate receiver (Floating-rate payer)
3. An investor may increase portfolio duration by entering this position in a swap contract	C. Neither a fixed-rate payer nor a fixed-rate receiver

Solution:

1. C is correct. A swap contract establishes a set of *certain* fixed future cash flows that are exchanged for a set of *expected* (*uncertain*) floating future cash flows. Therefore, *neither* a fixed-rate payer nor a fixed-rate receiver knows the *net* future cash flows of a swap at inception.
2. A is correct. A fixed-rate payer realizes an MTM gain on a swap contract if the expected future floating-rate payments increase.
3. B is correct. A fixed-rate receiver may increase portfolio duration by entering this position on a swap, because receiving fixed is similar to a long bond position.

4. Determine the correct answers to fill in the blanks: The value of a swap on any settlement date equals the ______ settlement value plus the present value of all remaining ______ swap settlements.

   Solution:

   The value of a swap on any settlement date equals the *current* settlement value plus the present value of all remaining *future* swap settlements.

5. Describe how an investor may use an interest rate swap to reduce the duration of a fixed-income portfolio, and justify your response.

   Solution:

   A pay-fixed swap is similar to a short bond position that reduces duration, because the fixed-rate payer (floating-rate receiver) is effectively long a floating-rate note priced at the MRR and short a fixed-rate bond with a coupon equal to the fixed swap rate.

PRACTICE PROBLEMS

The following information relates to questions 1-6

Ace Limited is a financial intermediary that is active in forward and swap markets with its issuer and investor clients. You have been asked to consult on a number of client situations to determine the best course of action.

1. Identify which of the following statements is associated with which Ace counterparty swap position.

1. Ace's counterparty with this swap position will realize an MTM gain if implied forward rates rise.	A. A receive-fixed interest rate swap
2. Ace's counterparty with this swap position will make a net payment if the initial market reference rate sets above the fixed swap rate.	B. A pay-fixed interest rate swap
3. Ace's counterparty with this position will face an initial swap contract value (ignoring transaction and counterparty credit costs) of zero.	C. Both a receive-fixed and a pay-fixed interest rate swap

2. Ace's client is an asset manager with a significant portion of its fixed-rate bond investment portfolio maturing soon. Ace intends to reinvest the proceeds in five-year bond maturities. Which of the following describes the *best* course of action in the derivatives market for Ace's client to address its bond reinvestment risk?

   A. Ace's client should consider *receiving* fixed on a cash-settled five-year forward-starting swap that starts and settles in three months in order to best address its bond reinvestment risk.

   B. Ace's client should consider *paying* fixed on a cash-settled five-year forward-starting swap starting in three months in order to best address its bond reinvestment risk.

   C. Ace's client should consider entering a *series* of forward rate agreements (FRAs) from today until five years from now under which it pays a fixed rate and receives a floating rate each period ending in five years to address its bond reinvestment risk.

3. Ace enters a 10-year GBP interest rate swap with a client in which Ace receives an initial six-month GBP MRR of 1.75% and pays a fixed GBP swap rate of 3.10% for the first semiannual period. Which of the following statements best describes the value of the swap from Ace's perspective three months after the inception of the trade?

   A. Ace has an MTM *loss* on the swap, because it owes a net settlement payment to its counterparty equal to 1.35% multiplied by the notional and period.

B. Ace has an MTM *gain* on the swap, because once it makes the first known net payment to its counterparty, the remainder of the future net fixed versus floating cash flows must have a positive present value from Ace's perspective.

C. While the present value of fixed and future cash flows was set to zero by solving for the swap rate at inception, we do not have enough information to determine whether the swap currently has a positive or negative value from Ace's perspective following inception.

4. Ace enters a 10-year GBP interest rate swap with a client in which Ace receives an initial six-month GBP MRR of 1.75% and pays a fixed GBP swap rate of 3.10% for the first semiannual period. Six months later, Ace and its counterparty settle the first swap payment, and no change has occurred in terms of future interest rate expectations. Which of the following statements best describes the value of the swap from Ace's perspective?

   A. Ace has an MTM gain on the swap, because once it makes the first known net payment to its counterparty, the remainder of the future net fixed versus floating cash flows must have a positive present value from Ace's perspective.

   B. Ace has an MTM loss on the swap, because once it receives the first known payment from its counterparty, the remainder of the future net fixed versus floating cash flows must have a negative present value from Ace's perspective.

   C. While the present value of fixed and future cash flows was set to zero by solving for the swap rate at inception, we do not have enough information to determine whether the swap currently has a positive or negative value from Ace's perspective following inception.

5. At time $t = 0$, Ace observes the following zero rates over three periods:

Periods	Zero Rates
1	2.2727%
2	3.0323%
3	3.6355%

   Which of the following best describes how Ace arrives at a three-period par swap rate (s_3)?

   A. Since the par swap rate represents the fixed rate at which the present value of fixed and future cash flows equal one another, we discount each zero rate back to the present using zero rates and solve for s_3 to get 2.961%.

   B. Since the par swap rate represents the fixed rate at which the present value of fixed and future cash flows equal one another, we first solve for the implied forward rate per period using zero rates, then discount each implied forward rate back to the present using zero rates, and solve for s_3 to get 3.605%.

C. Since the par swap rate represents the fixed rate at which the present value of fixed and future cash flows equal one another, we first solve for the implied forward rate per period using zero rates, then discount each zero rate back to the present using implied forward rates, and solve for s_3 to get 3.009%.

6. Ace's issuer client has swapped its outstanding fixed-rate debt to floating to match asset portfolio cash flows that generate an MRR-based return. Which of the following statements *best* describes how Ace's MTM credit exposure to the issuer changes if interest rates rise immediately following trade inception?

   A. Since the client receives fixed and pays floating swap, it faces an MTM loss on the transaction as rates rise, *increasing* Ace's MTM exposure to the client.

   B. Since the client receives fixed and pays floating swap, it faces an MTM gain on the transaction as rates rise, *decreasing* Ace's MTM exposure to the client.

   C. Since the swap's value is equal to the current settlement plus future expected settlement amounts, we do not have enough information to determine whether Ace's MTM exposure to the client increases or decreases.

SOLUTIONS

1. 1. B is correct. A pay-fixed swap counterparty will realize an MTM gain if implied forward rates rise.

   2. A is correct. A receive-fixed swap counterparty will make a net payment if the initial market reference rate sets above the fixed swap rate.

   3. C is correct. Both a receive-fixed and a pay-fixed swap counterparty will face an initial swap contract value (ignoring transaction and counterparty credit costs) of zero.

2. A is correct. Ace's client should consider *receiving* fixed on a five-year swap. A receive-fixed swap has a risk and return profile similar to that of a *long* fixed-rate bond position. Ace's client would therefore expect to have a similar MTM gain or loss on the swap position as if it had purchased a five-year bond at inception.

3. C is correct. At time $t = 0$, the present value of fixed and future cash flows was set to zero by solving for the swap rate at inception. Although the current settlement value is known, we cannot determine whether the swap has a positive or negative value from Ace's perspective three months later without further information—specifically, the current level of future forward rates.

4. A is correct. Ace makes the first net payment because the fixed-rate payment is greater than the floating rate received. Given no change in forward interest rates, this implies that the remaining net cash flows must have positive present value to Ace. B is incorrect as this response states the opposite compared to the prior response. C is incorrect because we have information about forward rate expectations.

5. B is correct. Since the expected floating cash flows on the swap are the implied forward rates, we first use zero rates to solve for IFRs using Equation 1:

   $(1 + z_A)^A \times (1 + \text{IFR}_{A,B-A})^{B-A} = (1 + z_B)^B.$

   We may solve for these rates as $\text{IFR}_{0,1} = 2.2727\%$, $\text{IFR}_{1,1} = 3.7975\%$, and $\text{IFR}_{2,1} = 4.8525\%$. We then substitute the respective IFRs discounted by zero rates into the following equation to solve for s_3:

   $$\frac{IFR_{0,1}}{(1+z_1)} + \frac{IFR_{1,1}}{(1+z_2)^2} + \frac{IFR_{2,1}}{(1+z_3)^3} = \frac{s_3}{(1+z_1)} + \frac{s_3}{(1+z_2)^2} + \frac{s_3}{(1+z_3)^3}.$$

   Solving for the left-hand side of the equation, we get

   $$0.10159 = \frac{2.2727\%}{1.022727} + \frac{3.7975\%}{(1.030323)^2} + \frac{4.8525\%}{(1.036355)^3}$$
   $$= \frac{2.2727\%}{1.022727} + \frac{3.7975\%}{(1.030323)^2} + \frac{4.8525\%}{(1.036355)^3}$$

   Solving for the right-hand side, we get

   $$2.81819 s_3 = \left[\frac{1}{1.022727} + \frac{1}{(1.030323)^2} + \frac{1}{(1.036355)^3}\right] \times s_3.$$

   $s_3 = 3.605\% = 0.10159 \div 2.81819.$

   A is incorrect, because it discounts zero rates, not IFRs, back to the present using zero rates, while C incorrectly discounts zero rates by the respective IFRs.

6. A is correct. Since the client receives fixed and pays floating swap, in a rising-rate environment, Σ PV(Floating payments) > Σ PV(Fixed payments), and it will

therefore owe more in future floating-rate settlements than it will receive in fixed-rate settlements, resulting in an MTM loss for the client and an *increase* in Ace's MTM exposure.

LEARNING MODULE

8

Pricing and Valuation of Options

LEARNING OUTCOMES	
Mastery	*The candidate should be able to:*
☐	explain the exercise value, moneyness, and time value of an option
☐	contrast the use of arbitrage and replication concepts in pricing forward commitments and contingent claims
☐	identify the factors that determine the value of an option and describe how each factor affects the value of an option

INTRODUCTION

1

Option contracts are contingent claims in which one of the counterparties determines whether and when a trade will settle. Unlike a forward commitment with a value of zero to both counterparties at inception, an option buyer pays a premium to the seller for the right to transact the underlying in the future at a pre-agreed price. The contingent nature of options affects their price as well as their value over time.

In the first lesson, we explore three features unique to contingent claims related to an option's value versus the spot price of the underlying: the exercise, or intrinsic, value; the relationship between an option's spot price and its exercise price, referred to as "moneyness"; and the time value. We then turn to how the arbitrage and replication concepts introduced earlier for forward commitments differ when applied to contingent claims with an asymmetric payoff profile. Finally, we identify and describe factors that determine the value of an option. These lessons focus on European options, which can be exercised only at expiration.

LEARNING MODULE OVERVIEW

- An option's value comprises its exercise value and its time value. The exercise value is the option's value if it were *immediately* exercisable, while the time value captures the *possibility* that the passage of time and the variability of the underlying price will increase the profitability of exercise at maturity.

- Option moneyness expresses the relationship between the underlying price and the exercise price. A put or call option is "at the money" when the underlying price equals the exercise price. An option is more likely to be exercised if it is "in the money"—with an underlying price above (for a call) or below (for a put) the exercise price—and less likely to be exercised if it is "out of the money."
- Due to their asymmetric payoff profile, options are characterized by no-arbitrage price bounds. The lower bound is a function of the present value of the exercise price and the underlying price, while the upper bound is the underlying price for a call and the exercise price for a put.
- As in the case of forward commitments, the replication of option contracts uses a combination of long (for a call) or short (for a put) positions in an underlying asset and borrowing or lending cash. The replicating transaction for an option is based on a proportion of the underlying, which is closely associated with the moneyness of the option.
- The underlying price, the exercise price, the time to maturity, the risk-free rate, the volatility of the underlying price, and any income or cost associated with owning the underlying asset are key factors in determining the value of an option.
- Changes in the volatility of the underlying price and the time to expiration will usually have the same directional effect on put and call option values. Changes to the exercise price, the risk-free rate, and any income or cost associated with owning the underlying asset have the opposite effect on call options versus put options.

LEARNING MODULE SELF-ASSESSMENT

These initial questions are intended to help you gauge your current level of understanding of this learning module.

1. Which of the following statements correctly describes the lower bound of a call option's value?

   A. The underlying's price minus the present value of the option's exercise price

   B. The underlying's price minus the option's exercise price or zero, whichever is greater

   C. The underlying's price minus the present value of the option's exercise price or zero, whichever is greater

   Solution:

   C is correct. The lower bound of a call price is the underlying's price minus the present value of its exercise price or zero, whichever is greater. A is incorrect as the response omits the fact that the lower bound is zero if the underlying's price is less than the present value of the exercise price. B is incorrect as it omits the present value term.

2. Match the following statements about replication strategies with their associated derivative instrument(s):

1. At time $t = 0$, lend at the risk-free rate and sell the underlying at S_0.	A. Neither a call option nor a put option replication strategy
2. The replication strategy is executed at inception and is settled at maturity with no adjustment over time.	B. A put option replication strategy
3. At time $t = T$, sell the underlying at S_T and repay the loan of X.	C. A call option replication strategy if exercised

Solution:

1. B is correct. At time $t = 0$, a put option replication strategy involves lending at the risk-free rate and selling the underlying at S_0.
2. A is correct. As both call and put options involve a non-linear payoff profile, their replication strategy requires adjustment over time as the likelihood of exercise changes.
3. C is correct. A call option replication strategy if exercised involves repaying the loan of X and selling the underlying at S_T at time $t = T$.

3. A European call option with three months remaining to maturity on an underlying stock with no additional cash flows has an exercise price (X) of GBP 50, a risk-free rate of 2%, and a current underlying price (S_t) of GBP 57.50. If the current call option price is GBP 10, which response below most closely shows the correct exercise value and the time value of the option?

A. Exercise value = GBP 7.50; Time value = GBP 2.50

B. Exercise value = GBP 7.75; Time value = GBP 2.25

C. Exercise value = GBP 0; Time value = GBP 10

Solution:

B is correct. An option's value comprises its exercise value plus its time value. The exercise value of a call option is Max (0, S_t – PV(X)) and is calculated as follows:

$$\text{Call Option Exercise Value} = \text{Max}\left(0,\ S_t - X(1+r)^{-(T-t)}\right)$$

$$\text{Max}(0, \text{GBP } 57.50 - \text{GBP } 50(1.02)^{-0.25})$$

$$= \text{GBP } 7.75$$

The exercise value is positive, as the current underlying price exceeds the present value of the exercise price. The time value is the difference between the option price and the exercise value, representing the possibility that the option payoff at maturity will exceed the current exercise value due to a favorable price change:

$$\text{Call Option Time Value} = c_t - Max\left(0,\ S_t - X(1+r)^{-(T-t)}\right)$$

$$= \text{GBP } 2.25\ (= \text{GBP } 10 - \text{GBP } 7.75)$$

The time value is always positive and declines to zero at maturity ($t = T$). A is incorrect as the present value term is omitted from the exercise value calculation. C is incorrect as it implies the option has zero exercise value.

4. Match the following underlying price and exercise price relationships with their associated put option:

1. S_T = 100, X = 100	A. An at-the-money put option
2. S_T = 110, X = 100	B. An in-the-money put option
3. S_T = 90, X = 100	C. An out-of-the-money put option

Solution:

Put options are in the money when $S_T < X$, at the money when $S_T = X$, and out of the money when $S_T > X$. Therefore:

1. A is correct. Since $S_T = X = 100$, this is an at-the-money put option.
2. C is correct. Since $S_T > X$, this is an out-of-the-money put option.
3. B is correct. Since $S_T < X$, this is an in-the-money put option.

5. Match the following changes in a factor affecting option value (holding other factors constant) with their corresponding option value change:

1. A higher exercise price (X)	A. Decreases the value of both a call option and a put option
2. A higher underlying price (S_T)	B. Decreases the value of a call option
3. A decline in the volatility of the underlying price	C. Decreases the value of a put option

Solution:

1. B is correct. A higher exercise price decreases the value of a call option; for a given underlying price at maturity (S_T), the call option settlement value of Max (0, $S_T - X$) will decrease for a higher X.
2. C is correct. A higher underlying price (S_T) will decrease the value of a put option. Since a put option is the right to sell an underlying, the put option settlement value of Max (0, $X - S_T$) will fall as S_T rises.
3. A is correct. A decline in the volatility of the underlying price will decrease the value of both a call option and a put option. Lower price variability of the underlying will reduce the probability of a higher positive exercise value for a call or a put option without affecting the downside case where the option expires unexercised.

6. Which of the following statements provides the correct description as to how a call option's value changes if the income on the underlying declines unexpectedly, holding all else equal.

A. The call option value increases.

B. The call option value decreases.

C. The call option value does not change.

Solution:

A is correct. Income or other, non-cash benefits (such as convenience yield) accrue to the owner of an underlying asset but not to the owner of a derivative, whose value is based on the underlying. A call option on an underlying with income has lower value than an identical call option on the same underlying without income. Thus, a decline in income on an underlying asset increases the value of a call option.

OPTION VALUE RELATIVE TO THE UNDERLYING SPOT PRICE

2

☐ explain the exercise value, moneyness, and time value of an option

As shown in earlier lessons, the non-linear or asymmetric payoff profile of an option causes us to approach these derivative instruments differently than for a forward commitment. When evaluating these derivatives, whose value depends critically on whether the spot price crosses an exercise threshold at maturity, buyers and sellers frequently rely on three measures—exercise value, moneyness, and time value—to gauge an option's value over the life of the contract. Recall from an earlier lesson that American options can be exercised at any time, while European options can be exercised only at maturity. This lesson focuses solely on European options with no additional cost or benefit of owning the underlying asset.

OPTION EXERCISE VALUE

3

☐ explain the exercise value, moneyness, and time value of an option

An option buyer will exercise a call or put option at maturity only if it returns a positive payoff—that is:

- $(S_T - X) > 0$ for a call
- $(X - S_T) > 0$ for a put

If not exercised, the option expires worthless and the option buyer's loss equals the premium paid.

At any time *before* maturity ($t < T$), buyers and sellers often gauge an option's value by comparing the underlying spot price (S_t) with the exercise price (X) to determine the option's exercise value at time t. This is the option contract's value *if* the option were exercisable at time t. The exercise value for a call and a put option at time t incorporating the time value of money is the difference between the spot price (S_t) and the present value of the exercise price (PV(X)), as follows:

$$\text{Call Option Exercise Value: } Max\left(0,\ S_t - X(1+r)^{-(T-t)}\right) \quad (1)$$

$$\text{Put Option Exercise Value: } Max\left(0,\ X(1+r)^{-(T-t)} - S_t\right) \quad (2)$$

If we assume an exercise price, X, equal to the forward price, $F_0(T)$, the exercise value of a call option is the *same* as the value of a long forward commitment at time t ($V_t(T)$). This forward commitment was shown earlier to equal S_t – PV($F_0(T)$), *provided that* S_t > PV(X). That is, for a call option where $F_0(T) = X$:

If S_t > PV(X): $S_t - \text{PV}(F_0(T)) = \text{Max}(0, S_t - \text{PV}(X))$

Note that this comparison *ignores* the upfront call option premium paid by the option buyer (c_0 at time $t = 0$).

EXAMPLE 1

Put Option Exercise Value

Consider the case of a one-year put option with an exercise price (X) of EUR 1,000 and a risk-free rate of 1%. What is the exercise value of the option in six months if the spot price (S_t) equals EUR 950?

Use Equation 2 to solve for Max (0, PV(X) – S_t):

$$X(1 + r)^{-(T-t)} - S_t$$

$$= \text{EUR } 45.04\ (= \text{EUR } 1{,}000(1.01)^{-0.5} - \text{EUR } 950)$$

4 OPTION MONEYNESS

☐ explain the exercise value, moneyness, and time value of an option

An option's exercise value at any time t was shown to be its current payoff. The relationship between the option's total value and its exercise price expresses the option's **moneyness**. Examples of in-the-money (ITM) options include a call option whose underlying spot price is *above* the exercise price (X) and a put option with an underlying spot price *below* the exercise price. When the underlying price is *equal to* the exercise price, the put or call option is said to be at the money (ATM). When the underlying price is *below* (*above*) the exercise price for a *call* (*put*) option, the option is less likely to be exercised and is said to be out of the money (OTM).

Also, the *degree* to which an option is in or out of the money affects the sensitivity of an option's price to underlying price changes. For example, a so-called **deep-in-the-money option**, or one that is highly likely to be exercised, usually demonstrates a nearly one-to-one correspondence between option price and underlying price changes. A **deep-out-of-the-money option**, which is very *unlikely* to be exercised, demonstrates far less option price sensitivity for a given underlying price change. In contrast, relatively small price changes in the underlying for an at-the-money option often determine whether the option will be exercised. Moneyness is often used to compare options on the same underlying but with different exercise prices and/or times to maturity. Exhibit 1 shows the moneyness of a call option at maturity and summarizes these relationships.

Exhibit 1: Call Option Moneyness at Maturity

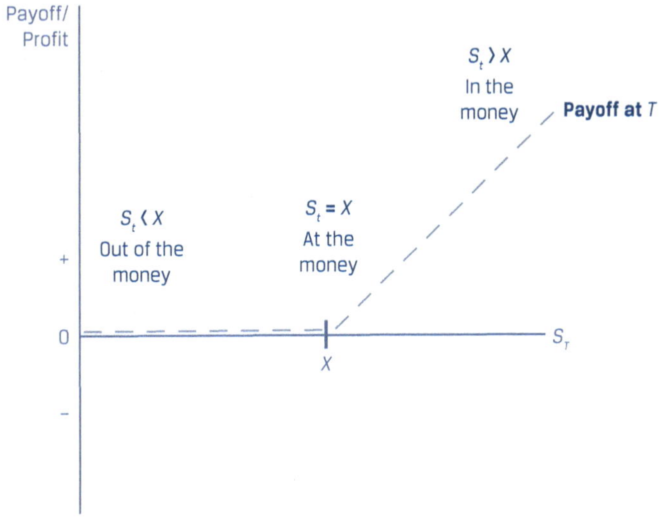

Moneyness	Call option (c_t)	Put option (p_t)
In the money (ITM)	$S_t > X$	$S_t < X$
At the money (ATM)	$S_t = X$	$S_t = X$
Out of the money (OTM)	$S_t < X$	$S_t > X$

EXAMPLE 2

Put Option Moneyness

Recall in Example 1 that at time t, a put option with six months remaining to maturity had an exercise price (X) of EUR 1,000 and an underlying spot price (S_t) of EUR 950. Describe the moneyness of the put option at time t.

Given that the underlying spot price is below the exercise price, the put option is in the money by EUR 50.

OPTION TIME VALUE 5

☐ explain the exercise value, moneyness, and time value of an option

While the exercise value of an option reflects its *current* payoff, an additional component of an option's value is derived from its remaining *time* to maturity. Although European options can be exercised only at maturity, they can be purchased or sold prior to maturity at a price (c_t or p_t, for a call or put, respectively) that reflects the option's *future expected* payoff. A longer time until expiration usually means a higher potential dispersion of the future underlying price for a given level of volatility.

Similarly, an increase in volatility at a specific underlying price for a given time to expiration increases option value for the same reason. We will explore these factors further in a later lesson.

The time value of an option is equal to the difference between the current option price and the option's current payoff (or exercise value):

Call Option Time Value: $Max\left(0,\ S_t - X(1+r)^{-(T-t)}\right)$ (3)

or: $c_t = Max\left(0,\ S_t - X(1+r)^{-(T-t)}\right) + \text{Time Value}$

Put Option Time Value: $p_t - Max\left(0,\ X(1+r)^{-(T-t)} - S_t\right)$ (4)

or: $p_t = Max\left(0,\ X(1+r)^{-(T-t)} - S_t\right) + \text{Time Value}$

That is, the current option price is equal to the sum of its exercise value and time value. As Exhibit 2 shows, the time value of an option is always positive but declines to zero at maturity, a process referred to as **time value decay**.

Exhibit 2: Exercise Value and Time Value of a Call Option

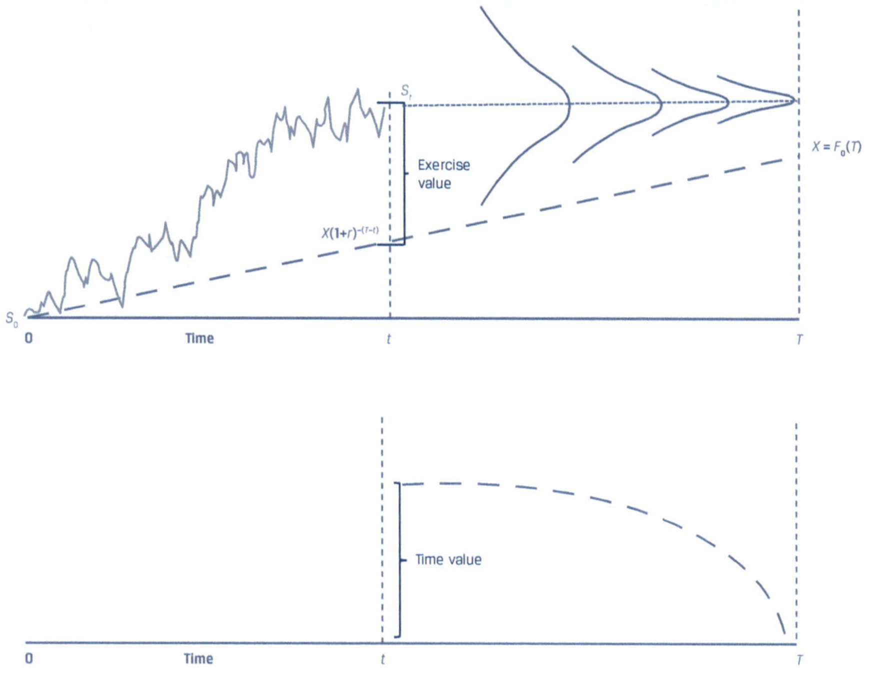

C_t = Exercise value$_t$ + Time value$_t$

EXAMPLE 3

Put Option Time Value

Example 1 showed that a one-year put option with an exercise price (X) of EUR 1,000 had an exercise value of EUR 45.04 with six months remaining to maturity when the spot price (S_t) was EUR 950. If we observe a current put option price (p_t) of EUR 50, what is the time value of the put option?

Use Equation 4 to solve for p_t – Max (0, PV(X) – S_t):

$$p_t - \max\left(0,\ X(1+r)^{-(T-t)} - S_t\right)$$

= EUR 4.96 (= EUR 50 − EUR 45.04)

QUESTION SET

Option Value relative to Underlying Spot Price

1. Describe the similarities and differences between the exercise value of a long put option position with an exercise price (X) equal to the forward price, $F_0(T)$, and a short forward position payoff at maturity with the same underlying details.

   Solution:

   The exercise value of a put option with an exercise price of $X = F_0(T)$ at maturity (Max $(0, X - S_T)$) is the *same* as the payoff of a short forward commitment at maturity ($F_0(T) - S_T$) *as long as* the exercise price is greater than the underlying price. That is, for $F_0(T) = X$:

   If $X > S_T$: $F_0(T) - S_T =$ Max $(0, X - S_T)$

   These payoff profiles will *differ* if $S_T > X$, since the short forward payoff at maturity will require a payment from the seller to the buyer, while the put option owner will allow the option to expire unexercised. Note that this payoff comparison ignores the upfront option premium paid by the put option buyer (p_0) at time $t = 0$.

2. A European put option with three months remaining to maturity on an underlying stock with no additional cash flows has an exercise price (X) of GBP 50, a risk-free rate of 2%, and a current underlying price (S_t) of GBP 55. If the current put option price is GBP 5, calculate the exercise value and the time value and interpret the results.

   Solution:

   An option's value comprises its exercise value plus its time value. The exercise value of a put option is Max (0, PV(X) − S_t) and can be calculated as follows:

   $$\text{Put Option Exercise Value} = Max\left(0,\ X(1+r)^{-(T-t)} - S_t\right)$$

   $$\text{Max}(0,\ \text{GBP } 50(1.02)^{-0.25} - \text{GBP } 55)$$

   $$= 0$$

   The exercise value is zero, as the current underlying price exceeds the present value of the exercise price. The time value is the difference between the option price and the exercise value and represents the possibility that the likelihood and profitability of exercise at maturity may increase due to a favorable price change:

   $$\text{Put Option Time Value} = p_t - Max\left(0,\ X(1+r)^{-(T-t)} - S_t\right)$$

= GBP 5 (= GBP 5 − GBP 0)

The time value is always positive and declines to zero at maturity ($t = T$). Since the put option is out of the money, its value consists *solely* of time value.

3. Match the following underlying price and exercise price relationships with their associated call option:

1. $S_T = 60, X = 50$	A. An at-the-money call option
2. $S_T = 50, X = 50$	B. An in-the-money call option
3. $S_T = 40, X = 50$	C. An out-of-the-money call option

Solution:

Call options are in the money when $S_T > X$, at the money when $S_T = X$, and out of the money when $S_T < X$. Therefore:

1. B is correct. Since $S_T > X$, this is an in-the-money call option.
2. A is correct. Since $S_T = X = 50$, this is an at-the-money call option.
3. C is correct. Since $S_T < X$, this is an out-of-the-money call option.

4. Describe how the moneyness of an option affects how the option's value will change for a given change in the price of the underlying.

Solution:

An increase in the moneyness of an option will increase the sensitivity of its value to changes in the underlying price. For example, an option that is very likely to be exercised will have a nearly one-to-one change in option value for a given change in the underlying price, while an option that is unlikely to be exercised will have a relatively small change in value for a given change in the underlying price.

6 ARBITRAGE

☐ contrast the use of arbitrage and replication concepts in pricing forward commitments and contingent claims

An earlier lesson showed that riskless arbitrage opportunities arise if the "law of one price" does not hold—that is, an identical asset trades at different prices in different places at the same time. In the case of a derivative, we establish no-arbitrage conditions based on the payoff profile at maturity. As shown earlier, forward commitments with a *symmetric* payoff profile settle based on the difference between the forward price, $F_0(T)$, at contract inception ($t = 0$) and the underlying price, S_T, at contract maturity ($t = T$), or $(S_T - F_0(T))$ for a long forward position. For an underlying with no additional cash flows, it was shown that assets with a known future price must have a spot price equal to the future price discounted at the risk-free rate, r: $S_0 = S_T(1 + r)^{-T}$. For purposes of this lesson, we ignore any costs or benefits of owning the underlying other than the opportunity cost (or the risk-free rate, r).

Contingent claims are characterized by *asymmetric* payoff profiles, introduced earlier. In the case of European options representing the right to purchase an underlying (or call option, *c*) or the right to sell an underlying (or put option, *p*) at a given exercise price (*X*) at maturity, the payoff profiles at maturity for an option buyer were shown to be:

$$c_T = \text{Max}\ (0, S_T - X) \quad (5)$$

$$p_T = \text{Max}\ (0, X - S_T) \quad (6)$$

Exhibit 3: European Option Exercise at Expiration

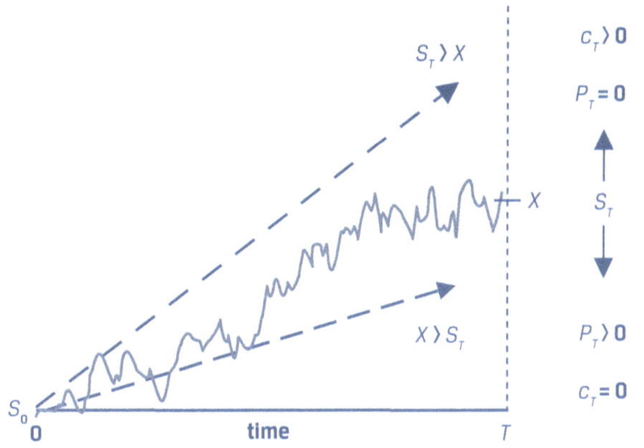

Recall that, unlike forward commitments with an initial price of zero, the option buyer pays the seller a premium (c_0 for a call and p_0 for a put at time $t = 0$), so the option buyer's *profit* at maturity was introduced earlier as follows (ignoring the time value of money):

$$\Pi - \text{Max}\ (0, S_T - X) - c_0 \quad (7)$$

$$\Pi - \text{Max}\ (0, X - S_T) - p_0 \quad (8)$$

Equations 7 and 8 show the key distinction between forward commitments and contingent claims for purposes of arbitrage. The forward buyer enters into the contract with no cash paid upfront and has an unlimited gain or loss (bounded by zero for an underlying such as a stock that cannot have a negative price) at maturity as the underlying price rises or falls. The option buyer, in contrast, will exercise an option at maturity only if it is in the money. This *conditional* nature of option payoff profiles leads us to establish upper and lower no-arbitrage price bounds at any time *t*.

A call option buyer will exercise only if the spot price (S_T) exceeds the exercise price (*X*) at maturity. The *lower* bound of a call price is therefore the underlying's price minus the present value of its exercise price or zero, whichever is greater. In other words, an option which trades below its exercise value violates the no-arbitrage condition. The call buyer will not pay more for the right to purchase an underlying than the price of that underlying, which is the *upper* bound:

$$Max\left(0,\ S_t - X(1+r)^{-(T-t)}\right) < c_t \le S_t \quad (9)$$

$$c_{t,Lower\ bound} = Max\left(0,\ S_t - X(1+r)^{-(T-t)}\right) \quad (10)$$

$$c_{t,Upper\ bound=S_t} \quad (11)$$

A put option buyer will exercise only if the spot price, S_T, is below X at maturity. The exercise price, X, therefore represents the *upper* bound on the put value. The *lower* bound is the present value of the exercise price minus the spot price or zero, whichever is greater:

$$Max\left(0,\ X(1+r)^{-(T-t)} - S_t\right) < p_t \leq X \tag{12}$$

$$p_{t,Lower\ bound} = Max\left(0,\ X(1+r)^{-(T-t)} - S_t\right) \tag{13}$$

$$p_{t,Upper\ bound} = X \tag{14}$$

EXAMPLE 4

Call Option Upper and Lower Bounds

Consider a one-year call option with an exercise price, X, of EUR 1,000. The underlying asset, S_0, trades at EUR 990 at time $t = 0$ and the risk-free rate, r, is 1%. What are the no-arbitrage upper and lower bounds in six months' time if the underlying asset price, S_t, equals EUR 1,050?

As the option buyer will exercise only if $S_T > X$ at $t = T$, the *lower* bound is equal to S_t – PV (X) or zero, whichever is greater:

$$c_{t,Lower\ bound} = Max\left(0,\ S_t - X(1+r)^{-(T-t)}\right)$$

$$c_{t,\text{Lower bound}} = \text{Max}(0,\ \text{EUR } 1{,}050 - \text{EUR } 1{,}000(1.01)^{-0.5})$$

$$c_{t,\text{Lower bound}} = \text{Max}(0,\ \text{EUR } 54.96)$$

The call buyer will not pay more than S_t for the right to purchase the underlying:

$$c_{t,Upper\ bound} = S_t$$

$$c_{t,\text{ Upper bound}} = \text{EUR } 1{,}050$$

7 REPLICATION

- [ ] contrast the use of arbitrage and replication concepts in pricing forward commitments and contingent claims

In an earlier lesson, we used replication to create forward commitment cash flows, utilizing a combination of long or short positions in an underlying asset and borrowing or lending cash. The ability of market participants to use replication strategies ensures that the law of one price holds and no riskless arbitrage profit opportunities exist.

Recall from an earlier lesson that a call option is *similar to* a long forward position in that it increases in value as the underlying price rises but *differs* in that the call option settles only if there is a gain upon exercise. This apparent symmetry for positive outcomes is shown in Exhibit 4, where the exercise price, X, is equal to the forward price, $F_0(T)$.

Exhibit 4: Call Option versus Long Forward Position

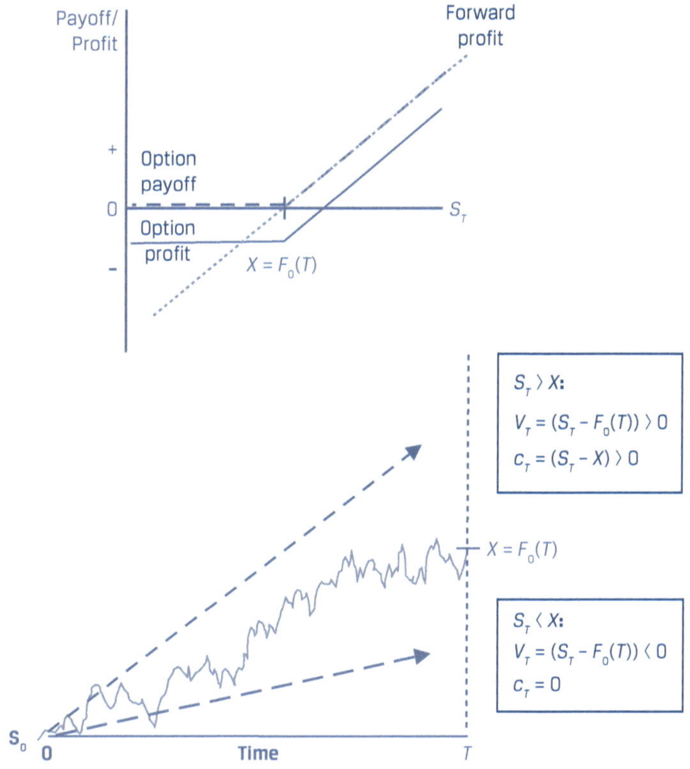

In order to replicate the call option at contract inception ($t = 0$), we also must borrow at the risk-free rate, r, and use the proceeds to purchase the underlying at a price of S_0. At option expiration ($t = T$), unlike in the case of the forward commitment, there are two possible replication outcomes:

- **Exercise** ($S_T > X$): Sell the underlying for S_T and use the proceeds to repay X.
- **No exercise** ($S_T < X$): No settlement is required.

If exercise were certain, we would borrow $X(1 + r)^{-T}$ at inception, as in the case of the forward. However, since it is uncertain, we instead borrow a *proportion* of $X(1 + r)^{-T}$ based on the *likelihood* of exercise at time T, which is closely associated with the moneyness of an option. The non-linear payoff profile of an option requires that the replicating transaction be adjusted as this likelihood changes, while the replicating trades for a forward commitment remain constant. Option replication will be addressed in greater detail in later lessons.

We now turn our attention to put option replication. It was shown earlier that a *short* put position with an exercise price equal to the forward price ($X = F_0(T)$) mirrors the outcomes for a *long* forward position when the underlying price at maturity is *below* the forward price ($S_T < X = F_0(T)$). The sold put *decreases* in value as the underlying price falls, but it settles only if there is a gain upon exercise. This relationship is shown in Exhibit 5, where the exercise price (X) is equal to the forward price, $F_0(T)$.

Exhibit 5: Put Option versus Short Forward Position

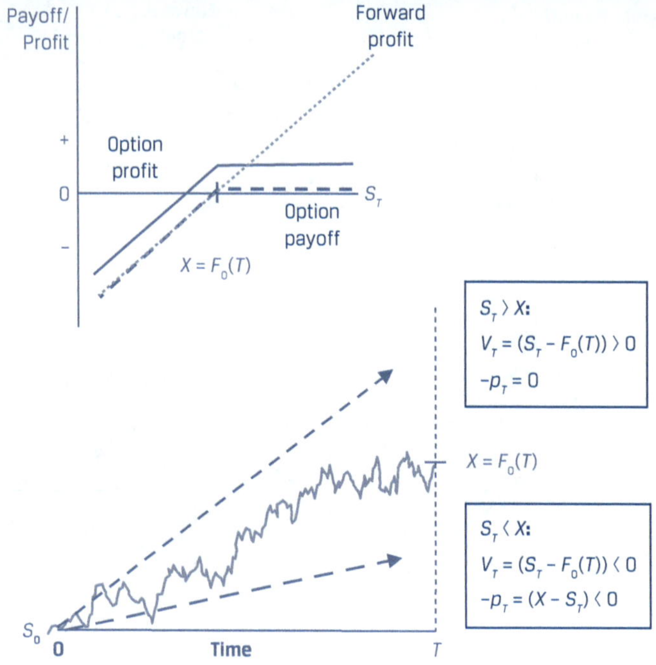

In order to replicate the put option at contract inception (t = 0), we must sell the underlying short at a price of S_0 and lend the proceeds at the risk-free rate, r. At option expiration (t = T), unlike in the case of the forward commitment, there are two possible replication outcomes:

- **Exercise** ($S_T < X$): Purchase the underlying for S_T from the proceeds of the risk-free loan.
- **No exercise** ($S_T > X$): No settlement is required.

If exercise were certain, we would lend $X(1 + r)^{-T}$ at inception, as in the case of the forward. However, as in the case of the call option, the asymmetric payoff profile requires adjustment over time based on the *likelihood* of exercise.

In the next lesson, we will turn our attention to the factors that drive the likelihood of option exercise prior to maturity.

QUESTION SET

Arbitrage and Replication

1. Determine the correct answers to complete the following sentence: The lower bound of a call price is the underlying's price ______ the present value of its ________ price or zero, whichever is greater.

   Solution:

   The lower bound of a call price is the underlying's price *minus* the present value of its *exercise* price or zero, whichever is greater.

2. A six-month European call option on an underlying stock with no additional cash flows has an exercise price (X) of GBP 50, an initial underlying price

(S_0) of GBP 49.75, and a risk-free rate of 2%. Calculate the lower bound of the call price in three months' time if S_t = GBP 65.

Solution:

As the call option buyer will exercise only if $S_T > X$ at maturity, the lower bound is equal to S_t – PV (X) or zero in three months' time, whichever is greater:

$$c_{t,Lower\ bound} = Max\left(0,\ S_t - X(1+r)^{-(T-t)}\right)$$

Given S_t = GBP 65, X = GBP 50, r = 2%, and (T – t) = 0.25, we can solve for the call option's lower bound as follows:

$$c_{t,Lower\ bound} = Max\left(0,\ \text{GBP}65 - \text{GBP}50(1.02)^{-(0.25)}\right)$$

$$= \text{GBP } 15.25$$

3. Match the following statements about replication strategies with their associated derivative instrument(s):

1. At time t = 0, borrow at the risk-free rate and purchase the underlying at S_0.	A. Both a call option and a put option replication strategy
2. The strategy requires adjustment over time as the likelihood of exercise changes.	B. A call option replication strategy
3. At time t = T, receive the loan repayment and purchase the underlying at S_T.	C. A put option replication strategy if exercised

Solution:

1. B is correct. At time t = 0, a call option replication strategy involves borrowing at the risk-free rate and purchasing the underlying.
2. A is correct. As both call and put options have a non-linear payoff profile, the replication strategy requires adjustment over time as the likelihood of exercise changes.
3. C is correct. A put option replication strategy if exercised involves receiving the loan repayment and purchasing the underlying at S_T at time t – T.

4. Explain the key difference between the changes in the replication of a contingent claim versus a forward commitment over the life of the contract.

Solution:

An option has an *asymmetric* payoff profile, since the option buyer will exercise only if the exercise value of the option is positive. Since the likelihood of option exercise changes over time, transactions replicating an option contract must be adjusted over time. A forward commitment has a *symmetric* payoff profile that will settle with certainty at a future date, and therefore the replicating transactions do not require adjustment over the contract life.

8 FACTORS AFFECTING OPTION VALUE

- [ ] identify the factors that determine the value of an option and describe how each factor affects the value of an option

We now turn our attention to identifying and describing factors that affect an option's value. Several of these factors are common to both forward commitments and options, and a number are unique to contingent claims. Factors that determine the value of an option include the value of the underlying, the exercise price, the time to maturity, the risk-free rate, the volatility of the underlying price, and any income or cost associated with owning the underlying asset.

Value of the Underlying

Changes in the value of the underlying will have the same directional effect on the *right* to transact the underlying under an option contract as on the *obligation* to transact under a forward commitment. For example, a call option and a long forward position will both *appreciate* if the spot price of the underlying *rises*, while a put option and a short forward position will both *appreciate* if the spot price of the underlying *falls*, as shown in Exhibit 6.

Exhibit 6: Call and Put Option Value versus Underlying Value

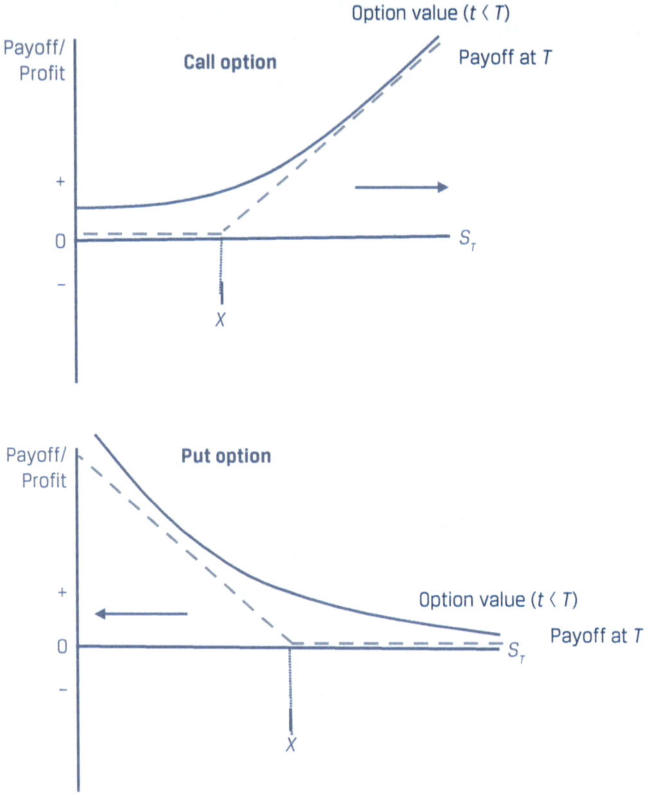

A key distinction between forward commitments and contingent claims is the *magnitude* of a derivative's price change for a given change in the underlying value. For a forward commitment, the derivative's value is a *linear* (one-for-one) function of the underlying price, while for an option it is a *non-linear* relationship that depends on the likelihood that an option buyer will exercise in the future. The more likely it is that the option buyer will exercise (e.g., when the option is in the money), the more sensitive the option's value to the underlying price. This likelihood depends on the relationship between the value of the underlying and the exercise price, a feature unique to option contracts that we turn to next.

Exercise Price

The exercise price is the threshold that determines whether an option buyer chooses to transact at contract maturity. For a call option representing the right to buy the underlying, the exercise price represents a *lower* bound on the option's exercise value at maturity, leading to a *higher* option value for a *lower* exercise price. As call options settle based on Max (0, $S_T - X$) at expiry, a lower X will increase both the likelihood of exercise and the settlement value if exercised.

The exercise price of a put option, in contrast, is an *upper* bound on its exercise value at maturity. A *higher* exercise price at which a put option buyer has the right to sell the underlying will therefore *increase* the value of the option. Exhibit 7 shows these differing effects of exercise price changes for both call and put options.

Exhibit 7: Call and Put Option Value versus Exercise Price

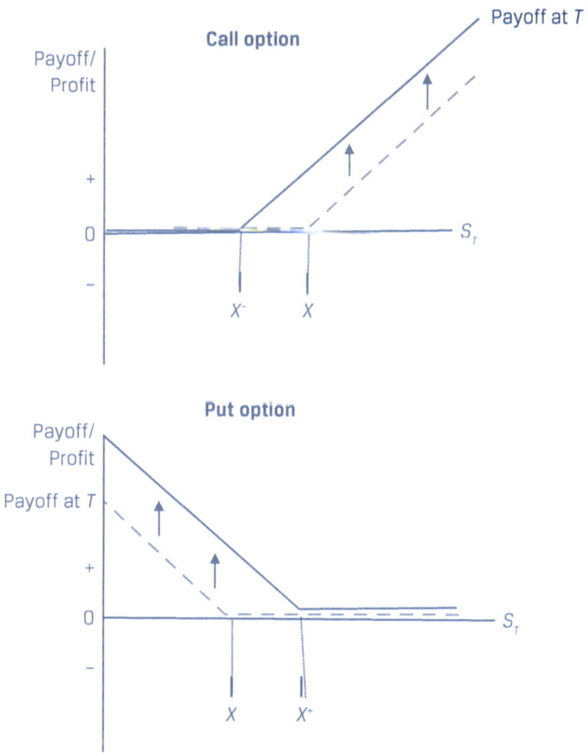

Time to Expiration

Recall from a prior lesson that the time value, or difference between an option's price and its exercise value, represents the likelihood that favorable changes to the underlying price will increase the profitability of exercise. Unlike a long forward position where the buyer is equally likely to experience an increase or a decrease in the underlying price over a longer period, the one-sided (or asymmetric) payoff profile of an option allows the buyer to ignore any outcomes where the option will expire unexercised.

For a call option, a longer time to expiration will increase the option's value in *all* cases. The price appreciation potential of an underlying is essentially unlimited and increases over longer periods, while the downside is limited to the loss of the premium.

A put option representing the right to sell the underlying also usually benefits from the passage of time. In the case of a put option, a longer time to expiration offers greater potential for price *depreciation* below the exercise price, while the loss is limited to the premium if the underlying price rises. However, as put option buyers await the *sale* of the underlying in order to receive $(X - S_T)$ upon exercise, a longer time to expiry *reduces* the present value of the payoff. While less common, in some cases a longer time to expiration will *lower* a put's value, especially for deep-in-the-money puts with a longer time to expiration and a higher risk-free rate of interest.

Risk-Free Interest Rate

An earlier lesson showed the risk-free rate to be the opportunity cost of holding an asset, which extends to the no-arbitrage valuation of derivatives. For example, an option's exercise value was shown to be equal to the difference between the spot price and the *present value* of the exercise price:

Call Option Exercise Value: $\text{Max}(0, (S_t - \text{PV}(X)))$

Put Option Exercise Value: $\text{Max}(0, (\text{PV}(X) - S_t))$

A *higher* risk-free rate therefore *lowers* the present value of the exercise price *provided* an option is in the money. A higher risk-free rate will *increase* the exercise value of a call option and *decrease* the exercise value of a put option. Note that the risk-free rate does not directly affect the time value of an option.

Volatility of the Underlying

Volatility is a measure of the expected dispersion of an underlying asset's future price movements. Higher price volatility of the underlying increases the likelihood of a higher positive exercise value without affecting the downside case in which the option expires unexercised, as shown in Exhibit 8. Note that this effect will be the same for both call options and put options.

For example, as volatility *rises*, a wider range of possible underlying prices *increases* an option's time value and the likelihood that it will end up in the money. *Lower* volatility will *reduce* the time value of both put and call options.

Exhibit 8: Volatility and Option Value

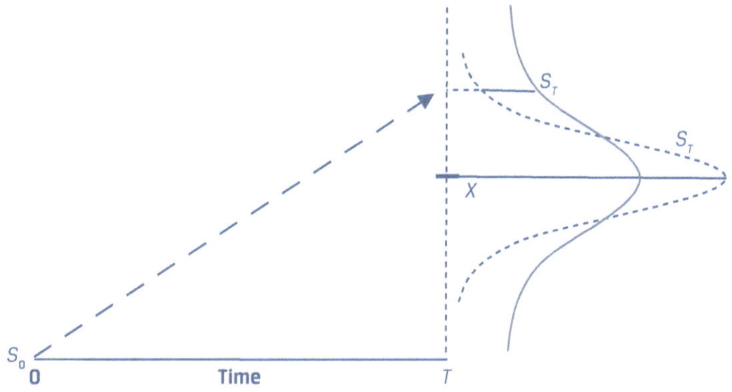

Income or Cost Related to Owning Underlying Asset

In a prior lesson, the benefits and costs of owning an underlying asset over time were shown to affect the relationship of spot versus forward prices. For example, income or other, non-cash benefits (such as convenience yield) accrue to the owner of an underlying asset but not to the owner of a derivative. This effect holds for both forward commitments and contingent claims. Income or other benefits of ownership *decrease* the value of a call and *increase* the value of a put. Carry costs (such as storage and insurance for commodities) have the opposite effect, *increasing* the value of a call option and *decreasing* the value of a put. A summary of the factors that affect an option's value is provided in Exhibit 9, with the sign on the option value referring to the impact (positive or negative) of an *increase* in the factor.

Exhibit 9: Factors That Affect the Value of an Option

Factor	Call Value	Put Value
Value of the underlying	+	−
Exercise price	−	+
Time to expiration	+	+/−
Risk-free interest rate	+	−
Volatility of the underlying	+	+
Income/cost related to owning the underlying	−/+	+/−

QUESTION SET

Factors That Affect Option Value

1. Determine the correct answers to complete the following sentence: For a call option representing the right to buy the underlying, the exercise price represents a ______ bound on an option's exercise value at maturity, leading to a ______ option value for a lower exercise price.

   Solution:

   For a call option representing the right to buy the underlying, the exercise price represents a *lower* bound on an option's exercise value at maturity, leading to a *higher* option value for a lower exercise price.

2. Match the following changes in factors affecting option value (holding other factors constant) with their corresponding option value change:

1. A lower exercise price (X)	A. Increases the value of both a call option and a put option
2. A lower underlying price (S_T)	B. Increases the value of a call option
3. A rise in the volatility of the underlying price	C. Increases the value of a put option

   Solution:

   1. B is correct. A lower exercise price increases the value of a call option, since for a given underlying price at maturity of S_T, the call option settlement value of Max $(0, S_T - X)$ will increase for a lower X.
   2. C is correct. A lower underlying price (S_T) will increase the value of a put option. Since a put option is the right to sell an underlying at the exercise price (X), the put option settlement value of Max $(0, X - S_T)$ will increase as S_T declines.
   3. A is correct. A rise in the volatility of the underlying price will increase the value of both a call option and a put option. Greater price variability of the underlying will increase the probability of a higher positive exercise value for a call or a put option without affecting the downside case where the option expires unexercised.

3. Determine the correct answers to complete the following sentences: A key distinction between forward commitments and contingent claims is the __________ of a derivative's price change for a given change in the underlying value. For a forward commitment, the derivative value is a ______ function of the underlying price, while for an option it is a _______ relationship.

   Solution:

   A key distinction between forward commitments and contingent claims is the *magnitude* of a derivative's price change for a given change in the underlying value. For a forward commitment, the derivative value is a *linear* function of the underlying price, while for an option it is a *non-linear* relationship.

4. Explain the effect of a *decrease* in the risk-free rate of interest on the value of put and call options and justify your answer.

Solution:

A *decrease* in the risk-free rate *increases* the present value of an option's exercise *price* (PV(X)). The exercise value for an *in-the-money call* option will fall, since (S_t – PV(X)) is lower for a higher PV(X), while the exercise value for an *in-the-money put* option will rise, since (PV(X) – S_t) rises for a higher PV(X). Note that the time value of an option is not directly affected by the risk-free rate.

PRACTICE PROBLEMS

The following information relates to questions 1-9

The Viswan Family Office (VFO) owns non-dividend-paying shares of Biomian Limited that are currently priced (S_0) at INR 295 per share. VFO's CIO is considering an offer to sell shares at a forward price ($F_0(T)$) of INR 300.84 per share in six months based on a risk-free rate of 4%. You have been asked to advise on the purchase of a put option or the sale of a call option with an exercise price (X) equal to the forward price ($F_0(T)$) as alternatives to a forward share sale.

1. Which of the following statements correctly describes the put option and call option premiums given the relationship between Biomian's current price of INR 295 and the exercise price equal to the forward price of INR 300.84?

   A. The call option's premium consists solely of time value, and the put option's premium consists solely of exercise value.

   B. The call option's premium consists solely of exercise value, and the put option's premium consists solely of time value.

   C. The call option's premium consists solely of time value, and the put option's premium consists solely of time value.

2. Which of the following statements correctly describes an important distinction between the two strategies of buying a put option and selling a call option with respect to option time value decay?

   A. Time value decay is a benefit to both option strategies.

   B. Time value decay is a cost to both option strategies.

   C. Time value decay is a benefit to selling a call option and a cost to buying a put option.

3. VFO is considering the purchase of the put option to hedge against a decline in Biomian's share price. Which of the following statements best characterizes the trade-off between the put and the forward based on no-arbitrage pricing?

   A. The gain on the forward sale will *equal* the purchased put option's profit at maturity *provided* the put option ends up in the money at maturity.

   B. The loss on the forward sale will *exceed* the loss on the purchased put at maturity if Biomian's share price exceeds the forward price by more than the initial put premium paid.

   C. We do not have enough information to answer this question, since we do not know the time value of the option at maturity.

4. In evaluating the purchased put strategy (with $X = F_0(T)$), the CIO has asked you to consider selling the put in three months' time if its price appreciates over that period. Which of the following best characterizes the no-arbitrage put price at

that time?

A. As VFO will exercise only if the spot price is below the exercise price, the lower bound of the put price is the greater of zero and the present value of the spot price minus the exercise price.

B. As VFO will exercise only if the spot price is below the exercise price, the upper bound of the put price equals the present value of the exercise price minus the spot price.

C. The put price can be no greater than the forward price and no less than the greater of zero and the present value of the exercise price minus the spot price.

5. VFO is considering a sold call strategy to generate income from the sale of a call. In your scenario analysis of the sold call option alternative, VFO has asked you to value the call option in three months' time if Biomian's spot price is INR 325 per share. Given an estimated call price of INR 46.41 at that time, which of the following correctly reflects the relationship between the call's exercise value and its time value?

A. The call's exercise value is INR 24.16, and its time value is INR 22.25.

B. The call's exercise value is INR 27.10, and its time value is INR 19.31.

C. The call's exercise value is INR 20.99, and its time value is INR 25.42.

6. Which of the following statements correctly describes how VFO could replicate selling a call option on Biomian if exercise is certain?

A. Borrow $X(1 + r)^{-T}$ at the risk-free rate and use the proceeds to buy Biomian stock at the current spot price, S_0. At expiration, sell the Biomian stock and use the proceeds to pay off the loan.

B. Sell short Biomian stock at the current spot price, S_0, and use the proceeds to lend $X(1 + r)^{-T}$ at the risk-free rate. At expiration, receive X as repayment of the risk-free loan and buy back the Biomian stock.

C. Sell short Biomian stock at the current spot price, S_0, and borrow $X(1 + r)^{-T}$ at the risk-free rate. At expiration, pay off the risk-free loan of X and buy back the Biomian stock.

7. In comparing the sold call and purchased put strategies at the forward price, VFO's CIO is concerned about how an increase in the volatility of the underlying Biomian shares affects option premiums. Which of the following statements about volatility change and its effect on strategy is most accurate?

A. An increase in the volatility of the underlying shares has the *same* effect on call and put option values, so this change should not affect VFO's strategy decision.

B. Since changes in the volatility of the underlying shares have the *opposite* effect on put versus call options, this change will increase the attractiveness of the put strategy versus the call strategy.

C. An increase in the volatility of the underlying shares will increase both the *cost* of the purchased put strategy and the premium received on the sold call strategy, so this change will increase the attractiveness of the call strategy versus the put strategy.

8. In comparing the Biomian purchased put and sold call strategies, which of the following statements is most correct about how the call and put values are affected by changes in factors other than volatility?

   A. Changes in the time to expiration and the risk-free rate have a similar directional effect on the put and call strategies, while changes in the exercise price tend to have the opposite effect.

   B. Changes in the time to expiration tend to have a similar directional effect on the put and call strategies, while changes in the exercise price and the risk-free rate tend to have the opposite effect.

   C. Changes in the risk-free rate have a similar directional effect on the put and call strategies, while changes in the exercise price and the time to expiration tend to have the opposite effect.

9. VFO is concerned about the potential for increasing interest rates in the future. Which of the following statements provides the most correct description as to how rising rates after entering into the two option strategies would affect the option valuations?

   A. Rising risk-free rates would make the selling a call option strategy more advantageous to VFO because call options increase in value with higher risk-free rates.

   B. Rising risk-free rates would make the buying a put option strategy more advantageous to VFO because the company locks in the put option premium at lower interest rates.

   C. Rising risk-free rates are a negative for both option strategies.

SOLUTIONS

1. C is correct. The exercise value of both the call and put options are zero because the present value of the exercise price is INR 295, which is equivalent to the stock price of INR 295. Thus, both option premiums reflect time value only. A is incorrect as this statement does not properly account for the discounting of the exercise price. B is incorrect as the call option's premium does not reflect exercise value.

2. C is correct. The time value component of an option premium declines toward zero as time passes toward the expiration date. A purchased option declines in value, all else equal, because of the time value decline. A sold option increases in value, all else equal, because of the time value decline. A is incorrect as time value decay is a cost to the purchased put option strategy, and B is incorrect as time value decay is a benefit to the sold option strategy.

3. The correct answer is B. The loss on the forward sale will be greater than the loss on the purchased put at maturity if Biomian's share price exceeds the forward price by more than the initial put premium. VFO's downside return is limited to the put premium paid, while the forward sale has unlimited downside as Biomian shares appreciate. A is incorrect as it does not take the put premium paid into account, while C is incorrect as the time value of an option is equal to zero at maturity.

4. The correct answer is C. The put exercise price, X (equal to $F_0(T)$ in this case), represents the *upper* bound on the put value, while the *lower* bound is the greater of the present value of the exercise price minus the spot price and zero:

   $$\text{Max}\left(0,\ X(1+r)^{-(T-t)} - S_t\right) < p_t \leq X$$

   A is incorrect, as the *lower* bound of the put price is the greater of zero and the present value of the exercise price minus the spot price, not the present value of the spot price minus the exercise price. B is incorrect, as the *lower*, not the upper, bound of the put price equals the present value of the exercise price minus the spot price.

5. The correct answer is B. The option price is equal to the sum of the exercise value and the time value. A call option's exercise value is equal to the greater of zero and the spot price minus the present value of the exercise price:

   $$Max\left(0,\ S_t - X(1+r)^{-(T-t)}\right)$$

   $= \text{Max}(0, \text{INR}325 - \text{INR}300.84(1.04)^{-0.25})$

   $= \text{INR}27.10$

   The time value is equal to the call price minus the exercise value, or INR 19.31 (= INR46.41 – INR27.10). A is incorrect as it takes the spot price minus the exercise price as the exercise value, while C calculates the exercise value as the present value of the spot price minus the exercise price.

6. B is correct. To replicate selling a call option, combine shorting the underlying with risk-free lending. This is exactly the opposite strategy to replicate buying a call option in which the underlying is purchased with proceeds from risk-free borrowing. A is incorrect as this statement describes replicating buying a call option. C is incorrect as selling short and borrowing initially creates two cash

inflows at $t = 0$ followed by two cash outflows at $t = T$.

7. The correct answer is C. An increase in the volatility of the underlying share price will increase both the upfront premium received on the sold call option and the premium paid on the purchased put option. Therefore, since the purchased put strategy involves an increased upfront payment made by VFO and the sold call strategy involves an increased premium received, the volatility increase will increase the attractiveness of the call strategy versus the put strategy.

8. The correct answer is B. Changes in the time to expiration tend to have a similar directional effect on the put and call strategies (the only exception being deep-in-the-money put options in some cases), while changes in the exercise price and the risk-free rate tend to have the opposite effect.

9. C is correct. Because both option strategies (buy a put or sell a call) are short strategies, VFO is delaying cash inflows so higher risk-free rates are negative. A is incorrect as this statement describes the value effect from buying a call option, not from selling. B is incorrect as the locked-in premium will decline after rising risk-free rates.

LEARNING MODULE

9

Option Replication Using Put–Call Parity

LEARNING OUTCOMES

Mastery	The candidate should be able to:
☐	explain put–call parity for European options
☐	explain put–call *forward* parity for European options

INTRODUCTION

1

Previous lessons examined the payoff and profit profiles of call options and put options, the upper and lower bounds of an option's value, and the factors impacting option values. In doing so, we contrasted the asymmetry of one-sided option payoffs with the linear or symmetric payoff of forwards and underlying assets.

We now extend this analysis further to show that there are ways to *combine* options to have an equivalent payoff to that of the underlying and a risk-free asset as well as a forward commitment. In the first lesson, we demonstrate that the value of a European call may be used to derive the value of a European put option with the same underlying details, and vice versa, under a no-arbitrage condition referred to as put–call parity. In the second lesson, we show how this may be extended to forward commitments and how the put–call parity relationship may be applied to option and other investment strategies. We will focus on European options on underlying assets with no income or benefit.

LEARNING MODULE OVERVIEW

- Put–call parity establishes a relationship that allows the price of a call option to be derived from the price of a put option with the same underlying details and vice versa.
- Put–call parity holds for European options with the same exercise price and expiration date, representing a no-arbitrage relationship between put option, call option, underlying asset, and risk-free asset prices.
- If put–call parity does not hold, then riskless arbitrage profit opportunities may be available to investors.

- Put–call forward parity extends the put–call parity relationship to forward contracts given the equivalence of an underlying asset position and a long forward contract plus a risk-free bond.
- Under put–call forward parity, we may demonstrate that a purchased put option and a sold call option are equivalent to a long risk-free bond and short forward position, and a sold put and purchased call are equivalent to a long forward and short risk-free bond.
- Put–call parity may be applied beyond option-based strategies in finance—for example, to demonstrate that equity holders have a position equivalent to a purchased call option on the value of the firm with unlimited upside, while debtholders have a sold put option position on firm value with limited upside.

LEARNING MODULE SELF-ASSESSMENT

These initial questions are intended to help you gauge your current level of understanding of this learning module.

1. Which of the following statements correctly describes the equivalent to a long position in an underlying according to put–call parity?

   A. Long a put option on the underlying, short a call option on the underlying, and long a risk-free bond

   B. Short a put option on the underlying, long a call option on the underlying, and long a risk-free bond

   C. Short a put option on the underlying, long a call option on the underlying, and short a risk-free bond

   Solution:

   B is correct. Put–call parity demonstrates that a long underlying position is equivalent to a sold put option, a purchased call option, and a long risk-free bond. This is shown in the following equation:

   Put–call parity: $S_0 + p_0 = c_0 + X(1 + r)^{-T}$ implies $S_0 = -p_0 + c_0 + X(1 + r)^{-T}$.

2. Identify which of the following positions has the same no-arbitrage value as which portfolio under put–call parity:

1. Long call option (c_0)	A. Long underlying, short risk-free bond, and short call option
2. Short risk-free bond ($-X(1 + r)^{-T}$)	B. Long underlying, long put option, and short risk-free bond
3. Short put option ($-p_0$)	C. Short underlying, long call option, and short put option

   Solution:

   Recall that the put–call parity relationship may be expressed as

   $S_0 + p_0 = c_0 + X(1 + r)^{-T}$.

   1. B is correct. A long call option position is the no-arbitrage equivalent of a long underlying position, a long put option, and a short risk-free bond position.

2. C is correct. A short risk-free bond position is equivalent to a short underlying position, a long call option, and a short put option.

3. A is correct. A short put option is equivalent to a long underlying position, a short risk-free bond, and a short call option.

3. Which of the following statements correctly describes a synthetic protective put position according to put–call forward parity?

   A. A long forward contract on the underlying, a long put option on the underlying, and short a risk-free bond

   B. A short forward contract on the underlying, a long put option on the underlying, and short a risk-free bond

   C. A short forward contract on the underlying, a short put option on the underlying, and short a risk-free bond

Solution:

A is correct. The formula for put–call forward parity is as follows:

$F_0(T)(1 + r)^{-T} + p_0 = c_0 + X(1 + r)^{-T}$.

Rearranging the terms as follows shows the synthetic protective put position on the left-hand side of the equation:

$F_0(T)(1 + r)^{-T} + p_0 - X(1 + r)^{-T} = c_0$.

4. Which of the following statements best describes a shareholder's claim in terms of an option payoff?

   A. Shareholder payoff resembles the payoff of a put option on firm value.

   B. Shareholder payoff resembles the payoff of a covered call option on firm value.

   C. Shareholder payoff resembles the payoff of a call option on firm value.

Solution:

C is correct. When considering shareholder claims in option terms, the shareholder payoff resembles a call option on firm value.

PUT–CALL PARITY 2

☐ explain put–call parity for European options

A prior lesson contrasted no-arbitrage pricing conditions and the replication of cash flows for forward commitments and contingent claims. Forwards have zero initial value and their *certain* payoff, which is replicated at inception by borrowing to purchase the underlying or selling the underlying and lending the sale proceeds. Option buyers pay an upfront premium, and their *contingent* payoff profiles lead us to establish upper and lower no-arbitrage price bounds. Option replication is similar to that of a forward but involves borrowing or lending to buy or sell a *proportion* of the underlying, which is adjusted as the moneyness of an option changes. We now extend this analysis using a combination of positions.

In this section, we show how combining cash and derivative instruments into a portfolio in a certain way enables us to price and value these positions without directly modeling them using no-arbitrage conditions. Consider an investor whose goal is to benefit from upward movements in the value of an underlying but who wants to protect her investment from downward movements in the underlying's value. Consider the following two portfolios, shown in Exhibit 1:

1. At $t = 0$, an investor purchases a call option (c_0) on an underlying with an exercise price of X and a risk-free bond today that pays X at $t = T$. The cost of this strategy is $c_0 + X(1 + r)^{-T}$, where we assume the option expires at time T.
2. At $t = 0$, an investor purchases an underlying unit (S_0) and a put option on the underlying (p_0) with an exercise price of X at $t = T$. The cost of this strategy is $p_0 + S_0$.

Exhibit 1 shows the payoff of the individual components of these two portfolios.

Exhibit 1: Payoffs at Time T for Two Portfolios

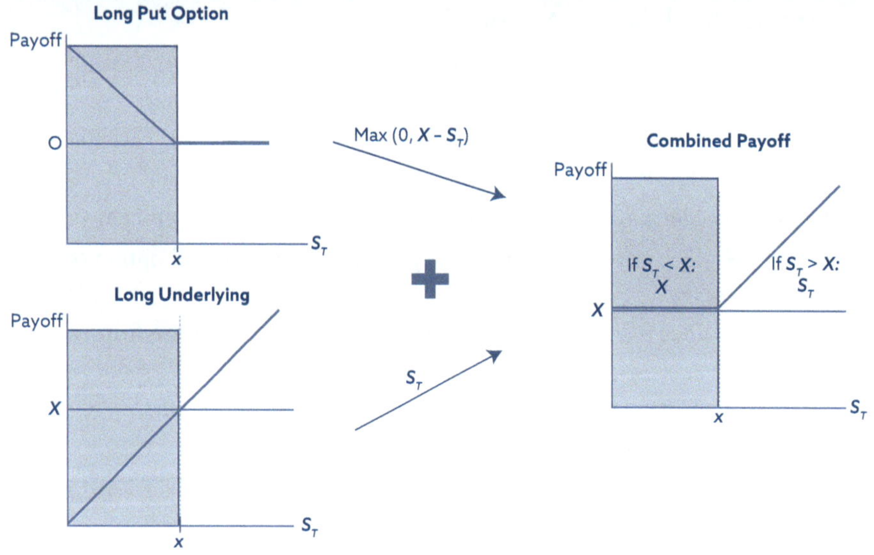

At first glance, these portfolios appear to offer the investor a similar opportunity to benefit from underlying asset appreciation without exposure to an underlying price decline below the exercise price.

In the first case (Portfolio 1), the investor buys a call option with a positive payoff if the underlying asset price rises above the exercise price ($S_T > X$) and invests cash in a risk-free bond. Since the risk-free asset pays X at time T, the investor pays $c_0 + X(1 + r)^{-T}$ at time $t = 0$. This combination of a purchased call and a risk-free bond is known as a **fiduciary call** and is shown in Exhibit 2.

Exhibit 2: Portfolio 1 (Fiduciary Call) Payoff at Time *T*

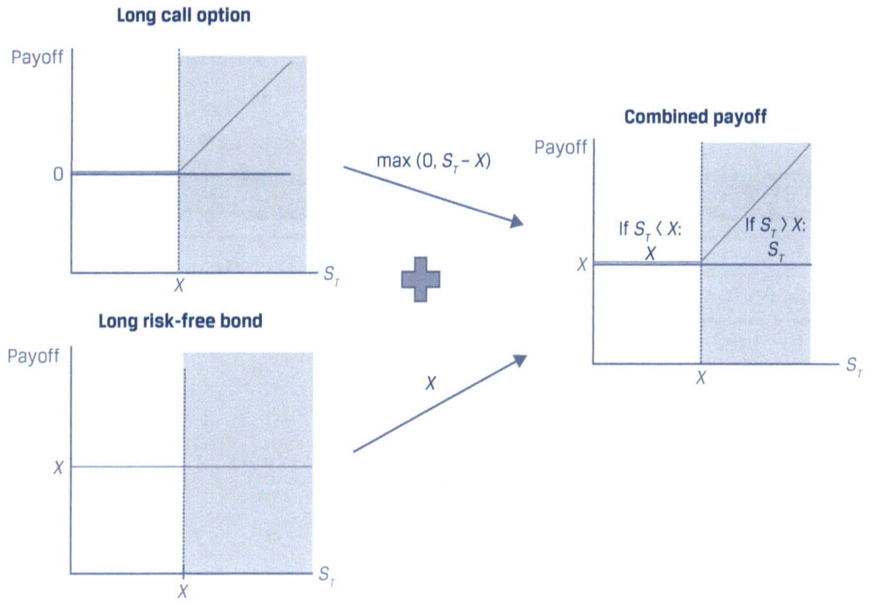

In the second instance (Portfolio 2) in Exhibit 1, the investor pays $S_0 + p_0$ at inception and is hedged if the underlying price falls below X. This strategy of holding an underlying asset and purchasing a put on the same asset is sometimes called a **protective put**. The payoff for Portfolio 2 at time T is shown in Exhibit 3.

Exhibit 3: Portfolio 2 (Protective Put) Payoff at Time *T*

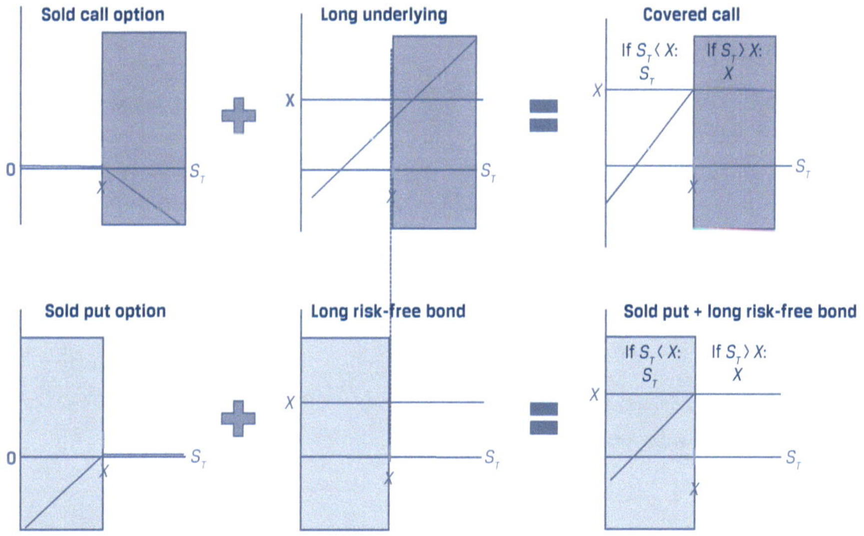

Despite their differences, these two portfolios have identical payoff profiles, as evidenced by Exhibit 2 and Exhibit 3. Recall that no-arbitrage conditions require two assets with identical future cash flows to trade at the same price, ignoring transaction costs. In Exhibit 4, we evaluate this in the case of the two portfolios by comparing their cash flows under all possible scenarios at time $t = T$.

Exhibit 4: Protective Put vs. Fiduciary Call at Expiration

Portfolio Position	Put Exercised ($S_T < X$)	No Exercise ($S_T = X$)	Call Exercised ($S_T > X$)
Protective Put:			
Underlying Asset	S_T	S_T	S_T
Put Option	$X - S_T$	0	0
Total:	X	$S_T (= X)$	S_T
Fiduciary Call:			
Call Option	0	0	$S_T - X$
Risk-Free Asset	X	X	X
Total:	X	$X (= S_T)$	S_T

These two portfolios have cash flows that are identical at time T under each scenario, and the prices of these portfolios must be equal at $t = 0$ to satisfy the no-arbitrage condition in a relationship commonly referred to as **put–call parity**:

$$S_0 + p_0 = c_0 + X(1 + r)^{-T}.$$

In other words, under put–call parity, at $t = 0$ the price of the long underlying asset plus the long put must equal the price of the long call plus the risk-free asset.

EXAMPLE 1

Biomian Put–Call Parity

In an earlier example, the Viswan Family Office (VFO) held non-dividend-paying Biomian shares currently priced (S_0) at INR295 per share. VFO is considering the purchase of a six-month put on Biomian shares at an exercise price, X, of INR265. If VFO's chief investment officer observes a traded six-month call option price of INR59 per share for the same INR265 exercise price, what should he expect to pay for the put per share if the relevant risk-free rate is 4%?

From Equation 1, the put–call parity relationship was shown as

$$S_0 + p_0 = c_0 + X(1 + r)^{-T}.$$

We can solve for the risk-free bond price as INR259.85 (= INR265(1.04)$^{-0.5}$) and substitute into Equation 1:

$$\text{INR295} + p_0 = \text{INR59} + \text{INR259.85}.$$

$$p_0 = \text{INR23.85}.$$

VFO should expect to pay a six-month put option premium of p_0 = INR23.85.

Arbitrage profit opportunities arise if these portfolios trade at different prices. As in the case of individual assets, an investor able to borrow and lend at the risk-free rate can earn a riskless profit if either portfolio is mispriced, as shown in the following example.

EXAMPLE 2

VFO Put–Call Parity Arbitrage Opportunity

As in Example 1, the Viswan Family Office holds non-dividend-paying Biomian shares at a price (S_0) of INR295 per share. VFO is considering the purchase of a put for which it expects to pay INR23.85 but which is instead currently priced at INR30. Assuming a risk-free rate of 4%, identify the arbitrage opportunity and the steps VFO might take to earn a riskless profit.

From Equation 1, the put–call parity relationship is

$$S_0 + p_0 = c_0 + X(1 + r)^{-T}.$$

Substituting the values from Example 1 and the current put price into Equation 1 gives us the following result:

$$\text{INR295} + \text{INR30} > \text{INR59} + \text{INR259.85},$$

$$\text{so, } S_0 + p_0 > c_0 + X(1 + r)^{-T}.$$

By selling the put and the shares and purchasing the call and the risk-free asset at $t = 0$, VFO has a positive cash flow of INR6.15 (= INR295 + INR30 – INR59 – INR259.85), or $S_0 + p_0 - c_0 - X(1 + r)^{-T}$, as shown in the following diagram.

Arbitrage Position	Cash Flow at $t = 0$	Put Exercised ($S_T < X$)	No Exercise ($S_T = X$)	Call Exercised ($S_T > X$)
Protective Put:				
Sell Underlying Asset	S_0	$-S_T$	$-S_T$	$-S_T$
Sell Put Option	p_0	$-(X - S_T)$	0	0
Total:	$S_0 + p_0$	$-X$	$-S_T (= X)$	$-S_T$
Fiduciary Call:				
Buy Call Option	$-c_0$	0	0	$(S_T - X)$
Buy Risk-Free Asset	$-X(1 + r)^{-T}$	X	X	X
Total:	$-c_0 - X(1 + r)^{-T}$	X	$X (= S_T)$	S_T
Overall Portfolio:	$S_0 + p_0 - c_0 - X(1 + r)^{-T}$	0	0	0

Note that the combined cash flows of the two portfolios are equal to zero under each scenario at time $t = T$, leaving VFO with an arbitrage profit of INR6.15.

OPTION STRATEGIES BASED ON PUT–CALL PARITY 3

☐ explain put–call parity for European options

The put–call parity relationship established between call option, put option, underlying asset, and risk-free asset pricing in the previous section provides the foundation for thinking about replication and pricing of individual derivative positions, cash positions, and option-based strategies.

For example, if we rearrange Equation 1 to solve for the put option premium, p_0, we find that it may be derived from a combination of a long call option (c_0), a long risk-free bond ($X(1 + r)^{-T}$), and a short position in the underlying ($-S_0$), as shown in Equation 2 and Exhibit 5.

$$p_0 = c_0 + X(1 + r)^{-T} - S_0. \quad (1)$$

Note that Equation 2 is both a statement of what the price of the put option should be and also sets out a replicating portfolio for that put option using a call option, the underlying, and a risk-free bond, as shown in Exhibit 5.

Exhibit 5: Put Option as a Long Call, Long Bond, and Short Underlying

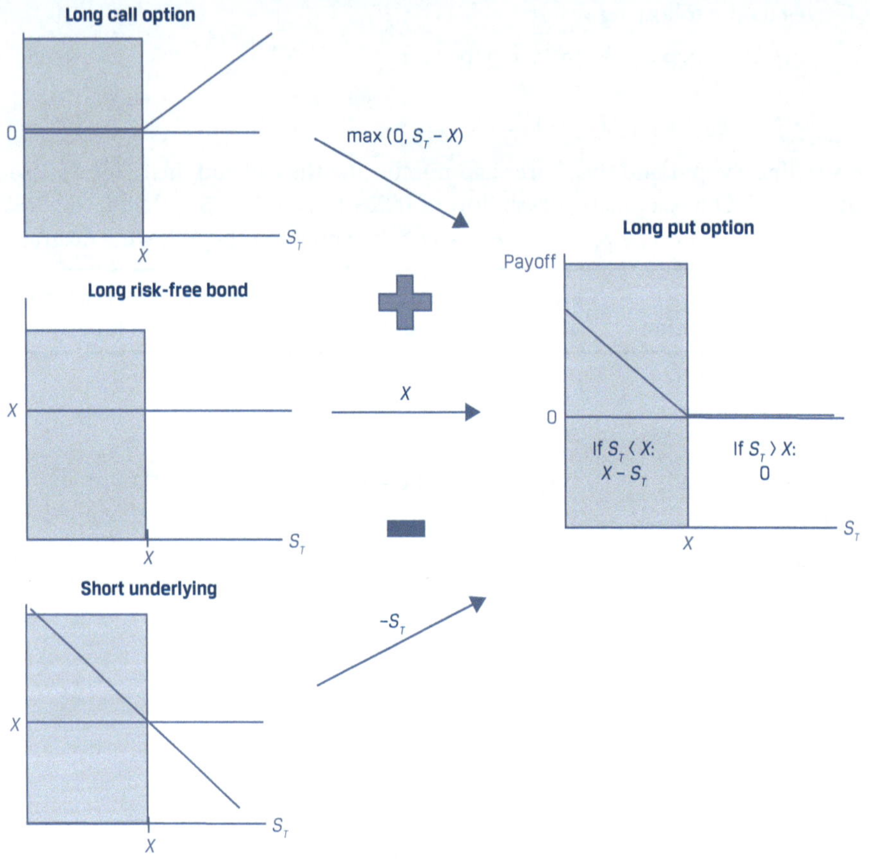

What is more, we may also demonstrate that the asymmetric payoff profiles of put and call options effectively offset one another in a no-arbitrage condition when combined to solve for the price of the underlying, as follows:

$$S_0 = c_0 - p_0 + X(1 + r)^{-T}. \quad (2)$$

Exhibit 6 summarizes the equivalence of these individual positions in terms of replicating positions using other cash and derivative positions.

Exhibit 6: Replication of Individual Positions under Put–Call Parity

Position	Underlying (S_0)	Risk-Free Bond ($X(1 + r)^{-T}$)	Call Option (c_0)	Put Option (p_0)
Underlying (S_0)	—	Long	Long	Short
Risk-free bond ($X(1 + r)^{-T}$)	Long	—	Short	Long
Call option (c_0)	Long	Short	—	Long
Put option (p_0)	Short	Long	Long	—

These building blocks are used not only to generate riskless profits in the case of mispricing but also to create other option-based strategies, such as in the following example.

EXAMPLE 3

VFO Covered Call Strategy

Recall from an earlier example that the Viswan Family Office holds non-dividend-paying Biomian shares currently priced (S_0) at INR295 per share. Since VFO's chief investment officer believes Biomian's share price will appreciate over the long term but remain relatively unchanged for the next six months, he would like to *sell* a six-month call option at a INR325 exercise price (X) to generate short-term income in what is known as a covered call strategy.

Using put–call parity, how can he replicate this position using a risk-free bond (the risk-free rate is 4%) and a put option, and what is the expected call option premium if the put option has a price of INR56?

The covered call strategy consists of a *long* position in the underlying and a *short* call option, or ($S_0 - c_0$) at inception. Recall from Equation 1 that put–call parity is shown as

$$S_0 + p_0 = c_0 + X(1 + r)^{-T}.$$

We may rearrange these terms to solve for ($S_0 - c_0$):

$$S_0 - c_0 = X(1 + r)^{-T} - p_0.$$

The covered call position is therefore equivalent to a *long* risk-free bond and a *short* put option, as shown in the following diagram.

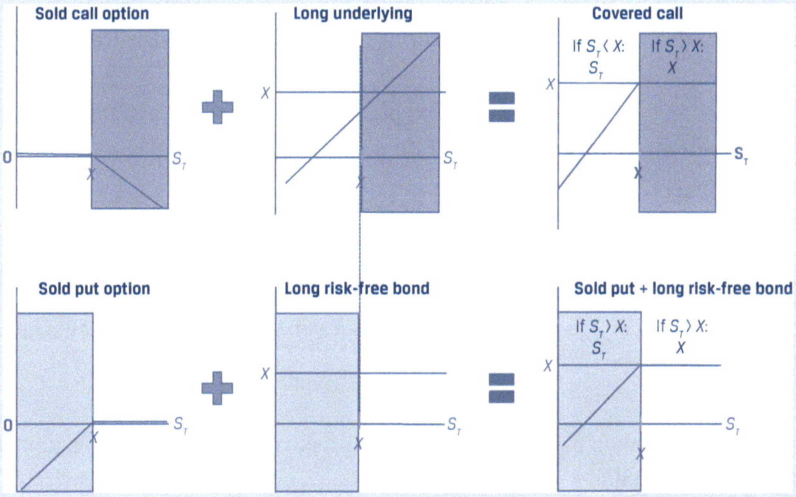

We may solve for the no-arbitrage call price, c_0, using put–call parity by substituting terms into the following equation:

$S_0 - c_0 = X(1 + r)^{-T} - p_0$.

INR295 – c_0 = INR325$(1.04)^{-0.5}$ – INR56.

c_0 = INR32.31.

QUESTION SET

Put–Call Parity

1. Determine the correct answers to complete the following sentence: If two portfolios have cash flows that are ________ at time T under each scenario, then the no-arbitrage prices of those portfolios must ________ one another at $t = 0$ in a relationship commonly referred to as put–call parity.

Solution:

If two portfolios have cash flows that are *identical* at time T under each scenario, then the no-arbitrage prices of those portfolios must *equal* one another at $t = 0$ in a relationship commonly referred to as put–call parity.

2. Identify which of the following positions has the same no-arbitrage value as which portfolio under put–call parity:

1. Short call option ($-c_0$)	A. Short underlying, long risk-free bond, and long call option
2. Long risk-free bond ($X(1 + r)^{-T}$)	B. Short underlying, short put option, and long risk-free bond
3. Long put option (p_0)	C. Long underlying, short call option, and long put option

Solution:

Recall that the put-call parity relationship may be expressed as

$S_0 + p_0 = c_0 + X(1 + r)^{-T}$.

1. B is correct. A short call option position is the no-arbitrage equivalent of a short underlying position, a short put option, and a long risk-free bond position.

2. C is correct. A long risk-free bond position is equivalent to a long underlying position, a short call option, and a long put option.

3. A is correct. A long put option is equivalent to a short underlying position, a long risk-free bond, and a long call option.

3. Determine the correct answer to complete the following sentence: The combination of a ________ call and a risk-free bond position is known as a fiduciary call.

Solution:

The combination of a *purchased* call and a risk-free bond position is known as a fiduciary call.

4. Identify the following statement as true or false, and justify your answer: The covered call strategy consists of a long position in the underlying and a long call option, or ($S_0 + c_0$) at inception.

   Solution:

   The statement is false. The covered call strategy consists of a *long* position in the underlying and a *short* call option, or ($S_0 - c_0$) at inception.

PUT–CALL FORWARD PARITY AND OPTION APPLICATIONS 4

☐ explain put–call *forward* parity for European options

Forward commitment replication was shown in earlier lessons to involve borrowing at the risk-free rate to purchase the underlying in the case of a long position or selling the underlying short and lending the proceeds at the risk-free rate for a short position. We also showed that a long underlying position combined with a short forward resulted in a risk-free return. We now incorporate these forward commitment building blocks into the put–call parity relationship shown in the prior lesson.

PUT–CALL FORWARD PARITY 5

☐ explain put–call *forward* parity for European options

In an earlier lesson, we learned that a long underlying asset position can be replicated by entering a long forward contract and purchasing the risk-free asset. Combining the synthetic asset with the put–call parity relationship—so, substituting the present value of $F_0(T)$ for S_0 in Equation 1—we have what is referred to as **put–call forward parity**:

$$F_0(T)(1 + r)^{-T} + p_0 = c_0 + X(1 + r)^{-T}. \quad (3)$$

We can demonstrate put–call forward parity by comparing a synthetic protective put position to the protective put and fiduciary call positions. Consider a modification of the portfolios used earlier to demonstrate put–call parity, as follows:

1. At $t = 0$, an investor purchases a forward contract and a risk-free bond with a face value equal to the forward price, $F_0(T)$, and a put option on the underlying (p_0) with an exercise price of X at $t = T$.
2. At $t = 0$, an investor purchases a call option (c_0) on the same underlying with an exercise price of X and a risk-free bond that pays X at $t = T$.

The first portfolio has replaced the *cash* underlying position with a *synthetic* underlying position using a forward purchase and a risk-free bond. The combination of the synthetic underlying position and a purchased put on the underlying is known as a **synthetic protective put**. Exhibit 7 demonstrates the equivalence of the protective and synthetic protective puts by comparing their cash flows at both $t = 0$ and contract maturity, T.

Exhibit 7: Protective Put vs. Synthetic Protective Put

Position	Cash Flow at $t = 0$	Put Exercised ($S_T < X$)	No Exercise ($S_T \geq X$)
Protective Put:			
Purchased Put (p_0)	p_0	$X - S_T$	0
Cash Underlying (S_0)	S_0	S_T	S_T
Total:	$p_0 + S_0$	X	S_T
Synthetic Protective Put:			
Purchased Put (p_0)	p_0	$X - S_T$	0
Forward Purchase	0	$S_T - F_0(T)$	$S_T - F_0(T)$
Risk-Free Bond $F_0(T)(1 + r)^{-T}$	$F_0(T)(1 + r)^{-T}$	$F_0(T)$	$F_0(T)$
Total:	$p_0 + F_0(T)(1 + r)^{-T}$ (= $p_0 + S_0$)	X	S_T

Exhibit 8 compares the future cash flows of the synthetic protective put with the fiduciary call under all possible scenarios at expiration.

Exhibit 8: Synthetic Protective Put vs. Fiduciary Call

Portfolio Position	Put Exercised ($S_T < X$)	No Exercise ($S_T = X$)	Call Exercised ($S_T > X$)
Synthetic Protective Put:			
Purchased Put (p_0)	$X - S_T$	0	0
Forward Purchase	$S_T - F_0(T)$	$S_T - F_0(T)$	$S_T - F_0(T)$
Risk-Free Bond $F_0(T)(1 + r)^{-T}$	$F_0(T)$	$F_0(T)$	$F_0(T)$
Total:	X	S_T (= X)	S_T
Fiduciary Call:			
Purchased Call (c_0)	0	0	$S_T - X$
Risk-Free Asset	X	X	X
Total:	X	X (= S_T)	S_T

It follows that the cost of the fiduciary call must equal the cost of the synthetic protective put, thereby demonstrating the put–call forward parity relationship:

$$F_0(T)(1 + r)^{-T} + p_0 = c_0 + X(1+ r)^{-T}.$$

If we rearrange these terms, we can demonstrate that a long put and a short call are equivalent to a long risk-free bond and short forward position:

$$p_0 - c_0 = [X - F_0(T)](1 + r)^{-T}. \quad (4)$$

Consider the earlier put–call parity example using a synthetic underlying position, as in the following example.

EXAMPLE 4

VFO Put–Call Forward Parity

Consider the Viswan Family Office example using a long forward and a risk-free bond, rather than a cash underlying position as in the prior example. Biomian shares trade at a price (S_0) of INR295 per share. VFO is considering the purchase of a six-month put on Biomian shares at an exercise price (X) of INR265. If VFO's chief investment officer observes a traded six-month call option price of INR59 per share for the same INR265 exercise price, what should he expect to pay for the put option per share if the relevant risk-free rate is 4%?

From Equation 5, the put–call forward parity relationship is

$$p_0 - c_0 = [X - F_0(T)](1 + r)^{-T}.$$

Substituting terms and solving for $F_0(T)$ = INR300.84 (= INR295$(1.04)^{0.5}$),

$$p_0 - \text{INR}59 = (\text{INR}265 - \text{INR}300.84)(1.04)^{-0.5}.$$

$$p_0 = \text{INR}23.86.$$

VFO should expect to pay a six-month put option premium of p_0 = INR23.86.

OPTION PUT–CALL PARITY APPLICATIONS: FIRM VALUE 6

- ☐ explain put–call parity for European options
- ☐ explain put–call *forward* parity for European options

The insights established by the put–call parity relationship go well beyond option trading strategies, extending to modeling the value of a firm to describe the interests and financial claims of capital providers—namely, the owners of a firm's equity and the owners of its debt.

Assume that at time $t = 0$, a firm with a market value of V_0 has access to borrowed capital in the form of zero-coupon debt with a face value of D. The market value of the firm's assets, V_0, is equal to the present value of its outstanding debt obligation, PV(D), and equity, E_0: $V_0 = E_0 + \text{PV}(D)$.

When the debt matures at T, the firm's debt and assets are distributed between shareholders and debtholders with two possible outcomes depending on the firm's value at time T (V_T):

1. **Solvency ($V_T > D$)**: If the value of the firm (V_T) *exceeds* the face value of the debt, or $V_T > D$, at time T, we say the firm is *solvent* and able to return capital to *both* its shareholders and debtholders.

   - Debtholders receive D and are repaid in full.
   - Shareholders receive the residual: $E_T = V_T - D$.

2. **Insolvency ($V_T < D$)**: If the value of the firm (V_T) is *below* the face value of the debt, or $V_T < D$, at time T, we say the firm is *insolvent*. In the event of insolvency, shareholders receive nothing and debtholders are owed more than the value of the firm's assets. Debtholders therefore receive V_T to settle their debt claim of D at time T.

   - Debtholders have a priority claim on assets and receive $V_T < D$.
   - Shareholders receive the residual, $E_T = 0$.

Unlike the *risk-free* bond shown in the prior put–call parity lesson, the firm has *risky* debt, because the bondholders receive D *only* in the case of solvency (when $V_T > D$). Debtholders therefore demand a premium similar to a put option premium from shareholders in order to assume the risk of insolvency.

Shareholders retain *unlimited* upside potential (if the firm remains solvent and can pay off its debt) and *limited* downside potential (if the firm becomes insolvent). In contrast, debtholder upside is *limited* to receiving debt repayment in the event of solvency, and principal and interest are at risk in the downside event of insolvency.

Next, we examine the respective payoff profiles at maturity more closely. At $t = T$,

- shareholder payoff is $\max(0, V_T - D)$ and
- debtholder payoff is $\min(V_T, D)$.

Consider these payoff profiles in terms of options:

- Shareholders hold a long position in the underlying firm's assets (V_T) and have purchased a put option on firm value (V_T) with an exercise price of D; that is, $\max(0, D - V_T)$.
- Debtholders hold a long position in a risk-free bond (D) and have sold a put option to shareholders on firm value (V_T) with an exercise price of D.

The payoff profiles for shareholders versus debtholders is shown in Exhibit 9.

Exhibit 9: Shareholder and Debtholder Payoff at Time *T*

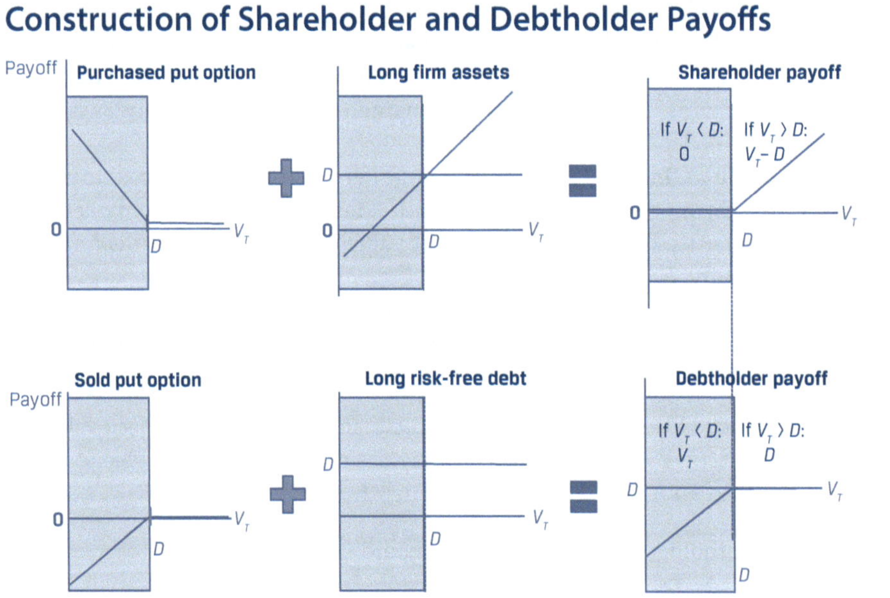

Firm Value Distribution Between Shareholders and Debtholders

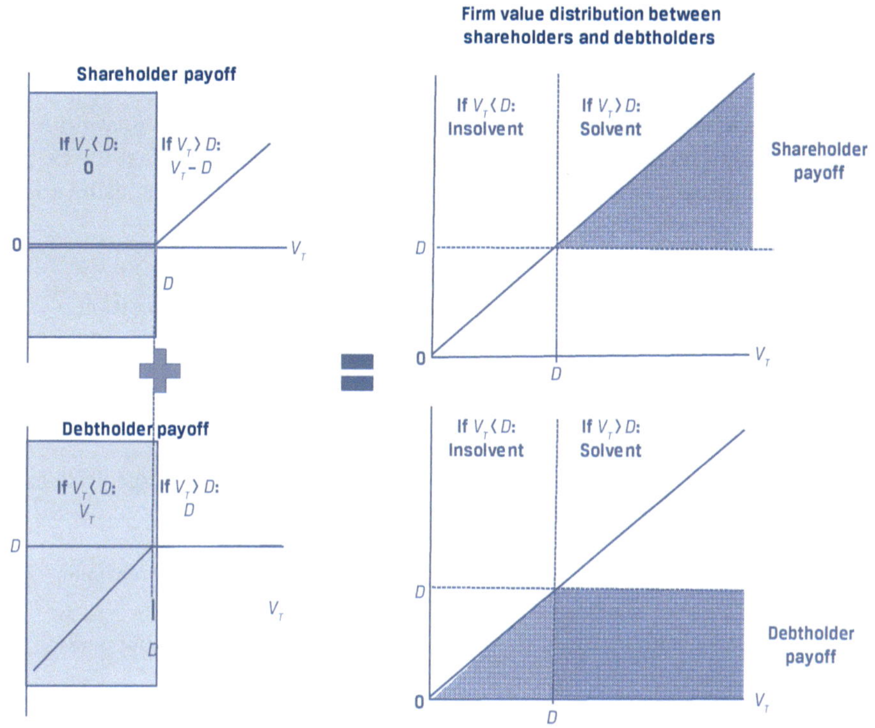

Note that the shareholder's combination of a purchased put option and a long position in the firm's assets is equivalent to a *call* option on the firm's assets. The risky debt held by the debtholders is a combination of the risk-free debt, D, and the put option sold to shareholders.

Revisiting the put–call parity relationship, $S_0 + p_0 = c_0 + \text{PV}(X)$, from Equation 1, we may substitute the value of the firm at time 0 (V_0) for the underlying asset (S_0), substitute the debt (D) for the risk-free bond (X), and solve for V_0 as follows:

$$V_0 + p_0 = c_0 + \text{PV}(D).$$

$$V_0 = c_0 + \text{PV}(D) - p_0. \quad (5)$$

Equation 6 captures the value of the firm's assets at $t = 0$ from a shareholder and debtholder perspective. The *shareholder* has a position with a payoff similar to that of a call option on firm value (c_0). The *debtholder* has a position of $\text{PV}(D) - p_0$, or risk-free debt of the firm *plus* a sold put option on firm value. The put option (p_0) may be interpreted as the *credit spread* on the firm's debt, or the premium above the risk-free rate the firm must pay to debtholders to assume insolvency risk. This put option increases in value to shareholders as the likelihood of insolvency increases. From a debtholder's perspective, the more valuable the sold put, the more credit risk is present in the firm's debt.

QUESTION SET

Put–Call Forward Parity and Option Applications

1. Identify the following statement as true or false, and justify your answer: A key link between put–call parity and put–call forward parity is that the cash underlying position is replaced by a synthetic underlying position using a forward purchase and a risk-free bond.

Solution:

The statement is true. The replacement of the cash underlying position by a synthetic underlying position using a forward purchase and a risk-free bond links call option, put option, and forward prices under put–call forward parity.

2. Identify which of the following positions has the same no-arbitrage value as which portfolio under put–call forward parity:

1. Long call option (c_0)	A. Forward sale, long risk-free bond, and long call option
2. Long risk-free bond ($X(1 + r)^{-T}$)	B. Forward purchase, long put option, and short risk-free bond
3. Long put option (p_0)	C. Long forward purchase, short call option, and long put option

Solution:

Recall that the put–call forward parity relationship may be expressed as

$F_0(T)(1 + r)^{-T} + p_0 = c_0 + X(1 + r)^{-T}$.

1. B is correct. A long call option position is the no-arbitrage equivalent of a forward purchase, a long put option, and a short risk-free bond position.

2. C is correct. A long risk-free bond position is equivalent to a long forward purchase, a short call option, and a long put option.

3. A is correct. A long put option is equivalent to a forward sale, a long risk-free bond, and a long call option.

3. Describe the cash flows at the time of option expiration for a synthetic protective put.

Solution:

A synthetic protective put is the combination of a *synthetic* underlying position (using a forward purchase and a long risk-free bond position equal to the exercise price) and a purchased put.

At the time of option expiration, time T, there are two possible scenarios:

Put option exercised ($X > S_T$): If the put option is exercised, an investor receives $(X - S_T)$. The risk-free asset returns $F_0(T)$, and the forward purchase returns $S_T - F_0(T)$.

The total return equals $(X - S_T) + [S_T - F_0(T)] + F_0(T) = X$.

Put option unexercised ($X \leq S_T$): If the put option is unexercised, it will expire worthless. The risk-free asset returns $F_0(T)$, and the forward purchase returns $S_T - F_0(T)$.

The total return equals $[S_T - F_0(T)] + F_0(T) = S_T$.

4. Describe how a debtholder's position may be considered similar to the sale of a put option on firm value.

   Solution:

   If the value of the firm (V_T) is *below* the face value of its debt outstanding, or $V_T < D$ at time T, we say the firm is *insolvent* and debtholders receive less than the face value (D) to settle their debt claim. Stated differently, a debtholder's payoff is $\min(D, V_T) = D - \max(0, D - V_T)$ and equals the debt face value (D) minus a put option on firm value (V_T) with an exercise price of D, which represents a *sold* put on firm value.

PRACTICE PROBLEMS

The following information relates to questions 1-6

South China Sprintwyck Investments (SCSI)

South China Sprintwyck Investments (SCSI) has a Chinese equity portfolio that has outperformed in the first half of the year due to an overweight position in health care industry shares. SCSI is considering option-based alternatives for one of its current overweight positions, ChinaWell Inc. (CWI). CWI has a current price (S_0) of CNY127.50 and pays no dividends. The current risk-free rate is 4%. You are a new SCSI analyst hired to evaluate several alternatives for CWI stock.

1. SCSI is considering the sale of a three-month call on CWI shares. If you observe a traded put price with the same underlying details, which of the following statements best describes how to derive the no-arbitrage call price?

   A. Using put–call parity, the call price may be derived by *subtracting* the traded put price from the underlying price less the present value of the exercise price.

   B. Using put–call parity, the call price may be derived by *adding* the traded put price to the underlying price less the present value of the exercise price.

   C. Using put–call parity, the call price may be derived by *adding* the traded put price to the present value of the exercise price minus the underlying price.

2. Due to the recent sharp rise in CWI's share price, SCSI is recommending that clients consider protective put strategies for three- to six-month tenors. If you observe that a six-month CWI call option at an exercise price of CNY120 is trading at a price of CNY22.60, which answer is closest to what you would expect to pay for a six-month put option with the same underlying terms?

   A. CNY15.10

   B. CNY9.83

   C. CNY12.77

3. You realize that the six-month put option on CWI shares is overpriced relative to the no-arbitrage price from Question 2. Which of the following statements best describes the steps you would take to earn a riskless arbitrage profit under this scenario?

   A. Sell the six-month put option and sell CWI short, investing the proceeds in a call option and a risk-free bond.

   B. Sell the six-month put option, buy a call option, and borrow at the risk-free rate to buy CWI shares.

   C. Sell the six-month put option, buy a call option, enter a forward purchase of CWI, and invest in a risk-free bond.

4. In her most recent research note on CWI, SCSI's equity analyst specifically mentions an increase in CWI's leverage ratio as a reason for her bearish outlook on the stock. Applying the put–call parity relationship to the value of the firm, which of the following statements most accurately describes the CWI outlook in terms of option pricing?

   A. The shareholder payoff has improved versus debtholders, because they have sold a put option on the firm value that has appreciated.

   B. The debtholder payoff has deteriorated versus the shareholders, because they are effectively short a put option on the value of the firm equal to the value of debt, which has appreciated in value.

   C. The shareholder payoff has improved versus the debtholders, because the debtholders have sold a call option on the firm's assets to the shareholders.

5. Which of the following choices best describes how SCSI could replicate a long risk-free bond return using a forward contract on CWI and call and put options on CWI?

   A. Short a forward contract on CWI, short a put option on CWI, and long a call option on CWI

   B. Long a forward contract on CWI, long a put option on CWI, and short a call option on CWI

   C. Long a forward contract on CWI, long a put option on CWI, and long a call option on CWI

6. SCSI observes that a 3-month call option on CWI with an exercise price of CNY 130 trades at a premium of CNY 3. A 3-month forward contract on CWI trades at a forward price of CNY 128.76. Which of the following choices is closest to the correct premium for a 3-month put option with an exercise price of CNY 130 on CWI?

   A. CNY 4.20

   B. CNY 1.20

   C. CNY 0.50

SOLUTIONS

1. The correct answer is B. From Equation 1, the put–call parity relationship is

   $S_0 + p_0 = c_0 + X(1 + r)^{-T}$.

   We can rearrange these terms to solve for c_0: $c_0 = S_0 + p_0 - X(1 + r)^{-T}$, which shows that the call price may be derived by *adding* the traded put price to the underlying price less the present value of the exercise price.

2. The correct answer is C. If c_0 = CNY22.60, S_0 = CNY127.50, and PV(X) = CNY117.67 (= $120(1.04)^{-0.5}$), we can solve for p_0 using put–call parity:

   $S_0 + p_0 = c_0 + X(1 + r)^{-T}$.

   $p_0 = c_0 + X(1 + r)^{-T} - S_0$.

   CNY12.77 = 22.60 + 117.67 – 127.50.

3. The correct answer is A. Since the put option is overpriced, we would sell it to earn the difference between the price at which it is sold and the no-arbitrage price. The put–call parity relationship, from Equation 1, is

   $S_0 + p_0 = c_0 + X(1 + r)^{-T}$.

   We can rearrange this to demonstrate that the put option value is equivalent to a long call option, a long risk-free bond, and a short position in CWI shares:

   $p_0 = c_0 + X(1 + r)^{-T} - S_0$.

   Answer A reflects this long risk-free bond and short CWI combination, which has a payoff of $X - S_T$ at expiration matching that of the put payoff, whereas Answer B involves a long cash position in CWI and Answer C involves a long synthetic (forward purchase) position in CWI stock.

4. The correct answer is B. The debtholder payoff has deteriorated versus the shareholders, because they are effectively short a put option on the value of the firm equal to the value of debt, which has appreciated in value.

   The debtholder payoff is min(D, V_T) = D – max(0, $D - V_T$) and equals the debt face value (D) *minus* a put option on firm value (V_T) with an exercise price of D. Answer A is incorrect because the debtholders, not the shareholders, have sold a put option. C is incorrect, because the shareholders own a call option, but it is not sold by the debtholders.

5. B is correct. Using the put–call forward parity equation as follows:

   $F_0(T)(1 + r)^{-T} + p_0 = c_0 + X(1 + r)^{-T}$

   And rearranging to solve for the risk-free bond gives the following:

   $F_0(T)(1 + r)^{-T} + p_0 - c_0 = X(1 + r)^{-T}$.

   The signs on the forward contract and put option positions are both positive, indicating long positions. The negative sign on the call option indicates a short position.

6. A is correct. The solution can be derived through either put–call parity or put–call forward parity. You can demonstrate the solution using put–call forward parity:

   $F_0(T)(1 + r)^{-T} + p_0 = c_0 + X(1 + r)^{-T}$

   $128.76(1.04)^{-0.25} + p_0 = 3 + 130(1.04)^{-0.25}$

$$127.50 + p_0 = 131.73$$
$$p_0 = 4.23.$$

LEARNING MODULE

10

Valuing a Derivative Using a One-Period Binomial Model

LEARNING OUTCOMES	
Mastery	***The candidate should be able to:***
☐	explain how to value a derivative using a one-period binomial model
☐	describe the concept of risk neutrality in derivatives pricing

INTRODUCTION

1

Earlier lessons explained how the principle of no arbitrage and replication can be used to value and price derivatives. The put–call parity relationship linked put option, call option, underlying asset, and risk-free asset prices. This relationship was extended to forward contracts given the equivalence of an underlying asset position and a long forward contract plus a risk-free bond.

Forward commitments can be priced without making assumptions about the underlying asset's price in the future. However, the pricing of options and other contingent claims requires a model for the evolution of the underlying asset's future price. The first lesson introduces the widely-used binomial model to value European put and call options. A simple one-period version is introduced, which may be extended to multiple periods and used to value more complex contingent claims. In the second lesson, we demonstrate the use of risk-neutral probabilities in derivatives pricing.

LEARNING MODULE OVERVIEW

- The one-period binomial model values contingent claims, such as options, and assumes the underlying asset will either increase by R^u (up gross return) or decrease by R^d (down gross return) over a single period that corresponds to the expiration of the derivative contract.
- The binomial model combines an option with the underlying asset to create a risk-free portfolio where the proportion of the option to the underlying security is determined by a hedge ratio.

CFA Institute would like to thank Don Chance, PhD, CFA, for his contribution to this section, which includes material derived from material that appeared in *Derivative Markets and Instruments*, featured in the 2022 CFA® Program curriculum.

- The hedged portfolio must earn the prevailing risk-free rate of return; otherwise, riskless arbitrage profit opportunities would be available.
- Valuing a derivative via risk-free hedging is equivalent to computing the discounted expected payoff of the option using *risk-neutral* probabilities rather than actual probabilities.
- Neither the actual (real-world) probabilities of underlying price increases or decreases nor the expected return of the underlying are required to price an option.
- The one-period binomial model can be extended to multiple periods as well to value more complex contingent claims.

LEARNING MODULE SELF-ASSESSMENT

These initial questions are intended to help you gauge your current level of understanding of this learning module.

1. Which of the following statements most correctly describes the binomial model for valuing options?

   A. The model uses the actual probabilities associated with stock price moves up or down.

   B. The model assumes that a risk-free portfolio can be created by combining the option and the underlying according to a hedge ratio.

   C. The model is similar to those used for valuing forward and futures contracts.

   Solution:

   B is correct. Unlike forward commitments, contingent claims, such as options, require that we model the future price behavior of the underlying asset because unlike forwards and futures, options have asymmetric payoffs. By modeling the future price behavior, the option and its underlying asset can be combined into a risk-free portfolio. The cost of this portfolio, where the proportion of the option and the underlying asset is set by a hedge ratio, determines the no-arbitrage price of the option. A is incorrect because the actual probabilities of up and down price moves do not factor into the model. C is incorrect because options have asymmetric payoffs, so they must be modeled differently than symmetric-payoff instruments like forward and futures contracts.

2. When using a one-period binomial model to price a call option, an increase in the actual probability of an upward move in the underlying asset will result in the call option price:

   A. decreasing.

   B. staying the same.

   C. increasing.

   Solution:

   The correct answer is B. The call option price will stay the same. The actual (real-world) probabilities of an up or a down price movement in a binomial model do not influence the (no-arbitrage) price of an option.

3. Identify which of the various factor changes has which effect on the no-arbitrage price of a put option based on the one-period binomial model:

1. The probability of an upward price movement, q, increases.	A. Put option price remains the same
2. The spread between the up and down factor, $R^u - R^d$, increases.	B. Put option price increases
3. The risk-neutral probability of price, π, increases.	C. Put option price decreases

Solution:

1. The correct answer is A. The probability of an upward price movement, q, has no impact on value in the one-period binomial option pricing model. Thus, this change would not have any impact on the price of a put option, and the price of the put option would remain the same.

2. The correct answer is B. The spread between the up and down factor, $R^u - R^d$, increases the range of potential prices, which increases the likelihood that the option ends up in the money. Thus, this change would increase the price of a put option.

3. The correct answer is C. The risk-neutral probability of price, π, captures the probability of the price of the underlying increasing. As π increases, the likelihood of the put option ending up in the money decreases.

4. A one-period binomial model assumes that the price of the underlying asset can change from \$16.00 today to either \$20.00 or \$12.00 at the end of the period. If the risk-free rate of return over the period is 5%, which of the following choices is closest to the risk-neutral probability of a price increase?

   A. 0.50

   B. 0.60

   C. 0.625

Solution:

B is correct. An increase from \$16.00 to \$20.00 or a decrease from \$16.00 to \$12.00 corresponds to:

R^u = \$20.00/\$16.00 = 1.25 and R^d = \$12.00/\$16.00 = 0.75.

Using the risk-neutral probability (π) of a price increase:

$\pi = (1 + r - R^d)/(R^u - R^d)$

$= (1 + 0.05 - 0.75)/(1.25 - 0.75) = 0.3/0.5 = 0.60.$

BINOMIAL VALUATION 2

- [ ] explain how to value a derivative using a one-period binomial model

The law of one price states that if the payoffs from any two assets (or portfolio of assets) at a given future time are identical in all possible scenarios, then the value of these two assets must also be identical *today*. Forward commitments offer symmetric payoffs at a predetermined price in the future, the value of which are independent of the future price behavior of the underlying asset.

The asymmetric payoff profile of options and other contingent claims makes valuation of these instruments more challenging. Assumptions about future prices are an important component in option valuation given the different payoffs under different scenarios whose likelihood changes over time. Option valuation therefore requires the specification of a model for the future (random) price behavior of the option's underlying asset.

The binomial model is a common tool used to determine the no-arbitrage value of an option. The simplicity of this model makes it attractive, as we only need to make an assumption about the magnitude of the potential upward and downward price changes of the underlying asset in a future time period.

3 THE BINOMIAL MODEL

☐ explain how to value a derivative using a one-period binomial model

The binomial model builds on a simple idea: Over a given period of time, the asset's price will either go up (u) to $S_1{}^u > S_0$ or go down (d) to $S_1{}^d < S_0$. We do not need to know the future price in advance, because it is determined by the outcome of a random variable. The movement from S_0 to either $S_1{}^u$ or $S_1{}^d$ can be interpreted as the outcome of a *Bernoulli trial.*

Let us denote q as the probability of an upward price movement and $1 - q$ as the probability of a downward price movement. With only two possible outcomes—the price either goes up or down—the sum of probabilities must equal 1. We will also find it useful to define the gross return from an up or a down price move as:

$$R^u = S_1{}^u/S_0 > 1 \quad (1)$$

$$R^d = S_1{}^d/S_0 < 1 \quad (2)$$

At first glance, it would appear that knowing q is crucial in determining the value of an option on any underlying asset. However, knowing q is not required; only specifying the values of $S_1{}^u$ and $S_1{}^d$ is needed. The difference between $S_1{}^u$ and $S_1{}^d$ measures the "spread" of possible future price outcomes. Specifying $S_1{}^u$ and $S_1{}^d$ (or R^uS_0 and R^dS_0) determines the *volatility* of the underlying asset, an important factor in valuing options as shown earlier. Simply stated, the size of the up and down price movements should match the underlying asset volatility, as shown in Exhibit 1.

Exhibit 1: Price Movement for the Underlying Asset

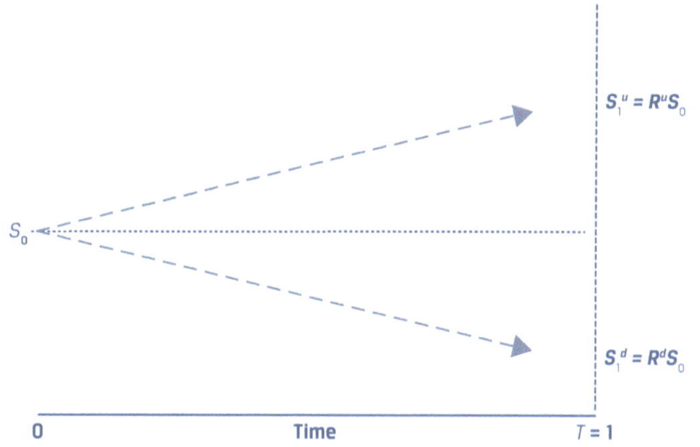

Binomial models may be extended to multiple periods where the underlying asset price can move up or down in each period. This extension creates a binomial tree, a powerful way to model more realistic price dynamics. A simple one-period binomial model is sufficient to introduce the pricing methodology and the required steps in the option pricing procedure.

PRICING A EUROPEAN CALL OPTION

4

☐ explain how to value a derivative using a one-period binomial model

Consider a one-year European call option with an exercise price (X) of €100. The underlying spot price (S_0) is €80. The one-period binomial model corresponds to the option's time to expiration of one year.

The binomial model specifies the possible values of the underlying asset in one year, where the option value is a known function of the value of the underlying asset. Further, we assume that $S_1^d < X < S_1^u$ (i.e., the exercise price of the option [X = €100] is between the value of the underlying in the two scenarios)—for example, setting S_1^d = €60 and S_1^u = €110. Then, R^u = 1.375 and R^d = 0.75. The value of the call option is as follows:

- At t = 0, the call option value is c_0.
- At t = 1, the call option value is either c_1^u (if the underlying price rises to S_1^u) or c_1^d (if the underlying price falls to S_1^d).
  - **Up move to S_1^u:** Call option ends up *in-the-money*

$$c_1^u = \text{Max}(0,\ S_1^u - X) = \text{Max}(0,\ €110 - €100) = €10.$$

  - **Down move to S_1^d:** Call option expires *out-of-the-money*

$$c_1^d = \text{Max}\left(0,\ S_1^d - X\right) = \text{Max}(0,\ €60 - €100) = 0.$$

Exhibit 2 summarizes the one-period binomial model and the value of the underlying asset and call option.

Exhibit 2: One-Period Binomial Option Pricing

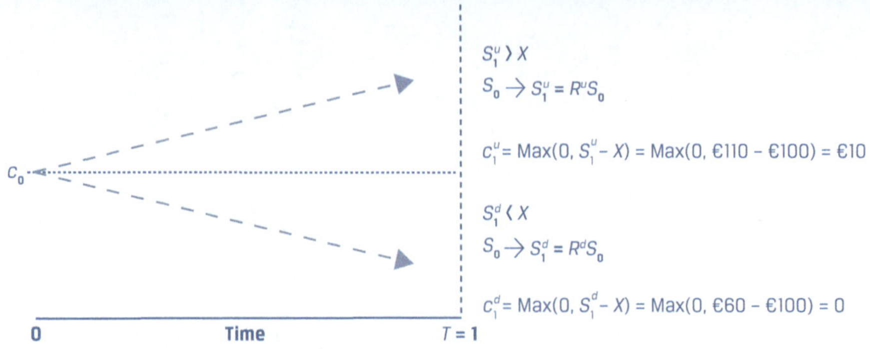

The only unknown value is c_0, which may be determined using replication and no-arbitrage pricing. That is, the value of both the option and its underlying asset in each future scenario may be used to construct a risk-free portfolio. For example, assume that at $t = 0$ we sell the call option at a price of c_0 and purchase h units of the underlying asset. Denoting the value of the portfolio as V, we have the following:

$$V_0 = hS_0 - c_0 \quad (3)$$

$$V_1^u = hS_1^u - c_1^u = h \times R^u \times S_0 - \text{Max}(0, S_1^u - X) \quad (4)$$

$$V_1^d = hS_1^d - c_1^d = h \times R^d \times S_0 - \text{Max}(0, S_1^d - X) \quad (5)$$

V_0 represents the initial portfolio investment in the portfolio, and V_1^u and V_1^d represent the portfolio value if the underlying price moves up or down, respectively. We must choose h so that $V_1^u = V_1^d$ (i.e., the portfolio value is the same in either scenario). The value of the combination, V_1, will not change if the underlying asset price changes. For portfolio V_0, the impacts of the changes are as follows:

- **Up move from S_0 to S_1^u by R^u:**
  - The asset value changes from €80 to €110 by 1.375, or 37.5%.
  - The call option ends up *in-the-money*:

$$c_1^u = \text{Max}(0, S_1^u - X) = \text{Max}(0, €110 - €100) = €10.$$

  - Total portfolio value: $V_1^u = hS_1^u - c_1^u$ = €110 × h – €10.
- **Down move from S_0 to S_1^d by R^d:**
  - The asset value changes from €80 to €60 by 0.75, or –25%.
  - The call option expires *out-of-the-money*:

$$c_1^d = \text{Max}\left(0, S_1^d - X\right) = \text{Max}(0, €60 - €100) = 0.$$

  - Total portfolio value: $V_1^d = hS_1^d - c_1^d$ = €60 × h.

Since we create two portfolios at time $t = 0$ with identical payoffs at option expiry at time $t = 1$, we must solve for h, the ratio between the underlying asset, S_0, and the call option, c_0, such that $V_1^u = V_1^d$, or $hS_1^u - c_1^u = hS_1^d - c_1^d$. Solving for h^* yields:

$$h^* = \frac{c_1^u - c_1^d}{s_1^u - s_1^d}, \quad (6)$$

where all quantities on the right-hand side are known at $t = 0$. Equation 6 gives us the **hedge ratio** of the option, or the *proportion* of the underlying that will offset the risk associated with an option. In our sold call option example,

$$h^* = \frac{c_1^u - c_1^d}{s_1^u - s_1^d} = \frac{€10 - €0}{€110 - €60} = \frac{10}{50} = 0.20.$$

For each call option unit sold, we buy 0.2 units of the underlying asset (or for each underlying asset unit, we must sell 5 call options to equate the portfolio values at $t =$ 1). Consider the two scenarios as follows:

- **Up move from S_0 to $S_1{}^u$ by R^u:**
  - Total portfolio value: $V_1{}^u = hS_1{}^u - c_1{}^u$

$= €110 \times 0.20 - €10 = €22 - 10 = €12.$

- **Down move from S_0 to $S_1{}^d$ by R^d:**
  - Total portfolio value $V_1{}^d = hS_1{}^d - c_1{}^d = €60 \times 0.20 = €12.$

The portfolio values are the same, $V_1{}^u = V_1{}^d$, which has two implications:

1. We can use either portfolio to value the derivative, and
2. The return $V_1{}^u / V_0 = V_1{}^d / V_0$ must equal one plus the risk-free rate.

Exhibit 3 summarizes these results.

Exhibit 3: Value of the Hedged Portfolio

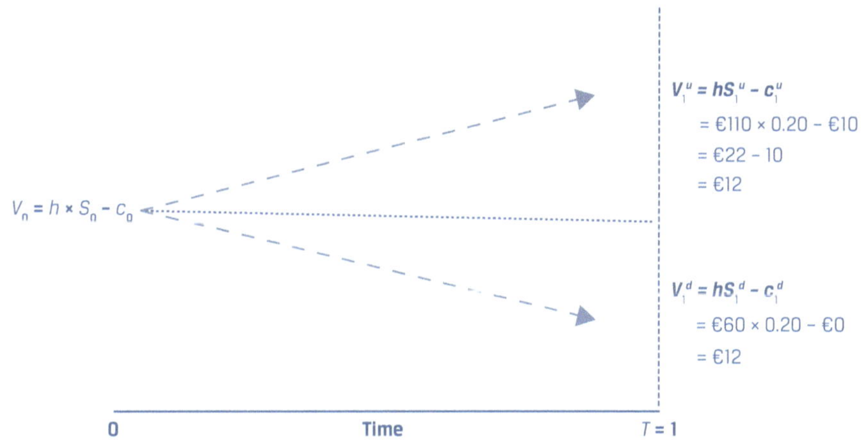

This hedging approach is not specific to call options and can be used for any derivative contract whose value is entirely determined by the underlying asset's value at $t = 1$.

To prevent arbitrage, the portfolio value at $t = 1$,

$$V_1 = h \times R^u S_0 - c_1^u = h \times R^d S_0 - c_1^d,$$

should be discounted at the risk-free rate so that:

$$hS_0 - c_0 = \frac{V_1}{1 + r}.$$

Based on no-arbitrage pricing and the certain portfolio payoff, V_1, the value of the call option may be shown as:

$$c_0 = h \times S_0 - V_1(1 + r)^{-1}. \quad (7)$$

Substituting the information from the previous example, we already established that V_1 = €12. For an annual risk-free rate of 5%:

$$c_0 = h \times S_0 - V_1(1 + \mathrm{r})^{-1}$$

$$=0.2 \times €80 - €12\ (1.05)^{-1} = €16 - €11.43 = €4.57.$$

The call option price c_0 is therefore €4.57. We may confirm an investor in the hedge portfolio would earn the risk-free rate (r) of 5% by comparing the initial portfolio value V_0 with the portfolio value after one period of V_1 (recalling that $V_1{}^u = V_1{}^d$) equal to €12:

$$V_0 = h \times S_0 - c_0$$

$$V_0 = €11.43 = €16 - €4.57$$

$$V_1 = V_0(1 + r) \quad (8)$$

$$V_1 = €12 = €11.43\ (1 + 0.5)$$

EXAMPLE 1

Hightest Capital

Hightest Capital believes that a particular non-dividend-paying stock is currently trading at $50 and is considering the sale of a one-year European call option at an exercise price of $55. Answer the following questions:

1. If the stock price is expected to either go up or down by 20% over the next year, what price should Hightest expect to receive for the sold call option? Assume a risk-free rate of 5%.
2. How would the call option price change if the stock price were expected to either go up or down by 40% over the next year?
3. If Hightest had a more optimistic outlook on the future stock price (i.e., they estimated a higher probability of the option ending up in-the-money), how would the expected call option price change?
4. What would be the price of a one-year put option at an exercise price of $55 if the stock price were expected to change by 20%? 40%?

Solution to 1:

Denote the initial price of the underlying stock as S_0= $50 and the exercise price of the call option as X = $55. If the stock price moves up or down by 20%, then:

$$S_1^u = R^u S_0 = 1.2 \times \$50 = \$60.$$

$$S_1^d = R^d S_0 = 0.8 \times \$50 = \$40.$$

The price will either move up to $60 or down to $40. Given that the payoff of a call option at expiry is Max(0, $S_T - X$):

$$c_1^u = \text{Max}(0,\ S_1^u - X) = \text{Max}(0,\ \$60 - \$55) = \$5.$$

$$c_1^d = \text{Max}\left(0,\ S_1^d - X\right) = \text{Max}(0,\ \$40 - \$55) = \$0.$$

The call option value is $5 if the underlying stock increases in price by 20% and zero if it decreases by 20%. The hedge ratio of the option is:

$$h^* = \frac{(c_1^u - c_1^d)}{(S_1^u - S_1^d)} = \frac{\$5.00 - \$0}{\$60.00 - \$40.00} = \frac{\$5.00}{\$20.00} = 0.25.$$

To create a risk-free portfolio, we can sell a call option and purchase 0.25 units of the underlying asset today. At maturity, the hedged portfolio value is:

$$V_1 = V_1^u = h^* S_1^u - c_1^u = 0.25 \times \$60.00 - \$5.00 = \$10.00.$$

$$V_1 = V_1^d = h^* S_1^d - c_1^d = 0.25 \times \$40.00 - \$0.00 = \$10.00.$$

We can use either $V_1{}^u$ or $V_1{}^d$ to compute the certain value, V_1, and the present value of the hedged position today is:

$$V_0 = V_1(1 + r)^{-1} = \$10.00 \times 1.05^{-1} = \$9.52.$$

The call option value is:

$$c_0 = h^* S_0 - V_0 = 0.25 \times \$50.00 - \$9.52 = \$12.50 - \$9.52 = \$2.98.$$

The no-arbitrage price of the call option should be \$2.98. If not, then investors would be able to construct a synthetic risk-free asset using the option and its underlying asset with a higher return than the risk-free rate.

Note that the hedge ratio (0.25 units in this example) is positive in this case since the derivative is sold and the underlying is purchased. A negative hedge ratio implies that *both* the derivative and the underlying are purchased or sold to create the hedge. Also, while the hedge ratio is usually expressed as a fraction of an underlying unit, option contracts are usually traded in larger size, allowing a round number of underlying assets to be purchased or sold as a hedge. It is important that the *ratio* (4:1 in this case) of options to underlying units is maintained in the portfolio.

Solution to 2:

If the stock price changes by 40%, then the call option payoff at expiry is:

$$c_1^u = \text{Max}(0, S_1^u - X) = \text{Max}(0, \$70 - \$55) = \$15.$$

$$c_1^d = \text{Max}\left(0, S_1^d - X\right) = \text{Max}(0, \$30 - \$55) = 0.$$

The hedge ratio of the option is:

$$h^* = \frac{\left(c_1^u - c_1^d\right)}{\left(S_1^u - S_1^d\right)} = \frac{\$15 - \$0}{\$70 - \$30} = \frac{\$15}{\$40} = 0.375.$$

At maturity, the perfectly hedged portfolio is worth:

$$V_1 = V_1^u = h^* S_1^u - c_1^u = 0.375 \times \$70 - \$15 = \$11.25.$$

$$V_1 = V_1^d = h^* S_1^d - c_1^d = 0.375 \times \$30 - \$0 = \$11.25.$$

The present value of the hedged position at $t = 0$ is:

$$V_0 = V_1(1 + \text{r})^{-1} = \$11.25 \times 1.05^{-1} = \$10.71.$$

Then, the call option price at $t = 0$ is:

$$c_0 = h^* S_0 - V_0 = 0.375 \times \$50 - \$10.71 = \$18.75 - \$10.71 = \$8.04.$$

A higher expected price change indicates higher volatility. An increase in the range of future price changes increases the value of the call option.

Solution to 3:

Since the actual probabilities of an up or a down move in the underlying asset do not affect the no-arbitrage value of the option, the option price that Hightest may charge should not change. Hightest can offset the risk of selling the call by purchasing h^* units of the underlying asset, so any directional views on the stock price do not affect the hedge position.

Solution to 4:

Using put–call parity, $c_0 - p_0 = S_0 - X(1 + r)^{-T}$, and rearranging terms to solve for the put price, when the stock price changes by 20% and the call option price is \$2.98, the result can be calculated as:

$$p_0 = c_0 - S_0 + X(1 + r)^{-T} = \$2.98 - \$50 + \$55(1 + 0.05)^{-1} = \$5.36.$$

When the underlying stock price changes by 40% and the call option price is \$8.04, the put option price is:

$$p_0 = c_0 - S_0 + X(1 + r)^{-T} = \$8.04 - \$50 + \$55(1 + 0.05)^{-1} = \$10.42.$$

QUESTION SET

Binomial Valuation of Options

1. Determine the correct answers to fill in the blanks: To price a contingent claim, such as an option, a model for the __________ of the underlying asset is needed due to the __________ nature of the contract's payoff.

   Solution:

   To price a contingent claim, such as an option, a model for the *future price behavior* of the underlying asset is needed due to the *asymmetric* nature of the contract's payoff.

2. Describe the main difference between pricing a contingent claim and pricing a forward commitment.

   Solution:

   The symmetric nature of a forward commitment's payoff (i.e., the obligation to transact at maturity) allows the commitment to be perfectly replicated without the need to model the future price behavior of the underlying asset. However, the asymmetric nature of a contingent claim's payoff (i.e., the right but *not* the obligation to transact at maturity) *does* require the future price behavior to be modeled.

3. If a one-period binomial model is used to price an at-the-money put option, which of the following statements is *most* accurate? The option will be:

   A. in-the-money if the price moves up.

   B. out-of-the-money if the price moves up.

   C. at-the-money if the price moves up or down.

   Solution:

   The correct answer is B; the option will be out-of-the-money if the price moves up. An at-the-money put option has an exercise price equal to the underlying asset price. Therefore, a price decrease will result in the put option moving *in the money*, and a price increase will result in the put option moving *out of the money*.

4. Explain how increasing the up gross return, R^u, and/or decreasing the down gross return, R^d, in a one-period binomial model would influence the price of a call and a put option.

Solution:

In a one-period binomial model, the volatility of the underlying asset is represented by the spread between the up gross return, R^u, and the down gross return, R^d. Therefore, if either the up gross return increases or the down gross return decreases (or both), the price of the underlying asset at maturity will be more volatile. If all else remains equal, then the price of both call and put options will increase when the underlying asset is expected to have a higher volatility over the life of the option.

5. A put option on a non-dividend-paying stock has an exercise price, X, of £21 and six months left to maturity. The current stock price, S_0, is £20, and an investor believes that the stock's price in six months' time will be either 10% higher or 10% lower.

   a. Describe how the investor can construct a perfectly hedged portfolio using the put option and its underlying stock.

   b. What will the value of the hedged portfolio be in the scenario that the stock price rises and the scenario that the stock price falls (assume a risk-free rate is 4%)?

   c. What is the no-arbitrage price of the put option?

Solution:

a. Denote the initial price of the underlying stock as S_0= £20.00 and the exercise price of the put option as X = £21.00. If the stock price moves up by 10%, then:

$$S_1^u = R^u S_0 = 1.1 \times £20.00 = £22.00.$$

If the stock price moves down by 10%, then

$$S_1^d = R^d S_0 = 0.9 \times £20.00 = £18.00.$$

Given that the payoff of a put option at expiry is Max(0, $X - S_T$):

$$p_1^u = \text{Max}(0,\ X - S_1^u) = \text{Max}(0,\ £21.00 - £22.00) = £0.$$

$$p_1^d = \text{Max}\left(0,\ X - S_1^d\right) = \text{Max}(0,\ £21.00 - £18.00) = £3.00.$$

The put option will be worth £3.00 if the underlying stock decreases in price by 10% and worthless if it increases by 10%. The hedge ratio of the option is:

$$h^* = \frac{(p_1^u - p_1^d)}{(S_1^u - S_1^d)} = \frac{£0 - £3}{£22 - £18} = \frac{£3}{£4} = -0.75.$$

So, to create a risk-free portfolio, we can buy the put option and buy 0.75 units of the underlying asset.

b. At maturity, the value of the perfectly hedged portfolio is:

$$V_1 = V_1^u = h^* S_1^u + p_1^u = 0.75 \times £22 + £0 = £16.50.$$

$V_1 = V_1^d = h^* S_1^d + p_1^d = 0.75 \times £18 + £3.00 = £16.50.$

We can use either $V_1{}^u$ or $V_1{}^d$ to compute the certain value, V_1, and the present value of the hedged position today is:

$V_0 = V_1(1 + r)^{-1} = £16.50 \times 1.04^{-0.5} = £16.18.$

c. The price of the put option is:

$p_0 = V_0 - h^* S_0 - = £16.18 - 0.75 \times £20 = £16.18 - £15 = £1.18.$

The no-arbitrage price of the put option should be £1.18.

6. Determine the correct answers to fill in the blanks: When the _______________ applies, the rate of return on all (real or synthetic) risk-free assets should equal the __________.

Solution:

When the *law of one price* applies, the rate of return on all (real or synthetic) risk-free assets should equal the *risk-free rate.*

5 RISK NEUTRALITY

☐ describe the concept of risk neutrality in derivatives pricing

As shown in the prior lesson, an option's value is not affected by actual (real-world) probabilities of underlying price increases or decreases. This realization contributed to the growing use of options as it became easier to agree on a given option's value. As we will see in this lesson, only the expected volatility—that is, gross returns R^u and R^d introduced earlier—and not the expected return are required to price an option.

We may generalize the relationship between an option's value and that of the hedge portfolios from Equation 5 of the prior lesson using the example of a call option c_0 as follows:

$$c_0 = \frac{\left(\pi c_1^u + (1 - \pi) c_1^d\right)}{(1 + r)^T}. \quad (9)$$

The value of the call option today, c_0, is computed as the expected value of the option at expiration, $c_1{}^u$ and $c_1{}^d$, discounted at the risk-free rate, r. This shows the derivative's value as similar to any other asset in that it equals the present value of expected future cash flows. In this case, these cash flows are weighted by assumed probabilities that are consistent with risk-neutral returns on the underlying.

The **risk-neutral probability** (π) is the computed probability used in binomial option pricing by which the discounted weighted sum of expected values of the underlying, $S_1{}^u = R^u S_0$ and $S_1{}^d = R^d S_0$, equal the current option price. Specifically, this probability is computed using the risk-free rate and assumed up gross return and down gross return of the underlying as in Equation 7.

$$\pi = \frac{1 + r - R^d}{R^u - R^d}. \quad (10)$$

More specifically, π, is the risk-neutral probability of an increase in the underlying price to $S_1{}^u = R^u S_0$, and (1 − π) is that of a decrease, $S_1{}^d = R^d S_0$.

Substituting the details from our earlier example, where R^uS_0= €110, R^dS_0= €60, S_0= €80, and X = €100, R^u = 1.375 and R^d = 0.75 and assuming an annual risk-free rate of 5%:

$$\pi = \frac{1+r-R^d}{R^u-R^d} = \frac{1+0.05-0.75}{1.375-0.75} = 0.48.$$

$$c_0 = \frac{\left(\pi c_1^u + (1-\pi)c_1^d\right)}{(1+r)^T}$$

=[0.48 × Max(0, €110 − €100) + 0.52 × Max(0, €60 − €100)]/1.05

= €4.80/1.05 = €4.57, which matches our earlier result from the prior lesson.

In Equation 7, the risk-neutral probabilities are determined solely by the up and down gross returns, R^u and R^d, representing underlying asset volatility and the risk-free rate used to calculate the present value of future cash flows. This no-arbitrage derivative value established separately from investor views on risk is referred to as **risk-neutral pricing**.

The use of risk-neutral pricing goes well beyond the simple one-period binomial tree and may be applied to any model that uses future underlying asset price movements, as we will see later in the curriculum.

EXAMPLE 2

Hightest Capital (revisited)

Revisiting Example 1 and the European call option sold by Hightest Capital, we can now explore the option price using risk-neutral pricing. Answer the following questions:

1. What is the risk-neutral probability of an up move and a down move in the one-period binomial model described in Example 1?
2. Demonstrate how this risk-neutral probability can be used to arrive at the no-arbitrage price of the call option.
3. What would be the value of a European *put* option on the same stock with the same exercise price and expiration date?
4. Confirm that the call option price computed in question 2 and the put option price computed in question 3 both satisfy the put–call parity relationship.

Solution to 1:

The risk-neutral probability of an up move, denoted π, is:

$$\pi = \frac{1+r-R^d}{R^u-R^d} = \frac{1+0.05-0.8}{1.2-0.8} = 0.625.$$

The risk-neutral probability of a down move is therefore:

$1 - \pi = 1 - 0.625 = 0.375.$

Solution to 2:

The call option price today is given by the (risk-neutral) expected value of the option payoff at maturity, discounted at the risk-free rate, r. In Equation 6:

$$c_0 = \frac{\left(\pi c_1^u + (1-\pi)c_1^d\right)}{(1+r)^T}$$

=[0.625 × Max(0, \$60 − \$55) + 0.375 × Max (0, \$40 − \$55)]/1.05

$$= \frac{\$3.125}{1.05} = \$2.98$$

which matches the value in Example 1.

Solution to 3:

Since Equation 6 is valid for any European option, the put option value with an exercise price of $55 is:

$$p_0 = \frac{\left(\pi p_1^u + (1-\pi)p_1^d\right)}{(1+r)^T}$$

$$=[0.625 \times \text{Max}(0, \$55 - \$60) + 0.375 \times \text{Max}(0, \$55 - \$40)]/1.05$$

$$= \$5.625/1.05 = \$5.36.$$

Note that we have used the same risk-neutral probability π as in Questions 1 and 2, since these values are a function of the binomial model for the underlying asset for a given asset volatility and risk-free rate, not the specific option being priced.

Solution to 4:

European call and put options with the same exercise price and maturity date must satisfy put–call parity as defined by:

$$S_0 + p_0 = c_0 + X(1+r)^{-T} = \$50 + \$5.36 = \$2.98 + \$55 \times 1.05^{-1} = \$55.36,$$

which confirms the relationship.

QUESTION SET

Hedging and Risk Neutrality

1. Which of the following factors influences the value of an option price when using a binomial model?

   A. The risk-free rate of return

   B. The level of investors' risk aversion

   C. The probability of an upward price move

   Solution:

   The correct answer is A, the risk-free rate of return. The value of an option is determined by its risk-neutral expectation discounted at the risk-free rate. In a one-period binomial model, the risk-neutral probabilities are determined only by the risk-free rate over the life of the option and the underlying asset's volatility (as measured by the up and down gross returns, R^u and R^d). Because of the ability to construct a perfect hedge of the option using the underlying asset, an option's price is independent of investors' risk aversion and the probability of the underlying price moving up (or down).

2. If the underlying asset price in a one-period binomial model can increase by 15% or decrease by 10% over the period and the prevailing risk-free rate

over the period is 4%, what is the risk-neutral probability of an asset pricing decrease?

Solution:

If the underlying asset price in a one-period binomial model can increase by 15%, then the up gross return is $R^u = 1.15$. Similarly, if the price can decrease by 10%, then the down gross return is $R^d = 0.9$.

The risk-neutral probability of an upward price move is:

$$\pi = \frac{1 + r - R^d}{R^u - R^d} = \frac{1 + 0.04 - 0.9}{1.15 - 0.9} = 0.56.$$

The risk-neutral probability of a downward price move is $1 - 0.56 = 0.44$.

3. Which of the following *best* describes the risk-neutral pricing interpretation of the one-period binomial option pricing formula?

   A. The real-world expected payoff discounted at the risk-free rate

   B. The risk-neutral expected payoff discounted at the risk-free rate

   C. The risk-neutral expected payoff discounted at a risk-adjusted rate

   Solution:

   The correct answer is B, the risk-neutral expected payoff discounted at the risk-free rate. The risk-neutral pricing interpretation of the option pricing formula states that the value of an option today is its risk-neutral expected value at maturity, discounted at the risk-free rate.

4. Determine the correct answers to fill in the blanks: If a call option is trading at a higher price than that implied from the binomial model, investors can earn a return in excess of the risk-free rate by ________ at the risk-free rate, __________ the call, and _________ the underlying.

   Solution:

   If a call option is trading at a higher price than that implied from the binomial model, investors can earn a return in excess of the risk-free rate by *borrowing* at the risk-free rate, *selling* the call, and *buying* the underlying.

   A synthetic risk-free asset can be created by this strategy that earns a return higher than the risk-free rate. Selling the over-priced call will provide a higher cash inflow than is required to generate the risk-free rate of return.

5. A stock's price is currently ¥8,000. At the end of one month when its options expire, the stock price is either up by 5% or down by 15%. If the risk-free rate is –0.20% for the period, what is the value of a put option with a strike price of ¥7,950?

   A. ¥333.67

   B. ¥299.60

   C. ¥236.93

   Solution:

   The correct answer is B, ¥299.60. Using risk-neutral pricing, we can determine the risk-neutral probability as:

$$\pi = \frac{1 + r - R^d}{R^u - R^d} = \frac{1 - 0.002 - 0.85}{1.05 - 0.85} = 0.74.$$

   The risk-neutral probability of a down move is therefore $1 - \pi = 1 - 0.74 = 0.26$. The value of a put option with an exercise price of ¥7,950 is:

$$p_0 = \frac{\left(\pi p_1^u + (1-\pi)p_1^d\right)}{(1+r)^T}$$

=[0.74 × Max(0, ¥7,950 − ¥8,400) + 0.26 × Max(0, ¥7,950 − ¥6,800)]/(1 − 0.002)

=[0.26 × ¥1,150]/0.998 = ¥299.60.

PRACTICE PROBLEMS

The following information relates to questions 1-4

Privatbank Kleinert KGaA, a private wealth manager in Munich, has a number of clients with large holdings in the German fintech firm SparCoin AG. Kleinert's analyst is concerned about a drop in SparCoin's share price in the next year and is recommending to clients that they consider purchasing a one-year put with an exercise price of €100. SparCoin's spot price (S_0) is €105.25, and it pays no dividends. The risk-free rate is 0.37%.

1. Kleinert's analyst estimates a 50-50 chance that the price of SparCoin will either increase by 12% or decline by 10% at the put option's expiration date. Which of the following statements best describes the no-arbitrage option price implied by this assumption?

   A. Since there is a 50% chance that the stock will fall to €94.73, there is a 50-50 chance of a €5.27 payout upon exercise and the no-arbitrage put is therefore worth €2.64 (= €5.27 / 2).

   B. Since there is a 50% chance that the stock will fall to €94.73, there is a 50-50 chance of a €5.27 payout upon exercise and given the risk-neutral probability of 0.47, the no-arbitrage put price is €2.48 (= €5.27 × 0.47).

   C. Since there is a 50% chance that the stock will fall to €94.73 and the risk-neutral probability is 0.47, the no-arbitrage put price is €2.78 (= €5.27 × {[1 – 0.47]/1.0037}).

2. If Kleinert's clients observe that the one-year put option with a €100 exercise price is trading at €2.50, which of the following statements best describes how Kleinert's clients could take advantage of this to earn a risk-free return greater than 0.37% over the year.

   A. Kleinert should purchase the put option and also purchase approximately 0.23 shares per option to match the hedge ratio.

   B. Kleinert should purchase the put option and purchase 50% of the underlying shares given the 50-50 chance the stock will fall and the put option exercised.

   C. Kleinert should purchase the put option and purchase 47% of the underlying shares to match the risk-neutral probability of put exercise.

3. If risk-free investments yielded a higher return over the next year, which of the following statements best describes how this would affect the no-arbitrage value of the put option on SparCoin shares?

   A. An increase in the risk-free rate will have *no effect* on SparCoin's put option price, as it is solely a function of the probability and degree of share price increase or decrease upon option expiration.

B. An increase in the risk-free rate will *increase* the value of the put option, as it will increase the risk-neutral probability of a price decline.

C. An increase in the risk-free rate will *decrease* the value of the put option, as it will both increase the risk-neutral probability of a price increase π and decrease the present value of the expected option payoff.

4. If the expected percentage increase and decrease in SparCoin's share price were to *double*, which of the following is the closest estimate of the one-year put option price with an exercise price of €100?

   A. The one-year put option price will rise to €7.90.

   B. The one-year put option price will rise to €8.50.

   C. The one-year put option price will rise to €7.40.

SOLUTIONS

1. The correct answer is C. A 12% increase in the stock price gives:

   $S_1^u = R^u S_0 = 1.12 \times €105.25 = €117.88.$

   The put option will expire unexercised:

   $p_1^u = \text{Max}(0, X - S_1^u) = \text{Max}(0, €100 - €117.88) = €0.$

   Alternatively, a 10% price decrease gives:

   $S_1^d = R^d S_0 = 0.9 \times €105.25 = €94.73.$

   The put option will pay off:

   $p_1^d = \text{Max}\left(1, X - S_1^d\right) = \text{Max}(0, €100 - €94.73) = €5.27.$

   To price this option, the risk-neutral pricing formula gives the risk-neutral probability π as:

   $\pi = (1 + 0.0037 - 0.9)/(1.12 - 0.9) = 0.47.$

   The no-arbitrage price is:

   $$p_0 = \frac{\left(\pi \times p_1^u + (1 - \pi) p_1^d\right)}{(1 + r)}$$

   $p_0 = (0.47 \times €0 + 0.53 \times €5.27)/(1 + 0.0037) = €2.79/1.0037 = €2.78.$

2. The correct answer is A. If the put option can be purchased for less than the no-arbitrage price, then a potential arbitrage opportunity is available. In this case, Kleinert's clients should purchase the underpriced put option and buy h^* units of SparCoin's stock. The hedge ratio, h^*, is calculated as:

   $$h^* = \frac{\left(p_1^u - p_1^d\right)}{\left(S_1^u - S_1^d\right)} = \frac{€0 - €5.27}{€117.88 - €94.73} = \frac{-€5.27}{€23.15} = -0.2276.$$

   Note that the negative hedge ratio implies that both the put option and underlying are purchased or sold to create a hedge. This initial purchase of the put option and stock will cost:

   $€2.50 + 0.2276 \times €105.25 = €26.45.$

   Should the stock price decrease, the value of this portfolio will be:

   $V_1 = V_1^d = h^* S_1^d + p_1^d = 0.2276 \times €94.73 + €5.27 = €26.83.$

   The strategy generates a risk-free return of (€26.83 – €26.45)/€26.45 = 1.44%, which is greater than the 0.37% return on other available risk-free investments.

3. The correct answer is C. Rising interest rates reduce the value of a put option. Increasing the risk-free rate will increase the risk-neutral probability of a price increase π and decrease the present value of the expected option payoff. Since the value of a put option is inversely related to the price of the underlying asset, an increased probability of an upward price move will reduce the expected payoff from the put. Consequently, both of these effects will reduce the put option value as the return on risk-free investments increases.

4. The correct answer is B. A 24% (previously 12%) increase in the stock price gives:

$S_1^u = R^u S_0 = 1.24 \times €105.25 = €130.51.$

The put option will expire unexercised:

$p_1^u = \text{Max}(0, X - S_1^u) = \text{Max}(0, €100.00 - €130.51) = €0.$

Alternatively, a 20% (previously 10%) decrease gives:

$S_1^d = R^d S_0 = 0.8 \times €105.25 = €84.20.$

The put option will pay off:

$p_1^d = \text{Max}\left(0, X - S_1^d\right) = \text{Max}(0, €100 - €84.20) = €15.80.$

To price this option, the risk-neutral pricing formula gives the risk-neutral probability as:

$\pi = (1 + 0.0037 - 0.8)/(1.24 - 0.8) = 0.46.$

The no-arbitrage price is:

$$p_0 = \frac{\left(\pi \times p_1^u + (1-\pi)p_1^d\right)}{(1+r)} = \frac{(0.46 \times €0 + 0.54 \times €15.80)}{(1 + 0.0037)} = \frac{€8.53}{1.0037} = €8.50.$$

Glossary

Abandonment option The option to terminate an investment at some future time if the financial results are disappointing.

Abnormal return The amount by which a security's actual return differs from its expected return, given the security's risk and the market's return.

Absolute dispersion The amount of variability present without comparison to any reference point or benchmark.

Accelerated book build An offering of securities by an investment bank acting as principal that is accomplished in only one or two days.

Accounting profit Income as reported on the income statement, in accordance with prevailing accounting standards, before the provisions for income tax expense. Also called *income before taxes* or *pretax income*.

Accredited investors Investors that meet certain minimum regulatory net worth or other requirements in order to invest in certain types of alternative assets.

Accrued interest The amount of interest in currency or par value terms of a fixed-income instrument that accumulates from the last coupon payment until the trade settlement date. The amount is paid by the buyer to the seller.

Action lag Delay from policy decisions to implementation.

Active investment An approach to investing in which the investor seeks to outperform a given benchmark.

Active return The return on a portfolio minus the return on the portfolio's benchmark.

Activist Short for "activist shareholder." Managers secure sufficient equity holdings to allow them to seek a position in a company's board and influence corporate policies or direction.

Activity ratios Ratios that measure how well a company is managing key current assets and working capital over time.

Ad hoc committee A small group of lenders or bondholders who negotiate with an issuer on debt restructuring and refinancing before the issuer submits a final proposal to the wider group of all lenders and bondholders.

Add-on pricing A pricing approach based on high-margin optional features, customizations, and additional content.

Add-on rate A yield or pricing convention for money market instrument quotations. It is the interest earned on an instrument, derived from the difference between the price and face value, expressed as a percentage of the price and multiplied by the periodicity of the annual rate.

Agency costs Direct and indirect costs borne by the principal in a principal-agent relationship owing primarily to information asymmetries. Agency costs include the costs of monitoring and assessing the agent as well as missed opportunities.

Agency RMBS Securities created by the pooling of residential mortgage-backed securities in the United States by either the Federal National Mortgage Association (Fannie Mae) or the Federal Home Loan Mortgage Corporation (Freddie Mac). These RMBS carry the full faith and credit of the government, essentially a guarantee with respect to timely payment of interest and repayment of principal.

All-or-nothing (AON) orders An order that includes the instruction to trade only if the trade fills the entire quantity (size) specified.

Allocationally efficient A characteristic of a market, a financial system, or an economy that promotes the allocation of resources to their highest value uses.

Altcoin A cryptocurrency other than Bitcoin.

Alternative data Data that are generated from non-traditional sources, such as social media and sensor networks.

Alternative hypothesis The hypothesis that is accepted if the null hypothesis is rejected.

Alternative investment markets Market for investments other than traditional securities investments (i.e., traditional common and preferred shares and traditional fixed income instruments). The term usually encompasses direct and indirect investment in real estate (including timberland and farmland) and commodities (including precious metals); hedge funds, private equity, and other investments requiring specialized due diligence.

Alternative trading systems Trading venues that function like exchanges but that do not exercise regulatory authority over their subscribers except with respect to the conduct of the subscribers' trading in their trading systems. Also called *electronic communications networks* or *multilateral trading facilities*.

American depository receipt A US dollar-denominated security that trades like a common share on US exchanges.

American depository share The underlying shares on which American depository receipts are based. They trade in the issuing company's domestic market.

American options Options that may be exercised at any time from contract inception until maturity.

American-style Type of option contract that can be exercised at any time up to the option's expiration date.

Amortization The process of allocating the cost of intangible long-term assets having a finite useful life to accounting periods; the allocation of the amount of a bond premium or discount to the periods remaining until bond maturity.

Amortizing debt A loan or bond with a payment schedule that calls for the complete repayment of principal over the instrument's time to maturity.

Analysis of variance (ANOVA) A table that presents the sums of squares, degrees of freedom, mean squares, and F-statistic for a regression model.

Analytical duration Estimates of duration using mathematical formulas. Estimates of the impact of yield changes on bond prices using analytical duration implicitly assume that benchmark yields and spreads are independent variables and are uncorrelated.

Anchoring and adjustment bias An information-processing bias in which the use of a psychological heuristic influences the way people estimate probabilities.

Annual general meeting (AGM) A yearly meeting of the corporate board of directors and shareholders, typically held in person and digitally, during which votes on directors, compensation plans, shareholder resolutions, and any other matters properly brought forward at the meeting are held. Issuer management may also make presentations and hold events.

Anomalies Apparent deviations from market efficiency.

Antidilutive With reference to a transaction or a security, one that would increase earnings per share (EPS) or result in EPS higher than the company's basic EPS—antidilutive securities are not included in the calculation of diluted EPS.

Arbitrage (1) The simultaneous purchase of an undervalued asset or portfolio and sale of an overvalued but equivalent asset or portfolio in order to obtain a riskless profit on the price differential. Taking advantage of a market inefficiency in a risk-free manner. (2) The condition in a financial market in which equivalent assets or combinations of assets sell for two different prices, creating an opportunity to profit at no risk with no commitment of money. In a well-functioning financial market, few arbitrage opportunities are possible. (3) A risk-free operation that earns an expected positive net profit but requires no net investment of money.

Arbitrageurs Traders who engage in arbitrage. See *arbitrage*.

Arithmetic mean The sum of the observations divided by the number of observations.

Artificial intelligence (AI) Computer systems that are capable of performing tasks that previously required human intelligence. AI methods are sometimes better suited to identify complex, non-linear relationships than are traditional quantitative and statistical methods.

Ask The price at which a dealer or trader is willing to sell an asset, typically qualified by a maximum quantity (ask size). See *offer*.

Ask size The maximum quantity of an asset that pertains to a specific ask price from a trader. For example, if the ask for a share issue is $30 for a size of 1,000 shares, the trader is offering to sell at $30 up to 1,000 shares.

Asset allocation The process of determining how investment funds should be distributed among asset classes.

Asset class A group of assets that have similar characteristics, attributes, and risk–return relationships.

Asset utilization ratios Ratios that measure how efficiently a company performs day-to-day tasks, such as the collection of receivables and management of inventory.

Asset-backed commercial paper Secured form of commercial paper issuance. Loans or receivables are sold to a special purpose entity that issues the ABCP and makes interest and principal payments to investors from asset cash flows.

Asset-backed securities (ABS) A type of bond issued by a legal entity called a special purpose entity created solely to own assets such as loans, receivables, and mortgages and to distribute cash flows to ABS investors. Generally, ABS backed by mortgages are known as mortgage-backed securities (MBS) while ABS refer to non-mortgage ABS.

Asset-backed token A token that represents the ownership of a physical asset that does not exist on the blockchain and whose value is based on the underlying asset.

Asset-based valuation models Valuation based on estimates of the market value of a company's assets.

Asymmetric information Also known as *information asymmetry*; the differential of information between corporate insiders and outsiders regarding the company's performance and prospects. Managers typically have more information about the company's performance and prospects than owners and creditors.

At-the-money Describes a unique situation in which the price of the underlying is equal to an option's exercise price. Like an out-of-the-money option, the intrinsic value is zero.

Auction/reverse auction models Pricing models that establish prices through bidding (by sellers in the case of reverse auctions).

Autarky Countries seeking political self-sufficiency with little or no external trade or finance. State-owned enterprises control strategic domestic industries.

Automatic stabilizer A countercyclical factor that automatically comes into play as an economy slows and unemployment rises.

Availability bias An information-processing bias in which people take a heuristic approach to estimating the probability of an outcome based on how easily the outcome comes to mind.

Available-for-sale Under US GAAP, debt securities not classified as either held-to-maturity or held-for-trading securities. The investor is willing to sell but not actively planning to sell. In general, available-for-sale debt securities are reported at fair value on the balance sheet, with unrealized gains included as a component of other comprehensive income.

Average revenue (AR) Total revenue divided by quantity sold.

Backfill Bias A problem whereby certain surviving hedge funds may be added to databases and various hedge fund indexes only after they are initially successful and start to report their returns. Also see *survivorship bias*.

Backup line of credit A type of credit enhancement provided by a bank to an issuer of commercial paper to ensure that the issuer will have access to sufficient liquidity to repay maturing commercial paper if issuing new paper is not a viable option.

Backwardation A downward-sloping, or inverted, forward curve in a futures market.

Balance sheet ratios Financial ratios involving balance sheet items only.

Balanced With respect to a government budget, one in which spending and revenues (taxes) are equal.

Balloon payment A large payment required at maturity to retire a bond's outstanding principal amount.

Base rates The reference rate on which a bank bases lending rates to all other customers.

Base-rate neglect A type of representativeness bias in which the base rate or probability of the categorization is not adequately considered.

Basic EPS Net earnings available to common shareholders (i.e., net income minus preferred dividends) divided by the weighted average number of common shares outstanding.

Basis risk The possibility that the expected value of a derivative differs unexpectedly from that of the underlying.

Basket of listed depository receipts (BLDR) An exchange-traded fund (ETF) that represents a portfolio of depository receipts.

Bayes' formula The rule for updating the probability of an event of interest—given a set of prior probabilities for the event, information, and information given the event—if you receive new information.

Bearer bonds Bonds for which ownership is not recorded; only the clearing system knows who the bond owner is.

Behavioral finance A field of finance that examines the psychological variables that affect and often distort the investment decision making of investors, analysts, and portfolio managers.

Behind the market Said of prices specified in orders that are worse than the best current price; e.g., for a limit buy order, a limit price below the best bid.

Benchmark A bond used to compare against another bond to discern attributes, often a government bond with the same or similar time-to-maturity as the bond under analysis.

Benchmark spread The difference in yield-to-maturity between a bond and that of a benchmark bond.

Best bid The highest bid in the market.

Best effort offering An offering of a security using an investment bank in which the investment bank, as agent for the issuer, promises to use its best efforts to sell the offering but does not guarantee that a specific amount will be sold.

Best offer The lowest offer (ask price) in the market.

Best-in-class An ESG implementation approach that seeks to identify the most favorable companies and sectors based on ESG considerations. Also called *positive screening*.

Beta A measure of the sensitivity of a given investment or portfolio to movements in the overall market.

Bid The price at which a dealer or trader is willing to buy an asset, typically qualified by a maximum quantity.

Bid size The maximum quantity of an asset that pertains to a specific bid price from a trader.

Big data The vast amount of information being generated by both traditional sources—for example, stock exchanges, companies, governments—and non-traditional sources—for example, electronic devices, social media, sensor networks, and company exhaust.

Bilateralism The conduct of political, economic, financial, or cultural cooperation between two countries. Countries engaging in bilateralism may have relations with many different countries but in one-at-a-time agreements without multiple partners. Typically, countries exist on a spectrum between bilateralism and multilateralism.

Bimodal A distribution that has two most frequently occurring values.

Bitcoin A cryptocurrency using blockchain technology that was created in 2009.

Bivariate correlation Also known as Pearson correlation. A parametric measure of the relationship between two variables.

Black swan risk An event that is rare and difficult to predict but has an important impact.

Block brokers A broker (agent) that provides brokerage services for large-size trades.

Blockchain A type of digital ledger in which information is recorded sequentially and then linked together and secured using cryptographic methods.

Blue chip Widely held large market capitalization companies that are considered financially sound and are leaders in their respective industry or local stock market.

Board of directors A body or individual selected by a limited company's member(s) or shareholder(s), in a manner determined by the company's charter, that manages the company. Typically, for larger companies, boards of directors appoint and oversee executive management.

Bond equivalent yield A money market interest rate quoted on a 365-day add-on rate basis.

Bond indenture A legal document between a bond issuer and investors that governs each party's rights and responsibilities.

Bond market vigilantes Bond market participants who might reduce their demand for long-term bonds, thus pushing up their yields.

Bondholders Investors in an entity's securitized debt claims, such as commercial paper, notes, and bonds. Common types of bondholders include investment funds and institutional investors.

Bonds Contractual agreements between an issuer and bondholders.

Bonus issue of shares A type of dividend in which a company distributes additional shares of its common stock to shareholders instead of cash.

Book building Investment bankers' process of compiling a "book" or list of indications of interest to buy part of an offering.

Book value Shareholders' equity (total assets minus total liabilities) minus the value of preferred stock; common shareholders' equity.

Boom An expansionary phase characterized by economic growth "testing the limits" of the economy.

Bootstrap A resampling method that repeatedly draws samples with replacement of the selected elements from the original observed sample. Bootstrap is usually conducted by using computer simulation and is often used to find standard error or construct confidence intervals of population parameters.

Bottom-up analysis An investment selection approach that focuses on company-specific circumstances rather than emphasizing economic cycles or industry analysis.

Box and whisker plot A graphic for visualizing the dispersion of data across quartiles. It consists of a box with "whiskers" connected to the box.

Breakeven point Represents the price of the underlying in a derivative contract in which the profit to both counterparties would be zero.

Bridge financing Interim financing that provides funds until permanent financing can be arranged.

Broker An agent who executes orders to buy or sell securities on behalf of a client in exchange for a commission.

Brokered market A market in which brokers arrange trades among their clients.

Broker–dealer A financial intermediary (often a company) that may function as a principal (dealer) or as an agent (broker) depending on the type of trade.

Brownfield investments The third stage of development of an infrastructure asset. Brownfield investments involve expanding existing facilities and may involve privatization of public assets or a sale leaseback of completed greenfield projects. They are characterized by a shorter investment period with immediate cash flows and an operating history.

Budget surplus/deficit The difference between government revenue and expenditure for a stated fixed period of time.

Bullet bond A bond whose principal repayment is made entirely at maturity.

Bundling A pricing approach that refers to combining multiple products or services so that customers are incentivized or required to buy them together.

Business cycles Are recurrent expansions and contractions in economic activity affecting broad segments of the economy.

Business model A concise description of how a business works and makes revenues and profits, including its customers, products or services, channels for reaching customers, and pricing.

Businesses Organization entities formed and managed for the purpose of providing a return or economic benefits to its investors and owners.

Buy-side firm An investment management company or other investor that uses the services of brokers or dealers (i.e., the client of the sell side firms).

Buyback A transaction in which a company buys back its own shares. Unlike stock dividends and stock splits, share repurchases use corporate cash.

Cabotage The right to transport passengers or goods within a country by a foreign firm. Many countries—including those with multilateral trade agreements—impose restrictions on cabotage across transportation subsectors, meaning that shippers, airlines, and truck drivers are not allowed to transport goods and services within another country's borders.

Call market A market in which trades occur only at a particular time and place (i.e., when the market is called).

Call money rate The interest rate that buyers pay for their margin loan.

Call option The right to buy an underlying.

Call period The time during which the issuer of a callable bond can exercise the call option.

Call price The price at which the issuer of a callable bond has the right to purchase the bond from investors.

Call protection period The time during which the issuer of a callable bond is not allowed to exercise the call option.

Call risk The uncertain maturity and limited price appreciation associated with callable bonds.

Callable bond A bond containing an embedded call option that gives the issuer the right to buy the bond back from the investor at specified prices on predetermined dates.

Cannibalization A transfer of sales or market share from one product to another product owned by the same company. It tends to occur when the two products are actual or perceived substitutes.

Capacity The ability of the borrower to make its debt payments on time.

Capital Other company resources available that reduce reliance on debt.

Capital allocation The process that companies use for decision making on capital investments—those projects with a life of one year or longer.

Capital allocation line (CAL) A graph line that describes the combinations of expected return and standard deviation of return available to an investor from combining the optimal portfolio of risky assets with the risk-free asset.

Capital asset pricing model (CAPM) An equation describing the expected return on any asset (or portfolio) as a linear function of its beta relative to the market portfolio.

Capital expenditure Expenditure on physical capital (fixed assets).

Capital investments An expenditure for an asset or resource with a useful life of more than one year.

Capital market expectations (CME) Expectations concerning the risk and return prospects of asset classes.

Capital market line (CML) The line with an intercept point equal to the risk-free rate that is tangent to the efficient frontier of risky assets; represents the efficient frontier when a risk-free asset is available for investment.

Capital market securities Fixed-income securities with original maturities greater than one year.

Capital markets Financial markets that trade securities of longer duration, such as bonds and equities.

Capital restrictions Controls placed on foreigners' ability to own domestic assets and/or domestic residents' ability to own foreign assets.

Capital structure The mix of debt and equity that a company uses to finance its business; a company's specific mix of long-term financing.

Capital-indexed bond A type of index-linked bond for which changes in the index are captured with adjustments to the principal. A common example is Treasury Inflation Protected Securities (TIPS) issued by the United States government.

Capital-intensive businesses Companies or business activities that are characterized by a relatively low fixed asset turnover, a high percentage of capital expenditures to sales, or a high net-working-capital-to-sales ratio.

Capital-light businesses Also known as *asset light businesses*, companies or business activities characterized by relatively high fixed asset turnover, a low percentage of capital expenditures to sales, or a low net-working-capital-to-sales ratio.

Carried interest A performance fee (also referred to as an incentive fee, or carry) that is applied based on excess returns above a hurdle rate.

Carrying Investing and holding an asset for a period of time.

Carrying amount The amount at which an asset or liability is valued according to accounting principles.

Carrying value Of a fixed-income instrument is the purchase price plus (minus) the amortized amount of the discount (premium) if the bond is purchased at a price below (above) par value.

Cartel Participants in collusive agreements that are made openly and formally.

Cash conversion cycle The amount of time between an issuer paying its suppliers in cash and receiving cash from its customers.

Cash flow additivity principle The principle that dollar amounts indexed at the same point in time are additive.

Cash flow from operations A cash profit measure over a period for an issuer's primary business activities. It includes cash from customers as well as interest and dividends received from financial investments, less cash paid to employees and suppliers as well as taxes paid to governments and interest paid to lenders.

Cash flow hedge Refers to a specific **hedge accounting** classification in which a derivative is designated as absorbing the variable cash flow of a floating-rate asset or liability, such as foreign exchange, interest rates, or commodities.

Cash markets Markets in which specific assets are exchanged at current prices. Cash markets are often referred to as **spot markets**.

Cash prices The current prices prevailing in **cash markets**.

Cash ratio A measure of liquidity that is the ratio of cash and marketable securities to current liabilities.

Catch-up clause A clause in an agreement that favors the GP. For a GP who earns a 20% performance fee, a catch-up clause allows the GP to receive 100% of the distributions above the hurdle rate *until* she receives 20% of the profits generated, and then every excess dollar is split 80/20 between the LPs and GP.

CDS credit spread Reflects the credit spread of a credit default swap (CDS) derivative contract. As with cash bonds, CDS credit spreads depend on the probability of default (POD) and the loss given default (LGD).

Central bank digital currencies (CBDCs) A tokenized version of the currency issued by the central bank, such as a digital bank note or coin, and a digital liability of the central bank.

Central bank funds market The market in which deposit-taking banks that have an excess reserve with their national central bank can lend money to banks that need funds for maturities ranging from overnight to one year. Called the federal or fed funds market in the United States.

Central bank funds rate The interest rate at which central bank funds are bought (borrowed) and sold (lent) for maturities ranging from overnight to one year. Called federal or fed funds rate in the United States.

Central clearing mandate A requirement instituted by global regulatory authorities following the 2008 global financial crisis that most **over-the-counter (OTC)** derivatives be **cleared** by a **central counterparty (CCP)**.

Central counterparty (CCP) An economic entity that assumes the **counterparty credit risk** between derivative **counterparties**, one of which is typically a financial intermediary. CCPs provide **clearing** and **settlement** for most **derivative contracts**.

Central limit theorem The theorem that states the sum (and the mean) of a set of independent, identically distributed random variables with finite variances is normally distributed, whatever distribution the random variables follow.

Certificate of deposit (CD) An instrument that represents a specified amount of funds on deposit with a bank for a specified maturity and interest rate. CDs are issued in various denominations and can be negotiable or non-negotiable.

Channels Venues where a company markets and/or delivers its products and services.

Character The quality of a debt issuer's management.

Checking accounts Bank deposits with no stated maturity available for transactional purposes that pay little or no interest. Also known as a *demand deposit*.

Circuit breaker A pause in intraday trading for a brief period if a price limit is reached.

Classical cycle Refers to fluctuations in the level of economic activity when measured by GDP in volume terms.

Clawback A requirement that the general partner return any funds distributed as incentive fees until the limited partners have received their initial investment and a percentage of the total profit.

Clearing An exchange's process of verifying the execution of a transaction, exchange of payments, and recording of participants.

Clearing instructions Instructions that indicate how to arrange the final settlement ("clearing") of a trade.

Clearinghouse An entity associated with a futures market that acts as middleman between the contracting parties and guarantees to each party the performance of the other.

Closed-end fund A mutual fund in which no new investment money is accepted. New investors invest by buying existing shares, and investors in the fund liquidate by selling their shares to other investors.

Cluster sampling A procedure that divides a population into subpopulation groups (clusters) representative of the population and then randomly draws certain clusters to form a sample.

Co-investing In co-investing, the investor invests in assets *indirectly* through the fund but also possesses rights (known as co-investment rights) to invest *directly* in the same assets. Through co-investing, an investor is able to make an investment *alongside* a fund when the fund identifies deals.

Code of ethics An established guide that communicates an organization's values and overall expectations regarding member behavior. A code of ethics serves as a general guide for how community members should act.

Coefficient of determination (R^2) The percentage of the variation of the dependent variable that is explained by the independent variable. It is a measure of goodness of fit of a regression model.

Coefficient of variation The ratio of a set of observations' standard deviation to the observations' mean value.

Cognitive cost The effort involved in processing new information and updating beliefs.

Cognitive dissonance The mental discomfort that occurs when new information conflicts with previously held beliefs or cognitions.

Cognitive errors Behavioral biases resulting from faulty reasoning; cognitive errors stem from basic statistical, information-processing, or memory errors.

Coincident economic indicators Turning points that are usually close to those of the overall economy; they are believed to have value for identifying the economy's present state.

Collateral Assets or financial guarantees underlying a debt obligation that are above and beyond the issuer's promise to pay.

Collateral manager Buys and sells debt obligations for and from the CDO's collateral pool to generate sufficient cash flows to meet the obligations to the CDO bondholders.

Collateralized bond obligations (CBOs) CDOs backed by high-yield corporate and emerging market bonds.

Collateralized debt obligations (CDOs) Securities backed by a diversified pool of one or more debt obligations. CDOs can be backed by a broad range of debt.

Collateralized loan obligations (CLOs) Investment vehicle with exposure to a portfolio of leveraged loans separated into tranches with different cash flow claims and exposure to losses based on a waterfall.

Collateralized mortgage obligations Securitize mortgage pass-through securities or multiple pools of loans. CMOs are structured to redistribute the cash flows to different bond classes or tranches and create securities that have different exposures to prepayment risk.

Commercial paper (CP) Short-term, negotiable, unsecured promissory note that represents a debt obligation of the issuer.

Committed (regular) lines of credit Bank commitments to extend credit; the commitment is considered a short-term liability and is usually in effect for 364 days (one day short of a full year).

Committed capital The amount that the limited partners have agreed to provide to the private equity fund.

Commodities A product or service from a firm that is indistinguishable from products or services of competing firms, usually conforming to a common standard or grade imposed by convention or regulation.

Commoditization A process by which competing products become less differentiated over time and become interchangeable "commodities" in the eyes of customers. This process is typically associated with declining profitability for the selling firms.

Commodity producers A firm that makes and/or sells commodities.

Commodity swap A type of swap involving the exchange of payments over multiple dates as determined by specified reference prices or indexes relating to commodities.

Common market Level of economic integration that incorporates all aspects of the customs union and extends it by allowing free movement of factors of production among members.

Common shares A type of security that represents an ownership interest in a company. Also called *common stock*.

Common stock A type of security that represents an ownership interest in a company. Also called *common shares*.

Common-size analysis The restatement of financial statement items using a common denominator or reference item that allows one to identify trends and major differences; an example is an income statement in which all items are expressed as a percent of revenue.

Companies Organization entities formed and managed for the purpose of providing a return or economic benefits to its investors and owners.

Company research report A document that presents an analyst's investment recommendation on an issuer and its securities, supported by financial modeling, industry overviews and competitive analyses, valuation scenarios, ESG considerations, and investment risks.

Complete markets Informally, markets in which the variety of distinct securities traded is so broad that any desired payoff in a future state-of-the-world is achievable.

Concession agreement A contractual arrangement under which an entity (also known as a grantor) establishes terms and conditions with a developer or operator (referred to as a concessionaire) to plan, build, operate, finance, and maintain an infrastructure asset for a specific period.

Conditional expected value The expected value of a stated event given that another event has occurred.

Conditional pass-through covered bonds Convert to pass-through securities after the original maturity date if all bond payments have not yet been made.

Conditional variances The variance of one variable, given the outcome of another.

Conditions The general economic, competitive, and business environment faced by all borrowers that may affect their ability to service or refinance debt.

Confidence level The complement of the level of significance.

Confirmation bias A type of cognitive bias that makes individuals view information that confirms beliefs they already hold as more salient.

Consensus protocol A set of rules governing how blocks can join the blockchain that is designed to resist attempts at malicious manipulation up to a certain level of security; it can be either a proof of work or a proof of stake.

Conservatism bias A belief perseverance bias in which people maintain their prior views or forecasts by inadequately incorporating new information.

Constant yield-price trajectory A graphical depiction of the relationship between time to maturity and a bond price, assuming no default, that shows that a bond price approaches par as time passes.

Constituent securities With respect to an index, the individual securities within an index.

Contango Refers to spot price below forward price in a futures market.

Contingency provision Clause in a legal document that allows for some action if a specific event or circumstance occurs.

Contingency table A table of the frequency distribution of observations classified on the basis of two discrete variables.

Contingent claim A type of derivative in which one of the *counterparties* determines whether and when the trade will settle. An *option* is a common type of contingent claim.

Contingent convertible bonds Bonds that automatically convert to equity if a specific event or circumstance occurs, such as the issuer's equity capital falling below the minimum requirement set by regulators.

Continuous trading market A market in which trades can be arranged and executed any time the market is open.

Continuously compounded return The natural logarithm of 1 plus the holding period return, or equivalently, the natural logarithm of the ending price over the beginning price.

Contract manufacturers Companies that make products for other companies that meet specific terms and specifications.

Contract size Amount(s) used for calculation to price and value the derivative. The contract size is often referred to as "notional amount or notional principal."

Contraction The period of a business cycle after the peak and before the trough; often called a *recession* or, if exceptionally severe, called a *depression*.

Contraction risk The risk of earlier repayment of a mortgage-backed security than expected.

Contractionary Tending to cause the real economy to contract.

Contractionary fiscal policy A fiscal policy that has the objective to make the real economy contract.

Contribution margin A profitability measure using variable costs: unit price less unit variable cost. It can also be expressed as a percentage of price or sales.

Controlling shareholder An individual or entity that owns a majority of the voting rights in a corporation.

Convenience sampling A procedure of selecting an element from a population on the basis of whether or not it is accessible to a researcher or how easy it is for a researcher to access the element.

Convenience yield A non-cash benefit of holding a physical commodity versus a derivative.

Conversion price Predetermined share price at which convertible debt may be fully exchanged for common shares during the conversion period.

Conversion ratio The number of common shares a convertible bond or noteholder may receive in exchange for a specific bond par value.

Conversion value The current contingency feature value derived by comparing a convertible bond's price with its value if a bondholder were to exchange bonds for shares.

Convertible bond A bond that gives the bondholder the right to exchange the bond for a specified number of common shares in the issuing company.

Convertible debt A fixed-income instrument which combines the features of debt with equity via a contingent feature, allowing debtholders to exchange their claim for common shares at a predetermined fixed price in the future.

Convertible preference shares A type of equity security that entitles shareholders to convert their shares into a specified number of common shares.

Convexity The second order, usually a positive change in the price of a bond for a given change in yield, which can be negative for a callable bond such as a high-yield bond.

Convexity adjustment A measure that is used to complement modified duration to capture the second-order effect of yield changes on a bond's price. It is equal to the annual convexity statistic times one-half times the given change in the yield-to-maturity squared.

Convexity bias Refers to the difference in price changes for a given change in yield between interest rate futures and interest rate forward contracts. That is, interest rate forwards exhibit a non-linear or convex relationship between price and yield, while the price–yield relationship is linear for interest rate futures.

Cooperation The process by which countries work together toward some shared goal or purpose. These goals may, and often do, vary widely—from strategic or military concerns, to economic influence, to cultural preferences.

Cooperative country A country that engages and reciprocates in rules standardization; harmonization of tariffs; international agreements on trade, immigration, or regulation; and allowing the free flow of information, including technology transfer.

Core real estate strategies Strategies with exposure to well-leased, high-quality commercial and residential real estate in the best markets, generally offered by open-end funds. Investors expect core real estate to deliver stable returns, primarily from income from the property.

Core-plus real estate strategies Value-add investments that require modest redevelopment or upgrades to lease any vacant space together with possible alternative use of the underlying properties. Compared to core real estate strategies, these may be appealing for investors seeking higher returns and willing to accept additional risks from development, redevelopment, repositioning, and leasing.

Corporate issuers Limited companies or corporations that seek financing in financial markets by, for example, issuing debt or equity securities.

Corporations Another term for limited companies, though often used to refer to public limited companies. See *limited company*, *private limited company*, and *public limited company*.

Correlation A measure of the linear relationship between two random variables.

Correlation coefficient A number between −1 and +1 that measures the consistency or tendency for two investments to act in a similar way. It is used to determine the effect on portfolio risk when two assets are combined.

Cost averaging The periodic investment of a fixed amount of money.

Cost of capital The cost of financing for a company; the rate of return that suppliers of capital require as compensation for their contribution of capital (also called *opportunity cost of funds*).

Cost of carry The net of the costs and benefits related to owning an underlying asset for a specific period.

Cost of debt The required return on debt financing for a company, such as when it issues a bond, takes out a bank loan, or leases an asset through a finance lease.

Cost of equity The return required by equity investors to compensate for both the time value of money and the risk. Also referred to as the required rate of return on common stock or the required return on equity.

Counterparty Legal entities entering a **derivative contract**.

Counterparty credit risk The likelihood that a **counterparty** is unable to meet its financial obligations under the contract.

Counterparty risk The risk that the other party to a contract will fail to honor the terms of the contract.

Country The geopolitical environment as well as the legal and political system faced by all issuers in a jurisdiction that may affect debt payment.

Coupon Periodic interest payments paid by a bond issuer to investors, typically expressed as a percentage of par on an annual basis.

Cournot assumption Assumption in which each firm determines its profit-maximizing production level assuming that the other firms' output will not change.

Covariance A measure of the co-movement (linear association) between two random variables.

Covenants The terms and conditions of lending agreements that the issuer must comply with; they specify the actions that an issuer is obligated to perform (affirmative covenant) or prohibited from performing (negative covenant).

Credit default swap (CDS) A type of credit derivative in which one party, the credit protection buyer who is seeking credit protection against a third party, makes a series of regularly scheduled payments to the other party, the credit protection seller. The seller makes no payments until a credit event occurs.

Credit enhancements Provisions or methods that allow a borrower improve their creditworthiness in a structured transaction.

Credit event An occurrence that triggers the settlement of a CDS contract, including failure to make a debt payment, debt restructuring, or a bankruptcy filing.

Credit facilities Loan agreements with pre-specified terms and limits but with fluctuating balances based on borrower-specific needs at different points in time, analogous to a credit card.

Credit migration risk The risk that a bond issuer's creditworthiness deteriorates, or migrates lower, leading investors to believe the risk of default is higher. Also called **downgrade risk**.

Credit rating Letter-grade, qualitative measures of an issuer's ability to meet its debt obligations based on both the probability of default and the expected loss under a default scenario.

Credit rating agencies Institutions that issue and maintain credit ratings. The three largest are Standard & Poor's, Moody's, and Fitch Ratings.

Credit risk The expected economic loss under a potential borrower default over the life of the contract.

Credit spread The compensation for the risk of default in a debt security, typically measured by the yield-to-maturity difference between a bond and a comparable government benchmark security.

Credit spread risk The risk of greater expected loss due to changes in credit conditions as a result of macroeconomic, market, and/or issuer-related factors.

Credit tranching Internal credit enhancement where cash flows into a senior/subordinate structure.

Credit-linked notes Bonds whose coupon changes when the bonds' credit rating changes.

Critical values Values of the test statistic at which the decision changes from fail to reject the null hypothesis to reject the null hypothesis.

Cross-default clause Covenant or contract clause that specifies borrowers are considered in default if they default on another debt obligation.

Cross-sectional analysis Analysis over a group as of a given time.

Crossing networks Trading systems that match buyers and sellers who are willing to trade at prices obtained from other markets.

Crowdsourcing A business model that enables users to contribute directly to a product, service, or online content.

Cryptocurrency An electronic medium of exchange that lacks physical form.

Cryptocurrency wallet A storage unit for public and/or private keys for cryptocurrency transactions. These wallets may be a physical device, program, or service.

Cryptography An algorithmic process to encrypt data, making the data unusable if received by unauthorized parties.

Cumulative preference shares Preference shares for which any dividends that are not paid accrue and must be paid in full before dividends on common shares can be paid.

Cumulative voting A voting process whereby shareholders can accumulate and vote all their shares for a single candidate in an election, as opposed to having to allocate their voting rights evenly among all candidates.

Currencies Monies issued by national monetary authorities.

Currency Money issued by national monetary authorities.

Currency swap A swap in which each party makes interest payments to the other in different currencies.

Current government spending With respect to government expenditures, spending on goods and services that are provided on a regular, recurring basis including health, education, and defense.

Current ratio A measure of liquidity that is the ratio of current assets to current liabilities.

Current yield The sum of the coupon payments received over the year divided by the flat price. Also called the income, interest yield, or running yield.

Customs union Extends the free trade area (FTA) by not only allowing free movement of goods and services among members, but also creating a common trade policy against nonmembers.

CVaR Conditional VaR, a tail loss measure. The weighted average of all loss outcomes in the statistical distribution that exceed the VaR loss.

Daily settlement A specific process of *mark-to-market* by a central clearing party in which the profits and losses of all counterparties to derivatives contracts are determined using settlement prices for each contract.

Dark pools Alternative trading systems that do not display the orders that their clients send to them.

Data mining The practice of determining a model by extensive searching through a dataset for statistically significant patterns. Also called *data snooping.*

Data science An interdisciplinary field that harnesses advances in computer science, statistics, and other disciplines for the purpose of extracting information from big data (or data in general).

Data snooping The subconscious or conscious manipulation of data in a way that produces a statistically significant result (i.e., the p-value is sufficiently small or the t-statistic sufficiently large to indicate statistical significance), such as by running multiple simulations and naively accepting the best result. Also known as p-hacking.

Day order An order that is good for the day on which it is submitted. If it has not been filled by the close of business, the order expires unfilled.

Days of inventory on hand (DOH) The average number of days it would take to sell the amount of inventory on hand. It is calculated as either the ending or average balance of inventories divided by (cost of goods sold/days in the period).

Days payable outstanding (DPO) The average number of days it takes a company to pay its suppliers. It is calculated as either the ending or average balance of accounts payable divided by (cost of goods sold/days in the period).

Days sales outstanding (DSO) The average number of days it takes for a company to receive payment from customers who purchase goods or services on credit. It is calculated as either the ending or average balance of accounts receivable divided by (revenues/days in the period).

Dealers Financial intermediaries, such as commercial banks or investment banks, who transact as **counterparties** with derivative end users.

Debt A claim against an entity to receive cash, stock, or other assets at a future date. From the perspective of the debtor or borrower, an obligation to pay cash, stock, or other assets at a future date. Generally, debt claims are unconditional and are senior to equity claims.

Debt service coverage ratio A key indicator of credit performance equal to the ratio of net operating income to debt service.

Debt tax shield The tax benefit from interest paid on debt being tax deductible from income, equal to the marginal tax rate multiplied by the value of the debt.

Debt-to-assets ratio A solvency ratio calculated as total debt divided by total assets.

Debt-to-capital ratio A solvency ratio calculated as total debt divided by total debt plus total shareholders' equity.

Debt-to-equity ratio A solvency ratio calculated as total debt divided by total shareholders' equity.

Debt-to-income ratio (DTI) Residential lending metric that compares an individual's monthly debt payments to their monthly pre-tax, gross income.

Debut issuer An issuer approaching the bond market for the first time.

Deciles Values that divide a distribution ranked smallest to largest into 10 equal parts.

Declaration date The day that the corporation issues a statement declaring a specific dividend.

Decreasing returns to scale When a production process leads to increases in output that are proportionately smaller than the increase in inputs.

Deductible temporary differences Temporary differences that result in a reduction of or deduction from taxable income in a future period when the balance sheet item is recovered or settled.

Deep learning An area of artificial intelligence in which a system uses neural networks to perform multistage, non-linear data processing to identify patterns. Also called *deep learning nets.*

Deep learning nets See *Deep learning.*

Deep-in-the-money option An option that is highly likely to be exercised.

Deep-out-of-the-money option An option that is highly unlikely to be exercised.

Default When a borrower on a mortgage loan fails to meet the obligations of the loan.

Default risk premium An extra return that compensates investors for the possibility that the borrower will fail to make a promised payment at the contracted time and in the contracted amount.

Defeasance Mechanism that allows prepayment on mortgage, but the borrower must purchase a portfolio of government securities that fully replicates the cash flows of the remaining scheduled principal and interest payments, including the balloon loan balance, on the loan.

Defensive interval ratio A liquidity ratio that estimates the number of days that an entity could meet cash needs from liquid assets; calculated as (cash + short-term marketable investments + receivables) divided by daily cash expenditures.

Deferred coupon bonds Bonds that pay no coupons for their first few years but then pay a higher coupon than they otherwise normally would for the remainder of their life. Also called *split coupon bonds*.

Deferred tax assets A balance sheet asset that arises when an excess amount is paid for income taxes relative to accounting profit. The taxable income is higher than accounting profit and income tax payable exceeds tax expense. The company expects to recover the difference during the course of future operations when tax expense exceeds income tax payable.

Deferred tax liabilities A balance sheet liability that arises when a deficit amount is paid for income taxes relative to accounting profit. The taxable income is less than the accounting profit and income tax payable is less than tax expense. The company expects to eliminate the liability over the course of future operations when income tax payable exceeds tax expense.

Defined benefit pension plans (DB plans) Plans in which the company promises to pay a certain annual amount (defined benefit) to the employee after retirement. The company bears the investment risk of the plan assets.

Defined contribution pension plans Individual accounts to which an employee and typically the employer makes contributions during their working years and expect to draw on the accumulated funds at retirement. The employee bears the investment and inflation risk of the plan assets.

Deflation Negative inflation.

Degree of financial leverage The ratio of percentage change in net income to percentage change in operating income over a period. It is a measure of how sensitive net income is to changes in operating income, driven by the firm's use of debt in its capital structure.

Degree of operating leverage The ratio of percentage change in operating income to percentage change in sales over a period. It is a measure of how sensitive operating income is to changes in sales, driven by the fixed and variable cost composition of operating expenses.

Delta The sensitivity of the derivative price to a small change in the value of the underlying asset.

Demand shock A typically unexpected disturbance to demand, such as an unexpected interruption in trade or transportation.

Dependent variable The variable that is explained by a regression model.

Depository bank A bank that raises funds from depositors and other investors and lends it to borrowers.

Depository institutions Commercial banks, savings and loan banks, credit unions, and similar institutions that raise funds from depositors and other investors and lend it to borrowers.

Depository receipt A security that trades like an ordinary share on a local exchange and represents an economic interest in a foreign company.

Depreciation The process of systematically allocating the cost of long-lived (tangible) assets to the periods during which the assets are expected to provide economic benefits.

Derivative A financial instrument that derives its value from the performance of an underlying asset or factor (e.g., stock price, interest rate, or exchange rate).

Derivative contract A legal agreement between counterparties with a specific **maturity**, or length of time, until the closing of the transaction, or **settlement**.

Derivative pricing rule A pricing rule used by crossing networks in which a price is taken (derived) from the price that is current in the asset's primary market.

Differentiated products A product or service from a firm that is distinguishable or distinct from those of competing firms. It is customers who determine and value whether a product is differentiated.

Diffuse prior The assumption of equal prior probabilities.

Diffusion index Reflects the proportion of the index's components that are moving in a pattern consistent with the overall index.

Digital assets The umbrella term covering assets that can be created, stored, and transmitted electronically and have associated ownership or use rights. Digital assets include a variety of assets, such as cryptocurrencies, tokens (security and utility), and digital collectables.

Diluted EPS The EPS that would result if all dilutive securities were converted into common shares.

Dilution An increase in the number of shares outstanding from share issuance that decreases the percentage of shares owned by existing shareholders.

Direct investing Occurs when an investor makes a direct investment in an asset without the use of an intermediary.

Direct lending Providing capital directly from private debt investors.

Direct listing Where the equity of a security is floated on the public markets directly, without underwriters, reducing the complexity and cost of the transaction.

Direct sales Marketing and/or delivering products and services to customers without an intermediary or third party between the customer and seller.

Direct taxes Taxes levied directly on income, wealth, and corporate profits.

Discount factor The price equivalent of a zero rate. Also may be stated as the present value of a currency unit on a future date.

Discount rate A yield or pricing convention for money market instrument quotations. It is the interest earned on an instrument, derived from the difference between the price and face value, expressed as a percentage of the face value and multiplied by the periodicity of the annual rate.

Discounted cash flow models Valuation models that estimate the intrinsic value of a security as the present value of the future benefits expected to be received from the security.

Discriminatory pricing rule A pricing rule used in continuous markets in which the limit price of the order or quote that first arrived determines the trade price.

Diseconomies of scale Increase in cost per unit resulting from increased production.

Dispersion The variability of a population or sample of observations around the central tendency.

Display size The size of an order displayed to public view.

Disposition effect A type of cognitive bias that makes individuals unwilling to sell their possessions at a loss.

Distressed debt Debt of mature companies in financial difficulty, in bankruptcy, or likely to default on debt.

Distressed/restructuring These strategies focus on securities of companies either in or perceived to be near bankruptcy. In one approach, hedge funds simply purchase fixed-income securities trading at a significant discount to par but that are still senior enough to be backed by sufficient corporate assets.

Distributed ledger A type of database that can be shared among entities in a network.

Distributed ledger technology (DLT) Technology based on a distributed ledger.

Diversification ratio The ratio of the standard deviation of an equally weighted portfolio to the standard deviation of a randomly selected security.

Dividend discount model (DDM) The model of the value of stock that is the present value of all future dividends, discounted at the required return on equity.

Dividend payout ratio The ratio of cash dividends paid to earnings for a period.

Dividends Distributions of profits and/or net assets from a corporation to its shareholders. While often in cash, dividends can be also be paid in stock or assets, such as property.

Divisor A number (denominator) used to determine the value of a price return index. It is initially chosen at the inception of an index and subsequently adjusted by the index provider, as necessary, to avoid changes in the index value that are unrelated to changes in the prices of its constituent securities.

Domestic bonds A type of bond for which the issuer's domicile and jurisdiction of issuance are the same.

Domestic content provisions Stipulate that some percentage of the value added or components used in production should be of domestic origin.

Double taxation Income is taxed twice.

Downside risk The potential for loss.

Drag on liquidity An action or event that reduces available funds or delays cash inflows.

Drivers Causative factors that explain the level of and changes in an output variable.

DSC ratio A property's annual net operating income (NOI) divided by the debt service.

Dual-class structure A capital structure that includes at least two classes of equity shares with unequal voting rights.

Dupont analysis An approach to decomposing return on investment, e.g., return on equity, as the product of other financial ratios.

Duration The first-order, linear change in a bond's price for a given yield change in yield, which is a negative or inverse relationship.

Duration gap the difference between a bond's Macaulay duration and its investor's investment horizon.

Dynamic pricing A pricing approach that charges different prices at different times. Specific examples include off-peak pricing, "surge" pricing, and "congestion" pricing.

Early repayment option May entitle the borrower to prepay all or part of the outstanding mortgage principal prior to maturity. This creates a risk from the lender's or investor's viewpoint because the cash flow amounts and timing cannot be known with certainty.

Earnings surprise The difference between reported EPS and expected EPS. Also referred to as *unexpected earnings*.

Economic indicators Economic statistics provided by government and established private organizations that contain information on an economy's recent past activity or its current or future position in the business cycle.

Economic infrastructure investments A category of infrastructure investments that support economic activity through transportation assets, information and communication technology assets, and utility and energy assets.

Economic stabilization Reduction of the magnitude of economic fluctuations.

Economic union Incorporates all aspects of a common market and in addition requires common economic institutions and coordination of economic policies among members.

Economies of scale A decline in costs per unit as output grows, generally resulting from having fixed costs in the cost structure that are spread over more units of output.

Economies of scope A decline in costs per unit as the number of product or business lines increases, generally resulting from having shared costs between the product lines.

Effective annual rate An interest rate with a periodicity of one.

Effective convexity An interest rate risk statistic that measures the non-linear/second-order effect of changes in the benchmark yield curve on a bond's price.

Effective duration The sensitivity of the bond's price to an instantaneous parallel shift in a benchmark yield curve—for example, the government par curve.

Efficient market A market in which asset prices reflect new information quickly and rationally. See also, *informationally efficient market.*

Either/or fee A custom fee arrangement whereby major investors are offered a structure where managers agree to charge *either* a lower management fee *or* a higher incentive fee, whichever is greater.

Electronic communications networks (ECNs) See *alternative trading systems* and *multilateral trading facilities.*

Embedded derivative A derivative within an underlying, such as a callable, putable, or convertible bond.

Embedded options Contingency provisions found in a bond's indenture representing rights that enable their holders to take advantage of interest rate movements. They can be exercised by the issuer, by the bondholder, or automatically depending on the course of interest rates.

Emotional biases Behavioral biases resulting from reasoning influenced by feelings; emotional biases stem from impulse or intuition.

Empirical duration Estimation of the price–yield relationship using historical bond market data in statistical models.

Employee stock ownership plan (ESOP) A type of employee benefit plan in which a company sets up a trust fund to receive contributions of newly issued shares or cash to buy existing shares. Contributions are tax deductible up to certain limits. Shares in the trust fund are allocated to individual employees based on relative pay or a formula.

Endowment bias An emotional bias in which people value an asset more when they hold rights to it than when they do not.

Enterprise risk management An overall assessment of a company's risk position. A centralized approach to risk management sometimes called firmwide risk management.

Enterprise value A measure of a company's total market value from which the value of cash and short-term investments have been subtracted.

Equal weighting An index weighting method in which an equal weight is assigned to each constituent security at inception.

Equity Ownership interest in an entity. A residual claim on the assets of an entity after more senior claims, such as debt, have been satisfied. Also known as *net assets*.

Equity swap A swap transaction in which at least one cash flow is tied to the return to an equity portfolio position, often an equity index.

Error term Represents the difference between the observed value of the independent variable and that expected from the true underlying population relation between the dependent and independent variable.

Estimated parameters In a simple linear regression, the estimated parameters are the intercept and slope of the fitted line.

Ether A programmable cryptocurrency created on the Ethereum blockchain in 2015 that allows for the execution of smart contracts.

Ethical principles Beliefs regarding what is good, acceptable, or obligatory behavior and what is bad, unacceptable, or forbidden behavior.

Ethics The study of moral principles or of making good choices. Ethics encompasses a set of moral principles and rules of conduct that provide guidance for our behavior.

Eurobonds A type of bond issued internationally, outside the jurisdiction of the country in whose currency the bond is denominated.

European options Options that may be exercised only at contract maturity.

European-style Said of an option contract that can only be exercised on the option's expiration date.

Event risk Risk that evolves around set dates, such as elections, new legislation, or other date-driven milestones, such as holidays or political anniversaries, known in advance. Example: Brexit referendum.

Ex-dividend date The first date that a share trades without (i.e., "ex") the right to receive the declared dividend for the period.

Excess kurtosis Degree of kurtosis (fatness of tails) relative to the kurtosis of the normal distribution.

Excess spread Surplus difference of yield remaining after payments to bondholders are made after expenses are made and losses are covered.

Exchange A rules-based, open access market venue where financial instruments are traded, with price and volume transparency accessible by issuers, investors, and their intermediaries.

Exchange-traded derivative (ETD) Futures, options, and other financial contracts available on exchanges.

Execution instructions Instructions that indicate how to fill an order.

Exercise The decision to transact the underlying by an option holder.

Exercise date The day that an option is exercised by its holder. For a call option, the day the strike price is paid and underlying is purchased. For a put option, when the strike price is received and the underlying is sold.

Exercise price The pre-agreed execution price specified in an option contract. Sometimes, this price is referred to as the strike price.

Exogenous risk A sudden or unanticipated risk that impacts either a country's cooperative stance, the ability of non-state actors to globalize, or both. Examples include sudden uprisings, invasions, or the aftermath of natural disasters.

Expansion The period of a business cycle after its lowest point and before its highest point.

Expansionary Tending to cause the real economy to grow.

Expansionary fiscal policy Fiscal policy aimed at achieving real economic growth.

Expected exposure (EE) The size of the investor's claim at the time of default.

Expected loss (EL) Default probability times loss severity given default.

Expected return on the portfolio Denoted as $(E\ (R_p))$. The weighted average of the expected returns (R_1 to R_n) on the component securities using their respective weights (w_1 to w_n).

Expected value of a random variable The probability-weighted average of the possible outcomes of a random variable.

Expert system A type of computer programming, often based on "if–then" rules, that attempts to simulate the knowledge base and analytical abilities of human experts in specific problem-solving contexts.

Export subsidy Paid by the government to the firm when it exports a unit of a good that is being subsidized.

Exposure at default (EAD) The size of the investor's claim at the time of default.

Extension risk The risk of later repayment of a mortgage-backed security than expected.

External credit enhancements Provisions or methods from a third party that allow a borrower improve their creditworthiness in a structured transaction.

External debt Sovereign debt owed to foreign creditors.

Extra dividend A dividend paid by a company that does not pay dividends on a regular schedule, or a dividend that supplements regular cash dividends with an extra payment.

Extraordinary general meetings (EGMs) Meetings besides an AGM of the corporate board and shareholders, typically held to deliberate and vote on urgent matters. Corporate charters and bylaws specify who can call an EGM and under what conditions.

Extreme value theory A branch of statistics that focuses primarily on extreme outcomes.

Face value The amount of principal on a bond, also known as par value.

Factoring arrangement When a company sells its accounts receivable to a lender (known as a factor) that assumes responsibility for the credit-granting and collection process.

Fair value A market-based measure of an investment based on observable or derived assumptions to determine a price that market participants would use to exchange an asset or liability in an orderly transaction at a specific time.

Fair value hedge Refers to a specific **hedge accounting** designation that applies when a derivative is deemed to offset the fluctuation in fair value of an asset or liability.

Fallen angels Formerly investment-grade-rated issuers whose bonds are downgraded to high yield due to credit deterioration.

Fat-Tailed Describes a distribution that has fatter tails than a normal distribution (also called leptokurtic).

Fed funds rate The US interbank lending rate on overnight borrowings of reserves.

Federal funds rate The US interbank lending rate on overnight borrowings of reserves. Also known as *Fed Funds rate*.

Fiat money Money that is not convertible into any other commodity.

Fiduciary call A combination of a purchased call option and investment in a risk-free bond with face value of the option's exercise price.

Fill or kill See *immediate or cancel order*.

Finance lease A type of lease which is more akin to the purchase or sale of the underlying asset.

Financial leverage The use of debt in the capital structure. Measured using ratios such as operating income to operating income less interest expense, total assets to total equity, or debt to equity.

Financial leverage ratio A measure of financial leverage calculated as average total assets divided by average total equity.

Financial risk The risk arising from a company's capital structure and, specifically, from the level of debt and debt-like obligations.

Fintech Technological innovation in the financial services industry, specifically with the design and delivery of financial services and products. It may also refer more broadly to companies involved in developing the new technologies and their applications, as well as the business sector that includes such companies.

Firm commitment A pre-determined amount (price and quantity) is agreed to be exchanged at settlement. Examples of firm commitments include forward contracts, futures contracts, and swaps.

First lien Also known as a priority lien, this investor protection grants a lender the right to take possession of property from a borrower which fails to repay debt.

First lien debt Debt secured by a pledge of certain assets that could include buildings, but it may also include property and equipment, licenses, patents, brands, etc.

First mortgage debt Debt secured by a pledge of a specific property.

Fiscal multiplier The ratio of a change in national income to a change in government spending.

Fiscal policy The use of taxes and government spending to affect the level of aggregate expenditures.

Fixed charge coverage A solvency ratio measuring the number of times interest and lease payments are covered by operating income, calculated as (EBIT + lease payments) divided by (interest payments + lease payments).

Fixed charge coverage ratio A measure of how well a company's earnings covers its fixed expenses, which may include debt payments, interest expense, and lease costs.

Fixed-income instruments Debt instruments such as loans or bonds.

Fixed-income securities Fixed-income instruments designed to be more easily tradeable than a loan, such as a bond.

Fixed-price call A contingency provision that grants an issuer the right to buy back a bond at a predetermined price in the future.

Fixed-rate payer The counterparty paying fixed cash flows in a swap contract. May also be referred to as the floating-rate receiver.

Flat price The full price of a bond minus accrued interest. Flat prices are usually quoted by bond dealers.

Float-adjusted market-capitalization weighting An index weighting method in which the weight assigned to each constituent security is determined by adjusting its market capitalization for its market float.

Floating-rate notes Notes on which interest payments are not fixed but instead vary from period to period depending on the current level of a reference interest rate. Also known as *floaters*.

Floating-rate payer The counterparty paying the variable cash flows in a swap contract. May also be referred to as the fixed-rate receiver.

Forecast object A variable on or related to an issuer's financial statements that an analyst makes a projection for. Examples include drivers of financial statements, financial statement lines, and summary measures like EBITDA.

Foreclosure Allows a lender to take possession of the property and ultimately sell the property to recover funds toward satisfying the outstanding debt obligation.

Foreign bonds A type of bond for which the issuer's domicile and jurisdiction of issuance are different.

Foreign currency reserves Holding by the central bank of non-domestic currency deposits and non-domestic bonds.

Foreign direct investments (FDI) Long-term investments in the productive capacity of a foreign country.

Foreign exchange gains (or losses) Gains (or losses) that occur when the exchange rate changes between the investor's currency and the currency that foreign securities are denominated in.

Forward contract A **derivative contract** for the future exchange of an **underlying** at a fixed price set at contract signing.

Forward price Represents the price agreed upon in a forward contract to be exchanged at the contract's maturity date, *T*. This price is shown in equations as $F_0(T)$.

Forward price-to-earnings ratio A P/E calculated on the basis of a forecast of EPS; a stock's current price divided by next year's expected earnings.

Forward rate agreement (FRA) An OTC derivatives contract in which counterparties agree to apply a specific interest rate to a future time period.

Founders class shares A way to entice early participation in startup funds whereby managers offer incentives that entitle investors to a lower fee structure and/or other favorable terms.

Framing bias An information-processing bias in which a person answers a question differently based on the way in which it is asked (framed).

Franchising A situation where an owner of an asset and associated intellectual property divests the asset and licenses intellectual property to a third-party operator (franchisee) in exchange for royalties. Franchisees operate under the constraints of a franchise agreement.

Free cash flow The actual cash that would be available to the company's investors after making all investments necessary to maintain the company as an ongoing enterprise (also referred to as free cash flow to the firm); the internally generated funds that can be distributed to the company's investors (e.g., shareholders and bondholders) without impairing the value of the company.

Free cash flow hypothesis The hypothesis that higher debt levels discipline managers by forcing them to make fixed debt service payments and by reducing the company's free cash flow.

Free float The portion of a listed company's equity securities that are not held by insiders, strategic investors, sponsors, founders, and so on, that are more freely available for trading.

Free trade areas One of the most prevalent forms of regional integration, in which all barriers to the flow of goods and services among members have been eliminated.

Free-cash-flow-to-equity models Valuation models based on discounting expected future free cash flow to equity.

Freemium business model A pricing approach that allows customers a certain level of usage or functionality at no charge. Those who wish to use more must pay.

Frequency table A representation of the frequency of occurrence of two discrete variables.

Full price The price of a bond including any accrued interest owed to the seller. It is the flat price plus accrued interest.

Fully amortizing loan A loan or bond with a payment schedule that calls for the complete repayment of principal over the instrument's time to maturity.

Fund investing In fund investing, the investor invests in assets indirectly by contributing capital to a fund as part of a group of investors. Fund investing is available for all major alternative investment types.

Fund of funds Funds that hold a portfolio of hedge funds; also called *funds of hedge funds*.

Fundamental analysis The examination of publicly available information and the formulation of forecasts to estimate the intrinsic value of assets.

Fundamental growth These strategies use fundamental analysis to identify companies expected to exhibit high growth and capital appreciation.

Fundamental long/short In this strategy, the hedge fund takes a long position in companies that are trading at inexpensive levels compared to their potential intrinsic value and shorts those that trade in the other direction, with the intention of reversing this trade to obtain alpha.

Fundamental value These strategies use fundamental analysis to identify undervalued and unloved companies for which there is a possibility that a corporate turnaround, with future revenue and cash flow growth, will result in higher valuations.

Fundamental weighting An index weighting method in which the weight assigned to each constituent security is based on its underlying company's size. It attempts to address the disadvantages of market-capitalization weighting by using measures that are independent of the constituent security's price.

Fungible Freely exchangeable, interchangeable, or substitutable with other things of the same type. Money and commodities are the most common examples.

Futures contract A variation of a forward contract that has essentially the same basic definition but with some additional features, such as a clearinghouse guarantee against credit losses, a daily settlement of gains and losses, and an organized electronic or floor trading facility.

Futures contract basis point value (BPV) The change in price of a futures contract given a 1 basis point (0.01%) change in yield.

Futures margin account An account held by an exchange clearinghouse for each derivatives counterparty. The funds in such an account are used to ensure that counterparties do not default on their contract obligation.

Futures price The pre-agreed price at which a futures contract buyer (seller) agrees to pay (receive) for the underlying at the maturity date of the futures contract.

FX swap The combination of a spot and a forward FX transaction.

G-spread Yield spread in basis points between a bond's yield-to-maturity and that of an actual or interpolated government bond. It represents the return for bearing risks relative to the government bond.

Game theory The set of tools decision makers use to incorporate responses by rival decision makers into their strategies.

Gamma A numerical measure of how sensitive an option's delta (the sensitivity of the derivative's price) is to a change in the value of the underlying.

Gate A provision that when implemented limits or restricts redemptions for a period of time.

General collateral repo Rather than involving a specific security, a repo that instead references a specific group of securities as eligible collateral (such as government bonds of a specific maturity).

General collateral repo rate The interest rate on a general collateral repo.

General obligation (GO) bonds Unsecured bonds issued by a non-sovereign government which are backed by the taxing authority of the issuer.

General obligation bonds Also known as GO bonds. Bonds issued by non-sovereign governments for general purposes and repaid from tax cash flows.

General partners (GPs) Private fund managers responsible for sourcing and deploying capital from limited partner investors over an investment life cycle and distributing returns to those investors over a finite investment holding period.

General partnership A business organizational form owned entirely by general partners.

Geophysical resource endowment Includes such factors as livable geography and climate as well as access to food and water, which are necessary for sustainable growth. Geophysical resource endowment is highly unequal among countries.

Geopolitics The study of how geography affects politics and international relations. These relations matter for investments because they contribute to important drivers of investment performance, including economic growth, business performance, market volatility, and transaction costs.

Gilts Bonds issued by the UK government.

Global depository receipt (GDR) A depository receipt that is issued outside of the company's home country and outside of the United States.

Global minimum-variance portfolio The portfolio on the minimum-variance frontier with the smallest variance of return.

Global registered share (GRS) A common share that is traded on different stock exchanges around the world in different currencies.

Globalization The process of interaction and integration among people, companies, and governments worldwide. It is marked by the spread of products, information, jobs, and culture across borders.

Gold standard With respect to a currency, if a currency is on the gold standard a given amount can be converted into a prespecified amount of gold.

Good-on-close An execution instruction specifying that an order can only be filled at the close of trading. Also called *market-on-close*.

Good-on-open An execution instruction specifying that an order can only be filled at the opening of trading.

Good-till-cancelled order An order specifying that it is valid until the entity placing the order has cancelled it (or, commonly, until some specified amount of time such as 60 days has elapsed, whichever comes sooner).

Goodwill An intangible asset that represents the excess of the purchase price of an acquired company over the value of the net identifiable assets acquired.

Governance tokens In permissionless networks, governance tokens serve as votes to determine how the particular network is run.

Government debt management Government policies that relate to the issuance of debt securities, typically handled by a treasurer or finance ministry.

Government equivalent yield Measures quoted using actual/actual day counts.

Grant date The day that terms of compensation are communicated by an issuer and accepted by an employee recipient.

Green bonds Bonds used to specifically finance environmental-related projects.

Greenfield investments New, "to-be-built" infrastructure projects and assets created to provide a specific essential service or to supply a public good.

Gross profit margin The ratio of gross profit to revenues.

Groupthink A behavioral bias that occurs when a team minimizes conflict and dissent in reaching and maintaining a consensus.

Growth cycle Refers to fluctuations in economic activity around the long-term potential trend growth level, focusing on how much actual economic activity is below or above trend growth in economic activity.

Growth option The option to make additional investments in a project at some future time if the financial results are strong. Also called an *expansion option*.

Growth rate cycle Refers to fluctuations in the growth rate of economic activity.

Haircut The difference between the market value of the security used as collateral and the value of the loan. Also called *repo margin*.

Halo effect An emotional bias that extends a favorable evaluation of some characteristics to other characteristics.

Hard commodities Traded natural resources, such as crude oil and metals, with markets often involving the physical delivery of the underlying upon settlement.

Hard hurdle rate Hurdle ratewhere the manager earns fees on annual returns in excess of the hurdle rate

Hard-bullet covered bonds Type of security where if payments do not occur according to the original schedule of a covered bond, a bond default is triggered and bond payments are accelerated.

Harmonic mean A type of weighted mean computed as the reciprocal of the arithmetic average of the reciprocals.

Hedge The **derivative contract** used in **hedging** an exposure.

Hedge accounting Accounting standard(s) that allow an issuer to offset a hedging instrument (usually a derivative) against a hedged transaction or balance sheet item to reduce financial statement volatility.

Hedge funds Private investment vehicles that may invest in public equities or publicly traded fixed-income assets, private capital, and/or real assets, but they are distinguished by their investment *approach* rather than by the investments themselves.

Hedge ratio The proportion of an underlying that will offset the risk associated with a derivative position.

Hedging The use of a derivative contract to offset or neutralize existing or anticipated exposure to an **underlying**.

Hegemony Countries that are regional or even global leaders and use their political or economic influence of others to control resources.

Held-to-maturity Debt (fixed-income) securities that a company intends to hold to maturity; these are presented at their original cost, updated for any amortisation of discounts or premiums.

Herding Clustered trading that may or may not be based on information.

Herfindahl-Hirschman Index (HHI) A measure of market concentration, calculated as the sum of the squares of competitor market shares. Antitrust regulators in some countries consider markets with an HHI between 1,500 and 2,500 moderately concentrated and consider markets with an HHI over 2,500 highly concentrated.

Heteroskedasticity Non-constant variance across all observations.

Hidden order An order that is exposed not to the public but only to the brokers or exchanges that receive it.

Hidden revenue business model Business models that provide services to users at no charge and generate revenues elsewhere.

High yield Bond issuers and issues rated BB+ (Ba1 on Moody's scale) or lower. Also known as speculative grade and junk.

High-water mark The highest value, net of fees, that a fund has reached in history. It reflects the highest cumulative return used to calculate an incentive fee.

Hindsight bias A type of cognitive bias that makes individuals misremember the past in ways that make them appear to have made better and more well-informed choices.

Holder-of-record date The date that a shareholder listed on the corporation's books will be deemed to have ownership of the shares for purposes of receiving an upcoming dividend.

Holding period return The single-period internal rate of return for a real estate property that includes property income and the change in property value over the period.

Home bias A preference for securities listed on the exchanges of one's home country.

Homogeneity of expectations The assumption that all investors have the same economic expectations and thus have the same expectations of prices, cash flows, and other investment characteristics.

Homoskedasticity Constant variance across all observations.

Horizon yield An investor's total rate of return on a fixed income instrument over their holding period, including reinvested coupon payments. It is an internal rate of return expressed as an annualized rate.

Hostile takeover When a potential acquirer seeks to acquire a company (the target) against the wishes of the target's board of directors. Typically, a tender offer is used to carry out the hostile takeover, against which a board might use a poison pill in its defense.

Household A person or a group of people living in the same residence, taken as a basic unit in economic analysis.

Human capital The present value of an individual's future expected labor income.

Hurdle rate Also called "preferred return." The minimum rate of return on investment that a fund must reach before a GP receives carried interest.

Hypothesis A proposed explanation or theory that can be tested.

Hypothesis testing The process of testing of hypotheses about one or more populations using statistical inference.

I-spread also known as interpolated spread, it is the yield spread for a bond over the standard swap rate in that currency of the same tenor.

Iceberg order An order in which the display size is less than the order's full size.

If-converted method A method for accounting for the effect of convertible securities on earnings per share (EPS) that specifies what EPS would have been if the convertible securities had been converted at the beginning of the period, taking account of the effects of conversion on net income and the weighted average number of shares outstanding.

Illusion of control bias A bias in which people tend to believe that they can control or influence outcomes when, in fact, they cannot.

Immediate or cancel order An order that is valid only upon receipt by the broker or exchange. If such an order cannot be filled in part or in whole upon receipt, it cancels immediately. Also called *fill or kill*.

Impact lag The lag associated with the result of actions affecting the economy with delay.

Implied forward rate An interest rate or yield over a future period implied by the current term structure of interest rates.

Import license Specifies the quantity of a good that can be imported into a country.

In-the-money Describes an option with a positive intrinsic value.

Income tax paid The actual amount paid for income taxes in the period; not a provision, but the actual cash outflow.

Income tax payable The income tax owed by the company on the basis of taxable income.

Increasing returns to scale When a production process leads to increases in output that are proportionately larger than the increase in inputs.

Incurrence test A financial ratio or other measurement taken prior to an action such as debt issuance, usually on a pro forma basis taking the action into account. Satisfaction of the test (e.g., leverage ratio below a certain value) is linked to covenants between the issuer and investors.

Indenture A written contract between a lender and borrower that specifies the terms of the loan, such as interest rate, interest payment schedule, or maturity.

Independent With reference to events, the property that the occurrence of one event does not affect the probability of another event occurring. With reference to two random variables X and Y, they are independent if and only if $P(X,Y) = P(X)P(Y)$.

Independent directors Members of a corporation's board of directors who do not have an employment or familial relationship with the company, nor do they have a relationship that would impair their independence such as an economic interest in a vendor or competitor of the company.

Independent variable An explanatory variable in a regression model.

Independently and identically distributed With respect to random variables, the property of random variables that are independent of each other but follow the identical probability distribution.

Index-linked bonds A bond whose coupon payments or principal repayment is linked to a specified index.

Indexing An investment strategy in which an investor constructs a portfolio to mirror the performance of a specified index.

Indicator variable A variable that takes on only one of two values, 0 or 1, based on a condition. In simple linear regression, the slope is the difference in the dependent variable for the two conditions. Also referred to as a *dummy variable*.

Indifference curve A curve representing all the combinations of two goods or attributes such that the consumer is entirely indifferent among them.

Indirect taxes Taxes such as taxes on spending, as opposed to direct taxes.

Inflation premium An extra return that compensates investors for expected inflation.

Inflation reports A type of economic publication put out by many central banks.

Inflation-linked bonds Debt instruments that link the principal and interest to inflation.

Information cascade The transmission of information from those participants who act first and whose decisions influence the decisions of others.

Information-motivated traders Traders that trade to profit from information that they believe allows them to predict future prices.

Informationally efficient market A market in which asset prices reflect new information quickly and rationally.

Infrastructure A type of real asset that is intended for public use and provides essential services. These assets are typically long-lived fixed assets, such as bridges and toll roads.

Initial coin offering (ICO) An unregulated process whereby companies raise capital by selling crypto-tokens to investors in exchange for fiat money or another agreed-upon cryptocurrency.

Initial margin The ratio of the price of collateral to the value of cash exchanged in a repo; a value over 1.0 or 100% indicates overcollateralization.

Initial margin requirement The margin requirement on the first day of a transaction as well as on any day in which additional margin funds must be deposited.

Initial public offering (IPO) The first issuance of common shares to the public by a formerly private corporation.

Inside directors Members of a corporation's board of directors who are not independent. Typically, inside directors are employees or founders (and their family) of the company.

Insolvency A situation in which an issuer's total liabilities exceed the market value of its assets.

Institution An established organization or practice in a society or culture. An institution can be a formal structure, such as a university, organization, or process backed by law; or it can be informal, such as a custom or behavioral pattern important to society. Institutions can, but need not be, formed by national governments. Examples of institutions include non-governmental organizations, charities, religious customs, family units, the media, political parties, and educational practice.

Intangible assets Assets without a physical form, such as patents and trademarks.

Interbank market The market of loans and deposits between banks for maturities ranging from overnight to one year.

Intercept The estimated value of the dependent variable when the independent variable is zero.

Interest coverage A solvency ratio calculated as EBIT divided by interest payments.

Interest coverage ratio A measure of an issuer's ability to service its debt, typically the ratio of operating income or EBIT to interest expense.

Interest rate A rate of return that reflects the relationship between differently dated cash flows; a discount rate.

Interest rate swap A swap in which the underlying is an interest rate. Can be viewed as a currency swap in which both currencies are the same and can be created as a combination of currency swaps.

Interest-indexed bond A type of index-linked bond for which changes in the index are captured with adjustments to interest payments.

Internal credit enhancements Provisions or methods a borrower initiates to improve their creditworthiness in a structured transaction, such as overcollateralization or excess spread.

internal rate of return The discount rate that makes net present value equal 0; the discount rate that makes the present value of an investment's costs (outflows) equal to the present value of the investment's benefits (inflows).

Internal rate of return (IRR) The uniform discount rate for a series of cash flows over n periods that returns a net present value of zero.

Internet of things The vast array of physical devices, home appliances, smart buildings, vehicles, and other items that are embedded with electronics, sensors, software, and network connections that enable the objects in the system to interact and share information.

Interquartile range The difference between the third and first quartiles of a dataset.

Intrinsic value The amount gained (per unit) by an option buyer if an option is exercised at any given point in time. May be referred to as the exercise value of the option.

Investment banks Financial intermediaries that provide advice to their mostly corporate clients and help them arrange transactions such as initial and seasoned securities offerings.

Investment grade Bond issuers and issues rated BBB- (Baa3 on Moody's scale).

Investment policy statement (IPS) A written planning document that describes a client's investment objectives and risk tolerance over a relevant time horizon, along with constraints that apply to the client's portfolio.

Issue rating A rating which seeks to capture the probability of default or expected loss of the issuer's senior unsecured bonds.

Issuer rating A rating which seeks to capture the credit risk of a specific financial obligation of an issuer which takes such factors as seniority into account.

J-curve effect Net income over a multiyear private investment holding period characterized by negative returns in an initial phase, followed by cash flow and income growth toward the end of the holding period.

Jackknife A resampling method that repeatedly draws samples by taking the original observed data sample and leaving out one observation at a time (without replacement) from the set.

January effect Calendar anomaly that stock market returns in January are significantly higher compared to the rest of the months of the year, with most of the abnormal returns reported during the first five trading days in January. Also called *turn-of-the-year effect.*

Joint probability function A function giving the probability of joint occurrences of values of stated random variables.

Judgmental sampling A procedure of selectively handpicking elements from the population based on a researcher's knowledge and professional judgment.

Junior debt Debt obligation with lower priority of payment than senior debt obligations.

Key rate duration Also known as partial duration, is a measure of a bond's sensitivity to a change in the benchmark yield at a specific maturity.

Keynesians Economists who believe that fiscal policy can have powerful effects on aggregate demand, output, and employment when there is substantial spare capacity in an economy.

Kurtosis The statistical measure that indicates the combined weight of the tails of a distribution relative to the rest of the distribution.

Lagging economic indicators Turning points that take place later than those of the overall economy; they are believed to have value in identifying the economy's past condition.

Law of one price A principle that states that if two investments have the same or equivalent future cash flows regardless of what will happen in the future, then these two investments should have the same current price.

Lead underwriter The lead investment bank in a syndicate of investment banks and broker–dealers involved in a securities underwriting.

Leading economic indicators Turning points that usually precede those of the overall economy; they are believed to have value for predicting the economy's future state, usually near-term.

Legal tender Something that must be accepted when offered in exchange for goods and services.

Lender of last resort An entity willing to lend money when no other entity is ready to do so.

Leptokurtic Describes a distribution that has fatter tails than a normal distribution (also called fat-tailed).

Lessee Tenant or property user that enters a lease with a property owner or lessor.

Lessor Property owner or manager that leases a property to a tenant or property user.

Level of significance The probability of a Type I error in testing a hypothesis.

Leverage A measure for identifying a potentially influential high-leverage point.

Leveraged buyout (LBO) A transaction in which a private acquiror uses equity and a high proportion of debt to acquire a public or private company in order to make changes to increase value over an investment period.

Leveraged loan Where private debt investor firms borrow money to make a direct loan to a borrower.

Leveraged loans Loans made to a borrower or issuer with relatively lower credit quality and/or higher leverage.

Liability-driven investing An investment industry term that generally encompasses asset allocation that is focused on funding an investor's liabilities in institutional contexts.

Licensing arrangements Rights to produce a product or have access to intangible assets using someone else's brand name in return for a royalty (often a percentage of revenues).

Lien A legal right or claim to property by a creditor.

Likelihood The probability of an observation, given a particular set of conditions.

Limit order Instructions to a broker or exchange to obtain the best price immediately available when filling an order, but in no event accept a price higher than a specified (limit) price when buying or accept a price lower than a specified (limit) price when selling.

Limit order book The book or list of limit orders to buy and sell that pertains to a security.

Limited company A business organizational form owned by shareholders or members with limited liability who elect a board of directors to appoint management. Generally, limited companies have indefinite life and easier transfer of ownership interests than limited partnerships.

Limited liability partnership (LLP) A business organizational form available in some jurisdictions owned entirely by limited partners with limited liability.

Limited partners (LPs) Outside investors in a private market fund who own a fractional interest in a limited, closed-end partnership managed by a general partner based on the investment commitment and other terms set out in a limited partner agreement.

Limited partnership Closed-end form of ownership frequently used in private market funds in which private market fund investors, or limited partners, commit capital that is invested, managed, and distributed by a private market fund manager, or general partner, over an investment holding period.

Limited partnership agreement (LPA) A legal document that outlines the rules of the partnership and establishes the framework that ultimately guides the fund's operations throughout its life.

lin-log model A functional form for transforming regression model data in which the dependent variable is linear but the independent variable is logarithmic.

Linear derivatives Firm commitment derivative contracts in which the contract's payoff/profit function is linear with respect to the price of the underlying.

Liquid market Said of a market in which traders can buy or sell with low total transaction costs when they want to trade.

Liquidity The extent to which a company is able to meet its short-term obligations using cash flows and those assets that can be readily transformed into cash.

Liquidity premium The compensation for liquidity risk that increases in proportion to the investment's illiquidity.

Liquidity ratios Financial ratios measuring the company's ability to meet its short-term obligations to creditors as they come due.

Liquidity risk The risk that an investment may not be readily sold at its true value.

Liquidity trap A condition in which the demand for money becomes infinitely elastic (horizontal demand curve) so that injections of money into the economy will not lower interest rates or affect real activity.

Load fund A mutual fund in which, in addition to the annual fee, a percentage fee is charged to invest in the fund and/or for redemptions from the fund.

Loan-to-value ratio (LTV) Ratio of the amount of the mortgage to the property's value. The lower the LTV, the higher the borrower's equity. From the lender's perspective, the higher the borrower's equity, the less likely the borrower is to default.

Loans Debt instruments agreed to between a borrower and lender, typically a bank.

Lockout or revolving period For an ABS with a non-amortizing collateral pool, such as credit card debt, is the period in which the cash proceeds from principal repayments are reinvested in additional loans with a principal equal to the principal repaid. During this period, there is no prepayment risk and potential default risk is generally limited. When the lockout period is over, principal repayments are used to pay off the outstanding principal on the ABS. Lockout period and revolving period are interchangeable.

Lockup period The minimum holding period before investors are allowed to make withdrawals or redeem shares from a fund. Its purpose is to allow the hedge fund manager the required time to implement and potentially realize a strategy's expected results.

log-lin model A functional form for transforming regression model data in which the dependent variable is logarithmic but the independent variable is linear.

log-log model A functional form for transforming regression model data in which both the dependent and independent variables are in logarithmic form.

Long A trading position in a **derivative contract** that gains value as the price of the **underlying** moves higher.

Long position A position in an asset or contract in which one owns the asset or has an exercisable right under the contract.

Long-run average total cost The curve describing average total cost when no costs are considered fixed.

Loss aversion The tendency of people to dislike losses more than they like comparable gains.

Loss given default (LGD) The amount a debtholder fails to recover if a default occurs, usually expressed as a percentage of par value.

Loss severity Portion of a bond's value (including unpaid interest) an investor loses in the event of default.

Loss-aversion bias A bias in which people tend to strongly prefer avoiding losses as opposed to achieving gains.

Low-cost producer A firm with lower production costs than its industry competitors.

M^2 A measure of what a portfolio would have returned if it had taken on the same total risk as the market index.

M^2 alpha Difference between the risk-adjusted performance of the portfolio and the performance of the benchmark.

Macaulay duration the present-value weighted average time to receipt of cash flows for fixed-income instrument, also the holding period needed to balance coupon reinvestment risk and price risk for a one-time instantaneous "parallel" shift in the yield curve once the bond purchase is settled. It is named after Frederick Macaulay, the Canadian economist who introduced the concept in 1938.

Machine learning (ML) Involves computer-based techniques that seek to extract knowledge from large amounts of data without making any assumptions about the data's underlying probability distribution. The goal of ML algorithms is to automate decision-making processes by generalizing, or "learning," from known examples to determine an underlying structure in the data.

Maintenance capital expenditures Investments in assets to keep them in operation or increase their efficiency without extending their useful lives.

Maintenance margin Minimum balance set below the initial margin that each contract buyer and seller must hold in the futures margin account from trade initiation until final settlement at maturity.

Maintenance margin requirement The margin requirement on any day other than the first day of a transaction.

Management buy-in A type of leveraged buyout where the current management team is replaced with the acquiring team involved in managing the company.

Management buyout A private sale to a strategic buyer that includes a company's existing management. The management team commits their own equity capital along with other investors as an incentive to grow the firm's cash flows and value.

Management guidance Management of public companies may publicly provide targets for earnings, revenues, and other measures (e.g., capital expenditures) for the next quarter, year, or longer term. Guidance can be detailed or rather directional and is often updated throughout the year. Initial guidance for next fiscal year might be provided during the fourth-quarter earnings call and updated for completed quarters, and new information provided at the first-, second-, and third-quarter earnings calls. Also known simply as *guidance*.

Margin call Request to a derivatives contract counterparty to immediately deposit funds to return the futures margin account balance to the initial margin.

Margin financing A financing arrangement whereby the prime broker lends shares, bonds, or derivatives and the hedge fund (or investment manager) deposits cash or other collateral into a margin account at the prime broker based on certain fractions of the investment positions.

Margin loan Money borrowed from a broker to purchase securities.

Marginal propensity to consume The proportion of an additional unit of disposable income that is consumed or spent; the change in consumption for a small change in income.

Marginal propensity to save The proportion of an additional unit of disposable income that is saved (not spent).

Mark to market (MTM) The practice in which a central clearing party assigns profits and losses to counterparties to derivative contracts. In exchange-traded markets, this practice takes place daily and is often referred to as daily settlement.

Market anomaly Change in the price or return of a security that cannot directly be linked to current relevant information known in the market or to the release of new information into the market.

Market bid–ask spread The difference between the best bid and the best offer.

Market discount rate The rate of return required by investors given the risk of the bond investment, also known as the required yield or required rate of return.

Market float The number of shares that are available to the investing public.

Market makers **Over-the-counter (OTC) dealers** who typically enter into offsetting bilateral transactions with one another to transfer risk to other parties.

Market model A regression model with the return on a stock as the dependent variable and the returns on a market index as the independent variable.

Market multiple models Valuation models based on share price multiples or enterprise value multiples.

Market neutral These strategies use quantitative, fundamental, and technical analysis to identify under- and overvalued equity securities. The hedge fund takes long positions in undervalued securities and short positions in overvalued securities, while seeking to maintain a market-neutral net position.

Market order Instructions to a broker or exchange to obtain the best price immediately available when filling an order.

Market reference rate (MRR) The interest rate underlying used in interest rate swaps. These rates typically match those of loans or other short-term obligations. Survey-based Libor rates used as reference rates in the past have been replaced by rates based on a daily average of observed market transaction rates. For example, the Secured Overnight Financing Rate (SOFR) is an overnight cash borrowing rate collateralized by US Treasuries. Other MRRs include the euro short-term rate (€STR) and the Sterling Overnight Index Average (SONIA).

Market risk Risk related to market movements, e.g., unexpected changes in share prices, interest rates, currency exchange rates, and commodity prices.

Market share A company's or product's revenue expressed as a percentage of its market size.

Market size Total sales for a good or service, which can be calculated on a global or more regional basis.

Market value The price at which an asset or security can currently be bought or sold in an open market.

Market-capitalization weighting An index weighting method in which the weight assigned to each constituent security is determined by dividing its market capitalization by the total market capitalization (sum of the market capitalization) of all securities in the index. Also called *value weighting*.

Market-on-close An execution instruction specifying that an order can only be filled at the close of trading.

Marketable limit order A buy limit order in which the limit price is placed above the best offer, or a sell limit order in which the limit price is placed below the best bid. Such orders generally will partially or completely fill right away.

Markowitz efficient frontier The graph of the set of portfolios offering the maximum expected return for their level of risk (standard deviation of return).

Master limited partnership (MLP) Has similar features to limited partnerships but is usually a more liquid investment that is often publicly traded.

Master repurchase agreement A legal document governing all repo trades between two parties.

Match funding Financing an asset with a source, such as a loan or bond, that is aligned with certain attributes of the asset, such as duration and the respective streams of income and financing costs.

Material (materiality) Refers to information that is decision-useful for a reasonable investor.

Matrix pricing An estimation process for financial instruments based on the prices of comparable instruments.

Maturity The date of a fixed-income instrument's final payment to investors.

Maturity premium An extra return that compensates investors for the increased sensitivity of the market value of debt to a change in market interest rates as maturity is extended.

Maturity structure of interest rates Also known as the term structure of interest rates, refers to the difference in interest rates or benchmark yields by time-to-maturity.

Mean absolute deviation With reference to a sample, the mean of the absolute values of deviations from the sample mean.

Mean square error (MSE) Calculated as the sum of squares error (SSE) divided by the degrees of freedom, which are the number of observations minus the number of independent variables minus one. Since simple linear regression has just one independent variable, the degrees of freedom calculation is the number of observations minus 2.

Mean square regression (MSR) Calculated as the sum of squares regression (SSR) divided by the number of independent variables in the regression model. In simple linear regression, there is only one independent variable, so MSR equals SSR.

Mean–variance analysis An approach to portfolio analysis using expected means, variances, and covariances of asset returns.

Measure of central tendency A quantitative measure that specifies where data are centered.

Measures of location Quantitative measures that describe the location or distribution of data. They include not only measures of central tendency but also other measures, such as percentiles.

Median The "middlemost" observation; i.e., in a set of observations that has been ranked from highest to lowest, the median will lie in the middle.

Meme coin A type of altcoin that is often inspired by a joke.

Mental accounting bias An information-processing bias in which people treat one sum of money differently from another equal-sized sum based on which mental account the money is assigned to.

Merger arbitrage Special situations investments related to business combinations in which investors seek to capitalize on price discrepancies of securities issued by the target company.

Mesokurtic Describes a distribution with kurtosis equal to that of the normal distribution, namely, kurtosis equal to three.

Mezzanine debt Refers to private credit subordinated to senior secured debt but senior to equity in the borrower's capital structure.

Mezzanine-stage financing Mezzanine venture capital that prepares a company to go public as it continues to expand capacity and enhance its growth trajectory. It represents the bridge financing needed to fund a private firm until it can execute an IPO or be sold.

Miner A validator of transactions on the blockchain that locks blocks of transactions into the blockchain and receives compensation for this process in the form of a digital asset.

Minimum efficient scale The smallest output that a firm can produce such that its long-run average total cost is minimized.

Minimum-variance portfolio The portfolio with the minimum variance for each given level of expected return.

Minority shareholder An individual or entity that owns less than a majority of the voting rights in a corporation.

Mode The most frequently occurring value in a distribution.

Modern portfolio theory (MPT) The analysis of rational portfolio choices based on the efficient use of risk.

Modified duration The first derivative of a bond's price with respect to its yield, this statistic is a measure of interest rate risk used to estimate the percentage price change for a given change in yield-to-maturity.

Monetarists Economists who believe that the rate of growth of the money supply is the primary determinant of the rate of inflation.

Monetary policy Actions taken by a nation's central bank to affect aggregate output and prices through changes in bank reserves, reserve requirements, or its target interest rate.

Monetary transmission mechanism The process whereby a central bank's interest rate gets transmitted through the economy and ultimately affects the rate of increase of prices.

Monetary union An economic union in which the members adopt a common currency.

Money convexity A measure that is used to complement modified duration to capture the second-order effect of yield changes on a bond's price, expressed in currency terms.

Money duration A measure of the price change of a fixed-income instrument in currency units from a change in yield-to-maturity. The money duration can be stated per 100 of par value or in terms of the actual position size. In the United States, money duration is commonly called "dollar duration."

Money market The market for short-term debt instruments (one-year maturity or less).

Money market securities Fixed-income securities with original maturities of one year or less.

Money-weighted return The internal rate of return on a portfolio, taking account of all cash flows.

Moneyness Expresses the relationship between an option's value and its exercise price across the full range of possible underlying prices.

Monopolistic competition Highly competitive form of imperfect competition; the competitive characteristic is a notably large number of firms, while the monopoly aspect is the result of product differentiation.

Monopoly In pure monopoly markets, there are no substitutes for the given product or service. There is a single seller, which exercises considerable power over pricing and output decisions.

Monte Carlo simulation A technique that uses the inverse transformation method for converting a randomly generated uniformly distributed number into a simulated value of a random variable of a desired distribution. Each key decision variable in a Monte Carlo simulation requires an assumed statistical distribution; this assumption facilitates incorporating non-normality, fat tails, and tail dependence as well as solving high-dimensionality problems.

Moral principles Beliefs regarding what is good, acceptable, or obligatory behavior and what is bad, unacceptable, or forbidden behavior.

Mortgage loan Agreement to finance real estate by the collateral of a specified property that obliges the borrower to make a predetermined series of payments to the lender.

Mortgage pass-through security Security created when mortgage lenders pool mortgages together and sell securities to investors. The cash flow from the mortgage pool––monthly payments of principal, interest, and prepayments––are "passed through" to the security holders.

Mortgage-backed securities (MBS) Debt obligations that represent claims to the cash flows from pools of mortgage loans, most commonly on residential property.

Multi-factor model A model that explains a variable in terms of the values of a set of factors.

Multi-market indexes Comprised of indexes from different countries, designed to represent multiple security markets.

Multilateral trading facilities See *alternative trading systems.*

Multilateralism The conduct of countries who participate in mutually beneficial trade relationships and extensive rules harmonization. Private firms are fully integrated into global supply chains with multiple trade partners. Examples of multilateral countries include Germany and Singapore.

Multiple of invested capital (MOIC) Also referred to as the multiple of money or total value to paid-in, this private market performance measure incorporates both the cumulative distributions received and the net asset value of a fund as a proportion of invested capital.

Multiple-price auction A debt securities auction in which bidders receive distinct prices based on their bids.

Multiplier models Valuation models based on share price multiples or enterprise value multiples.

Mutual fund A comingled investment pool in which investors in the fund each have a pro-rata claim on the income and value of the fund.

Nash equilibrium When two or more participants in a non-coop-erative game have no incentive to deviate from their respective equilibrium strategies given their opponent's strategies.

Nationalism The promotion of a country's own economic interests to the exclusion or detriment of the interests of other nations. Nationalism is marked by limited economic and financial cooperation. These actors may focus on national production and sales, limited cross-border investment and capital flows, and restricted currency exchange.

Natural language processing (NLP) A field of research within the field of text analytics and at the intersection of computer science, AI, and linguistics that focuses on developing computer programs to analyze and interpret human language.

Natural resources These include commodities (hard and soft), agricultural land (farmland), and timberland.

Negative externalities A cost to a third party because of the production or consumption of a good or service.

Negative pledge clause Limitations on investments, the disposal of assets, or issuance of debt senior to existing obligations. Negative covenants seek to ensure that an issuer maintains the ability to make interest and principal payments.

Net cash An issuer's total debt less cash and marketable securities. When the balance is negative it is referred to as net cash.

Net debt An issuer's total debt less cash and marketable securities. When the balance is positive it is referred to as net debt.

Net investment hedge Refers to a specific **hedge accounting** designation that applies when either a foreign currency bond or a derivative, such as an FX swap or forward, is used to offset the exchange rate risk of the equity of a foreign operation.

Net present value (NPV) The present value of an investment's cash inflows (benefits) minus the present value of its cash outflows (costs).

Net profit margin An indicator of profitability, calculated as net income divided by revenue; indicates how much of each dollar of revenues is left after all costs and expenses. Also called *profit margin* or *return on sales.*

Net tax rate The tax rate net of transfer payments.

Net working capital Working capital excluding short-term items unrelated to business operations, such as cash, marketable securities, and short-term debt.

Network effects A business model that enables users to contribute directly to a product, service, or online content.

Neural networks A type of computer program design based on how the human brain learns and processes information.

Neutral rate of interest The rate of interest that neither spurs on nor slows down the underlying economy.

No-load fund A mutual fund in which there is no fee for investing in the fund or for redeeming fund shares, although there is an annual fee based on a percentage of the fund's net asset value.

Node Each value on a binomial tree from which successive moves or outcomes branch.

Non-agency RMBS MBS backed by residential mortgages that are issued by private entities and not guaranteed by a federal agency or a GSE.

Non-amortizing loans Type of debt where there are no scheduled principal repayments.

Non-cooperative country A country with inconsistent and even arbitrary rules; restricted movement of goods, services, people, and capital across borders; retaliation; and limited technology exchange.

Non-cumulative preference shares Preference shares for which dividends that are not paid in the current or subsequent periods are forfeited permanently (instead of being accrued and paid at a later date).

Non-financial risks Risks that arise from sources other than changes in the external financial markets, such as changes in accounting rules, legal environment, or tax rates.

Non-fungible token (NFT) A unique cryptographic token on the blockchain that cannot be replicated and is used to represent ownership of physical assets, such as artwork, real estate, or other assets.

Non-linear derivatives Derivatives, such as options or other contingent claims, with payoff/profit profiles that are non-linear (asymmetric) with respect to the price of the underlying.

Non-participating preference shares Preference shares that do not entitle shareholders to share in the profits of the company. Instead, shareholders are only entitled to receive a fixed dividend payment and the par value of the shares in the event of liquidation.

Non-probability sampling A sampling plan dependent on factors other than probability considerations, such as a sampler's judgment or the convenience to access data.

Non-recourse loan Loan in which the lender does not have a claim against the borrower and thus can look only to the property to recover the outstanding mortgage balance.

Non-state actors Those that participate in global political, economic, or financial affairs but do not directly control national security or country resources. Examples of non-state actors are non-governmental organizations (NGOs), multinational companies, charities, and even influential individuals, such as business leaders or cultural icons.

Nonparametric test A test that is not concerned with a parameter or that makes minimal assumptions about the population from which a sample comes.

Nonsystematic risk Unique risk that is local or limited to a particular asset or industry that need not affect assets outside of that asset class.

Normal distribution A continuous, symmetric probability distribution that is completely described by its mean and its variance.

Normalized earnings The expected level of mid-cycle earnings for a company in the absence of any unusual or temporary factors that affect profitability (either positively or negatively).

Notching Ratings adjustment methodology where specific issues from the same borrower may be assigned different credit ratings.

Notice period The length of time (typically 30–90 days) in advance that investors may be required to notify a fund of their intent to redeem some or all of their investment. This allows a fund manager to liquidate a position in an orderly fashion without magnifying losses.

Novation process A process that substitutes the initial **swap execution facility (SEF)** contract with identical trades facing the **central counterparty (CCP)**. The CCP serves as **counterparty** for both financial intermediaries, eliminating bilateral **counterparty credit risk** and providing **clearing** and **settlement** services.

Null hypothesis The hypothesis that is tested.

Off-the-run Seasoned government bonds that are often less liquid.

Off-the-run securities Sovereign debt securities outstanding other than on-the-sun securities. Off-the-run securities are less liquid than on-the-run securities.

Offer The price at which a dealer or trader is willing to sell an asset, typically qualified by a maximum quantity (ask size).

Official interest rate An interest rate that a central bank sets and announces publicly; normally the rate at which it is willing to lend money to the commercial banks. Also called *official policy rate* or *policy rate.*

Official policy rate An interest rate that a central bank sets and announces publicly; normally the rate at which it is willing to lend money to the commercial banks.

Oligopoly Market structure with a relatively small number of firms supplying the market.

Omnichannel Refers to a company selling its products or services in multiple channels, such as in store and online.

On-the-run Most recently issued, and liquid, government bonds.

On-the-run securities The most recently issued and liquid sovereign debt securities.

Open interest The number of outstanding contracts.

Open market operations The purchase or sale of bonds by the national central bank to implement monetary policy. The bonds traded are usually sovereign bonds issued by the national government.

Open-end fund A mutual fund that accepts new investment money and issues additional shares at a value equal to the net asset value of the fund at the time of investment.

Operating cycle The length of time between a company's acquisition of goods or raw materials and the collection of cash from sales to customers.

Operating efficiency ratios Ratios that measure how efficiently a company performs day-to-day tasks, such as the collection of receivables and management of inventory.

Operating leases A type of lease which is more akin to the rental of the underlying asset.

Operating leverage The sensitivity of a firm's operating profit to a change in revenues, determined by the composition of fixed and variable operating costs.

Operating profit margin A profitability ratio calculated as operating income (i.e., income before interest and taxes) divided by revenue. Also called *operating margin.*

Operational deposits Bank deposits generated by clearing, custody, and cash management activities.

Operational independence A bank's ability to execute monetary policy and set interest rates in the way it thought would best meet the inflation target.

Operational risk The risk that arises from inadequate or failed people, systems, and internal policies, procedures, and processes, as well as from external events that are beyond the control of the organization but that affect its operations.

Operationally efficient Said of a market, a financial system, or an economy that has relatively low transaction costs.

Opportunistic real estate strategies Include major redevelopment, repurposing of assets, taking on large vacancies, or speculating on significant improvement in market conditions. These may be appealing for investors seeking higher returns and willing to accept additional risks from development, redevelopment, repositioning, and leasing.

Opportunity cost Reflects the foregone opportunity of investing in a different asset. It is typically denoted by the risk-free rate of interest, *r*.

Optimal capital structure The capital structure at which the value of the company is maximized.

Option A primary example of a **contingent claim**. A **derivative contract** that provides the buyer the right, but not the obligation, to buy or sell an **underlying**.

Option contract See *option.*

Option premium An amount that is paid upfront from the option buyer to the option seller. Reflects the value of the option buyer's right to exercise in the future.

Option-adjusted price The sum of a bond's flat price and value of an embedded option.

Option-adjusted spread or OAS for a bond is its Z-spread adjusted for the value of an embedded option.

Option-adjusted yield A yield measure for a bond adjusted for embedded options.

Order A specification of what instrument to trade, how much to trade, and whether to buy or sell.

Order precedence hierarchy With respect to the execution of orders to trade, a set of rules that determines which orders execute before other orders.

Order-driven markets A market (generally an auction market) that uses rules to arrange trades based on the orders that traders submit; in their pure form, such markets do not make use of dealers.

Ordinary shares Equity shares that are subordinate to all other types of equity (e.g., preferred equity). Also called *common stock* or *common shares.*

Organizational form A legal and tax classification of a business, specific to a jurisdiction, that determines the organization's legal identity, owner–manager relationship, owner liability, taxation, and access to financing.

Out-of-the-money Describes an option with zero intrinsic value because the option buyer would not rationally exercise the option. An example of such would be the case in which the price of the underlying is less than the option's exercise price for a call option.

Over-the-counter (OTC) Refers to derivative markets in which **derivative contracts** are created and traded between derivatives end users and **dealers**, or financial intermediaries, such as commercial banks or investment banks.

Overcollateralization Credit enhancement technique where collateral underlying the transaction exceeds the face value of the issued bonds.

Overconfidence bias A bias in which people demonstrate unwarranted faith in their own intuitive reasoning, judgments, and/or cognitive abilities.

Overfitting When a machine learning model learns the input and target dataset too precisely, making the system more likely to discover false relationships or unsubstantiated patterns that will lead to prediction errors.

P-value The smallest level of significance at which the null hypothesis can be rejected.

Par rate A yield-to-maturity that makes the present value of a bond's cash flows equal to par.

Par swap rate The fixed swap rate that equates the present value of all future expected floating cash flows to the present value of fixed cash flows.

Par value The amount of principal on a bond, also known as face value.

Parallel shift When all maturities along a yield curve increase or decrease in yield in the same direction by the same magnitude. A parallel shift in the yield curve is implicitly assumed in analytical duration and convexity.

Parameter A descriptive measure computed from or used to describe a population of data, conventionally represented by Greek letters.

Parametric test Any test (or procedure) concerned with parameters or whose validity depends on assumptions concerning the population generating the sample.

Pari passu clause A covenant or contract clause that ensures a debt obligation is treated the same as the borrower's other senior debt instruments and is not subordinated to similar obligations.

Partially amortizing bond A loan or bond with a payment schedule that calls for partial repayment of principle over the life of the bond, with the remaining principal paid at maturity.

Participating preference shares Preference shares that entitle shareholders to receive the standard preferred dividend plus the opportunity to receive an additional dividend if the company's profits exceed a pre-specified level.

Pass-through businesses Businesses that, by virtue of their organizational form and/or other legal and regulatory attributes, do not pay entity-level taxes on income or loss; income or loss is passed through to owners, who pay personal taxes.

Pass-through rate The coupon rate of a mortgage pass-through security that is received by the investor after administrative charges. It is lower than the weighted average mortgage rate earned on the underlying pool of mortgages because of administrative charges. The pass-through rate that the investor receives is said to be "net interest" or "net coupon."

Passive investment A buy-and-hold approach in which an investor does not make portfolio changes based on short-term expectations of changing market or security performance.

Payable date The day that the company actually mails out (or electronically transfers) a dividend payment.

Payment date The day that the company actually mails out (or electronically transfers) a dividend payment.

Payment-in-kind A bond feature whereby coupon payments can be fully or partially paid in the form of additional issuance or added to the principal amount.

Payments system The system for the transfer of money.

Pearson correlation A parametric measure of the relationship between two variables.

Pecking order theory The theory that managers consider how their actions might be interpreted by outsiders and thereby order their preferences for various forms of corporate financing. Forms of financing that are least visible to outsiders (e.g., internally generated funds) are most preferable to managers, and those that are most visible (e.g., equity issuance) are least preferable.

Penetration pricing A discount pricing approach used when a firm willingly sacrifices margins in order to build scale and market share.

Percentiles Values that divide a distribution into 100 equal parts.

Perfect competition A market structure in which the individual firm has virtually no impact on market price, because it is assumed to be a very small seller among a very large number of firms selling essentially identical products.

Performance evaluation The measurement and assessment of the outcomes of investment management decisions.

Performance fee Fee paid to the general partner from the limited partner(s) based on realized net profits.

Period costs Costs (e.g., executives' salaries) that cannot be directly matched with the timing of revenues and which are thus expensed immediately.

Periodicity Number of periods in a year, used for compound interest. The periodicity of a fixed-income instrument usually matches the frequency of its coupon payments.

Permanent differences Differences between tax and financial reporting of revenue (expenses) that will not be reversed at some future date. These result in a difference between the company's effective tax rate and statutory tax rate and do not result in a deferred tax item.

Permissioned networks Networks that are fully open only to select participants on a DLT network.

Permissionless networks Networks that are fully open to any user on a DLT network.

Perpetual bonds Bonds with no stated maturity date.

Perpetuity A perpetual annuity, or a set of never-ending level sequential cash flows, with the first cash flow occurring one period from now.

PESTLE analysis A framework for analyzing factors that influence an industry's economic outcomes.

Pet projects A capital investment that is pursued by management but is not economically justifiable by a disinterested party. Motivations for pet projects include self-dealing and vanity.

Physical risks Economic and financial losses from the increase in the severity and frequency of extreme weather due to climate change—for example, the loss of coastal real estate from a storm.

PIPE (private investment in public equity) A private offering to select investors with fewer disclosures and lower transaction costs that allows the issuer to raise capital more quickly and cost effectively.

Platykurtic Describes a distribution that has relatively less weight in the tails than the normal distribution (also called thin-tailed).

Pledge A legal right or claim to property by a creditor. Also called a lien.

Poison pill Officially known as a shareholder rights plan, a poison pill is a hostile-takeover defense adopted by boards of directors according to rules specified in the corporate charter. There are several types of poison pills. Generally, they allow shareholders, *excluding* the shareholder making the hostile bid and their affiliates, to buy newly issued shares at a discounted price. The share issuance would dilute the bidder's ownership percentage, rendering it impossible for the bidder to attain control.

Policy rate An interest rate that a central bank sets and announces publicly; normally the rate at which it is willing to lend money to the commercial banks.

Portfolio companies The individual companies owned by a private equity firm.

Portfolio investment flows Short-term investments in foreign assets, such as stocks or bonds.

Portfolio planning The process of creating a plan for building a portfolio that is expected to satisfy a client's investment objectives.

Position The quantity of an asset that an entity owns or owes.

Posterior probability An updated probability that reflects or comes after new information.

Power of a test The probability of correctly rejecting the null—that is, rejecting the null hypothesis when it is false.

Pre-funding period Allows the trust to acquire during a certain period of time after the close of the transaction.

Preference shares A type of equity interest which ranks above common shares with respect to the payment of dividends and the distribution of the company's net assets upon liquidation. They have characteristics of both debt and equity securities. Also called *preferred stock*.

Preferred stock See *preference shares*.

Premium In the case of bonds, premium refers to the amount by which a bond is priced above its face (par) value. In the case of an option, the amount paid for the option contract.

Prepayment option May entitle the borrower to prepay all or part of the outstanding mortgage principal prior to maturity. This creates a risk from the lender's or investor's viewpoint because the cash flow amounts and timing cannot be known with certainty.

Prepayment risk The risk that the some or all of a mortgage-backed security's principal is repaid at a different speed than expected, either in the form of contraction risk (or earlier repayment than expected) or extension risk (later repayment).

Present value models Valuation models that estimate the intrinsic value of a security as the present value of the future benefits expected to be received from the security. Also called *discounted cash flow models*.

Pretax margin A profitability ratio calculated as earnings before taxes divided by revenue.

Price discrimination A pricing approach that charges different prices to different customers based on their willingness to pay.

Price index Represents the average prices of a basket of goods and services.

Price limits Establish a band relative to the previous day's settlement price within which all trades must occur.

Price multiple A ratio that compares the share price with some sort of monetary flow or value to allow evaluation of the relative worth of a company's stock.

Price priority The principle that the highest priced buy orders and the lowest priced sell orders execute first.

Price return Measures *only* the price appreciation or percentage change in price of the securities in an index or portfolio.

Price return index An index that reflects *only* the price appreciation or percentage change in price of the constituent securities. Also called *price index*.

Price stability In economics, refers to an inflation rate that is low on average and not subject to wide fluctuation.

Price takers Producers that must accept whatever price the market dictates.

Price value of a basis point (PVBP) An estimate of the change in the full price of a bond given a 1 bp change in its yield-to-maturity. The PVBP is also called the "PV01," standing for the "price value of an 01" or "present value of an 01," where "01" means 1 bp. In the United States, it is commonly called the "DV01" for the "dollar value" of 1 bp.

Price weighting An index weighting method in which the weight assigned to each constituent security is determined by dividing its price by the sum of all the prices of the constituent securities.

Price-setting option The option to adjust prices when demand or supply varies from what is forecast.

Price-to-earnings ratio (P/E) The ratio of share price to earnings per share.

Pricing power A company's ability to set prices and other economic terms with customers without affecting its sales volumes.

Primary bond markets Fixed-income markets comprised of issuers issuing bonds to investors to raise capital, often intermediated by a third-party such as an investment bank.

Primary capital markets (primary markets) The market where securities are first sold and the issuers receive the proceeds.

Primary dealer Financial institution that is authorized to deal in new issues of sovereign bonds and that serves primarily as a trading counterparty of the office responsible for issuing sovereign bonds.

Primary market The market where securities are first sold and the issuers receive the proceeds.

Prime broker A broker that provides services that commonly include custody, administration, lending, short borrowing, and trading.

Prime loans Lending made to borrowers of high credit quality with strong employment and credit histories, a low DTI, substantial equity in the underlying property, and a first lien on the mortgaged property serving as the collateral for the loan.

Principal The amount that an issuer agrees to repay the debtholders on the maturity date.

Principal-agent relationship An arrangement in which one party (the agent) has authority to act for or on behalf of another party (the principal). Such an arrangement imposes a duty on the agent to act in the principal's best interest.

Prior probabilities Probabilities reflecting beliefs prior to the arrival of new information.

Priority of claims Priority of payment, with the most senior or highest ranking debt having the first claim on the cash flows and assets of the issuer.

Private capital Funding provided to companies that is not sourced from the public markets.

Private company A company, typically a limited company, that does not list its equity securities on an exchange.

Private debt Capital extended to companies through a loan or other form of debt.

Private debtholders Investors in an entity's non-securitized debt claims, such as a loan or lease. The most common type of private debtholder is a bank.

Private equity Equity investment capital raised from sources other than public markets and traditional institutions.

Private equity fund A hedge fund that seeks to buy, optimize, and ultimately sell portfolio companies to generate profits. See *venture capital fund*.

Private equity securities Securities that are not listed on public exchanges and have no active secondary market. They are issued primarily to institutional investors via non-public offerings, such as private placements.

Private investment in public equity (PIPE) An investment in the equity of a publicly traded firm that is made at a discount to the market value of the firm's shares.

Private limited company A type of limited company in many jurisdictions with pass-through taxation but restrictions on the number of shareholders or members and on the transfer of ownership interest.

Private placement A sale of debt or equity securities to a small group of investors on an unregulated basis. The terms of the offering are negotiated by the issuer and investors.

Probability of default (POD) The likelihood that a borrower fails to make full and timely payments of principal and interest according to debt terms, usually expressed in annual percentage terms.

Probability sampling A sampling plan that allows every member of the population to have an equal chance of being selected.

Probability tree diagram A diagram with branches emanating from nodes representing either mutually exclusive chance events or mutually exclusive decisions.

Production flexibility option The option to alter production when demand varies from what is forecast.

Profession An occupational group that has specific education, expert knowledge, and a framework of practice and behavior that underpins community trust, respect, and recognition.

Profit margin An indicator of profitability, calculated as net income divided by revenue; indicates how much of each dollar of revenues is left after all costs and expenses.

Profitability ratios Ratios that measure a company's ability to generate profitable sales from its resources (assets).

Prospectus Legal document in securitization that describes the structure of the transaction, including the priority and amount of payments to be made to the servicer, administrators, and the ABS holders, as well as the credit enhancements used in the securitization.

Protective put A strategy of purchasing an underlying asset and purchasing a put on the same asset.

Proxy contest When a shareholder or group of shareholders campaigns for certain matters they have submitted to a shareholder vote, often a slate of directors who oppose the incumbent board and management. The incumbent board and management simultaneously campaign for their side.

Proxy voting A form of casting a ballot in an election in which a voter authorizes a representative to vote on their behalf according to instructions. In corporate elections, proxy ballots are cast by shareholders that direct a representative, typically the corporate secretary, to enter their votes as instructed.

Public (listed) company A company with its equity securities traded on an exchange.

Public limited companies A type of limited company in many jurisdictions with entity-level taxation but no restrictions on the number of shareholders or transferability of ownership interest; the most suitable organizational form for a company that seeks to go public.

Public–private partnership A long-term contractual relationship between the public and private sectors for the purpose of having the private sector deliver a project or service traditionally provided by the public sector. Infrastructure is increasingly being financed privately through public–private partnerships by local, regional, and national governments.

Public–private partnership (PPP) An agreement between the public sector and the private sector to finance, build, and operate public infrastructure, such as hospitals and toll roads.

Pull on liquidity An action or event that accelerates cash outflows.

Purchase agreement Legal document in a securitization transaction that outlines the representations and warranties that the seller makes about the assets sold.

Pure discount bonds Bonds that do not pay interest during their life. They are issued at a discount to par value and redeemed at par. Also called zero-coupon bonds.

Put An option that gives the holder the right to sell an underlying asset to another party at a fixed price over a specific period of time.

Put option The right to sell an underlying.

Putable bonds Bonds that give the bondholder the right to sell the bond back to the issuer at a predetermined price on specified dates.

Put–call forward parity Describes the no-arbitrage condition in which at $t = 0$ the present value of the price of a long forward commitment plus the price of the long put must equal the price of the long call plus the price of the risk-free asset (with face value of the exercise price of both the call and the put).

Put–call parity Describes the no-arbitrage condition in which at $t = 0$ the price of the long underlying asset plus the price of the long put must equal the price of the long call plus the price of the risk-free asset (with face value of the exercise price of both the call and the put).

Quantile A value at or below which a stated fraction of the data lies. Also referred to as a fractile.

Quantitative easing An expansionary monetary policy based on aggressive open market purchase operations.

Quartiles Quantiles that divide a distribution into four equal parts.

Quick ratio A measure of liquidity that is the ratio of cash, marketable securities, and receivables to current liabilities.

Quintiles Quantiles that divide a distribution into five equal parts.

Quota rents Profits that foreign producers can earn by raising the price of their goods higher than they would without a quota.

Quotas Government policies that restrict the quantity of a good that can be imported into a country, generally for a specified period of time.

Quote-driven market A market in which dealers acting as principals facilitate trading.

Quoted margin Specified spread of a floating rate instrument over a market reference rate or benchmark.

Range The difference between the maximum and minimum values in a dataset.

Rapid amortization provisions Provisions in receivable ABS that may require early principal amortization if specific events occur. Such provisions are referred to as early amortization and are included to safeguard the credit quality of the issue, particularly during the revolving period.

Razor, razorblade pricing A pricing approach that combines a low price on a piece of equipment and high-margin pricing on repeat-purchase consumables.

Real assets Generally, these are tangible physical assets, such as real estate, infrastructure, and natural resources, but they also include such intangibles as patents, intellectual property, and goodwill. Real assets generate current or expected future cash flows and/or are considered a store of value.

Real estate Includes borrowed or ownership capital in buildings or land. Developed land includes commercial and industrial real estate, residential real estate, and infrastructure.

Real option A right, but not an obligation, for management to make a decision with respect to a capital investment that alters future cash flows from the original forecasted scenario.

Real risk-free interest rate The single-period interest rate for a completely risk-free security if no inflation were expected.

Rebalancing Adjusting the weights of the constituent securities in an index.

Rebalancing policy The set of rules that guide the process of restoring a portfolio's asset class weights to those specified in the strategic asset allocation.

Recapitalization Recapitalization via private equity describes the steps a firm takes to increase or introduce leverage to its portfolio company and pay itself a dividend out of the new capital structure.

Recognition lag The lag in government response to an economic problem resulting from the delay in confirming a change in the state of the economy.

Recourse loan Loan in which the lender has a claim against the borrower for the shortfall (deficiency) between the amount of the outstanding mortgage balance and the proceeds received from the sale of the property.

Recovery rate (RR) The percentage of an outstanding debt claim recovered when an issuer defaults

Redemption fee A fee charged to discourage redemptions and to offset the transaction costs for remaining investors in the fund.

Refinancing rate A type of central bank policy rate.

Regionalism In between the two extremes of bilateralism and multilateralism. In regionalism, a group of countries cooperate with one another. Both bilateralism and regionalism can be conducted at the exclusion of other groups. For example, regional blocs may agree to provide trade benefits to one another and increase barriers for those outside of that group.

Registered bonds Bonds for which ownership is recorded by either name or serial number.

Regression analysis Allows us to test hypotheses about the relationship between two variables, by quantifying the strength of the relationship between the two variables, and to use one variable to make predictions about the other variable.

Regression coefficients The collective term for the intercept and slope coefficients in the regression model.

Regret The feeling that an opportunity has been missed; typically, an expression of *hindsight bias*.

Regret-aversion bias An emotional bias in which people tend to avoid making decisions that will result in action out of fear that the decision will turn out poorly.

Relative dispersion The amount of dispersion relative to a reference value or benchmark.

Reopening Issuing bonds by increasing the size of an existing bond issue with a price significantly different from par.

Replication A strategy in which a derivative's cash flow stream may be recreated using a combination of long or short positions in an underlying asset and borrowing or lending cash.

Repo rate The interest rate on a repurchase agreement.

Representativeness bias A belief perseverance bias in which people tend to classify new information based on past experiences and classifications.

Repurchase agreement (Repo) A form of collateralized loan involving the sale of a security with a simultaneous agreement by the seller to buy back the same security from the purchaser at an agreed-on price and future date. The party who sells the security at the inception of the repurchase agreement and buys it back at maturity is borrowing money from the other party, and the security sold and subsequently repurchased represents the collateral.

Repurchase date The date when the party who sold the security at the inception of a repurchase agreement buys back the security from the cash lending counterparty.

Repurchase price The price at which the party who sold the security at the inception of the repurchase agreement buys back the security from the cash lending counterparty.

Required margin Also known as discount margin. The market-determined yield spread over or under the market reference rate such that a floating-rate loan is priced at par on a rate reset date following issuance.

Required rate of return The rate of return required by investors given the risk of the bond investment, also known as the market discount rate or required yield.

Required yield The rate of return required by investors given the risk of the bond investment, also known as the market discount rate of required rate of return.

Required yield spread The difference in yield-to-maturity between a bond and that of a government benchmark bond with the same or similar time-to-maturity.

Resampling A statistical method that repeatedly draws samples from the original observed data sample for the statistical inference of population parameters.

Reserve currency A currency held by global central banks in significant quantities and widely used to conduct international trade and financial transactions.

Reserve requirement The requirement for banks to hold reserves in proportion to the size of deposits.

Residual The amount of deviation of an observed value of the dependent variable from its estimated value based on the fitted regression line.

Restricted domestic currency A currency with limited convertibility into other currencies due to illiquidity.

Return on assets (ROA) A profitability ratio calculated as net income divided by average total assets; indicates a company's net profit generated per dollar invested in total assets.

Return on equity (ROE) A profitability ratio calculated as net income divided by average shareholders' equity.

Return on invested capital (ROIC) A measure of the profitability of a company relative to the amount of capital invested by the equityholders and debtholders.

Return on sales An indicator of profitability, calculated as net income divided by revenue; indicates how much of each dollar of revenues is left after all costs and expenses. Also referred to as *net profit margin*.

Return-generating model A model that can provide an estimate of the expected return of a security given certain parameters and estimates of the values of the independent variables in the model.

Revenue bonds Bonds issued by non-sovereign governments related to a government sponsored project expected to generate future cash flow as a primary source of repayment.

Reverse repurchase agreement A repurchase agreement viewed from the perspective of the cash lending counterparty.

Reverse stock split A reduction in the number of shares outstanding with a corresponding increase in share price but no change to the company's underlying fundamentals.

Revolving credit agreements The most reliable form of short-term bank borrowing facilities; they are in effect for multiple years (e.g., three to five years) and can have optional medium-term loan features. Also known as *revolvers*.

Rho The change in a given derivative instrument for a given small change in the risk-free interest rate, holding everything else constant. Rho measures the sensitivity of the option to the risk-free interest rate.

Ricardian equivalence An economic theory that implies that it makes no difference whether a government finances a deficit by increasing taxes or issuing debt.

Risk Exposure to uncertainty. The chance of a loss or adverse outcome as a result of an action, inaction, or external event.

Risk averse The assumption that an investor will choose the least risky alternative.

Risk aversion The dislike for risk such that compensation is required in terms of higher expected returns for assuming higher risk.

Risk budgeting The establishment of objectives for individuals, groups, or divisions of an organization that takes into account the allocation of an acceptable level of risk.

Risk exposure The state of being exposed or vulnerable to a risk. The extent to which an organization is sensitive to underlying risks.

Risk governance The top-down process and guidance that directs risk management activities to align with and support the overall enterprise.

Risk management The process of identifying the level of risk an organization wants, measuring the level of risk the organization currently has, taking actions that bring the actual level of risk to the desired level of risk, and monitoring the new actual level of risk so that it continues to be aligned with the desired level of risk.

Risk management framework The infrastructure, process, and analytics needed to support effective risk management in an organization.

Risk premium An extra return expected by investors for bearing some specified risk.

Risk shifting Actions to change the distribution of risk outcomes.

Risk tolerance The level of risk an investor is willing and able to bear.

Risk transfer Strategies implemented to mitigate the impact of specific risks by transferring them to an insurance company.

Risk-neutral pricing A no-arbitrage derivative value established separately from investor views on risk that uses underlying asset volatility and the risk-free rate to calculate the present value of future cash flows.

Risk-neutral probability The computed probability used in binomial option pricing by which the discounted weighted sum of expected values of the underlying equal the current option price. Specifically, this probability is computed using the risk-free rate and assumed up gross return and down gross return of the underlying.

Rollover risk The likelihood that a property owner will lose an existing tenant and forgo income until a new one is found.

Safety-first rules Rules for portfolio selection that focus on the risk that portfolio value or portfolio return will fall below some minimum acceptable level over some time horizon.

Sample correlation coefficient A standardized measure of how two variables in a sample move together. It is the ratio of the sample covariance to the product of the two variables' standard deviations.

Sample covariance A measure of how two variables in a sample move together.

Sample excess kurtosis A sample measure of the degree of a distribution's kurtosis in excess of the normal distribution's kurtosis.

Sample mean The sum of the sample observations divided by the sample size.

Sample skewness A sample measure of the degree of asymmetry of a distribution.

Sample standard deviation The positive square root of the sample variance.

Sample variance The sum of squared deviations around the mean divided by the degrees of freedom.

Sample-size neglect A type of representativeness bias in which financial market participants incorrectly assume that small sample sizes are representative of populations (or "real" data).

Sampling distribution The distribution of all distinct possible values that a statistic can assume when computed from samples of the same size randomly drawn from the same population.

Sampling error The difference between the observed value of a statistic and the estimate resulting from using subsets of the population.

Sampling plan The set of rules used to select a sample.

Saving deposits Bank deposits typically held for non-transactional purposes that often have a stated term.

Scatter plot A two-dimensional graphical plot of paired observations of values for the independent and dependent variables in a simple linear regression.

Scenario analysis A variation of the valuation process combining a base case with alternative outcomes, allowing the incorporation of more favorable or adverse scenarios in the valuation process.

Scraping An automated, large-scale, algorithm-driven approach that retrieves otherwise unstructured data available on websites and creates data in a more structured format.

Seasoned offering An offering in which an issuer sells additional units of a previously issued security.

Secondary bond markets Fixed-income markets comprised of investors trading existing bonds amongst themselves.

Secondary market The market where securities are traded among investors.

Secondary precedence rules Rules that determine how to rank orders placed at the same time.

Secondary sale Sale of a private company stake to another private equity firm or group of financial buyers.

Secondary-stage investments The second stage of development of an infrastructure asset. Secondary-stage investments involve existing infrastructure facilities or fully operational assets that do not require further investment or development over the investment horizon. These assets generate immediate cash flow and returns expected over the investment period.

Sector indexes Indexes that represent and track different economic sectors—such as consumer goods, energy, finance, health care, and technology—on either a national, regional, or global basis.

Secured With collateral; secured debt is backed by the cash flows of the issuer and the collateral as a secondary source of repayment.

Secured loans Loans collateralized by an asset of the borrower.

Security Evidence of equity or debt interest or in an entity or a related right, such as a derivative. Often standardized to conform to security exchange requirements.

Security characteristic line A plot of the excess return of a security on the excess return of the market.

Security market index A portfolio of securities representing a given security market, market segment, or asset class.

Security market line The graphical representation of the CAPM formula, showing the relationship between expected return and beta.

Security selection The process of selecting individual securities; typically, security selection has the objective of generating superior risk-adjusted returns relative to a portfolio's benchmark.

Security tokens Digitizes the ownership rights associated with publicly traded securities.

Segmenting A process of identifying and grouping customers by decision-useful attributes.

Self-attribution bias A bias in which people take too much credit for successes (*self-enhancing*) and assign responsibility to others for failures (*self-protecting*).

Self-control bias A bias in which people fail to act in pursuit of their long-term, overarching goals because of a lack of self-discipline.

Self-investment limits With respect to investment limitations applying to pension plans, restrictions on the percentage of assets that can be invested in securities issued by the pension plan sponsor.

Sell-side firm A broker/dealer that sells securities and provides independent investment research and recommendations to their clients (i.e., buy-side firms).

Semi-strong-form efficient market A market in which security prices reflect all publicly known and available information.

Semiannual bond basis yield Also known as a semiannual bond equivalent yield, it is an annualized interest rate with a periodicity of two.

Semiannual bond equivalent yield Also known as a semiannual bond basis yield, it is an annualized interest rate with a periodicity of two.

Senior debt A debt obligation with higher priority of payment than junior debt obligations.

Senior unsecured debt The highest-ranked debt in an issuer's capital structure which is a general obligation of the borrower.

Seniority Priority of payment of various debt obligations.

Sensitivity analysis A form of analysis used to determine the impact of a change in one or more key variables affecting investment returns or valuation.

Separately managed account (SMA) An investment portfolio managed exclusively for the benefit of an individual or institution.

Service period The time between the grant and vesting dates for an employee share-based award, usually measured in years.

Settlement The closing date at which the counterparties of a derivative contract exchange payment for the underlying as required by the contract.

Settlement price The price determined by an exchange's clearinghouse in the daily settlement of the mark-to-market process. The price reflects an average of the final futures trades of the day.

Share class Types of equity securities that have different voting rights—for example, an issuer may issue Class A shares that carry one vote per share and Class B shares that carry ten votes per share.

Share repurchase A transaction in which a company buys back its own shares. Unlike stock dividends and stock splits, share repurchases use corporate cash.

Shareholder activism A range of actions by a corporation's shareholders that are intended to result in some change in the corporation, typically a change in the board of directors, management, or business strategy.

Shareholder derivative lawsuit A legal action by a shareholder on behalf of a company, not the shareholder personally, against a third party. Often, the third party is a director or manager who the shareholder believes has harmed the company.

Shareholder engagement Shareholder engagement reflects active ownership by investors in which the investor seeks to influence a corporation's decisions on ESG matters, either through dialogue with corporate officers or votes at a shareholder assembly (in the case of equity).

Shareholder theory of corporate governance Espoused by Milton Friedman in his famous 1970 essay, the shareholder theory holds that the objective of a business is to increase profits and shareholder value.

Shareholders Hold a direct equity position in a firm, and both individual persons and financial institutions can be shareholders. The term comes from the individual or investment firm literally having a share of the company. It is most commonly used when talking about the rights and responsibilities that come with being an "owner" of a company, such as stewardship, voting, and engagement. This differentiates it from a situation where an individual or an investment firm lends money or invests in a bond (in other words, they are not an equityholder of a company). Because bond investors do not have a share and are not owners of a company, they cannot vote. Nonetheless, expectations around engagement are increasing for those who invest in loans and bonds as well, making the difference between the two terms more subtle.

Shares Units of ownership interest in a limited company.

Sharpe ratio The ratio of mean excess return to standard deviation (excess return).

Shelf registration A type of public offering that allows the issuer to file a single, all-encompassing offering circular that covers a series of bond issues.

Short A trading position in a **derivative contract** that gains value as the price of the **underlying** moves lower.

Short biased These strategies use quantitative, technical, and fundamental analysis to short overvalued equity securities with limited or no long-side exposures.

Short position A position in an asset or contract in which one has sold an asset one does not own, or in which a right under a contract can be exercised against oneself.

Short selling A transaction in which borrowed securities are sold with the intention to repurchase them at a lower price at a later date and return them to the lender.

Short-run average total cost The curve describing average total cost when some costs are considered fixed.

Shortfall risk The risk that portfolio value or portfolio return will fall below some minimum acceptable level over some time horizon.

Shutdown point The point at which average revenue is equal to the firm's average variable cost.

Side letter A side agreement created between the GP and specific LPs. These agreements exist *outside* the LPA. These agreements provide additional terms and conditions related to the investment agreement.

Signpost An indicator, market level, data piece, or event that signals a risk is becoming more or less likely. An analyst can think of signposts like a traffic light.

Simple linear regression (SLR) An approach for estimating the linear relationship between a dependent variable and a single independent variable by minimizing the sum of the squared deviations between the fitted line and the observed values.

Simple random sample A subset of a larger population created in such a way that each element of the population has an equal probability of being selected to the subset.

Simple random sampling The procedure of drawing a sample to satisfy the definition of a simple random sample.

Simple yield The sum of the coupon payments plus the straight-line amortized share of the gain or loss divided by the bond's flat price. Simple yields are used mostly to quote JGBs.

Simulation A technique for exploring how a target variable (e.g. portfolio returns) would perform in a hypothetical environment specified by the user, rather than a historical setting.

Simulation trial A complete pass through the steps of a simulation.

Single-price auction A debt securities auction in which all bidders pay the same price.

Sinking fund Provisions that reduce the credit risk of a bond issue by requiring the issuer to retire a portion of the bond's principal outstanding each year.

Situational influences External factors, such as environmental or cultural elements, that shape our behavior.

Skewed Not symmetrical.

Skewness A quantitative measure of skew (lack of symmetry); a synonym of skew. It is computed as the average cubed deviation from the mean standardized by dividing by the standard deviation cubed.

Slope coefficient The change in the estimated value of the dependent variable for a one-unit change in the value of the independent variable.

Small country A country that is a price taker in the world market for a product and cannot influence the world market price.

Smart beta Involves the use of simple, transparent, rules-based strategies as a basis for investment decisions.

Smart contracts Computer programs that are designed to self-execute on the basis of pre-specified terms and conditions agreed to by parties to a contract.

Social infrastructure investments A category of infrastructure investments that are directed toward human activities and include such assets as educational, health care, social housing, and correctional facilities, with the focus on providing, operating, and maintaining the asset infrastructure.

Soft commodities Standardized agricultural products, such as cattle and corn, with markets often involving the physical delivery of the underlying upon settlement.

Soft hurdle rate Hurdle rate where the fee is calculated on the entire return when the hurdle is exceeded. With a soft hurdle, GPs are able to catch up performance fees once the hurdle threshold is exceeded.

Soft power A means of influencing another country's decisions without force or coercion. Soft power can be built over time through actions, such as cultural programs, advertisement, travel grants, and university exchange.

Soft-bullet covered bonds Delay the bond default and payment acceleration of bond cash flows until a new final maturity date, which is usually up to a year after the original maturity date.

Solvency Refers to the condition in which firm value exceeds the face value of debt used to finance the firm's assets.

Solvency ratios Ratios that measure a company's ability to meet its long-term obligations.

Solvency risk The risk that an organization does not survive or succeed because it runs out of cash, even though it might otherwise be solvent.

Sophisticated investors Individuals or entities that are permitted in a jurisdiction to trade unregistered or, generally, less regulated securities, including shares of privately held companies; also called *accredited investors.*

Sovereign immunity A principle that limits legal recourse of lenders from forcing a sovereign borrower to declare bankruptcy or liquidate its assets to settle debt claims.

Spearman rank correlation coefficient A measure of correlation applied to ranked data.

Special dividend A dividend paid by a company that does not pay dividends on a regular schedule, or a dividend that supplements regular cash dividends with an extra payment.

Special purpose acquisition company A "blank check" company that exists solely for the purpose of acquiring an unspecified private company within a predetermined period or return capital to investors.

Special purpose entity (SPE) Also referred to as a special purpose vehicle (SPV), this legal entity is created for a specific economic purpose. In the case of a project SPV, the entity's sole purpose is to facilitate the construction, operation, and financing of an infrastructure asset over its contractual life.

Special purpose vehicle See *special purpose entity.*

Special situations An area of private capital investment which targets return by investing in stressed, distressed, or event-driven opportunities.

Split ratings Complex risks viewed very differently by rating agencies

Sponsored A type of depository receipt in which the foreign company whose shares are held by the depository has a direct involvement in the issuance of the receipts.

Spot curve Yields-to-maturity on a series of default-risk-free zero-coupon bonds.

Spot markets Markets in which specific assets are exchanged at current prices. Spot markets are often referred to as **cash markets.**

Spot prices The current prices prevailing in **spot markets.**

Spot rates Yields-to-maturity on default-risk-free zero-coupon bonds.

Spread The difference in yield-to-maturity between a bond and that of a another bond.

Spread risk Bond price risk arising from changes in the yield spread on credit-risky bonds; reflects changes in the market's assessment and/or pricing of credit migration (or downgrade) risk and market liquidity risk.

Spurious correlation Refers to: 1) correlation between two variables that reflects chance relationships in a particular dataset; 2) correlation induced by a calculation that mixes each of two variables with a third variable; and 3) correlation between two variables arising not from a direct relation between them but from their relation to a third variable.

Stablecoin A cryptocurrency that aims to maintain a stable value relative to a specified asset or to a pool or basket of assets.

Stackelberg model A prominent model of strategic decision making in which firms are assumed to make their decisions sequentially.

Staggered board A structure of board elections in which only part of the board is elected simultaneously—for example, only one-third of the board may be up for election each year, so the board can be replaced over three years, not in one year if all seats were elected annually. This structure fosters greater continuity of board members but is an obstacle for shareholders seeking to effect change.

Stakeholder theory of corporate governance An expansion of the shareholder theory of corporate governance under which the objective of a business is to maximize value for, and balance the interests of, a broad group of stakeholders, including shareholders, employees, society, and the non-human environment.

Stakeholders Any party with an interest, financial or non-financial, in an entity or its actions.

Standard deviation The positive square root of the variance; a measure of dispersion in the same units as the original data.

Standard error of the estimate A measure of the distance between the observed values of the dependent variable and those predicted from the estimated regression. The smaller this value, the better the fit of the model. Also known as the standard error of the regression and the root mean square error.

Standard error of the forecast Used to provide an interval estimate around the estimated regression line. It is necessary because the regression line does not describe the relationship between the dependent and independent variables perfectly.

Standard error of the slope coefficient Calculated for simple linear regression by dividing the standard error of the estimate by the square root of the variation of the independent variable.

Standardization The process of creating protocols for the production, sale, transport, or use of a product or service. Standardization occurs when relevant parties agree to follow these protocols together. It helps support expanded economic and financial activities, such as trade and capital flows that support higher economic growth and standards of living, across borders.

Standards of conduct Behaviors required by a group; established benchmarks that clarify or enhance a group's code of ethics.

Standing limit orders A limit order at a price below market and which therefore is waiting to trade.

State actors Typically national governments, political organizations, or country leaders that exert authority over a country's national security and resources. The South African President, Sultan of Brunei, Malaysia's Parliament, and the British Prime Minister are all examples of state actors.

Statement of cash flows A financial statement that details the movement of cash over a period. The statement is classified into operating, investing, and financing activities.

Static trade-off theory of capital structure A theory pertaining to a company's optimal capital structure; the optimal level of debt is found at the point where additional debt would cause the costs of financial distress to increase by a greater amount than the benefit of the additional tax shield.

Statistically significant A result indicating that the null hypothesis can be rejected; with reference to an estimated regression coefficient, frequently understood to mean a result indicating that the corresponding population regression coefficient is different from zero.

Status quo bias An emotional bias in which people do nothing (i.e., maintain the status quo) instead of making a change.

Statutory voting A common method of voting where each share represents one vote.

Step-up bonds Bonds for which the coupon, be it fixed or floating, increases by specified margins at specified dates.

Stock dividend A type of dividend in which a company distributes additional shares of its common stock to shareholders instead of cash.

Stock exchange An exchange in which equity securities are traded. See *exchanges*.

Stock split An increase in the number of shares outstanding with a consequent decrease in share price, but no change to the company's underlying fundamentals.

Stockholder overhang The downward pressure on the share price of stock as large blocks of shares are being sold on the open market.

Stop order An order in which a trader has specified a stop price condition. Also called *stop-loss order*.

Stop-loss order See *stop order*.

Stranded assets A resource that is no longer economically valuable owing to changes in demand, regulations, or availability of substitutes—for example, a newly discovered oil well that will not be brought into production.

Strategic asset allocation A long-term strategy that establishes target allocations for various asset classes and aims to optimize the balance between risk and reward by diversifying investments.

Stratified random sampling A procedure that first divides a population into subpopulations (strata) based on classification criteria and then randomly draws samples from each stratum in sizes proportional to that of each stratum in the population.

Street convention For yield measures on fixed-income instruments that assume payments are made on scheduled dates and ignore weekends and holidays.

Stress testing A specific type of scenario analysis that estimates losses in rare and extremely unfavorable combinations of events or scenarios.

Strong-form efficient market A market in which security prices reflect all public and private information.

Structural budget deficit Also known as the cyclically adjusted budget deficit. The deficit that would exist if the economy was at full employment (or full potential output).

Structural subordination Refers to the positioning of debt, which is issued by a legal entity, typically a holding company, which is separate and therefore one step removed from an operating company, which holds assets pledged under a security agreement to senior secured debtholders.

Structured notes A broad category of securities that incorporate the features of debt instruments and one or more embedded derivatives designed to achieve a particular issuer or investor objective.

Subordinated debt A class of unsecured debt that ranks below a firm's senior unsecured obligations.

Subordination A form of internal credit enhancement that relies on creating more than one bond tranche and ordering the claim priorities for ownership or interest in an asset between the tranches. The ordering of the claim priorities is called a senior/subordinated structure, where the tranches of highest seniority are called senior, followed by subordinated or junior tranches. Also called **credit tranching**.

Subprime loans Lending to borrowers with lower credit quality, high DTI, and/or are loans with higher LTV, and include loans that are secured by second liens otherwise subordinated to other loans.

Sum of squares error (SSE) A measure of the total deviation between observed and estimated values of the dependent variable. It is calculated by subtracting each estimated value $\hat{Y}_i$ from its corresponding observed value Y_i, squaring each of these differences, and then summing all of these squared differences.

Sum of squares regression (SSR) A measure of the explained variation in the dependent variable, calculated as the sum of the squared differences between the predicted value of the dependent variable, Y^_i, based on the estimated regression line, and the mean of the dependent variable, Y¯.

Sum of squares total (SST) A measure of the total variation in the dependent variable in a simple linear regression. It is calculated by subtracting the mean of the observed values $\overline{Y}$ from each of the observed values Y_i, squaring each of these differences, and then summing all of these squared differences.

Sunk costs A cost that has already been incurred.

Supervised learning A type of machine learning in which the system attempts to learn to model relationships based on labeled training data.

Supervisory board In some jurisdictions, a corporation's board of directors is formally composed of a supervisory board and a management board. The supervisory board appoints and oversees the management board and often includes representatives of employees and other non-shareholder stakeholders.

Supply chain The sequence of processes involved in the creation and delivery of a physical product to the end customer, both within and external to a firm, regardless of whether those steps are performed by a single firm.

Supply shock A typically unexpected disturbance to supply.

Survivorship bias Relates to the inclusion of only current investment funds in a database. As such, the returns of funds that are no longer available in the marketplace (have been liquidated) are excluded from the database. Also see *backfill bias*.

Swap A firm commitment involving a periodic exchange of cash flows.

Swap contract An agreement between two parties to exchange a series of future cash flows.

Swap execution facility (SEF) A swap trading platform accessed by multiple **dealers**.

Swap rate The fixed rate to be paid by the fixed-rate payer specified in a swap contract.

Syndicate A group of lenders, typically made up of banks.

Synthetic protective put The combination of a synthetic long underlying position (i.e., a long forward and risk-free borrowing) and a purchased put on the underlying.

Systematic risk Risk that affects the entire market or economy; it cannot be avoided and is inherent in the overall market. Systematic risk is also known as *non-diversifiable* or *market risk*.

Systematic sampling A procedure of selecting every *k*th member until reaching a sample of the desired size. The sample that results from this procedure should be approximately random.

Systemic risk Refers to risks supervisory authorities believe are likely to have broad impact across the financial market infrastructure and affect a wide swath of market participants.

Tactical asset allocation A proactive strategy that adjusts asset class allocations within a portfolio based on short-term market trends, economic conditions, or valuation changes to capitalize on temporary market inefficiencies or opportunities to improve returns or manage risk more effectively.

Target capital structure Management's desired proportions of debt and equity financing, usually stated on a book value basis or indirectly using a financial leverage metric, such as net or gross debt to EBITDA or credit rating.

Target independent A bank's ability to determine the definition of inflation that they target, the rate of inflation that they target, and the horizon over which the target is to be achieved.

Target semideviation A measure of downside risk, calculated as the square root of the average of the squared deviations of observations below the target (also called *target downside deviation*).

Tariffs Taxes that a government levies on imported goods.

Tax base The amount at which an asset or liability is valued for tax purposes.

Tax expense An aggregate of an entity's income tax payable (or recoverable in the case of a tax benefit) and any changes in deferred tax assets and liabilities. It is essentially the income tax payable or recoverable if these had been determined based on accounting profit rather than taxable income.

Taxable income The portion of an entity's income that is subject to income taxes under the tax laws of its jurisdiction.

Taxable temporary differences Temporary differences that result in a taxable amount in a future period when determining the taxable profit as the balance sheet item is recovered or settled.

Technical analysis A form of security analysis that uses price and volume data, often displayed graphically, in decision making.

Tender offer A solicitation by a current or prospective shareholder to other shareholders to acquire a substantial percentage, including 100%, of shares at a specified price. This action is usually undertaken by a potential acquirer whose bid was rejected by the issuer's board of directors, prompting the potential acquirer to appeal directly to shareholders.

Tenor Remaining time-to-maturity for a fixed-income instrument.

Term repos Repos with a maturity longer than one day.

Term structure of interest rates Also known as the maturity structure of interest rates, refers to the difference in interest rates or benchmark yields by time-to-maturity.

Terminal stock value The expected value of a share at the end of the investment horizon—in effect, the expected selling price. Also called *terminal value*.

Terminal value The expected value of a share at the end of the investment horizon—in effect, the expected selling price.

Test of the mean of the differences A statistical test for differences based on paired observations drawn from samples that are dependent on each other.

Text analytics Involves the use of computer programs to analyze and derive meaning typically from large, unstructured text- or voice-based datasets, such as company filings, written reports, quarterly earnings calls, social media, email, internet postings, and surveys.

Thematic risks Known risks that evolve and expand over a period of time. Climate change, pattern migration, the rise of populist forces, and the ongoing threat of terrorism fall into this category.

Thin-tailed Describes a distribution that has relatively less weight in the tails than the normal distribution (also called platykurtic).

Tiered pricing A pricing approach that charges different prices to different buyers, commonly based on volume purchased.

Timberland investment management organizations Entities that support institutional investors by managing their investments in timberland by analyzing and acquiring suitable timberland holdings.

Time tranching Structure of a securitization that allows for the redistribution of "prepayment risk" among bond classes by creating bond classes of different expected maturities.

Time value The difference between an option's premium and its intrinsic value.

Time value decay The process by which the time value of an option declines toward zero as the option's expiration date is approached.

Time-weighted rate of return The compound rate of growth of one unit of currency invested in a portfolio during a stated measurement period; a measure of investment performance that is not sensitive to the timing and amount of withdrawals or additions to the portfolio.

Tokenization The process of representing ownership rights to physical assets on a blockchain or distributed ledger.

Top-down analysis An investment selection approach that begins with consideration of macroeconomic conditions and then evaluates markets and industries based upon such conditions.

Total probability rule for expected value A rule explaining the expected value of a random variable in terms of expected values of the random variable conditional on mutually exclusive and exhaustive scenarios.

Total return Measures the price appreciation, or percentage change in price of the securities in an index or portfolio, plus any income received over the period.

Total return index An index that reflects the price appreciation or percentage change in price of the constituent securities plus any income received since inception.

Total working capital The difference between current assets and current liabilities.

Tracking error The standard deviation of the differences between a portfolio's returns and its benchmark's returns; a synonym of active risk.

Tracking risk The standard deviation of the differences between a portfolio's returns and its benchmarks returns. Also called *tracking error*.

Trade creation When regional integration results in the replacement of higher cost domestic production by lower cost imports from other members.

Trade diversion When regional integration results in lower-cost imports from non-member countries being replaced with higher-cost imports from members.

Trade sale A portion or division of a private company sold via either direct sale or auction to a strategic buyer interested in increasing the scale and scope of an existing business.

Trade settlement date The date when the buyer and seller transfer consideration and securities.

Traditional investment markets Markets for traditional investments, which include all publicly traded debts and equities and shares in pooled investment vehicles that hold publicly traded debts and/or equities.

Tranches A grouping of securities within an issue with characteristics that vary from other tranches, such as different credit quality and seniority.

Transfer payments Welfare payments made through the social security system that exist to provide a basic minimum level of income for low-income households.

Transition risks Economic and financial losses from the transition to a lower-carbon economy in response to climate change—for example, the abandonment of an oil well that is no longer economical.

Treasury Inflation-Protected Securities (TIPS) US Treasury bonds with a principal that is adjusted for changes in the Consumer Price Index. TIPS are issued in 5-, 10-, and 30-year maturities.

Treynor ratio A measure of risk-adjusted performance that relates a portfolio's returns in excess of the risk-free rate to a portfolio's beta.

Trimmed mean A mean computed after excluding a stated small percentage of the lowest and highest observations.

Triparty repo A repurchase agreement in which the transacting parties agree to use a third-party agent that provides access to a larger collateral pool and multiple counterparties, as well as valuation and safekeeping of assets.

True yield Measures on fixed-income instruments use actual payment dates, accounting for weekends and holidays. The true yield on an instrument is always lower than the street convention yield.

Turn-of-the-year effect Calendar anomaly that stock market returns in January are significantly higher compared to the rest of the months of the year, with most of the abnormal returns reported during the first five trading days in January.

Two-fund separation theorem The theory that all investors regardless of taste, risk preferences, and initial wealth will hold a combination of two portfolios or funds: a risk-free asset and an optimal portfolio of risky assets.

Two-way table A table of the frequency distribution of observations classified on the basis of two discrete variables. Also known as *Contingency table*.

Two-week repo rate The interest rate on a two-week repurchase agreement; may be used as a policy rate by a central bank.

Type I error The error of rejecting a true null hypothesis; a false positive.

Type II error The error of not rejecting a false null hypothesis; false negative.

Uncommitted lines of credit Sources of bank credit that a bank can refuse to honor. Uncommitted credit lines are made up to a certain principal amount for a pre-determined maximum maturity, charging a market reference rate plus an issuer-specific spread on only the principal outstanding for the period of use.

Underfitted When a machine learning model treats true parameters as if they are noise and is unable to recognize relationships in the training data, making the model more likely to fail to fully discover patterns that underlie the data.

Underlying The asset referred to in a **derivative contract**.

Underwritten offering A type of securities issue mechanism in which the investment bank guarantees the sale of the securities at an offering price that is negotiated with the issuer. Also known as *firm commitment offering*.

Unearned revenue A liability account for money that has been collected for goods or services that have not yet been delivered; payment received in advance of providing a good or service. Also called *deferred revenue* or *deferred income*.

Unimodal A distribution with a single value that is most frequently occurring.

Unit economics The expression of revenues and costs on a per-unit basis.

Unitranche debt A hybrid or blended loan structure combining different tranches of secured and unsecured debt into a single loan with a single, blended interest rate.

Unsecured Without collateral; unsecured debt is backed only by cash flows of the issuer.

Unsponsored A type of depository receipt in which the foreign company whose shares are held by the depository has no involvement in the issuance of the receipts.

Unsupervised learning A type of machine learning in which the system tries to learn the structure of unlabeled data.

Utility tokens Tokens that provide services within a network, such as paying for services and network fees.

Validity instructions Instructions which indicate when the order may be filled.

Value added resellers Businesses that distribute a product and also handle more complex aspects of product installation, customization, service, or support.

Value at risk A money measure of the minimum value of losses expected during a specified time period at a given level of probability.

Value chain The systems and processes in a firm that create value for its customers.

Value proposition The product or service attributes valued by a firm's target customer that lead those customers to prefer that firm's offering.

Value-add real estate strategies Strategies that involve larger-scale redevelopment and repositioning of existing assets and that may allow the investor to earn a higher return compared with core-plus real estate strategies.

Value-based pricing Pricing set primarily by reference to the value of the product or service to customers.

VaR See *value at risk.*

Variance The expected value (the probability-weighted average) of squared deviations from a random variable's expected value.

Variance of a random variable The expected value (the probability-weighted average) of squared deviations from a random variable's expected value.

Variation margin The difference between current margin required and the current collateral price in a repurchase agreement.

Vega A measure of the sensitivity of an option's price to changes in the underlying's volatility.

Velocity The pace at which geopolitical risk impacts an investor portfolio.

Venture capital Private equity investment in a startup or early-stage company involving high risk and a high rate of failure.

Venture capital fund A hedge fund that seeks to buy, optimize, and ultimately sell portfolio companies to generate profits. See *private equity fund.*

Venture debt Private debt funding that provides venture capital backing to start-up or early-stage companies that may be generating little or negative cash flow.

Vest To become unconditionally entitled to.

Vesting date The day that an employee becomes unconditionally entitled to compensation.

Vintage year The year in which a private capital fund makes its first investment.

Volatility The standard deviation of the continuously compounded returns on the underlying asset.

Vote by proxy A mechanism that allows a designated party—such as another shareholder, a shareholder representative, or management—to vote on the shareholder's behalf.

Voting rights The power of shareholders to cast votes in corporate elections for directors and other matters submitted to a shareholder vote.

Warrant Debt feature or security granting the right to purchase additional common equity shares issued by the company at a predetermined price for a given period.

Waterfall structures These represent the distribution order for cash flows and risk to different tranches in a financing structure.

Weak-form efficient market hypothesis The belief that security prices fully reflect all past market data, which refers to all historical price and volume trading information.

Weighted average coupon rate (WAC) Rate calculated for a mortgage pass-through security by weighting the mortgage rate of each mortgage in the pool by the percentage of the outstanding mortgage balance relative to the outstanding amount of all the mortgages in the pool.

Weighted average maturity (WAM) Calculated for a mortgage pass-through security by weighting the remaining number of months to maturity of each mortgage in the pool by the outstanding mortgage balance relative to the outstanding amount of all the mortgages in the pool.

Weighted-average cost of capital (WACC) A weighted average of the after-tax required rates of return on a company's equity, debt, preferred stock, and other long-term financing sources, where the weights are the fraction of each source of financing in the company's current market value or management's target capital structure.

Winsorized mean A mean computed after assigning a stated percentage of the lowest values equal to one specified low value and a stated percentage of the highest values equal to one specified high value.

Write-off/liquidation Refers to a transaction that has not gone well, and the investment is likely to lose value. The private equity firm revises the value of its investment downward or liquidates the portfolio company.

Yield curve A graphical depiction of yields-to-maturity of bonds from the same issuer across maturities.

Yield spread The difference in yield-to-maturity between a bond and that of a another bond.

Yield-to-call An internal rate of return on a fixed-income instrument's cash flows assuming cash flows are received on scheduled dates and the bond is called at a certain call price and date.

Yield-to-maturity Internal rate of return on a fixed-income instrument's cash flows assuming all cash flows are received on their scheduled dates.

Yield-to-worst The lowest among a fixed-income instrument's yields-to-call and yield-to-maturity. A commonly cited yield measure for fixed-rate callable bonds.

Z-spread or zero-volatility spread is a constant yield spread for a bond over a government or swap curve.

Zero-coupon bonds Bonds that do not pay interest during their life. They are issued at a discount to par value and redeemed at par. Also called pure discount bond.